Professional Baseball in North Carolina

Professional Baseball in North Carolina

An Illustrated City-by-City History, 1901–1996

by

J. CHRIS HOLADAY

with a foreword by

MILES WOLFF

McFarland & Company, Inc., Publishers
Jefferson, North Carolina, and London

Cover design by John Crabill

British Library Cataloguing-in-Publication data are available

Library of Congress Cataloguing-in-Publication Data

Holaday, J. Chris, 1966–
    Professional baseball in North Carolina : an illustrated city-by-city
history, 1901–1996 / by J. Chris Holaday ; with a foreword by Miles
Wolff.
        p.   cm.
    Includes bibliographical references (p.) and index.   ∞
    ISBN 0-7864-0532-5 (case binding : 50# alkaline paper)
    1. Baseball — North Carolina — History.   2. Baseball teams — North
Carolina — History.   I. Title.
    GV863.N8H65   1998   796.357'64'09756 — dc21   98-17879 CIP

Manufactured in the United States of America

McFarland & Company, Inc., Publishers
  Box 611, Jefferson, North Carolina 28640

Acknowledgments

I would like to thank all of the former players and those associated with minor league baseball in North Carolina that I have spoken with for their help in this project. This book is for them. Without their information, stories and photographs I never would have been able to complete it.

Thank you to those who allowed me to visit them in their homes and sharing their memories and scrapbooks: Walter Rabb, Harry Soufas, Russell Mincy, Billy Bevill, Janet Neville, Betty Fite, Bernie Keating, Uriah Norwood, Edna Tatum, Billy Arthur, Otis Stephens, Cecil Tyson, Gaither Riley, George Erath, Walt Sorgi, Claude Griffin, Fair Swaim, Mack Arnette, Charlie Roach, Jim Mills, Emo Showfety, Cotton Bagwell, Bill Fowler, Ralph Hodgin, Gene Summerlin, Bob Kendall, Harry Land, Worth Cuthbertson, Howard Auman, Hank Tillotson, Cotton Powell, Alex Cosmidis, William Davis, Buddy Payne, George Rimmer, Zeb Harrington, Buddy Frazier, Sherman Hoggard, Joe Plick, Pete Howard, the late Fred Chapman and especially the late Norman Small. I have been amazed at how many wonderful and truly friendly people I have met while working on this project.

I would also like to thank those who took the time to talk with me on the telephone or correspond in writing: Al Gettel, Johnny Klippstein, Ducky Detweiler, John Pyecha, Alton Brown, Red Hayworth, Vernon Mustian, Duncan Futrelle, Ford Jordan, Gus Zernial, Ed Mayer, Johnny Pesky, Harold Lambeth, Moses Crutchfield, Willie Bradshaw, Art Hoch, Elder White, Francis Essic, Alex Sherrill, Glenn Eury, Al Thomy, Fred McCall, Ray Baughn, Dwight Feimster, Merrill Wiles, Henry Brown, Dutch Hengeveld, Rose Cathay and Bill Moose.

John Marks at the High Point Museum and Stephen Catlett at the Greensboro Historical Museum were invaluable in their help with finding photographs. Special thanks also to Chris Smith and Ron McKee with the Asheville Tourists, North Johnson with the Kinston Indians and David Beal and Pete Fisch with the Winston-Salem Warthogs.

Very special thanks to fellow SABR members Bob Gaunt and Hank Utley for sharing their research and for their encouragement. Also to Miles Wolff, for his wealth of information and for his part in the revival of minor league baseball in general. Thanks also to Marshall Adesman, the head of the Carolinas Chapter of SABR, for his great baseball stories and knowledge.

Thanks to Kinsley Dey of Dey Photography in Durham and to everyone at CCI Photographic, also of Durham, for their help and expertise.

Thanks most of all to my wife Sue, for putting up with all of my weekend trips, phone calls, and late nights at the computer.

Author's Note

It is my intention with this book to lay the groundwork for future, more in-depth writings about North Carolina's professional baseball history. There are hundreds of great stories about people and teams, but there's just not room here to tell them all. This book can serve, however, as a general reference to team histories and prominent players. I thought it was sad when somebody gave me a clipping from a 1980s newspaper that showed Temple Park in Sanford. The article stated that professional baseball had never been played in Sanford, only semipro. In fact, Sanford fielded a professional team for seven seasons.

I also hope to give recognition to some of the great athletes who made baseball in the state what it was and still is. This book is for them.

Contents

Foreword

North Carolina has always been a great state for all forms of athletic endeavor. As this foreword is being written in the spring of 1998, reports abound that North Carolina may get a major league baseball team. Already major league football, basketball and hockey have come to the area. The state has long been noted for its outstanding college athletics, particularly college basketball. Outstanding amateur and professional golf, stock car racing, and high school sports have long been part of the sports scene.

However, minor league baseball was part of the North Carolina sports landscape before any of these other sports came into prominence, and it has been a fixture in the state for nearly 100 years. Most important, minor league professional baseball has been part of the fabric of almost every locale in the state. An amazing 72 cities have had professional teams. Towns as small as Elkin, Red Springs, and Snow Hill can all boast of professional baseball and in 1949 some 33 different towns in the state had teams.

Chris Holaday has done a phenomenal job in arranging, researching, and compiling the history of baseball in all of these 72 cities. From Albemarle and Ayden to Winston-Salem and Zebulon he writes of the good (the 1941 Wilson Tobbs), the bad (the 1980 Rocky Mount Pines) and the ugly (the 1951 Granite Falls Rocks) in North Carolina minor league baseball. He gives accounts of the notable players and club records in every season, and describes the causes for the rise and fall of baseball in the different cities. He has researched old stadium locations and nicknames, and he writes of all the leagues that have made up baseball in the state. In short, his knowledge of the history of minor league baseball in the state is tremendous.

This volume includes a section of biographies on 20 different players who were an important part of N.C. baseball history along with their career records. And in the appendix he has a comprehensive list of players from the North Carolina teams who have gone on to the major leagues. For any fan of North Carolina baseball, minor league baseball, or simply baseball this is a book that will be a treasured part of their baseball library. Chris Holaday has written the definitive volume on minor league baseball in the state of North Carolina.

Miles Wolff
Spring 1998

Introduction

The history of professional baseball in North Carolina is a rich and colorful one. It is a story involving over 70 towns and cities of all sizes, from large cities like Charlotte to small textile mill towns such as Cooleemee. It is also a story of boys barely out of high school trying to reach a dream of playing in the major leagues, and of veteran ballplayers well past their prime trying to hold on to a career in the sport they love. The story of professional baseball in North Carolina is a story of the minor leagues. All of the teams in the state's history have been members of the minor leagues and until 1993 no team had even been at the highest level of the minors.

Professional baseball was well established in other parts of the country before it took hold in North Carolina. The nation's first professional team, the Cincinnati Red Stockings, was founded in the late 1860s. From there professional baseball spread to the other large cities of the North and Midwest. The great urban growth these cities had witnessed was slow coming to the cities of North Carolina, just as it was to all of the South. Industrial growth really began in North Carolina in the last decade of the nineteenth century. The furniture and textile industries grew rapidly in the Piedmont area of the state, while in the Coastal Plain the tobacco industry boomed. The cities of the state grew, opening the way for professional baseball to become a commercially viable form of entertainment.

It is unclear when the first truly professional baseball team was founded in the state. Amateur teams were common in many towns in the 1890s and college baseball was played at the University of North Carolina as early as 1884. More than likely, the first professional teams in the state were those that were members of the Virginia–North Carolina League of 1901. There were a few earlier teams, though they may have been what would be considered semiprofessional.

In the early part of the century, several professional leagues were founded as baseball grew in popularity in the state. Many of the leagues failed to finish their seasons due to financial problems. The Virginia–North Carolina League of 1901 disbanded early as did another league bearing the same name in 1905. The North Carolina League of 1902 met with the same fate. In 1908, one of the state's two leagues, the Carolina Association, finally finished a season as scheduled. The other league, the Eastern Carolina League, called it quits a couple of weeks early. One of the reasons for these early failures was the difficulty of travel between cities. All travel had to be done by train, which could become expensive over long distances.

Finally in the teens, professional baseball seemed to be stable in the state's larger cities. The Carolina Association and its successor, the North Carolina State League, enjoyed several successful seasons with members in cities including Greensboro, Winston-Salem, Durham, Raleigh, Asheville and Charlotte. This ended in 1917, when minor league baseball all across the nation was thrown into disarray by the entry of the United States into World War I. The North Carolina State League shut down early as did 10 of the 21 minor leagues in the country. With players leaving for military service and with war time restrictions it was not feasible for the teams to continue.

The foundation of the Class D Piedmont League in 1920 marks the beginning of the next period in the state's minor league history. With franchises located in Greensboro, Raleigh, High Point, Winston-Salem, and Durham along with Danville, Virginia, the league was basically a reformation of the defunct North Carolina State League. Asheville, Charlotte, Henderson, Rocky Mount and Wilmington would also at various times be members of the league. The Piedmont League would prosper and be the predominant baseball league in the state, rising as high as the level of Class B, until 1942. The league existed until 1955 as a predominantly Virginia league but the last North Carolina team dropped out after the 1943 season.

The decade of the 1920s also saw baseball return to the eastern part of the state as the Class D Eastern Carolina League was reformed in 1928. Fayetteville, Goldsboro, Greenville, Kinston, Rocky Mount and Wilmington were the members of the league which would last only two seasons before failing.

In the 1930s, the popularity of minor league baseball began to spread, making it more feasible for the smaller towns and cities of the state to support professional teams. In 1934, the Class D Bi-State League, made up of towns in North Carolina as well as Virginia, was the first new league to form. Lasting until 1942, the league fielded teams in Mayodan, Reidsville, Mt. Airy, Leaksville-Spray-Draper, Sanford, Wilson and Burlington.

The 1937 season was an important one in the state's minor league history: Two new leagues, made up of teams only from North Carolina, were formed. Originally a semipro

league for college players formed in 1934, the Coastal Plain League joined the National Association in 1937. Designated Class D, the league originally consisted of Ayden, Goldsboro, Greenville, Kinston, New Bern, Snow Hill, Tarboro, and Williamston. Ayden and Snow Hill were later replaced by Wilson and Rocky Mount. Based in the textile mill towns of the Western Piedmont, the Class D North Carolina State League was also formed in 1937. Its original members were Cooleemee, Landis, Lexington, Mooresville, Newton-Conover, Salisbury, Shelby and Thomasville. Other prewar members were Concord, Gastonia and Kannapolis.

The only other league during this period which had North Carolina members was the Class B South Atlantic League. Charlotte (1919–1930), Gastonia (1923), and Asheville (1924–1930) were members of this league which was centered primarily in South Carolina.

During the 1941 season, North Carolina towns and cities were home to 25 different minor league teams. Minor league baseball as a whole was growing in popularity across the country. The future of all professional baseball became uncertain, however, after the Japanese attack on Pearl Harbor and the United States' subsequent declaration of war on Japan and Germany.

There was talk of suspending all baseball but President Roosevelt decided it should stay, as the game was important to stability and morale on the home front. All of the major league teams continued operation but many minor league teams shut down. The war left a shortage of players and team travel to games was made difficult by gasoline rationing. The rationing of gas also cut down on attendance at games.

The 1942 season saw the number of North Carolina teams drop to 18 after the Coastal Plain League suspended operations. All of these remaining teams managed to play a full season while across the country many other leagues and teams did not.

In 1943 only ten minor leagues in the entire country began play whereas in 1941 there had been 41 different leagues. All North Carolina teams — with the exception of Durham, still a member of the Piedmont League — ceased play. That league continued play in 1944 though Durham dropped out, leaving North Carolina without a single professional baseball team that season.

North Carolina was not without high quality baseball during the latter years of the war, however. Most military bases fielded baseball teams and the competition between them was strong. Since many of the nation's major and minor league players were serving in the military, most bases had at least some talented players available. In North Carolina, two of the top military teams were Fort Bragg and Greensboro's AAF Oversea's Replacement Depot. The Fort Bragg team, which won the state semipro title in 1944, included Dwight Wall, Van Harrington, Buster Maynard, Tige Harris, and Paige Dennis, all of whom had played minor league ball in the state. The Greensboro ORD represented the state at the national tournament in Wichita, Kansas, that year, finishing third. The Tech-Hawks, as the team was called, featured major leaguers Lee Gamble and Taffy Wright as well as minor leaguers Barney Deforge and Walter "Teapot" Frye.

As the 1945 season approached, it appeared that the war was winding down. Baseball returned to North Carolina as the North Carolina State League resumed play. That year also marked the founding of the Carolina League, a league which still exists today. A Class C circuit, the Carolina League was originally made up of teams from six North Carolina cities and two from Virginia. That summer saw the war end. For baseball, this meant the return of players and the lifting of all restrictions. Minor league baseball was about to boom and reach a level of popularity it had never before seen.

With the war over, the American people turned their attention to other things. They wanted to put the war and the pain it had caused behind them. The years after the war were times of great economic growth and prosperity. People had extra money to spend

on entertainment. What better or more American way to spend money than attend a baseball game? If one did not live in a major league city then that game would be a minor league game. The years 1946–51 saw minor league baseball in North Carolina reach its peak. Every town, it seemed, wanted a team to call its own. Professional baseball was played in all of the larger cities of the state but also in places like Elkin, with a population of less than 3,000, and Red Springs, with only around 2,200 people. Both towns drew over 33,000 in attendance in 1949, showing the true popularity and support teams in small towns had during this all-too-brief period.

The 1946 season saw 33 teams from North Carolina take the field in six different leagues. The Carolina and North Carolina State leagues continued play while the Coastal Plain League resumed play after postponement due to the war. Three new leagues began play: the Tobacco State League (made up of teams from the Southern Piedmont and Coastal Plain areas), the Blue Ridge League (teams from the mountains of North Carolina and Virginia) and the Tri-State League (teams from North Carolina, South Carolina and Tennessee).

The number of teams grew to 36 in 1947 as some of the leagues added members. Professional baseball in the state reached its peak in 1948 with 44 different towns and cities fielding teams. That year the Western Carolina League had been formed, adding eight more teams to the state's total.

In 1949, teams took to the field in 43 towns with only minor changes in the leagues. For many teams, attendance still increased. The years 1947–49 saw attendance figures that would not be rivaled until the 1980s. In 1947, the Winston-Salem Twins drew a Carolina League–leading 223,507 fans. By 1952 that number had dropped well below 100,000. A team from Winston-Salem — the only city in the state to have continuous minor league baseball since 1945 — did not break 100,000 in attendance again until 1986.

Towns fought to get their own minor

league team. It was a source of pride. As a team in one town would fail, other towns would scramble to take its place in the league. Other teams would be lured to relocate with promises of better attendance and town support. Towns were proud of their local teams and star players were considered heroes. Joe Di-Maggio and Ted Williams were far away in the cities of the North. Baseball heroes in the towns of North Carolina had names like Norman Small, Eddie Neville and Harry Soufas. Major league scores got little attention in many newspapers while local baseball results made headlines.

In the early '50s minor league baseball began to experience a decline in popularity. Before that time baseball had no real competition for entertainment dollars. Movies had always competed somewhat but they were more of a special occasion and not a social event like a baseball game. By the early '50s, however, the minor leagues met their greatest enemy: television.

Baseball, which had ruled unchallenged as the national game, also had growing competition from other sports. College athletics, particularly football and basketball, grew immensely in popularity. By the late '50s, professional football became widely popular. Though it had existed since the 1920s, pro football had been limited to the cities of the North and Midwest. Television brought it to the South for the first time. The late '40s had also seen the emergence of another pastime that competed directly with minor league baseball: stock car racing. In the South, and particularly in North Carolina, racing began to attract more and more fans. Its popularity continues to grow today. While many of these sports had seasons that did not directly compete with baseball, every year a few more fans would decide that they had a new favorite sport other than baseball.

The 1952 season marked the end of the golden age of minor league ball in the state. The three Class D leagues that operated in the state — the Coastal Plain, the Western Carolina, and the North Carolina State — all disbanded after that season. Though the Tar

Heel League would be organized from former NCSL and WCL members, it would last only a year-and-a-half before it too failed.

In the late 1950s, the state was represented in professional baseball only by the teams in the Carolina League, which had continued to hold on, and by Charlotte, a member of the South Atlantic League. Finally, in 1960, the Western Carolina League was reorganized, adding eight teams to the state's total. Two years later, however, that league had dropped to only four members.

It became apparent to the major league teams in the early 1960s that something would have to be done to save the minor leagues. The minors had always been the main source of talent, serving as an incubator for players until they were ready for major league play. In May of 1962, the major league teams adopted what was called the Player Development Plan for implementation in 1963. It restructured the entire minor league system, guaranteeing the survival of at least 100 minor league clubs, yet basically making the minor leagues their endentured servants. Gone was the era of the independent ball club. Now a team's survival hinged upon its ability to secure a major league working agreement or player development contract, as they came to be called.

Gone also were the league classifications of B, C and D. Now all teams would become either AAA, AA, A or Rookie level ball. The Western Carolina League and the Carolina League were both reclassified as single A level baseball. The South Atlantic League, which included Charlotte and Asheville, became double A.

This new agreement helped North Carolina's minor league teams to survive but not prosper. Throughout the 1960s and '70s, the teams struggled. Though players' salaries were now paid by the major league club that owned them, the minor league team was responsible for many of the other expenses such as ballpark upkeep, paying the power bill for the lights, and so on. This was hard to do if paying fans were not coming to the park every night.

The rebirth of professional baseball in North Carolina was sparked by the return to the game by two long-time baseball cities: Greensboro and Durham. When Greensboro dropped out of the Carolina League after the 1968 season, the city was left without baseball for ten years. When a new team was formed in the city in 1979 as a member of the Western Carolinas League, fan interest was renewed. Whereas the 1968 Greensboro team had drawn only 26,000 fans, the new team drew 165,596. The second place team in the league in attendance, Gastonia, drew only 58,000. Attendance figures like those of the 1979 Greensboro Hornets had not been seen in the state since the late 1940s.

The next season saw the return of the Durham Bulls to the Carolina League. The last team to play in that city had been the Raleigh-Durham Triangles of 1971, who split home games between those two cities. Much like Greensboro, the new team brought renewed fan interest. While the Triangles of 1971 had drawn only 40,000, the Bulls drew almost 176,000 in their first season back in the league. By 1995, with a growth in attendance nearly every year, the Bulls were drawing close to 400,000 fans.

The resurgence in the popularity of minor league baseball has helped return a lost sense of community to many cities and towns. In the 1970s, with few minor league teams in the state, fans had to turn to faraway major league teams. During this time most fans watched their favorite teams only on television as even Baltimore and Atlanta, the closest big league cities, were several hours away. Now fans in Raleigh can see baseball in person by driving a short distance to Zebulon or Durham. With the growth of the minors, many fans again have hometown teams to root for. Every team has its avid followers. Rivalries between the state's cities have returned. Durham's main rival was Kinston in the Carolina League; Asheville's is probably Hickory, and so on. Residents of each town take pride in their local teams.

Minor league baseball has lost some of its innocence, however. Rarely is a team today owned by some successful local businessman who happens to love baseball. In the past everyone knew the team owner and he was always at the game. Today, minor league teams are looked upon as a good business investment and several teams are owned by groups of nonlocal investors.

There is big money in minor league baseball today. In the past, teams struggled just to break even at the end of the season. Thanks to the renewed popularity of the game and the crowds that go with it, teams today turn healthy profits. That, combined with huge revenues from sales of souvenirs, adds greatly to the value of an investment in a minor league team. When teams are sold they now can easily bring a couple of million dollars.

Marketing has come to play a huge part in the success of minor league teams all across the country. The selling of T-shirts, hats, and so on, with a team's logo on it has become big business. With the popularity of the movie *Bull Durham* in 1988, Durham Bulls hats and shirts became immediately popular. They were followed by the Carolina Mudcats and the Hickory Crawdads. It is not uncommon to see someone wearing a hat from one of these teams on the other side of the country. These three teams led all other minor league teams in the country in marketing sales in 1994. Another team in the state, the Piedmont Phillies, changed their name from that of their parent team to become the Piedmont Boll Weevils in 1996. They hope to establish their own identity as well as increase sales of souvenirs.

It is easy to forget that the purpose of professional baseball is entertainment. It always has been and always will be. Just like movies or concerts, professional baseball games are played to attract paying spectators. Since there is so much competition for entertainment dollars, teams go out of their way to ensure fans enjoy themselves. In the past, minor league teams were run by a couple of guys who did everything from ticket sales to field maintenance. Today, some teams have staffs of dozens to assist fans in every way possible. The Durham Bulls have even sent staff members to "college" at Disney World to learn the finer points of customer service.

The players themselves are much different from those who played the game in the past. The biggest difference is age. Most players today in the minor leagues are in their late teens and early twenties. Only in Charlotte and Durham, with their Triple A franchises, might you see older players. In Burlington, the players are all in their first professional season. Most of them just graduated from high school a few weeks before the season begins. They are away from home for the first time as well as playing with wooden bats and before sizable crowds for the first time. Their enthusiasm is evident and every one of them thinks he will make the big leagues. In reality only one or two might ever play in a major league game. If a player doesn't improve at every level, the major league team that owns their contract will release them. Up until the early 1950s, it was not uncommon to see players in their late thirties playing Class D ball. These were players who had realized they would never make the major leagues but were successful at the minor league level so there they stayed. Remember, up until the early 1960s, there were only 16 major league teams. Today there are 30. There were also many more minor league teams than today. The odds of making it were much less.

Despite the changes in the game over the years, professional minor league baseball remains an important part of North Carolina's heritage. The number of towns and cities in the state that have fielded teams is second only to the much larger and more populous state of Texas. Even today, with 11 teams, North Carolina ranks third behind only Florida and California. North Carolina's teams (and their fans) have led the rediscovery of the minor leagues by the entire nation, a growth in popularity that continues to this day.

The Towns
and Their Teams

◆ —————— *Albemarle* —————— ◆

The Albemarle Rockets took to the field at Morton Park for their one and only season in 1948 as a member of the Class D North Carolina State League. The franchise had originally been located in Landis but was moved to Albemarle in hopes of better attendance. The Rockets went through three managers (Stanley Brown, Jim Miller, and George Motto) on their way to a terrible record of 32–78, 35 games out of first. The team had a good offense led by outfielders Hal Walters (.362, 81 RBIs), Claude Hathcock (.341) and shortstop Bob Deese (.327). No Rockets pitcher, however, had a winning record. The team was next to last in the league in attendance (with 28,025) and moved back to Landis after the season.

◆ —————— *Angier–Fuquay Springs* —————— ◆

The Angier–Fuquay Springs Colts were a charter member of the Class D Tobacco State League when it formed in 1946. The Colts finished the regular season with a record of 57–62, 14 games back, in fourth place. This did qualify them for the playoffs and in the first round they defeated regular season champ Sanford, four games to two. In the deciding game of the semifinals, Colts pitcher Jim House (11–10) pitched a no-hitter against the Spinners.

In the finals the Colts beat the Clinton Blues four games to three to take the championship. The team was led by first baseman Marvin Lorenz (.338, 86 RBIs, 87 runs), outfielder-manager Paul Dunlap (.361, 81 RBIs), and third baseman Joe Mills (.306). Outfielder Otis Stephens joined the team in midseason after being released from the military and hit .324. Overall, the Colts led the league with a .295 team batting average. The pitching staff, led by Ray Bomar (11–8), was not as strong but still had some decent talent.

Although successful, the team was sold to a group from Warsaw and subsequently relocated there.

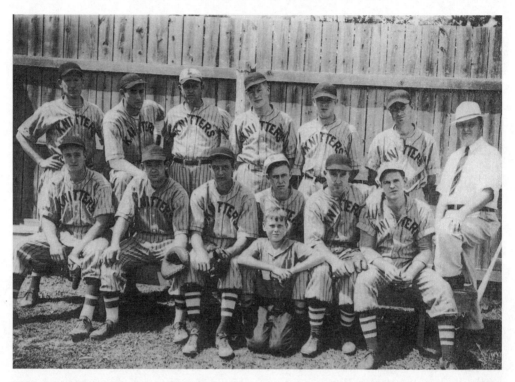

The 1935 Wiscassett Knitters, an Albemarle-based textile team that included many players who would also appear in the minor leagues: *Back:* Rip Tudor, Orge "Pat" Cooper, Shelby Burleson, Monk Watson, Skin Hatchcock, Bob Kendall, Hoyle Blalock (bus. mgr.); *Front:* Ike Williams, Jim Staton, Claude Hatcock, batboys, Snook Cooper, Bruce Staton (courtesy of Bob Kendall).

◆ ——————— *Asheville* ——————— ◆

The history of professional baseball in Asheville can be traced back as far as 1897. That summer, an Asheville team named the Moonshiners played in a league known as the Southeastern League. Little else is known except that the team had an 11–10 record when the league disbanded.

Organized baseball next appeared in the city in 1909 when an Asheville team was organized for play in an independent league known as the Western North Carolina League. The team, called the Red Birds, played against teams from Hendersonville, Waynesville and Canton. The league disbanded shortly before the season was scheduled to end.

In 1910, the Asheville Moonshiners became a charter member of the Class D Southeastern League. The team had a mediocre season and finished fourth in the six team league with a record of 44–41. The league divided after the season and Asheville went with the teams from Tennessee to form the new Class D Appalachian League in 1911. The Moonshiners had a decent season and turned in a third place, 53–44 finish. Returning to the league the following season, the team dropped to fifth place, winning 47 games and losing 58.

Now called the Mountaineers, Asheville became a charter member of the Class D North Carolina State League in 1913. It was a forgettable season as the team finished 58–55, good enough for fourth place. Third baseman Walter Barbare (.273) went on to spend eight seasons in the big leagues. The 1914 season was even more of a disappointment to Asheville

Top: The 1946 Angier Colts included: *Back:* Andrew Scrobola, Ray Bomar, Otis Stephens, Roscoe Gentry, James House, Marvin Lorenz, Joe Mills, Bill Ratteree; *Front:* Ray Hardee, unidentified, Harry Fortune, Sam Sellers, Paul Hunt, Ken Jackson, Gus Rogers (courtesy of Otis Stephens). *Bottom:* Several Angier–Fuquay Springs players were on the 1946 Tobacco State League All-Star team. Members were: *Back:* Smith, Marvin Lorenz, Ed Bass, Hank Nesselrode, Jim Taylor, Jim Stephenson, Jim House, Howard Auman, Ray Hardee, Bob Pugh, Bruce Hedrick; *Front:* Andrew Holliday, Phalti Shoffner, Granville "Shamrock" Denning, Jimmy Guinn, Paul Crawford, Zeb Harrington (mgr.), Joe Nessing, Joe Mills, Ken Jackson, Paul Hunt (courtesy of Howard Auman).

baseball fans; the team finished last with a lowly 43–73 record. The 1915 season, however, was a dramatic change. Called the Tourists for the first time, the team took the league pennant, winning both halves of the season. Led by manager and shortstop Jack Corbett, they compiled a record of 74–46. Pitcher Gary Fortune led the team to victory with his 22–10 record while outfielder Jim Hickman (.291) hit a league leading 14 home runs and scored 95 runs.

In 1916, the Tourists started strong and won the first half of the season. Slumping in the second half—possibly due to the fact that their home field at Riverside Park was washed away in a flood on July 16—the team finished with the league's fourth best record of 57–54. In the playoffs with second half champ Charlotte, the Tourists were swept in four games. Outfielder Jim Hickman, who won the league batting title with a .350 average, was called up to Brooklyn to finish the season. Catcher Earle Mack (.278) had already played briefly in the big leagues with the Philadelphia Athletics, a team owned by his father Connie Mack.

The North Carolina State League was one of nine minor leagues to begin but not finish the 1917 season. With the shortages caused by the United States' involvement in World War I, many teams and leagues found they could not make ends meet. Asheville and Raleigh both decided to drop out of the N.C. State League on May 18. The league tried to continue but called it quits on May 30.

Professional baseball finally returned to Asheville in 1924 when the city was granted a franchise in the Class B South Atlantic League. Named the Skylanders, the team did not have a particularly good season as they finished fifth in the six team league with a record of 55–62. Pitcher Sam Gibson (17–12), a native of King, N.C., led the league with 140 strikeouts. He made it to the big leagues for a few seasons but later found stardom in the Pacific Coast League. In 14 seasons in that league, which could almost have been considered a major league at that time, he compiled a 227–140 record. The 1924 season was also an important one for Asheville as it marked the opening of McCormick Field, the home of baseball in the city to this day.

In 1925 the team readopted the name Tourists. With the exception of the Asheville Orioles of 1972–75, this name has since been used by every Asheville team. The team finished at 66–63 in 1925, good enough for fifth place in the now eight team league. Outfielder Hal Anderson (.299, 47 SB) had a good season. He would return to Asheville to manage the Tourists from 1937 to 1939. The 1926 Tourists, managed by former big league third baseman Larry Gardner, rose to second place. However, with a record of 80–66, they were still 17 games behind first place Greenville (S.C.). Pitcher Gary Fortune, who had been with the Tourists in 1914 and '15, returned to the team for half a season and contributed a 5–2 record. Fourth place was the best the team could manage in 1927. The Tourists' record of 76–73 left them 16½ games out of first. Outfielder Stan Keyes, in the first of three seasons in Asheville, hit .320 with 22 home runs and 94 RBIs.

Finally winning the league pennant in 1928, the Tourists turned in an impressive record of 97–49. With a team batting average of .304, it was perhaps the greatest Tourists team ever. Manager Ray Kennedy hit .366, Ben Chapman hit .336 and Dusty Cooke (.362) hit an amazing 30 triples. The stars of the pitching staff were Bill Harris (25–9), Bud Shaney (21–11) and Joe Heving (13–5), who led the league with an ERA of 2.46. After the season the Tourists sold six players to the major leagues. Of those six, Dusty Cooke and Joe Heving had decent big league careers while Ben Chapman became a three-time All-Star with the Yankees and later spent four seasons as manager of the Phillies.

Asheville fielded another good team in 1929. Ray Kennedy led that season's Tourists to first place in the first half of the season. They dropped to third in the second half but still finished with the league's second best overall record at 84–62. The Tourists failed, however, to take a second consecutive pennant as they lost the playoff to Knoxville, four games to one. The Tourists featured the league's batting champion that season, outfielder Stan Keyes (.377, 108 RBIs), along with pitcher Johnny Allen (20–11), the league strikeout leader with 173. Keyes was sold to the Minneapolis Millers of the American Association after 110 games. Allen became one of the American League's best pitchers in the 1930s with the Yankees and the Indians. First baseman Bobby Hipps (.323) and catcher Chick Outen (.342, 105 runs) both had great seasons and joined Keyes on the league All-Star team. Pitcher Bud Shaney, in his fifth season with the Tourists, posted a 17–12 record.

The Tourists had another solid season in 1930. Their record of 79–61 put them in third place, eight games out of first. The team again had the league batting champ as All-Star outfielder Hal Sullivan hit .374.

Jumping to the Class C Piedmont League for the 1931 season, the Tourists took a step down in the minor league classifications. For the first time in their existence, the Tourists became affiliated with a higher level team as they signed a working agreement with the Hollywood Stars of the Pacific Coast League. The team had an unremarkable season and finished fourth in the eight team league with a record of 66–67. First baseman Bobby Hipps finished second in the league in batting with a .360 average while pitcher Monroe Mitchell (20–13) was one of the league's best.

The next season saw the Tourists sign a working agreement with Louisville of the American Association. They failed to complete the season, however. On July 7, the Tourists withdrew from the league (as did High Point) due to financial difficulties caused by the Depression. At the time of their withdrawal, the Tourists' record stood at 35–32. The manager of that short-lived team was outfielder Joseph Guyon (.364). A Chippewa Indian from Minnesota, Guyon had been an All-American football player at Georgia Tech. He spent eight seasons in the NFL (1920–27) and in 1971 was named to the National Football League Hall of Fame.

Asheville remained without a team in 1933 and it appeared 1934 would be the same.

On June 6 of that season, however, the Columbia franchise of the Piedmont League (now Class B) decided to relocate to Asheville. This new Tourists team, a Boston Red Sox farm club, had good hitting but desperately lacked pitching. Right fielder George Ferrell hit .361 with 20 home runs and 82 RBIs before being promoted to Class A Reading (Pa.) after 90 games. Left fielder Paul Dunlap hit .329 with 100 RBIs while first baseman Ivy Griffin, a former major leaguer, hit .325. No pitcher on the team had a winning record. Because of this the Tourists finished fifth out of six in the league with a record of 55–78. They disbanded after the season.

In 1935, the St. Louis Cardinals moved their Piedmont League farm club from Greensboro to Asheville. Managed by Billy Southworth, who would later spend 13 seasons as a big league manager, this new Tourists team won the first half of the season and finished with a league best record of 75–62. Outfielders Cap Clark (.358), league leader in RBIs with 129, and Stu Martin (.332) led the offense. Herb Moore (21–5) was the league's best pitcher. The Tourists advanced to play second half champ Richmond in a playoff but lost, four games to two. On March 28 of that year, before the season had begun, McCormick Field had been heavily damaged by fire. Most of the grandstand was destroyed but the field was not and the season began on schedule with fans sitting in temporary bleachers.

Going from the league's best team in 1935 to its worst in 1936, the Tourists finished the season with the horrible record of 40–103. No starting player hit over .300 and, without run support, no pitcher even came close to a winning record. Individual pitching records included 8–17, 4–12, 2–11, and 4–12. The worst record though, belonged to Tom Sunkel, who won 6 games and lost 26. Surprisingly, Sunkel debuted in the majors the next spring with the Cardinals and spent parts of several seasons there.

The Tourists continued their rollercoaster ride in 1937 as they were once again on top of the league. Led by the league MVP, third baseman Harl Maggert (.342, 23 HR, 139 RBIs, 122 runs), the team took the pennant with an 89–50 record. A well-balanced team, the Tourists had outstanding hitters in first baseman Jim Grilk (.320, 25 HR, 120 RBIs), second baseman Jimmy Gruzdis (.310, 125 runs) and catcher Sam Narron (.328, 95 RBIs). Manager and outfielder Hal Anderson hit .288 with 73 RBIs. The pitching staff featured two 20-game winners: Al Scherer (23–7) and Maywood Belcher (20–8). Despite all of this talent, the Tourists were upset in the playoffs by Portsmouth, three games to two.

With a record of 63–75, the Tourists dropped back to seventh place in 1938. Hank Gornicki (17–13, 2.57 ERA), named to the league All-Star team, pitched well but received little run support. The 1939 season, however, saw the team again win the pennant. With an 89–55 record, the Tourists finished first by 12 games. The team had an outstanding pitching staff led by Herschel Lyons (12–1, 1.82 ERA) and Hank Gornicki (9–0). The offense was powered by catcher Walker Cooper (.336, 80 RBIs) and All-Star first baseman John Angle (.326, 94 RBIs). Cooper would go on to be one of the major league's best catchers during the 1940s. Guided by manager Hal Anderson, the Tourists breezed through the playoffs, sweeping Richmond in the first round then taking the championship by defeating Rocky Mount, four games to two.

The 1940 season was also a good one for the Tourists. They won 75 games and lost 60, finishing second by a game-and-a-half. With a 20–6 record and a league leading 145 strikeouts, pitcher Ken Burkhart was one of the league's best. The team had no real offensive stars but Rocky Rhawn (.272), Emil Verban (.282) and Bill Hart (.267) all went on to play in the majors. Hart would later return to Asheville to manage the 1952 Tourists. The playoffs were not kind to the Tourists as they lost in the first round to Rocky Mount, four games to two. The 1940 season was also significant for another reason: For the first time permanent lights were installed at McCormick Field.

It was back to seventh place for the 1941 Tourists, as they finished 21 games out of first with a 64–76 record. Speedy center fielder Bill Shewy (.302) was the team's best player and led the league with 107 runs and 42 stolen bases. Outfielder and manager Nick Cullop (.266), whose playing career spanned 25 seasons, holds the career record for minor league RBIs with 1,857. The results of the 1942 season, the city's last in the Piedmont League, were also disappointing as the Tourists turned in a sixth place, 61–77 finish. Outfielder Dick Sisler (.271), who would spend eight seasons in the big leagues, was one of the team's best hitters. As did many other cities across the country, Asheville dropped out of professional baseball after the season due to the war.

With the end of the war, plans were made to bring professional baseball back to Asheville. In 1946, the reformed Tourists signed a working agreement with the Brooklyn Dodgers and joined the newly organized Class B Tri-State League, a league made up of teams from the Carolinas and Tennessee. Led by the league batting champ, catcher Dick Bouknight (.367), the Tourists played well. Their 83–57 record left them in second place, ten games behind Charlotte. They advanced to the playoffs but lost to Knoxville, four games to one. Pitcher Erv Palica (15–6, 2.51 ERA) made his debut with Brooklyn the following season. Lefty Morrie Martin, 14–6 for the Tourists, also made the big leagues.

Winning 65 games and losing 74, the Tourists of 1947 finished sixth out of the eight teams in the league. Future Brooklyn Dodger pitcher Clem Labine was 6–0 with a 2.07 ERA. The 1948 season was a much better one as the Tourists, managed by former Cubs pitcher Clay Bryant, ran away with the regular season title. Their record of 95–51 put them 17 games ahead of the second place team. Asheville had seven .300 hitters that season, led by first baseman Ray Hickernell (.332, 22 HR, 139 RBIs) and second baseman Forrest "Spook" Jacobs (.328, 92 RBIs, 47 SB), who was voted the league's Most Valuable Player. The pitching staff featured Tom Lakos (21–8) and Joe

Landrum (17–4). The playoffs were a disaster for the Tourists as they were upset by third place Rock Hill, three games to one in the first round.

The end of the 1949 season found the Tourists in third with a 76–71 record. Led by All-Star outfielder Alex Driskill (.319, 97 RBIs, 102 runs), they advanced to the playoffs but lost to Spartanburg, three games to one. Improving to 83–62 in 1950, the Tourists finished second. They had no trouble with Spartanburg in the first round of the playoffs as they swept the Peaches in three games. The finals went a full seven games before Asheville succumbed to Rock Hill.

The results of the 1951 season were much the same as the Tourists finished second with an 85–55 record. They then defeated Rock Hill in the first round of the playoffs, three games to two, but again falling short in the finals, the Tourists were swept by Spartanburg. Outfielder Bill Kerr (.339, 118 RBIs) and shortstop Chris Kitsos (.334, 134 runs), both named to the league All-Star team, led the Asheville offense that season while pitchers Ralph Butler (21–13, 2.68 ERA) and Jim Cater (16–7) were two of the league's best. First baseman Norm Larker (.297, 94 RBIs, 118 runs) would go on to spend six years in the majors.

The Tourists (65–75) had a losing season in 1952 and finished fifth in the league but improved in 1953 to second place, posting a 83–67 record. A talented ballclub, the Tourists hit .291 as a team. Catcher Joe Pignatano (.316, 82 RBIs), who hit a league-leading 13 triples, and pitcher Fred Kipp (15–5, 2.23 ERA), the league ERA leader, would both later play for the Dodgers. The team's most impressive performance, however, came from first baseman Danny Keith, who in only 58 games hit an amazing .420 with 59 RBIs, 50 runs, 9 triples and 15 stolen bases. In the playoffs that season, the Tourists were upset by fourth place Anderson, three game to one.

Manager Ray Hathaway led the Tourists to the pennant in 1954. With an 86–54 record they finished 13 games ahead of second place Knoxville. Shortstop Jackie Spears (.329, 120 runs, 82 RBIs) was the team's leading hitter while outfielder Oscar Sierra (.290) led the league with 104 RBIs. Both were named to the league's All-Star team along with pitcher Les Fessette (22–8). The Tourists defeated Greenville (S.C.) in the playoffs but were once again denied the postseason championship as they lost to Knoxville, three games to one, in the finals.

The Tri-State League had dropped from eight members to six for the 1953 season. After the 1954 season, two more league members dropped out. The financially strapped league decided to operate with only four teams in 1955, making it the smallest league in professional baseball that season. Asheville remained as the only North Carolina member. It was not a successful season for the Tourists as they finished third with a record of 53–63. Outfielder Edwin Allen (.342, 78 RBIs) and second baseman Ed Serrano (.270, 86 RBIs, 126 BB) were the team's top players. The league disbanded after the season.

Professional baseball was absent from Asheville for three seasons. On weekend nights during the summers of 1956–58, McCormick Field was used as a stock car racing track. A quarter mile loop was paved around the field and a concrete wall was built. In 1959 the asphalt track was torn up as a new baseball team was formed to begin play in the Class A South Atlantic League. It was an average season for the new team, again called the Tourists, as they finished the season fifth out of eight with an even 70–70 record. Attendance, however, was first in the league at 113,001. First baseman Nate Dickerson, named to the All-Star team, won the batting title with a .362 average.

After spending the 1959 season as an independent team, the Tourists signed a working agreement with the Philadelphia Phillies for 1960. They were not supplied with particularly good talent and finished sixth in the league with a 62–77 record. Attendance dropped to 73,276.

The next season was much more successful. The 1961 Tourists, guided by manager Ray Hathaway, won the league title by 13

games with their record of 87–50. A new working agreement had been signed with Pittsburgh and the Pirates sent Asheville many talented players. Eight players from the 1961 Tourists went on to appear in the big leagues. Future Hall of Famer Willie Stargell (.289, 22 HR, 89 RBIs) played center field. Catcher Jesus McFarlane (.301, 21 HR) and second baseman Gene Alley (.263) also made it up to Pittsburgh. Eighteen-year-old infielder Bob Bailey, recently signed by the Pirates for a $175,000 bonus, hit only .220 but spent 17 seasons in the majors. Pitchers Art Swanson (11–3) and Tommie Sisk (12–3) also went on to Pittsburgh. Surprisingly, the Tourists' best hitter in 1961, first baseman Gary Rushing (.311, 25 HR, 99 RBIs, 108 runs), never made the majors though he led the league in home runs, RBIs and runs scored.

The Tourists broke even in 1962 with a 70–70 record and finished sixth. Asheville did, however, have the league's best hitter — outfielder Elmo Plaskett (.349, 27 HR). The South Atlantic League went to a split-season format in 1963. Asheville (79–61) finished with the league's second best record but failed to win either half of the season. Second baseman Felix Santana (.300) and All-Star pitcher Troy Giles (18–7) both had good seasons.

The 1964 season saw the Tourists drop to the cellar of the league (which was now renamed the Southern League). With a record of 52–86, they were 28 games out of first. Outfielder George Spriggs (.322) was the star of the team, leading the league with 33 stolen bases.

Much improved in 1965, the Tourists finished at 80–60, tied for first with Columbus. First baseman Charlie Leonard (.270) led the league with 78 RBIs and catcher Jesus McFarlane (.292) led in home runs with 22. Luke Walker (12–7, 2.26 ERA, 197 strikeouts) was the league's best pitcher. An 88–61 finish put the 1966 Tourists in second place. First baseman Bob Robertson (.287, 32 HR, 99 RBIs) went on to a long major league career after leading the Southern League that season in home runs and RBIs. Pitcher Dave Roberts (14–5, 2.61 ERA) led the league in ERA; Dock Ellis was 10–9 with a 2.76 ERA.

For the 1967 season the Tourists jumped to the Class A Carolina League, becoming an affiliate of the Houston Astros. Outfielder Danny Walton (.302, 25 HR) led the team in hitting while catcher Hal King (.288) won the league home run title with 30, earning a September call-up to Houston. Mike Daniel (15–5, 2.63 ERA) was one of the league's best pitchers. The Tourists lacked depth, however, and finished last in their division with a 64–74 record.

The Tourists returned to the Southern League in 1968 as an affiliate of the Cincinnati Reds. Managed by future legendary big league manager Sparky Anderson, the Tourists (86–54) took the pennant. Outfielder Arlie Burge (.317) won the batting title while pitcher Grover Powell led the league with 16 wins and an ERA of 2.54. Outfielder Bernie Carbo (.281, 20 HR), shortstop Darrel Chaney (.231, 23 HR) and catcher Fred Kendall (.291) all had long major league careers. Relief pitcher Dan McGinn finished the season 6–3 with a 2.29 ERA and was promoted to Cincinnati in September.

Finishing at an even 69–69 in 1969, the Tourists placed third in the league. First baseman Don Anderson (.324, 100 RBIs) won the batting title and led the league in RBIs. His teammate and fellow All-Star, third baseman Kurt Bevacqua (.316, 91 RBIs), finished second in hitting. Shortstop and future Reds star Dave Concepcion hit .294 and led the league in fielding percentage at his position. The 1970 season was a poor one as the team dropped to last place with a record of 59–80. Attendance was at its postwar low with only 28,720, also last in the league.

For the 1971 season, the Southern League merged with the Texas League to form the Dixie Association. Asheville, now a White Sox farm club, played in the Eastern Division of the association. The Tourists (90–51) played well yet still finished second, 1½ games behind Charlotte. In a playoff with Charlotte the Tourists came out losers, two games to one. Outfielder Ken Hottman (.302) had a great season, leading the league in home runs (37), RBIs (116), and runs scored (99). The

The pennant-winning 1968 Asheville Tourists, managed by Sparky Anderson (kneeling, middle) (courtesy of Jim Mills).

Southern and Texas leagues split up again after the season.

At the insistence of their new parent team Baltimore, the team became the Asheville Orioles in 1972. It was the first time since 1924 that an Asheville team had not been called the Tourists. Managed by Cal Ripken, Sr., the Orioles turned in an 81–58 record, winning their division. They lost in the playoffs, however, to Montgomery, three games to none. Outfielder Mike Reinbach (.346, 30 HR, 109 RBIs, 123 runs) had an extraordinary season and was named league MVP. He dominated league pitching and led the league in almost every offensive category. Future Baltimore star outfielder Al Bumbry hit .347 in 26 games with Asheville before being promoted to AAA.

Asheville again featured the league batting champ in 1973 when second baseman Rob Andrews hit .309. Catcher Terry Clapp led the league in home runs (35) and RBIs (98) while shortstop and future big leaguer Bob Bailor hit .293 and stole 39 bases. As a team

the Orioles had an average season. They finished second in their division with a 71–69 record. The 1974 season was also a mediocre one as the Orioles (70–67) again turned in a second place divisional finish. The stars of that season's team were second baseman Kim Andrew (.317) and shortstop Kiko Garcia (.274), both of whom were named to the league All-Star team. Infielder Rich Dauer, who would go on to spend ten seasons in Baltimore, hit .328 in 53 games.

The 1975 season was the last one for the city in both the Southern League and at the AA level. Asheville's Orioles (63–75) had a poor season and finished last in their division though outfielder Chuck Heil (.322) did win the batting title. First baseman Eddie Murray, who had appeared briefly with Asheville in 1974, returned and hit .264 with 17 home runs. Reaching the majors in 1977, Murray had a career that will almost certainly lead to the Hall of Fame. Another future big league star, pitcher Dennis Martinez, won four games for the Tourists after being promoted from the Florida State League late in the season. After the 1975 season, Baltimore dropped Asheville in favor of Charlotte.

For 1976, Asheville was able to pick up a player development contract with the Texas Rangers and switched to the Class A Western Carolinas League. Renamed the Tourists, the team won the first half of a split season and finished with a league best record of 76–62. They faced second half champ Greenwood in the playoffs but lost, three games to one. Pitcher Harold Kelly led the league with 13 wins and an ERA of 3.02. First baseman Pat Putnam (.361, 24 HR, 142 RBIs) accomplished the rare feat of winning the Triple Crown. He was named Minor League Player of the Year by *The Sporting News*, the first player from a North Carolina team to be so honored since Johnny Vander Meer of the 1936 Durham Bulls.

The Tourists had another Triple Crown winner in 1977 as outfielder David Rivera hit .346 with 26 home runs and 118 RBIs. Rivera never made the major leagues but teammate Dave Righetti (11–3, 3.14 ERA) did. Named American League Rookie of the Year in 1981, Righetti spent the entire decade of the '80s with the New York Yankees and was one of the majors' best relief pitchers. As a team, the Tourists had a good season (81–58) and finished with the second best record in the league. However, they were not included in the playoffs since they won neither half of the season. The 1978 season was an average one for the team as they finished tied for third with a 73–67 record. All-Star first baseman Jim Barbe led the league in RBIs (99), runs (91) and home runs (18).

The 1979 Tourists (75–63) finished with the league's second best overall record but again won neither half of the season. Designated hitter Luis Gonzalez (.290, 26 HR, 87 RBIs) powered the offense while the pitching staff featured Jim Farr (14–7).

In 1980, the league was renamed the South Atlantic League and divided into North and South divisions. Asheville was assigned to the North with the three other league members from North Carolina. The Tourists had an unremarkable season on the field, finishing third in their division with a 69–71 record. All-Star first baseman Pete O'Brien (.295, 17 HR, 94 RBIs) and catcher Donnie Scott (.295, 78 RBIs) led the team in hitting. The 1981 team improved slightly to 74–68, finishing second though they were still 24½ games behind a Greensboro team that had run away with the league championship. Asheville did have the league's best hitter as outfielder Danny Murphy won the batting title with a .369 average. His fellow outfielder, Tom Dunbar (.296, 101 runs), also played well, leading the league with 33 doubles. Daryl Smith (16–5) was the league's winningest pitcher and reliever Tom Henke, who saved only three games, would go on to save 311 in the big leagues. That season marked the last one for Asheville as a Texas Rangers affiliate.

For the 1982 season, Asheville signed a player development contract with the Houston Astros. The 1982 and '83 seasons were forgettable ones. The 1982 Tourists finished in fourth place at 65–76 and featured All-Star first baseman Glenn Carpenter (.323) and third baseman Juan Delgado (.328). The 1983 team was last in the league with a 64–80 record.

The 1984 Tourists (73–70) started slow but recovered to win the second half of the season. They defeated first half champ Greensboro in the playoffs, two games to one, then took the league pennant by sweeping South Division champ Charleston in the finals.

In 1985, the Tourists finished with a division best record of 76–62. Unfortunately, they failed to win either half of the season so were excluded from the playoffs. The team's standouts were catcher Jaime Williams (.304), first baseman Pete Mueller (.297, 28 HR, 93 RBIs) and pitcher Chris Huchingson (10–5). The next season was much better as the Tourists, led by third baseman and league batting champ Carlo Colombino (.339), won both halves of the season. Their 90–50 overall record put them 11½ games ahead of the second place team. The playoffs were not so kind, however, as the Tourists lost to Columbia, three games to one. The 1986 season marked the first time since 1959 that attendance had risen above the 100,000 mark.

The 1987 Asheville Tourists were one of the most talented teams in the city's long baseball history. Led by third baseman and league MVP Ed Whited (.323, 28 HR, 126 RBIs), the team won the first half of the season by half-a-game with a 37–32 record. In the second half the Tourists dominated. They won 54 games and lost only 16, 18 games ahead of the second place team. Besides Whited, the offense also starred first baseman Mike Simms (.273, 39 HR, 100 RBIs), outfielder Victor Hithe (.302) and catcher Craig Biggio (.375, 31 SB), who joined the team in midseason as the Astros' number one pick in the June draft. Shortstop Art Frazier led the team with 75 stolen bases as the Tourists set the league record with 335 steals as a team. The equally talented pitching staff consisted of four of the league's best: Sam August (12–1, 1.72 ERA), Ryan Bowen (12–5), Guy Normand (16–5) and Mike Stoker (13–5). Despite having one of the best teams in league history, the Tourists were upset in the playoffs by Myrtle Beach. The hard fought series went a full five games with four of them being decided by one run. The Tourists blew a ninth inning lead in the final game to lose 6–5.

The Tourists struggled in the first half of the 1988 season and finished fourth with a 29–41 record. They managed to rise above .500 in the second half, improving to 36–34, but overall it was a disappointing season. The only real star of the team was outfielder Eric Anthony (.273, 29 HR, 89 RBIs), the league home run leader.

The results of the 1989 season were much the same as the Tourists struggled in the first half (30–36) but improved slightly in the second (38–34). Highly regarded shortstop prospect Andujar Cedeño hit .300 with 14 home runs and 93 RBIs despite striking out 124 times. Pitcher Gordon Farmer went 9–2 while Ed Ponte compiled an 11–3 record as a reliever. Led by second baseman Larry Lamphere's 67 steals, the Tourists again topped the 300 mark in team stolen bases. Outfielder Kenny Lofton (.329) was promoted to Asheville late in the season and stole 14 bases in 22 games.

Once again, in 1990, the Tourists played poorly in the first half of the season and with a 28–43 record, finished last in their division. The second half saw improvement, however, as the Tourists rose to a third place, 38–34 finish. Though the team's pitching staff was weak, the offense did have a couple of talented players, namely shortstop Orlando Miller (.313, 62 RBIs) and All-Star second baseman David Hajek (.313, 43 SB).

The 1991 season was another disappointing one for Tourists fans. The team played poorly in both halves of the season and finished with the league's worst overall record (55–83). Shortstop Tom Nevers (.251, 16 HR, 71 RBIs) and reliever Jim Dougherty (1.52 ERA, 28 SV) were the Tourists' best that season.

Led by outfielder Gary Mota (.291, 23 HR, 89 RBIs), the league MVP, the Tourists had a better season in 1992. Though they still didn't qualify for the playoffs, their 74–66 record was a great improvement. Besides Mota, the son of former big league standout Manny Mota, the Tourists also featured the talents of outfielder Bob Abreu (.292) and pitchers Tom Anderson (11–5) and Alvin Morman (8–0, 1.55 ERA, 15 SV).

It was back to the league cellar for the 1993 Tourists. They finished last in both halves of the season with a combined record of 51–88, 41½ games out of first. Second baseman Donovan Mitchell (.291, 28 SB) did earn the honor of being named to the league All-Star team. That season marked the end of a 12-year relationship with the Houston Astros as the Tourists switched their working agreement to the expansion Colorado Rockies. Supplied with average talent, the Tourists improved slightly in 1994. They finished the first half of the season in fourth place but slipped to seventh in the second half for an overall record of 60–73. The team was led by first baseman Nate Holdren, who only hit .236 but tied for the league lead in home runs with 28, and third baseman Pedro Carranza (.282). Relief pitcher Jake

Viano (4–1, 1.35 ERA, 23 SV) was one of the league's best.

In 1995, the Tourists got off to a slow start and finished the first half in sixth place (32–36), 12 games out of first. In the second half the Tourists were a different team, winning the division with a 44–27 record. The pitching staff had several outstanding performers, including All-Star Brent Crowther (12–3, 2.28 ERA), left-hander Mike Kusiewicz (8–4, 2.06 ERA) and reliever Luis Colmenares (21 SV, 2.29 ERA). The offense featured the talents of the All-Star outfielder Derrick Gibson, the Rockies' number one prospect. Gibson hit .292, drove in 115 runs, and was the only 30–30 player in the minor leagues as he hit 32 home runs and stole 31 bases.

Led by P.J. Carey, the South Atlantic League's manager of the year, the Tourists dominated the first half of the 1996 season. With a record of 47–20, they won their division by 10 games. The second half was not quite as successful as the Tourists were hurt by midseason promotions but, at 84–52, they still finished with the league's best overall record. In the first round of the playoffs the Tourists swept Capital City (Columbia, S.C.) but lost in the second round to Delmarva (Salisbury, Md.). Two members of the offense, catcher Ben Petrick (.235, 14 HR) and outfielder David Feuerstein (.286) — were named to the All-Star team but the real strength of the Tourists was their pitching staff. Scott Randall (14–4, 2.74 ERA), Neil Garrett (12–4) and Heath Bost (5–2, 1.32 ERA, 15 SV) were its leaders.

◆ ──────── *Ayden* ──────── ◆

The Ayden Aces were a charter member of the semipro Coastal Plain League in 1934. They had a strong team with a winning record every year, taking the league championship in 1936. The league teams during the semipro years were made up primarily of college players. Each team had an unofficial alliance with a different school and many of Ayden's players came from the University of Alabama. First baseman Jim Whatley, who played for the Aces in 1936, had been an All-American tackle at Alabama in 1935. He later spent 25 years as the head baseball coach at the University of Georgia. His Ayden teammate and fellow Alabama native, third baseman Jim Tabor, went on to spend seven seasons in the big leagues with the Red Sox and the Phillies. George Turbeville, Woody Upchurch and Doyt Morris, all of whom played for the semipro Aces, made it up to the Philadelphia Athletics for brief trials.

The Aces remained in the league when it became a true professional circuit in 1937, operating as an independent team with no major league working agreement. Home games, as before, were played at the tiny high school ballpark. The team turned in an average finish that first year as pros with a fifth place, 47–46 record, 12½ games out of first. Outfielder-manager Alfred "Monk" Joyner of the Aces had a great season, winning the Triple Crown as the league leader in batting average (.380), hits (136), RBIs (97), and co-leader in home runs with 24. He made the All–Coastal Plain team as left fielder. Second baseman John Schuerholz had a good season and hit .280. His son, John, Jr., would go on to achieve baseball success as the general manager of the Atlanta Braves.

The Aces of 1938 did not fare quite as well as they had the previous year. The team finished in the league cellar with a 38–76 record, 26 games back. Ayden did, however, have the batting champion for a second year as first baseman Phil Morris, who began the season with Greenville, hit .377. With an 18–11 record, pitcher Bill Herring accounted for nearly half of the team's wins. He was successful at the plate as well, hitting .332 with 9 home runs and was named to the

All–Coastal Plain team. Shortstop Jiggs Gasaway made honorable mention with his .321 batting average and 81 RBIs.

Ayden's small size ultimately led to poor attendance and the financial troubles that go with it. The ballpark was really too small to be used for professional baseball and its lo-

cation did not permit expansion. It also lacked lights, an investment the struggling team could not afford. In January of 1939 it was announced that the team's assets were sold to a group from Wilson and that the team would be moved there.

Belmont

The Belmont Chiefs took to the field at Davis Park for their one and only year in 1961. The team entered that season as a transferred franchise in the Class D Western Carolina League, having played previously as the Rutherford County Owls. The Chiefs, who began the season with a 17 game losing streak, finished the year in fifth place (out of six teams), 24 games out of first, with a record of 39–61. The Chiefs went through three managers beginning with Jim Poole, a North Carolina native and former major leaguer who was also part owner of the team. Poole was replaced by Whitey Ries, who was later replaced by another North Carolina native and long time big league pitcher, Max Lanier. The leading players were relief pitcher Barry Huntzinger (10–9, 3.72 ERA),

who led the league in appearances with 49, and All-Star second baseman Mario "Buddy" Cia, the league leader with 86 walks and whose .271 batting average led the team. These two players, along with utilityman Kermit Williams (.266) were the only members of the Chiefs to play the complete season with the team. The Chiefs had a lowly team batting average of .229 and the whole team hit a total of only 16 home runs.

Though the Western Carolina League continued on, professional baseball in Belmont did not. The Chiefs had managed to draw only 10,081 in attendance, an average of only around 100 spectators per game. Seven hundred fans showed up for the home opener on May 4, but attendance dropped off quickly as the Chiefs failed to win games.

Burlington

Burlington's first professional baseball team was the 1942 Burlington Bees, members of the Class D Bi-State League. Made up of members from Virginia and North Carolina, the league had suffered financially and was desperately looking for new members. Minor leagues all across the country, including North Carolina's Coastal Plain League, were shutting down due to the war. Several members of the Bi-State League wanted to continue play, however, and team organizers in Burlington saw this as an opportunity to

enter professional baseball. The city was granted a franchise to give the league an even six teams. Burlington's home games were played at Hillcrest Park, which was located on High Street just off Hillcrest Avenue.

The Bees finished at an even 62–62 that season, fourth in the league standings. The offense had several good hitters as Harry Clifton (.311), Hal Wilson (.309, 94 RBIs) and Steve Collins (.306,19 HR, 101 runs) led the team. The otherwise weak pitching staff featured Tracy Hart (19–5), one of the league's best. The Bees qualified for the playoffs but were defeated in the first round by Sanford. The Bi-State League could no longer face the inevitable and disbanded after that season.

Three former members of the Bi-State League — Burlington, Leaksville and Danville — met in the fall of 1944 to discuss resuming play. They invited four North Carolina cities and one from Virginia to join them. This led to the formation of the Class C Carolina League, which was one of only 12 minor leagues to play in 1945. Burlington's Bees finished fourth with a 67–70 record, 26½ games out of first. They advanced to face Raleigh in the playoffs and were up two games to none but lost the series to the Capitols, four games to three. Third baseman Richard Meyers (.294, 75 RBIs) was named to the league All-Star team.

The Bees moved from Hillcrest Park to the Elon College baseball park in 1946. The team finished fourth yet again, winning 69 games and losing 71. Like the previous season, the Bees lost to Raleigh in the playoffs. The stars of the team were first baseman Jim Blair (.331) and outfielder Gus Zernial (.336, 111 RBIs), who led the league with 41 home runs. Zernial would reach the majors in 1949, where he would spend 11 seasons with four different American League teams and hit a total of 237 home runs.

In 1947, Burlington signed a working agreement with the Atlanta Crackers of the Class AA Southern Association. The Bees took the pennant that season with an 87–55 record, led by three outstanding pitchers: Lamar Chambers (21–6), Pete Bryant (22–12), and Ken Deal (23–7). Deal's 275 strikeouts stood as the Carolina League record until broken by Dwight Gooden in 1983. No other team in league history has had three 20-game winners on the same team. Surprisingly, none of the three ever made the major leagues. The Bees also had some outstanding hitting from outfielders Buddy Bates (.361, 82 RBIs, 116 runs), who was also the team's manager, and Charles Woodail (.323, 118 RBIs, 120 runs). Outfielder Emo Showfety, one of the league's top power hitters, played

much of the season with the Bees before being sold to Greensboro. Unfortunately for the Bees, they lost in the first round of the playoffs to Raleigh (for the third straight year), four games to three.

The Bees slipped to third place in 1948 with an 80–62 record, four games behind first place Raleigh. Buddy Bates again played outfield and managed the team, hitting .332. Fellow outfielder Dick Woodward hit .336 while catcher Norm Wilson hit .311 with 102 RBIs. The pitching staff was led by Larry Hartley (11–5) and Max Wilson (13–3), who had begun that season as the manager of the Coastal Plain League's Wilson franchise. In the playoffs the Bees finally got past Raleigh in the first round. Unfortunately, they lost to Martinsville in the finals, four games to two.

The Carolina League moved from Class C to Class B in 1949. Four teams, including Burlington, voted against the change (because player salaries would increase) but the president of the league broke the tie in favor of the move. Burlington's Bees finished the regular season in fourth place at 72–72. They went on to take the league championship by upsetting Danville, the regular season pennant winner, and then Raleigh, four games to three, in the final. Outfielder Pat Cooper (.323, 26 HR, 110 RBIs) led the offense that season while Larry Hartley (13–6) was again the ace of the pitching staff.

The Bees fielded another good team in 1950. Their record of 83–70 put them in third place and they went on to reach the league championships before falling to Winston-Salem, four games to one. The team was lead by league Player of the Year, center fielder Bill Evans. Evans won the batting title with a .338 average, while scoring 111 runs and collecting 207 hits. Evans never made the major leagues but two of his teammates that season — fellow outfielders Jim "Buster" Maynard (.310) and Pat Cooper (.302) — had already played there and were on the way back down.

The Bees slid down to the league cellar in 1951, posting a 47–93 record. This was probably due to the fact that the club had

1948 Burlington Bees: *Back:* Bob Gailey, Doc Faucette, Larry Hartley, unidentified, Dave Baxter; *Middle:* Herb Young, Ray Williams, Jim Burns, Buddy Bates, Claude Swiggett, Bob Falk; *Front:* Dick Woodward, Pete Howard, Mike Hefner, Norm Wilson, Maxie Wilson (courtesy Pete Howard).

signed a working agreement with the Pittsburgh Pirates, leaving less room on the roster for veteran players. Attendance dropped well below 50,000, less than half of what it had been just a couple of years earlier. Outfielder Don MacLean, in his third season with the team, was Burlington's leading hitter at .304.

The 1952 team, now using the nickname of its parent team, was no better, again finishing last with a 45–92 record. The Burlington Pirates did have an exciting prospect in pitcher Ron Necciai. "Rocket" Ron began the season in the Appalachian League but was soon promoted after he posted some amazing strikeout numbers. In Burlington, Necciai won seven games and lost nine. This, however, was for a last place team. His earned

run average was only 1.37, showing the poor run support he received from his own team. In 126 innings, Necciai struck out 176 batters. He was promoted to Pittsburgh in August but never reached his potential, going only 1–6 with a 7.08 ERA. Necciai never made it back to the majors after that season. One of his fellow Burlington pitchers, Ron Kline (3–6), went on to a 17 year major league career, mainly as a reliever. Burlington outfielder Dick Hall (.242), who had started the season with Pittsburgh, later converted to a pitcher and went on to spend a total of 19 seasons in the big leagues.

In 1953 the Burlington team began playing home games in Graham Athletic Park and became known as the Burlington-Graham (or Bur-Gra for short) Pirates. The team

Burlington shortstop Pete Howard batting before a sold out crowd at Elon College Park, 1949 (courtesy Pete Howard).

played well, finishing in third at 75–65, and attendance was up. The Pirates had good talent including outfielder Bob Honor (.328, 96 RBIs) and first baseman George Hott (.308). Catcher Jack McKeon hit only .181 but went on to manage four different major league teams. Pitcher Jim Waugh was 6–3 with a 1.34 ERA before being promoted to Pittsburgh. Ron Necciai was back in Burlington

briefly, going 1–1 in six games. In the playoffs, the Pirates lost to Danville in the first round, three games to one.

Led by player-manager Stan Wentzel (.318, 20 HR, 108 RBIs), the Bur-Gra Pirates improved to second place in 1954. With an 82–56 record, the team advanced to the playoffs. There they beat Greensboro in the first round but lost to Fayetteville in the finals, four games to one. Burlington had two black team members for the first time that season: first baseman R. C. Stevens (.293, 25 HR, 115 RBIs) and outfielder Herb Bush (.343 in 30 games). Stevens made it to the majors in 1958 where he spent parts of four seasons. Burlington pitcher Don Schultz (17–11) pitched a no-hitter and led the league in strikeouts with 178. Pitcher Andrew Olsen (11–4) turned to umpiring when his minor league playing days were over. As an umpire he made the big leagues, calling games in the National League from 1969 to 1981.

It was back to the cellar for the Pirates in 1955. The team turned in a record of 60–78, finishing 20 games behind first place High Point–Thomasville. Catcher Larry Dorton (.309) and first baseman Anthony Bartirome (.328) were the team's top players. Attendance suffered and was last in the league at 33,605. Because of this, the team moved to Kinston after the season, leaving Burlington without professional baseball.

In 1958, Burlington regained admission to the Carolina League. The new team signed a working agreement with Cleveland and became known as the Alamance Indians. The Indians had an average season, finishing in fourth with a record of 70–67. In the playoffs, however, they upset regular season champ Danville and then took the pennant by defeating Greensboro in the finals, two games to one. In the deciding game of that series the Indians scored a tie-breaking run in the eighth inning and held on to win the game, 6 to 5. The team had several outstanding players that season, including outfielder Walt Bond (.296) and infielder Ken Kuhn (.309). Bond would go on to reach the majors while Kuhn had already spent parts of the past three seasons with Cleveland. Pitcher Steve Hamilton (15–14) went on to spend 12 seasons in the majors, most of them with the Yankees, as a relief pitcher. Outfielder Sonny Siebert hit a lowly .147 playing part of the season in Burlington. He would return to the team in 1960 as a pitcher.

The Alamance Indians of 1959, who finished in last place at 49–81, were perhaps the worst Burlington team of all time. They improved to fourth place in 1960 with a 67–73 overall record. Outfielder Mitchell June (.320, 24 HR, 90 RBIs) had a great season but missed winning the batting title by .0002 of a percentage point to Phil Linz of Greensboro. Catcher Howard "Doc" Edwards went on to play parts of five seasons in the big leagues while pitcher Sonny Siebert would play 12 seasons in the majors, winning 140 games. The Indians started the season off slow (26–44) but recovered to win the second half of a split season with a 41–29 record. They faced Greensboro in the playoffs but lost four games to one. Burlington got a new ballpark that season as Fairchild Park was completed. The grandstand had originally been located in Danville, Virginia, but the city of Burlington bought it for $5,000, moved it to town piece by piece, and then reassembled it.

Managed by Bill Herring, the 1961 Indians finished fifth in the first half of the season at 32–36 but improved in the second half to 39–30. Their overall record of 71–66 was second best in the league. Catcher Duke Sims, on his way to an 11 year big league career, hit .304 for the Indians with 21 home runs. Pitcher David Seeman was promoted to Burlington after going 17–3 for Selma of the Alabama-Florida League. With the Indians he won seven straight games, giving him a combined record of 24–3 and the best winning percentage in all of professional baseball that season.

The Indians turned in a fourth place 66–74 finish in 1962 and with the league no longer using the split season format, qualified for the playoffs. They lost to Durham, however, two games to none in the first round. Shortstop Gil Garrido, outfielder Tommie Agee (.258) and first baseman Bob Chance (.285) all went on to spend several seasons in the major leagues.

In 1963, future major league star pitcher Luis Tiant (14–9, 207 strikeouts) led the 1963 Indians to a 77–66 third place finish in the West Division of the league. Now designated a Class A league in minor league baseball's new arrangement, the Carolina League was divided into East and West divisions. Burlington led their division for most of the season but an injury caused Tiant to miss three weeks of the season, resulting in a team slump. The team also had two other excellent pitchers, Chuck Kovach (17–11) and George Pressley (16–7), though neither ever made the major leagues.

Bill Herring returned as manager of the 1964 Indians. Unfortunately, he didn't have much to work with, especially in the area of pitching. Outfielder Sam Parilla (.315, 16 HR, 77 RBIs), who made it to the major leagues for 11 games in 1970, led the team in hitting. Outfielder Richie Scheinblum (.309) would go on to spend several years in the majors, primarily as a reserve. Gene Conley, a two sport star who had played in the NBA and pitched in the major leagues, came to Burlington in an unsuccessful attempt to recover from a sore arm.

Burlington became a farm team of the Washington Senators in 1965, beginning an eight year relationship with that franchise. The team, managed by former major leaguer Owen Friend, changed its name to that of its parent club. Burlington's Senators played poorly and finished last in the West Division of the league with a 63–81 record. Catcher Paul Casanova (.287, 76 RBIs) went on to spend most of ten seasons in the majors with Washington and later Atlanta. Pitcher Joe Coleman, though only 2–10 with a 4.56 ERA, received a September call-up to Washington. The Senators proved to be right in their assessment of his potential; Coleman went on to win 142 big league games, twice winning 20 or more in a season.

Managed in 1966 by another former major leaguer — Wayne Terwilliger — the Senators improved to second place in their division. Their 76–62 record qualified them for the playoffs but they lost to Winston-Salem, two games to none. Outfielder Dick Billings (.312) led the team's offense while the top pitchers were Bill Hayward (17–9), Rupe Toppin (13–4) and Bill Gogolewski (11–9). Attendance for the season was poor at only 22,041.

The 1967 season was a forgettable one for the Burlington Senators. They finished third in their division with a 70–69 record. In an expanded playoff format the Senators faced Durham but lost the one-game first round. The next season was even worse as the team finished last in the West with the league's worst record (56–84). Shortstop Toby Harrah hit only .239 for Burlington that season but went on to have an above average 17 year major league career.

The Senators improved to an even 71–71 in 1969. They finished third in their division but advanced through the playoffs all the way to the finals. There the Senators lost to Raleigh in the deciding third game of the series, 8–2. Toby Harrah was back with the team after missing much of the season for military duty and showed more talent as he hit .306 in 46 games before being promoted to AA. Attendance was still pitiful as the team drew only 20,550 fans, half as many as the next-to-last-place team.

For the 1970 season, the Carolina League went back to a split-season format. Burlington finished sixth in the first half at 32–38 but came back strong to win the second half of the season with a 40–27 record. However, in the playoff they lost to first-half champ Winston-Salem, two games to none. Outfielder Dave Moates (.311, 44 SB) was the star of the team.

The Senators were back in the league cellar in 1971. They finished eighth in the first half of the season and seventh in the second to have a combined record of 54–84, the league's worst. After that season the Washington Senators moved to Texas, becoming the Rangers. They kept their affiliation with Burlington, that team also changing its name. Burlington's Rangers improved greatly in 1972, winning the first half of the season. The team had some good talent, including outfielder Dane Iorg (.321) and second baseman Mike Cubbage (.281). Both went on to decent big league careers. Pitcher Steve Foucalt, who had been 1–2 with a 6.33 ERA for Burlington the previous season, began the 1972 season with a 7–0 record and an amazing ERA of 0.45. He was promoted to AAA at midseason. Partially due to the loss of Fou-calt, Burlington stumbled in the second half, finishing fourth at 34–36. In the playoffs with second half champ Salem, the Rangers held a 4–1 lead in the deciding game but wound up losing the game and the pennant. Burlington's attendance, even though the team played well, was only 18,222. This is the lowest total in Carolina League history. By comparison, the Durham Bulls in 1997 were drawing more than Burlington's season total in a *weekend*. Needless to say, the team moved after the season (to Wilson where it was also unsuccessful). That season proved to be the last for Burlington as a member of the Carolina League.

Burlington finally got another chance to enter professional baseball in 1986. That season the Burlington Indians were granted membership in the rookie Appalachian League as an affiliate of the Cleveland Indians. Only average that first season, the team turned in a 36–31 record. In attendance, however, the Indians broke the league record with 62,701, nearly twice the total of the second place team.

It was almost a short-lived relationship between the Appalachian League and the city of Burlington. League president Bill Halstead informed the team that they would have to leave the league after the 1987 season due to Burlington's distance from other league members. All of the other league members were located in West Virginia, eastern Tennessee and western Virginia. Despite an uncertain future, the Indians played outstanding baseball that season. Led by the league's top two hitters, outfielder Beau Allred (.341, 10 HR) and shortstop Bill Narleski (.324), they ran away with the pennant, finishing at 51–19. The pitching staff, with a league best team ERA of 2.85, was the real strength of the team. Dave Harwell (4–1, 1.69 ERA) and left-hander Kevin Bearse (7–1, 1.71 ERA) were its top members. The Indians went on to take the league championship by sweeping Johnson City in the playoffs, two games to none. They also broke their own league attendance record as 76,653 passed through the gate at Burlington Athletic Park.

Fortunately, league president Halstead changed his mind about forcing Burlington out after seeing the support for the team. Instead, he made plans to expand the league toward Burlington by placing teams in Martinsville and Danville, Virginia.

The Indians again played well in 1988 and won their division with a 37–32 record. They advanced to the playoffs but were swept by Kingsport (Tenn.), two games to none. Cleveland's number one draft pick, shortstop Mark Lewis, hit .264 with 43 RBIs for Burlington that season.

The 1989 season was a mediocre one as the Indians finished with a 31–37 record, third in their division. Catcher Jesse Levis, recently drafted out of the University of North Carolina, hit .344 and later reached the major leagues. The results of the 1990 season were not much different. The Indians finished with the league's sixth best record, winning 35 games and losing 37. Third baseman and future Cleveland star Jim Thome was hitting .373 with 12 home runs when promoted at midseason.

Led by outfielder and league MVP Manny Ramirez in 1991 (.326, 19 HR, 63 RBIs), the Indians won their division with a 40–27 record. Unfortunately, they were swept in the playoff by Pulaski, two games to none. The next season the Indians dropped to second place (35–31). Outfielder Derek Hacopian (.324) and pitcher Mike Mathews (7–0, 1.01 ERA), both named as league All-Stars, led the team.

Burlington tied for first in their division in 1993 with Bluefield. Though their records were identical at 44–24, the Indians were declared the winner since they had won seven out of the ten games in which the teams had played each other. The Indians then went on to take the league pennant by sweeping Elizabethton (Tenn.) in the playoffs. Outfielder Rich Lemons (.329) and catcher Einar Diaz (.299) led the offense but the real strength of the team was the pitching staff. Jason Mackey (6–0, 2.15 ERA), Johnny Martinez (6–1, 2.22 ERA) and reliever Cesar Ramos (14 saves, 1.88 ERA) were among the league's best.

The 1994 season was a disappointment to Burlington fans; the Indians finished in the league cellar with a record of only 23–42. Pitcher Bartolo Colon (7–4, 3.14 ERA) and first baseman Chan Perry (.314) were the team's top players.

The 1995 season saw only slight improvement as the team finished fourth at 26–38. Third baseman Christian Mota (.282,

36 RBIs) and outfielder Milton Anderson (.257, 38 SB), the league stolen base leader, both had good seasons.

Again in 1996, the Indians failed to improve much in the league standings as they finished with another losing record (29–38). Pitcher Mike Bacsik earned league All-Star honors.

Charlotte

The first appearance of organized baseball in Charlotte probably took place in the summer of 1900 when the semipro North Carolina Baseball Association was formed. Charlotte was one of six teams in the short-lived league that disbanded early after only about a month of play. The first truly professional league in the state, the six team Virginia–North Carolina League, was formed in 1901. Charlotte was not an original member but became the new home for the Portsmouth franchise when it failed in that city at the end of June. The league continued play though it was plagued by difficulties in finances and the long travel distances between some cities. The two remaining Virginia teams then decided to drop out because they did not want to travel to Charlotte, leaving just four North Carolina members. The Charlotte team called it quits a few weeks later and the league was forced to halt play. At that time their record stood at 50–55.

Professional baseball returned to Charlotte in 1902 when it was one of the six North Carolina cities that banded together to form the Class C North Carolina League. (The National Association of Professional Baseball Leagues had been created in the winter of 1901 to serve as a governing body of the minor leagues. It classified leagues A, B, C and D according to their level of play, with D being the players with little or no experience.) The Charlotte Athletic Association was formed to run the team and local lumber

merchant J.H. Wearn was elected as its president. Wearn became an important figure in Charlotte baseball. He later donated land adjacent to his lumber yard for use as the city's baseball park. The park, which bore his name, was the home of baseball in the city until the 1930s. Wearn would also serve as the president of the Class D Carolina Association from 1908 to 1912 and the North Carolina State League in 1913.

The Charlotte Hornets took to the field in 1902 with veteran minor leaguer Ed Ashenback at the helm. Home games were played at Latta Park in the Dilworth section of the city. The Hornets played outstanding baseball and at one point they won 25 consecutive games, a winning streak that to this day is the second longest in minor league history. Though they were successful, the Hornets were forced to withdraw from the league due to poor attendance and the expense of traveling by train to the league's other cities, which included distant Wilmington and New Bern. At the time of their demise, the Hornets' record stood at 39–8. Buck Weaver (not the same Buck Weaver of Black Sox fame) won the batting title with a .325 average. Another member of the Hornets was outfielder Archie "Moonlight" Graham. A former baseball star at the University of North Carolina, his name would become famous when used in the popular movie *Field of Dreams*. Like the character in the movie, Graham did appear in one game in the outfield

1909 batting champ Al Humphrey of Charlotte (from the collection of the author).

league's winningest pitcher with his 13–4 record. The results of the 1909 season were similar as the Hornets were again fifth, this time with a 46–63 record. The team did feature the batting champion, however, as Al Humphrey hit .296. That season marked the first of three with the Hornets for player-manager Lave Cross. A former big league star, Cross, then 43 years old, hit .316 playing at second base.

The Hornets improved to 56–50 in 1910 to finish in second place. Pitcher O.W. Brazile led the league with 21 wins. Manager Cross, who played third base, hit .295. The 1911 season saw the Hornets drop one spot to finish third. Their 52–58 record left them 20½ games out of first. Hornets outfielder F.P. Wofford claimed the batting title with a .392 average while manager Cross hit .322. The Hornets played well and turned in a record of 61–46 in 1912. It was still a third place finish as they were 3½ games out of first. Outfielder Harry Weiser (.318) led the team in hitting while manager-shortstop Champ Osteen, a former big leaguer, hit .283. The Carolina Association disbanded after that season.

In 1913 a new league, the Class D North Carolina State League, was formed. Charlotte became one of the six North Carolina cities to join. Unfortunately for the Hornets, it was not a successful season as they finished in fifth place with a 47–67 record. Manager and third baseman Burleigh Emery led the team with his .283 batting average.

The next season, the Hornets made great improvements as they rose to a first place tie with a 72–49 record. Outfielder Harry "Bud" Weiser was the star of the team as he won the batting title with a .333 average and scored a league leading 102 runs. He began the next season with the Philadelphia Phillies. Charlotte pitcher Ralph "Razor" Ledbetter (26–12) was the league's best.

The Hornets dropped to fourth place in 1915 as they finished below .500 with a 56–66 record. Pitchers Bob Geary (19–12) and Razor Ledbetter (17–12) had good seasons. For the 1916 season the league played a split

with the New York Giants (though it was in 1905), never getting an at bat. A native of Fayetteville, North Carolina, he really did go on to become a small-town doctor in Minnesota.

It was 1905 before professional baseball returned to Charlotte. A new Hornets team was formed for entry into the Class D Virginia–North Carolina League. The league also consisted of teams from Greensboro, Winston-Salem and Danville, Virginia. The Hornets finished the season in second place with a record of 40–42, 11½ games behind Danville. No official statistics for the league exist.

In 1908, the Carolina Baseball Association was formed with the Charlotte Hornets as a charter member. The team fared poorly and finished fifth in the six team league with a 40–47 record. Phifer Fulenwider was the season. Asheville won the first half but the Hornets came on strong and took the second half. Their combined record of 68–43 was the league's best. The Hornets then advanced to a playoff with Asheville and took the championship by sweeping the series. Outfielder Ben Paschal (.285), later a member of the legendary New York Yankee teams of the 1920s, led the league with 15 home runs. Pitcher Phil Redding (23–10, 1.34 ERA), who had spent parts of two seasons with the St. Louis Cardinals, dominated the league, leading it in wins and ERA.

The N.C. State League began play in 1917 but soon ran into difficulties. The United States had entered World War I in April of that year, resulting in travel restrictions and a shortage of ballplayers. The low level minor league teams, most of which operated on the verge of bankruptcy anyway, were the hardest hit. The N.C. State League was no different and on May 18 two clubs dropped out. The other four continued on until May 30 before giving up. At that time the Charlotte Hornets were in second place with a 20–16 record.

After going without professional baseball in 1918, Charlotte joined the newly formed Class C South Atlantic League for the 1919 season. The team played well and finished second, one game out of first with a 55–41 record. The Hornets' star pitcher, left-hander Rube Eldridge (20–12, 2.59 ERA), was the league's best. The 1920 season was not as successful as the Hornets dropped to fifth, winning 58 games while losing 68. The team did have the league's batting champ as Clarence Marshall hit .320. Outfielder Ben Paschal returned to the team after two years of military service and hit .284. He was sold to the Boston Red Sox in September and played nine games.

The Hornets dropped all the way to the league cellar in 1921, with their record of 52–93 leaving them 41 games out of first. Ben Paschal was back with the team and hit .316 with 28 stolen bases but he alone could not save the team. Rookie pitcher Bill Harris (3–4, 2.22 ERA), who would play through

1945, would eventually win 257 minor league and 24 major league games. In 1922, led by second baseman Ernie Padgett (.333), the league batting champ, and Ben Paschal (.326, 131 runs, 114 RBIs, 18 HR), who led the league in almost every other offensive category, the Hornets improved greatly. With a 73–59 record the team finished second.

Ben Paschal returned to Charlotte for a final season in 1923 and led the Hornets to the pennant. He hit .351 with 122 RBIs, 26 home runs and 147 runs scored. Outfielder Roy Carlyle (.337, 81 RBIs) and pitcher Lee Bolt (20 wins) also had good seasons. The Hornets finished the season with a record of 89–56 and in the playoffs had little trouble with Macon, winning four games to one. Ben Paschal would make it up to the New York Yankees the next season and stay there through 1929, mainly as a backup outfielder. For the legendary 1927 Yankees team, Paschal hit .317 in 50 games. Roy Carlyle played for the Yankees in 1926, hitting .385 in 35 games after being traded from the Red Sox.

The Hornets just missed another pennant in 1924. They finished 73–48, one game behind Augusta. Outfielder Cleo Carlyle, younger brother of Roy, batted .355 with 103 RBIs and a league leading 25 triples. Again denied the pennant by one game in 1925, the Hornets (79–50) finished second to Spartanburg. Outfielder Art Ruble had a great season, hitting .385 with 110 RBIs and 129 runs scored.

The 1926 Hornets had an average season and finished fourth with a 77–72 record. The team dropped below .500 to finish the 1927 season 72–78, sixth in the eight team league. Pitcher Jake Levy, however, was one of the league's best, turning in a 22–12 record with a 2.73 ERA. The Hornets continued their slide in 1928, dropping to a seventh place finish. Their record of 60–86 left them 37 games out of first. Manager Heinie Groh, recently retired from a long major league career, led the team in hitting with a .333 average.

The Hornets improved greatly in 1929, turning in the league's third best record as they won 79 games and lost 67. All-Star third baseman Harry Daughtry (.296, 86 RBIs), outfielder Albie Hood (.334, 97 RBIs, 41 2B) and pitcher Earl Brown (21–8) were the team's best. The 1930 season saw the Hornets slump again, however, as they finished next to last with a record of 61–78. The team did feature the league strikeout leader, All-Star pitcher Jim Mooney (185 SO). On July 19, 1930, in the league's first night game at Augusta, Mooney struck out 23 batters (some credit this to the poor lighting system). He debuted in the big leagues with the Giants the next season.

Charlotte, along with Asheville, jumped to the Class C Piedmont League for the 1931 season. There they joined the other larger cities of the state. The Hornets of 1931 proved to be one of the greatest teams in the state's baseball history. They ran away with the regular season pennant, finishing 13½ games ahead of second place Raleigh, with a record of 100–37. They then took the championship by defeating Raleigh in a playoff, four games to two.

Led by second baseman and manager Guy Lacy (.311, 86 RBIs), the Hornets totally dominated the league that season. Shortstop Vern Brandes hit .335 and stole a league leading 44 bases. Third baseman Emory Culbreth hit .358 while first baseman Jimmy Hudgens hit .290 and drove in 103 runs. The star of the offense, however, was left fielder Frank Packard. Leading the league in almost every offensive category, Packard won the Triple Crown (.366, 21 HR, 123 RBIs). Fellow outfielders Bill Carrier (.313, 96 RBIs) and George Rhinehardt (.325, 71 RBIs) also made great contributions to the offense. The Hornets' pitching may have been even more impressive than the offense. Bud Shaney (24–10) led the league in wins while Jim Lyle (21–6) had a league best 1.92 ERA. The other three starting pitchers — Merle Settlemire (18–8), Frank Wical (16–3) and Chet Martin (13–4) — also posted outstanding records.

The Hornets were once again the league's best team in 1932. Again managed by Guy Lacy, they finished with 80 wins against 52

losses. Led by pitcher Jim Lyle (22–7, 2.55 ERA) and third baseman Emory Culbreth (.356, 118 RBIs), the league MVP, it was again a great team but nowhere near what the 1931 team had been. With the death of team owner Felix Hayman that year, the Hornets were sold to the Boston Red Sox.

With an 80–61 record in 1933, the Hornets finished second to Greensboro, who won both halves of a split season. Pitcher Al Veach (12–4, 2.42 ERA) was one of the league's best. He would have a major league career consisting of two games with the Athletics in 1935. Outfielder Taffy Wright (.330, 90 RBIs) led the team in hitting. He went on to a solid major league career as did pitcher Hugh Casey (19–9).

In 1934 the Hornets (87–51) started the season well and won the first half as the league again used a split season format. They stumbled in the second half, though, and lost out to Norfolk. In the playoffs Norfolk took the pennant, four games to two. The Hornets' strength that season was a pitching staff that consisted of Bob Durham (21–8), Chet Martin (16–7), Jim Lyle (13–8), John Lanning (11–7) and Guy Green (8–3). The offense was led by center fielder Emile "Red" Barnes (.324, 81 RBIs), a former big leaguer. Thirty-eight-year-old third baseman Tommy Taylor, a long time minor league veteran, hit .304 for the Hornets that season.

The Hornets finished in the league cellar in 1935 with a 62–75 record. Pitcher Bill Humphrey (20–7) and outfielder Cecil Trent (.319, 88 RBIs) were two of the team's top players. After the season, a dispute erupted between the city of Charlotte and the Boston Red Sox, who owned the Hornets. The Red Sox wanted the team to add Sunday games to its schedule to increase revenues. The city refused to allow it since Sunday baseball in Charlotte was illegal, just as it was in many towns in the so-called "Bible Belt." Since the city refused to budge, the Red Sox moved the team to Rocky Mount, where Sunday baseball was allowed.

In 1936, another Hornets team was formed in Charlotte for membership in the newly organized Carolina League, which was considered an "outlaw" league since it was professional but not a member of the National Association. Players who participated in the league were threatened with being declared ineligible to ever return to organized ball. Despite this, many players were lured to the new league by the offer of high salaries as the league imposed no salary limits. The Hornets played well in 1936, winning 61 games and losing 36, and finished the season in second place out of the eight teams. Minor league veteran Frank Packard, who had been a star with the Hornets a few seasons earlier, managed the team for the first half of the season. He was replaced shortly after midseason by another long time veteran and former Hornet, pitcher Bud Shaney. Though it was a hitters' league, the 36-year-old Shaney had a legendary season on the mound, winning 17 consecutive games. The only statistics available for that year are from midseason. At that time shortstop Russell Maxey was hitting .347 while outfielder Bill Carrier was at .325 with 50 RBIs.

A new Charlotte Hornets team rejoined the Piedmont League in 1937. Owned by Clark Griffith, the Hornets became a member of the farm system of his Washington Senators. The relationship between Griffith's big league team (which later became the Minnesota Twins) and the city of Charlotte was one that would last through the 1972 season. The 1937 Hornets' lack of pitching led to a seventh place finish for the team. Only one regular starting pitcher, Elmer Riddle (13–6), achieved a winning record. He went on to have a couple of standout seasons for the Cincinnati Reds in the early '40s. The Hornets did feature the league batting and home run champ that season as outfielder Bobby Estalella hit .349 with 33 home runs.

Estalella returned in 1938 and led the Hornets to the league championship. The team finished the regular season in second place, half a game behind Norfolk. Advancing to the playoffs, the Hornets survived a close series with Portsmouth before facing Rocky Mount for the championship. Char-

lotte prevailed, four games to one. Estalella was the league MVP that season as he won the Triple Crown. He hit .378, drove in 123 runs, scored 134, drew 117 bases on balls and hit 38 home runs. Durham outfielder Norman Small recalled the power that Estallela displayed in 1938:

> That Bobby Estalella was a good hitter. One game, in Durham, he hit a ball that went just over my head. It rolled up the hill in centerfield into the corner against the fence. By the time I got to it and threw it back to home, Estalella was back in the dugout havin' a drink of water.

Estalella's fellow Cuban, Gil Torres, also had a good season for the Hornets. A versatile player, he hit .328 while playing several infield positions as well as posting a 10–6 record as a pitcher. Catcher Jake Early hit .316. He would spend nine seasons in the big leagues, eight of them with Washington. Pitcher Early Wynn (10–11), in the first of three seasons in Charlotte, would eventually spend 23 seasons in the big leagues. A 300-game winner, Wynn was elected to the Hall of Fame in 1972. The Hornets' best pitcher that season, Joe Haynes (18–9), also had a long major league career.

The Hornets dropped to seventh in the league standings in 1939. An overall average team, they were hurt by the midseason call-up of outfielder Bob Prichard (.339), the team's best hitter. Early Wynn (15–14) and Bill Holland (10–7) were two of the team's best pitchers. Second baseman Morris Aderholt (.297, 21 HR, 90 RBIs) received a September call-up to Washington. Again mediocre in 1940, the Hornets finished fifth with a 68–65 record. First baseman Jack Sanford (.317, 84 RBIs) and shortstop Sherry Robertson (.249, 23 HR, 90 RBIs) led the otherwise weak offense. Sanford would have three short stays with Washington while Robertson would spend ten seasons as a big league utility player.

Continuing their lackluster play, the Hornets finished the 1941 season with a record of 65–70, sixth in the league. Outfielder Roberto Ortiz (.301, 35 2B), the team's only .300 hitter, was called up to Washington and spent much of six seasons with the Senators. The 1942 Hornets showed some improvement and rose to fourth place. They qualified for the playoffs but were swept in the first round by Greensboro. Versatile veteran Gil Torres (17–5) and former big league catcher Cliff Bolton (.281) were the team's only real players of note. Though the Piedmont League continued on after that season, Charlotte dropped out due to the war.

In 1946, Charlotte joined with cities in both Carolinas as well as Tennessee to form the new Class B Tri-State League. The Hornets, managed by Spencer Abbott, had a great team in the league's inaugural season and took the pennant with a 93–46 record. In the first round of the playoffs, the Hornets defeated Shelby, four games to two. They then took the championship as they won a hard fought series with Knoxville, four games to three. Charlotte players dominated the league All-Star team as first baseman Carl Miller, second baseman Lawrence Womack, third baseman Bob Morem, outfielder Al Kvasnak and pitcher John Dixon were all honored.

The Hornets (72–68) dropped back to fourth place in 1947. They qualified for the playoffs, however, and upset regular season champ Spartanburg in the first round, four games to one. In a finals series that went a full seven games, the Hornets prevailed and again took the league championship. All-Star shortstop Sam Meeks made it to Washington the following April. Sixty-nine-year-old manager Spencer Abbott retired on June 21 of that season, ending a managerial career that had begun in 1903. He is the fifth all-time winningest manager in minor league history with 2,180 victories.

With a fifth place finish in 1948, the Hornets (72–74) just missed the playoffs. Legendary minor league slugger Leo "Muscle" Shoals (.287) played first base, hitting 21 home runs and driving in 82. The 1949 season was even less successful as the team dropped to seventh place with a 62–80 record. First baseman Don Stafford (.290) and pitcher Howard Sutherland (18–10) were

the team's top performers. The 1950 Hornets improved to 72–73 but again missed the playoffs as they finished fifth. Don Stafford had another good season and was named as the All-Star team's first baseman.

Finally, in 1951, the Hornets returned to the top of the league standings. With a team just as dominant as the 1931 Hornets had been, they finished first by 15 games with an impressive record of 100–40. Managed by second baseman Cal Ermer (.297) the main strength of the Hornets was the pitching staff. Levi "Buck" Fleshman (20–9), Jerry Lane (17–7), Survern Wright (7–0), Bob Danielson (11–3) and Harley Grossman (10–2) combined to lead the talented staff. Surprisingly, the Hornets' offense featured only one real star, Cuban outfielder Francisco Campos (.368, 103 RBIs), the league's batting champ and MVP. Despite the Hornets' talent and pitching depth, they were upset in the first round of the playoffs by Spartanburg, three games to one.

Led by All-Star outfielder and batting champ Bruce Barmes (.360) along with pitcher Dean Stone (17–10), the Hornets finished second in 1952 with an 87–51 record. They went on to take the championship by defeating first Anderson and then Spartanburg in the playoffs.

The 1953 season was Charlotte's last in the Tri-State League. After finishing the regular season in third place, the Hornets (74–71) advanced to the playoffs. They bid farewell to the league by taking their second consecutive championship, sweeping both Spartanburg and Anderson. Shortstop Pompeyo "Yo-Yo" Davalillo (.305, 24 SB) had a great season as he led the Hornets in hitting. The league's best fielding shortstop, he was promoted to Washington at the beginning of August. In 19 games, Davalillo hit .293 but never made it back to the big leagues. (Interestingly, at a height of only five feet, three inches, Davalillo is one of the smallest men to ever play major league baseball.) Another member of the 1953 Hornets, pitcher Dick Hyde (9–8, 3.32 ERA), had a longer stay in the big leagues where he spent six seasons as a reliever.

The Hornets jumped to the Class A South Atlantic League in 1954. Facing tougher competition in the new league, the team finished only sixth with a 62–77 record. The league change did raise fan interest in the team, however, as attendance increased by over one third to nearly 93,000.

Attendance was still good in 1955 though the Hornets finished last. With a 54–86 record, they were 35 games behind first place Columbia. The team was much improved in 1956 and finished second, winning 79 games while losing 61. They advanced to the playoffs but lost to Jacksonville. Outfielder Ken Wood (.267, 17 HR, 96 RBIs) and pitchers Herman Brown (13–9, 2.28 ERA) and Matt Saban (15–7, 2.65 ERA) were that season's stars.

The 1957 season brought another second place finish as the Hornets finished 86–67. The offense had no real standout players but the strong pitching staff included Matt Saban (16–7, 2.17 ERA), Garland Shifflett (14–10, 2.73 ERA) and Angel Oliva (16–10). The Hornets went on to sweep Knoxville in the first round of the playoffs and then upset regular season champ Augusta, two games to one, to take the championship.

The Hornets of 1958 dropped below .500 to finish 69–71, good enough for third place. They lost a one-game first round playoff to Jacksonville. Pitcher Woody Rich, in the final season of a 22-year baseball career that included stints with the Red Sox before and during World War II, was 1–5 in 16 games for the Hornets. Improving to 75–65 in 1959, the Hornets finished second in the league. They again lost in the first round of the playoffs, this time to Gastonia. The results of the 1960 season were similar as the Hornets (79–61) finished in second place but were ousted in the first round of the playoffs by Knoxville. All-Star outfielder Lamar "Jake" Jacobs played well and finished the season in Washington.

A seventh place, 61–79 finish was all the Hornets could manage in 1961. They wound up the 1962 season in the league cellar with a 54–86 record. Outfielder Tony Oliva (.350, 17 HR, 93 RBIs), did play well, however, and was named a league All-Star. It was an honor he would also achieve six times while in the big leagues with Minnesota.

In May of 1962 a new "Player Development Plan" was announced for minor league baseball which would take effect for the 1963 season. It involved a major restructuring of the minors, basically making them dependant on the major league clubs for survival. Each major league team was required to have five minor league farm clubs and be responsible for some of their minor league teams' costs (such as paying for spring training). While minor league teams had been classified either AAA, AA, A, B, C or D, the new system grouped everyone into just AAA, AA, A and Rookie level ball. The South Atlantic League was designated AA.

The changes in the minor leagues had no real effect on the Charlotte Hornets in 1963 since they were already owned and operated by the Minnesota Twins. On the field there was little improvement as the Hornets (58–82) rose only to seventh place. First baseman Al Barth (.284, 80 RBIs) led the team.

In 1964, the South Atlantic League changed its name to the Southern League, remaining class AA . The Hornets actually improved that season to finish with a 73–67 record, leaving them in fourth place. Third baseman Minnie Mendoza hit .302 while catcher Ron Henry hit .307 with 17 home runs in 54 games. The next season was another mediocre one. The Hornets played average ball and finished 72–68, eight games out of first.

The 1966 Hornets were one of six Southern League teams to finish below .500; their 64–74 finish left them in sixth place. Pitcher Garland Shifflett was the league's best reliever as he appeared in 63 games and had an ERA of only 1.98. Led by league batting champ Minnie Mendoza (.297) in 1967, the Hornets improved to 75–65, landing them in fourth place. Future major league All-Star third baseman Graig Nettles (.232, 19 HR, 86 RBIs) tied for the league lead in home runs and finished the season with Minnesota. Catcher George Mitterwald (.242) also made it to Minnesota and would spend 11 seasons in the big leagues. Garland Shifflett had another outstanding season out of the bullpen, appearing in 69 games and compiling a 12–7 record with a 1.45 ERA.

First in attendance by nearly 30,000 in 1968, the Hornets finished the season in third with a 72–68 record. Pitcher Tom Hall (6–3, 1.36 ERA) had a great start to the season before being promoted to AAA. By June he was in Minnesota. In 1969, Charlotte finally won the league pennant. The Hornets won 81 games and lost 59 to finish three games ahead of Birmingham. The team featured the two best pitchers in the league, starter Bill Zepp (15–3, 2.34 ERA) and reliever Bob Gebhard (13–3, 1.23 ERA, 19 saves). Attendance rose that season to 146,141, nearly 100,000 more than the league's second place team.

The 1970 season saw the Hornets drop back below .500 as they posted a 66–73, sixth place finish. Outfielder Steve Brye (.307) won the batting title and finished the season with the Twins.

In 1971, the Southern League played an interlocking schedule with the Texas League to form what was known as the Dixie Association, an experiment that lasted only one season. The Hornets, closely pursued by the Asheville Tourists, finished the season with the Association's best record, 92–50. They then defeated Asheville in the Southern League playoffs, two games to one. Advancing to face the Arkansas Travelers of the Texas League in the "Dixie Series," the Hornets took the championship, three games to none. Infielder Minnie Mendoza (.316), the league batting champ, and pitchers Dick Rusteck (17–8) and Greg Jaycox (15–5) led the team to victory. Pitcher Steve Luebber (9–1, 1.97 ERA) dominated the league in the first half before being called up to Minnesota.

The Minnesota Twins, Charlotte's parent club, tried a unique experiment in 1972: They made Charlotte home to both their single A and AA franchises. While the Hornets were on the road, the Class A Twins of the Western Carolina League would play in Griffith Park. It was not a successful arrangement as the two teams combined drew over 25,000 fewer fans than the 1971 Hornets had by themselves. On the playing field, the Hornets broke even with a 70–70 record, third in their division. Pitcher Bill Campbell (13–10, 204 SO) would go on to spend 15 seasons in the major leagues as a reliever, saving 126 games. The Charlotte Twins were even less successful than the Hornets as they won 50 games and lost 79, avoiding the league cellar by half a game. After the season Minnesota transferred both franchises to other locations, ending a relationship between that franchise and the city of Charlotte that had lasted over 30 years.

For the next three seasons, Charlotte was without professional baseball. After failing to find a buyer for Griffith Park, Clark Griffith announced plans to have it torn down. Charlotte businessman Jim Crockett stepped in and bought the park for $87,000, renaming it Crockett Park. Baseball returned to the city as the Asheville Orioles of the Southern League were moved to Charlotte for the 1976 season. Named the Charlotte O's, the team had a decent season and finished second in their division with a 74–66 record. They lost a one-game playoff to the Orlando Twins, Charlotte's former franchise. Pitcher Dave Ford (17–7, 121 SO) was one of the league's best while first baseman Eddie Murray (.298, 12 HR), promoted during the season, became one of the game's all-time great hitters and is guaranteed a place in Cooperstown.

The 1977 and '78 seasons found the O's in the divisional cellar, as they finished below .500 both seasons. The 1977 team did feature the league batting champ, outfielder Mark Corey (.310), and two future big league pitchers, Sammy Stewart (9–6) and Bryn Smith (15–11). Finally in 1979, the O's (73–69) posted a winning record. The team started strong and won the first half of the season but slumped in the second half. Finishing with the second best record in their division, the O's advanced to the playoffs but

were promptly swept by the Columbus Astros. Attendance, which only been 64,163 in
1978, doubled in 1979, signaling the beginning of a new era for minor league baseball
in Charlotte.

Like the previous season, the 1980 O's
started strong and won the first half of the
season. Again they had trouble in the second
half and finished with an overall record of
72–72, third best in their division. Advancing
to the playoffs, the O's swept Savannah in the
first round. They then took the league championship by defeating Memphis, three games
to one. Outfielder Drungo Hazewood (.261,
28 HR) and third baseman and future big
league superstar Cal Ripken, Jr. (.276, 25
HR), provided Charlotte's offensive power.
Both were named to the league All-Star team.

The O's finished the 1981 season with a
record of 74–69, second best in their division. They failed, however, to win either half
of the season so were not involved in the
playoffs. Catcher Willie Royster (.265, 31
HR) and second baseman Vic Rodriguez
(.306) led the team. Attendance topped the
200,000 mark for the first time that season.

The 1982 season saw the O's (66–77) return to the divisional cellar. The next season
they showed only slight improvement as they
posted a 69–77 record, the league's fifth best.
Future Baltimore outfielder Larry Sheets
(.288) led the league with 25 home runs. All-
Star second baseman Vic Rodriguez would
also make it to Baltimore for a few games.

The O's were Southern League champs
in 1984. After a terrible start, they improved
to win the second half of the season, and with
an overall record of 75–72 the O's advanced
to the playoffs to face the Greenville Braves.
They took the series, three games to one, and
moved on to meet Knoxville in the finals,
taking the pennant in three straight games.
Pitcher Ken Dixon (16–8, 211 SO) was the
star of the team, leading the league in wins,
strikeouts and complete games.

On March 16, 1985, in a fire suspected
as arson, Crockett Park burned. Temporary
seating was put up and the O's began play in
what was left of their ballpark. The team

(78–65) played well and won the Eastern Division of the league by defeating Columbus
in a playoff, three games to one. They then
advanced to the championship but lost the
series to Hunstville, three games to two.
Pitcher John Habyan (13–5) was named to
the league All-Star team and received a September call-up to Baltimore.

The O's finished the 1986 season with a
71–73 record, fourth in their division. Second baseman Billy Ripken (.268) was named
to the All-Star team. The team improved the
next season, winning the East Division's
first-half title. With their 85–60 record, the
O's advanced to the playoffs to face Jacksonville. They won the first round but lost
the league championship to Birmingham,
three games to one. Designated hitter and
league MVP Tom Dodd (.289, 37 HR, 127
RBIs) and All-Star first baseman Dave Fal-
cone (.293, 92 RBIs) powered the Charlotte
offense that season. The pitching staff was
average but one member, future big leaguer
Bob Milacki (11–9), turned in a legendary
performance; on May 28, he pitched 11⅓ no-
hit innings against Chattanooga. He pitched
13 of the game's 14 innings and came out with
a 2–1 victory.

Led by All-Star outfielder Butch Davis
(.301, 82 RBIs), the team, now named the
Knights, finished the 1988 season in fourth
place (69–75). The long relationship with
Baltimore ended after that season and the
team became a Chicago Cubs affiliate. The
results of the 1989 season were much the
same as the Knights (70–73) were again
fourth. Laddie Renfroe was named the league's
most outstanding pitcher as he posted a
record of 19–7 with 15 saves.

Knight's Castle, the team's new 10,000
seat, $12 million ballpark, opened in 1990.
The result was a huge jump in attendance.
The Knights had drawn 157,720 in 1989 and
then led the league with 271,502 in 1990, the
highest attendance figure for any AA team in
the nation. On the field the Knights were not
as successful as they again finished fourth in
their division, 20 games out of first. The
team batting average was a lowly .234, worst

Billy Ripken enjoyed an All-Star season for Charlotte in 1986 (from the collection of the author).

in the league. The pitching staff did have two outstanding performances, however, from Kevin Coffman (7–3, 2.03 ERA) and Heathcliff Slocumb (3–1, 2.15 ERA, 12 SV).

The Knights (74–70) improved to finish above .500 in 1991 but still could do no better than fourth in the division standings. First baseman Elvin Paulino (.257) led the league in home runs (24) and RBIs (81). With a 70–73 record, the Knights finished second in 1992. They were, however, still 30 games out of first as Greenville dominated the league. The Knights met Greenville in the divisional playoff but were easily swept.

The 1993 season began a new era in North Carolina baseball as Charlotte became a triple A franchise. Never before in the state's long minor league history had a team been at the minor's highest level. The Knights became an expansion franchise in the International League as an affiliate of the Cleveland Indians.

It was a great season for baseball in Charlotte as the Knights won the league pennant in their inaugural season. With a league-best record of 86–55, the team defeated Richmond and then Rochester to take the championship. In another great season for ticket sales, the Knights' attendance rose by 65,000 to top the 400,000 mark. On the field the Knights were led by third baseman

and league MVP Jim Thome. Thome won the batting title with a .332 average and led in RBIs with 102. Designated hitter Sam Horn (.269, 96 RBIs) led the league (as well as all other minor leagues) with 38 home runs. The pitching staff featured the talents of Chad Ogea (13–8) and relievers Jerry DiPoto (6–3, 1.93 ERA) and Bill Wertz (7–2, 1.95 ERA).

The Knights (77–65) were not as successful in 1994. After leading the division in the final month of the season, the team hit a slump. They lost four out of five games to Richmond in a series that decided the division championship. In the playoffs, the Knights again faced Richmond but lost that series, three games to one. All-Star first baseman Herbert Perry (.327, 70 RBIs) led the Charlotte offense while Albie Lopez (13–3) and Julian Tavarez (15–6) had excellent seasons on the mound.

For the 1995 season the Knights became the Florida Marlins triple A affiliate. It proved to be a disappointing season for the team as they finished last in their division with a 59–81 record. Fifty-eight different players appeared in a Knights uniform that season. Of those, first baseman Russ Morman (.314, 36 RBIs in 44 games), catcher Rob Natal (.314 in 53 games), and former Red Sox outfielder Bob Zupcic (.295, 11 HR in 72 games) were the best offensively while lefthander Joel Adamson (8–4, 3.29 ERA) led the pitching staff.

Again in 1996, the Knights finished last in their division though their record improved slightly to 62–79. The star of the team was All-Star outfielder Billy McMillon, who won the league batting title with a .352 average and was named as the International League's Rookie of the Year. Third baseman Jose Olmeda (.320) and first baseman Russ Morman (.332, 18 HR, 77 RBIs) also had outstanding seasons.

Clinton

When the Class D Tobacco State League formed in 1946 the Clinton Sampson Blues (Clinton is located in Sampson County) joined as a charter member. The Blues, as they were called for short, played at Clinton High School Park and had a talented team that first year. They finished the season in second place, half a game back, with a record of 70–48. Manager-outfielder Willie Duke (27 HR, 109 RBIs) won the batting title with a .393 average while fellow All-Star third baseman Lonnie Smith (.304, 21 HR) led the league in runs with 117. Pitchers Bob Keane (23–4) and Earl Mossor (21–8) were two of the best in the league. In the first round of the postseason, the Blues easily beat Smithfield, four games to one. They lost the finals in seven games, however, to Angier-Fuquay Springs.

The 1947 season was not as successful as the previous one. The Blues went through three managers, including former major league pitcher Van Lingle Mungo (who batted .362 in 33 games at first base), and finished with a record of only 56–67, 29 games out of first. Shortstop Theron Evans was the Blues' offensive leader, batting .334 with 60 RBIs. Though they had no real stars the team hit for a surprising .290 average. Suvern Wright was the leading pitcher on an otherwise weak staff at 14–9 (he also hit .305). Attendance for the season was 36,778.

The Blues, signed a working agreement with the Detroit Tigers in 1948 but turned in another mediocre finish with a record of 70–67. The team finished in sixth place (out of eight), 10½ games behind first place Sanford. Manager Marvin Lorenz, who played first base and occasionally pitched, hit .333 with 103 RBIs and 127 runs scored. Outfielders Jim Williams (.378 in 83 games) and Don MacLean (.358, 115 RBIs) were also among the best players in the league. Though they had a strong offense, the Blues

were hindered by an unreliable pitching staff.

The 1949 Blues, again managed by Marvin Lorenz (.286, 89 RBIs), dropped another rung on the ladder as they finished in seventh place. The team won 60 games while losing 72 and was 22½ games behind regular season champion Dunn-Erwin. Outfielder Andrew Scrobola (.315, 100 runs) was the team's best hitter and pitcher Billy Price (12–5) dominated opposing hitters and had a league best ERA of 2.19. Other than these two players, the only other performance of note was by second baseman Nick Purchia (.277), who led the league with 118 runs scored.

In 1950 the Blues' record was almost the same as the previous year. They went 61–72 and finished in fifth place. Marvin Lorenz, who had managed the Blues the two previous seasons, began the year as the manager of the Smithfield-Selma Leafs. He was rehired by the Blues (to become their third manager of the season) when the Leafs withdrew from the league on August 16.

Catcher Al Kluttz (.373 in 61 games) and All-Star second baseman Nick Purchia (.281, 89 RBIs) were the team's top hitters. Outfielder Bill Kay (.275, 131 runs) led the league with 57 stolen bases and an amazing 180 bases on balls.

A decline in attendance caused many teams in the league to suffer financial difficulties. Attendance in Clinton dropped from 37,496 in 1949 to 29,060 in 1950 and though this was a substantial drop it was slight compared to some league members. The Tobacco State League decided to break up after the 1950 season and most towns that fielded a team in that league, Clinton included, have been without professional baseball ever since.

◆ ——————— *Concord* ——————— ◆

In the mill town of Concord, baseball had long been played in the textile leagues of the area. In 1935 a team was formed for membership in the Carolina Textile League, a circuit that allowed teams to have four players with professional experience. Most of the members of that league, Concord included, joined to form a new league in 1936. Called the Carolina League, it allowed unlimited salaries and was thus a professional league, though it was not a member of the National Association.

For the three seasons it was in existence, Concord was a member of this so-called "outlaw league." The Weavers, as the team was called, played well and won the pennant in 1936 with a record of 66–33. In 1937, they finished third (52–45) but won the postseason championship. Catcher Bill Steinecke, whose minor league playing and managing career lasted nearly 40 years, led the team in hitting with a .364 average. First baseman and manager Bobby Hipps, a former Asheville Tourists star, hit .317 while shortstop Dick Culler, who would go on to the major leagues, hit .315. Ken Chitwood was the leading pitcher with an 11–4 record. The 1938 Weavers finished the season in fourth place with an even 47–47 record. Bill Steinecke (.340) again led the team in hitting, tied with another longtime minor league star, first baseman Holt "Cat" Milner. Witt "Lefty" Guise, who would appear in two games for Cincinnati in 1940, won 13 and lost 7.

With the demise of the Carolina League, the Weavers joined the Class D North Carolina State League in 1939. They finished at 60–50 and qualified for the playoffs with a third place finish. They lost to league champion Mooresville in the first round, however, three games to one. Second baseman Ulmont Baker (.333, 44 2B) led the team in hitting, followed by outfielder-manager Gerry Fitzgerald (.318). Both, along with catcher John Pare (.295), were named to the league

All-Star team. John Berry (21–5, 2.69 ERA) was the ace of the pitching staff.

The 1940 season saw the Weavers finish at 58–54, good enough only for fifth place. All-Star third baseman Ulmont Baker (.335, 103 RBIs) was the team's best player. In 1941, despite the performances of Ulmont Baker (.333), who had taken over at manager, and outfielders George Brown (.333) and Willie Mauney (.325), the team again finished fifth (51–49).

In 1942 the Weavers won the league pennant with a record of 64–34. They were led by pitcher Herman Drefs (23–5), third baseman–manager Marvin Watts (.318) and outfielder George Brown (.332). The Weavers were upset, however, in the first round of the playoffs by Thomasville, three games to one.

The Weavers returned when league play resumed in 1945, yet their winning ways did not: They finished in last place with a record of 34–79. That season marked the first time that a Concord team had signed a major league working agreement as the Weavers joined up with the Philadelphia Phillies. A 17-year-old pitcher named Tommy Lasorda made his professional baseball debut with Concord that season, turning in a 3–12 record.

The next year the Weavers, once again independent, nearly reversed their record of the previous season. The team won 77 games and lost only 34, dominating the league and taking the pennant by 15½ games. Their pitching staff, undeniably the best in the league, had strong performances from Lacy James (22–7, 247 SO), Bob Ennis (19–3, 1.05 ERA), Richard Aldridge (13–7) and Charlie Vartanian (12–5). Second baseman Lewis Davis (.349, 81 RBIs) finished second in the league batting race but did lead with 67 stolen bases. Outfielders Jim Thomas (.332) and Willie Mauney (.301, 44 SB) also contributed greatly to the offense. The Weavers swept Thomasville in the first round of the playoffs but unfortunately were upset in the

The 1942 Concord Weavers included: *Back:* Buck Glover, Marvin Watts, Herman Drefs, Glenn Miller, Zeke Graham, unidentified, George Motto, unidentified; *Front:* Willard Mauney, unidentified, John Shoe, unidentified, Herman "Ginger" Watts, unidentified, George Brown, unidentified (courtesy Hank Utley).

finals by the Mooresville Moors, a team the Weavers had finished 19 games ahead of in the regular season.

The 1947 and '48 seasons saw the Weavers post losing records. They finished seventh both seasons with records of 48–63 and 44–62. Pitcher Furman Taylor (10–4), who led the league with a 2.43 ERA, was the most notable member of the 1947 Weavers. The 1948 team was led by outfielder-manager Jim Mills (.322) and pitcher Charlie Cudd (12–10).

After the 1948 season the team was purchased by the big league Washington Senators. The team name was changed to the Concord Nationals but the losing continued. In 1949, the team finish in sixth place at 50–72. Seventh place was the best the team could do in 1950, finishing 24 games out of first with a record of 44–68. Third baseman Len Cross (.303, 25 HR, 95 RBIs) was that season's best player.

The next season, 1951, was the last for professional baseball in Concord. The independent team, no longer part of the Washington organization, became the Concord Sports. With only a slight improvement, they finished in sixth, winning 56 games and losing 70. First baseman Jim Thomas (.327, 23 HR, 111 RBIs), put in a good effort for the Sports, as did pitcher Ray Nesbit (14–6), but it wasn't enough. The team disbanded after the season.

 ———————— *Cooleemee* ————————

Cooleemee is another of the many small textile mill towns located in the Piedmont section of the state that has a long history of baseball. Textile league ball had been played for many seasons before a truly professional team was fielded. In 1935 the town took a big step toward professional baseball by entering a team named the Weavers in the Carolina Textile League. A very competitive league, it allowed teams to have four players with

Fair Swaim (left) and Lawrence "Ty" Tysinger, members of the 1938 Cooleemee ball club (courtesy Fair Swaim).

professional experience and paid good salaries to attract quality ballplayers. The Weavers had a good team that season and featured future big-league shortstop Dick Culler (.354), a native of High Point, North Carolina.

The Weavers became a charter franchise in the Class D North Carolina State League when it formed in 1937. In the five years Cooleemee fielded a team in the league it never finished better than sixth place (out of eight) and twice finished last. The 1937 team posted a record of 45–67, seventh in the league. They did have several talented players, however, including first baseman Glen Stafford (.333, 91 RBIs) and outfielder Lawrence Tysinger (.320). Pitcher Firpo Creason (16–17, 3.22 ERA) would undoubtedly have won more games had he played for a better team.

In 1938 the Weavers signed a working agreement with the Winston-Salem Twins of the Piedmont League, who were in turn a Brooklyn Dodgers farm club. Unfortunately it still proved to be an unsuccessful season on the field as the Weavers again finished in seventh place (42–69), avoiding the cellar by one game. First baseman Vick Koslowski (.321) was the team's top hitter while Jim Reid (17–10, 207 SO) led the pitching staff.

Cooleemee's best season came in 1939 when the team finished with a record of 49–62, sixth in the eight-team league. That team, called the Cools, was managed by outfielder Otis "Blackie" Carter (.306), who was near the end of a long, outstanding minor league career. Catcher Luther Whitlock led the team in hitting with a .345 average, followed by third baseman George Motto (.332) and center fielder Claude Wilborn (.339), both of whom were named to the league All-Star team. Wilborn went on to appear in five games with the Boston Bees at the end of the following season.

The team was known as the Cooleemee

Cards for their final two seasons as they became a member of the St. Louis Cardinals' huge, 29-team farm system. Supplied with little talent, it was a miserable two seasons, as the Cards could do no better than last place with records of 27–84 in 1940 and 28–72 in 1941. Nearly 50 different players appeared in a Cooleemee uniform in 1940 but only two— catcher Oscar Galipeau (.258) and pitcher Joe Yockman (5–20)— remained for the entire season. Second baseman Dutch Dorman (.343 in 18 games), whose minor league playing career lasted more than 25 years, was player-manager for the Cards in the middle part of the 1940 season. Outfielder Jim Matthews (.321 in 35 games) would also have a long minor league career, including a 50 home run season in the West Texas–New Mexico League in 1953.

The 1941 team had a couple of good hitters — outfielders Forrest Rogers (.315) and Conrad Graff (.308)— but they alone were not enough to help the weak team. The lone player from a Cooleemee team ever to lead the league in a category was pitcher Merle Muhl, who led in ERA (2.17) in 1941. His won-lost record, however, was only 4–7, attesting to the fact that he played for a poor team.

The smallest town in the league, Cooleemee was not big enough to give the team the kind of crowds necessary to make it a financial success. No money at the gate meant no money to buy good players to make a competitive team. Therefore, Cooleemee dropped out of the league after the 1941 season.

Dunn-Erwin

When the Class D Tobacco State League formed in 1946, the Dunn-Erwin Twins became a charter franchise. That first year they did not fare well as they finished last in the league with a 48–70 record, 22½ games behind first place Sanford. Outfielders Eddie Bass (.323, 19 HR, 110 RBIs) and Granville "Shamrock" Denning (.304, 80 RBIs) were the team's leading hitters.

Dunn-Erwin outfielder and manager Gaither Riley was placed on baseball's ineligible list for assaulting umpire Robert Mann in a game at Dunn on August 28, 1946. In that game, Mann called a strike that was disputed by Riley and several other Twins players. Mann then ordered Riley off the field for using profanity. Riley, who later stated that the umpire called him a son of a bitch, proceeded to punch Mann in the eye and knock him down. The decision of Judge William Bramham, president of the National Association, read: "Riley's conduct is not disputed. I have talked with this player and he merely says he lost his head and does not

know what prompted him to do such a thing. He is very sorry and has apologized to Umpire Mann." Riley's suspension was later lifted.

The 1947 Twins, managed by second baseman Jack Bell and later Bill Aurette, finished a little better. They turned in a .500 record going 62–62, 23½ games behind Sanford. They qualified for the playoffs but lost in the first round to Lumberton, four games to one. Attendance for the year was a respectable 49,262, third in the league. Outfielder Carl McQuillan and outfielder-catcher Shamrock Denning had outstanding seasons. Denning hit .333 with 101 runs scored, 25 stolen bases, and, though he hit only five home runs, 96 RBIs. McQuillan, named to the league All-Star team, hit .331 with 19 home runs, 121 RBIs and 103 runs scored. Pitcher John Komar was 10–5 with a 1.86 ERA.

In 1948 the Twins were back in the cellar with a 48–89 record, this time 32 games behind perennial front-runner Sanford. The team went through three managers that year:

1946 Dunn-Erwin Twins (courtesy Gaither Riley).

Carl McQuillen, Babe Bost and Gaither Riley (from June 21 on). Shamrock Denning had another great season, hitting .323 with 105 runs and 92 RBIs, but the pitching staff was weak with no one winning more than seven games. Attendance dropped considerably to 26,475, last in the league.

The Twins made a complete turn-around for the 1949 season. They won the league pennant, five games ahead of their nearest rival, with a record of 81–54. The team, managed by Jim Staton, had several stars. Among them were veteran Shamrock Denning (.354) — the league leader in hits (185), runs (118) and RBIs (119) — outfielder John Richards (.351, 105 RBIs, 107 runs) and pitcher Clarence Condit (20–9), who led the

league in wins and strikeouts (264). Richards, Condit and catcher Steve Marko (.326) were all named to the league's postseason All-Star team. Having a winning team helped attendance, as it rose to 39,335. In the playoffs the Twins had little trouble with Lumberton, winning four games to one. However, they managed to lose the finals to Red Springs, also four games to one.

The Twins returned in 1950 with James Staton as manager and Shamrock Denning as probably the best offensive player in the league. Due to poor attendance, however, the team decided to move to Whiteville during the middle of the season. This spelled the end of professional baseball in the Dunn-Erwin area.

◆ ———————— *Durham* ———————— ◆

Durham's Bulls are perhaps the state's most famous team. Thanks in part to the popular movie *Bull Durham* in 1987, the Bulls became famous nationwide. It became common to see Bulls baseball caps

being worn in any part of the country. The Bulls were popular even before the movie, however, as they helped lead the renaissance of minor league baseball. Beginning in 1980, Miles Wolff's Bulls helped to spark a new popularity for the minor leagues that has since spread across the country. Though the Bulls of the 1980s and '90s may be the most well-known, the history of the team goes back much further.

The first professional baseball team to call Durham home took to the field in 1902. The team played in the short-lived Class C North Carolina League and was named the Bulls, after the locally produced Bull Durham brand of tobacco. The league disbanded in mid–July, leaving Durham in fifth place with a 21–27 record. Games were played at Hanes Field on the campus of Trinity College (now Duke University's East Campus). The playing field had been upgraded, a new grandstand built, and an outfield wall added to get ready for the season.

It was 1913 before professional baseball returned to Durham. A new team, again named the Bulls, was formed to join the new Class D North Carolina State League. Led by outfielder James Kelly (.321), the league batting champ, the team played well and finished in second place with a 65–49 record, only half a game behind first place Winston-Salem. The Bulls again came close to winning the league in 1914 with their 70–50 record but finished 1½ games behind co-leaders Charlotte and Winston-Salem.

The results of the 1915 season were similar as the Bulls (69–52) again finished second. Manager and outfielder James Kelly led the team in hitting with a .296 average while pitcher C.H. Frye won 22 games and lost 13. In 1916, the Bulls dropped to third place as they posted a 62–51 record. Outfielder Warren Butts (.279) had a good season, leading the league in stolen bases (87) and runs scored (90).

The 1917 baseball season was filled with uncertainty as the United States entered World War I. Many minor leagues, the N.C. State League included, began the season but didn't finish it, forced to shut down by a shortage of players and by travel restrictions. Unfortunately for the Durham Bulls,

they were in first place with a 24–12 record when their league disbanded on May 30. At the time of the demise, Bulls first baseman Ray Grimes was leading the league with six home runs while his twin brother, shortstop Roy Grimes, was hitting .321. Pitcher N.L. Elliott was the league's best with his 10–1 record.

Durham remained without professional baseball until 1920, when the Bulls returned and became a charter member of the new Class D Piedmont League. The team had a tough first season and finished in the cellar with a 53–65 record. Pitcher George Nelson (19–9), responsible for more than a third of the team's wins, tied for the league's best record. The results of the 1921 season were not much different as the Bulls (57–64) rose only one place to fifth. Outfielder Jim Conley led the team with a .331 batting average while pitcher George Price, the league strikeout leader with 158, compiled a 19–10 record.

The Bulls improved in 1922. They started slowly but came on strong to win the second half of the season; their overall record of 69–58 was the second best in the league. In a playoff with first half champ High Point, the Bulls prevailed, four games to three, to take the pennant. Outfielder and manager Lee Gooch (.350), a native of Oxford, North Carolina, who had played briefly in the major leagues, was the offensive star of the team.

The 1923 season saw the Bulls drop back to the league cellar. Twenty-three games out of first, the team finished with a record of 50–73. First baseman-manager Art Bourg (.321, 27 SB) led the Bulls back to the top in 1924. The team finished first with a 72–48 record. Second baseman Hobart Brummitt (.356, 72 RBIs) won the batting title while pitchers Bill Hackney (19–12) and Walt Masters (17–5) were among the league's best. Rookie outfielder Leroy "Cowboy" Jones, who would go on to be one of the great all-time minor league hitters, batted .292 with a league leading 16 triples. No playoff was held that season.

Art Bourg led the Bulls to their second

straight pennant in 1925. Winning the first half of the season, the team (68–58) went on to defeat Winston-Salem in seven games for the championship. Bourg hit .318 and led the league with 108 runs and 49 stolen bases. Outfielder Jule Mallonee (.366) had a great year and finished the season with the Chicago White Sox. The star of the team, however, was outfielder Harry Smith. The league batting champion, Smith hit .385, scored 105 runs and drove in 95.

After a slow start, the Bulls (73–71) recovered to win the second half of the 1926 season. The team's strong offense featured veterans Harry Smith (.337, 89 RBIs), Hobart Brummitt (.291, 84 RBIs) and Jule Mallonee (.323, 103 runs, 17 HR, 85 RBIs). Despite a talented team, the Bulls lost in the playoffs to Greensboro, four games to one.

Back in the cellar in 1927, the Bulls finished 48–95. The team had a good offense but horrible pitching. No pitcher on the team even came close to posting a winning record. Shortstop Bill Akers (.330) went on to spend a few seasons in the big leagues. The Bulls won even fewer games in 1928 as they finished with a 40–91 record, again the worst in the league. Again the pitching staff was inept as members posted records of 10–21, 5–10, 6–15, 5–15 and 1–10. The team's only real star was outfielder Fred Tauby, who hit .343.

With an 85–51 record, the 1929 Bulls once again took the league pennant. The offense was powered by outfielders Tom Wolfe (.345, 27 HR, 134 RBIs) and Fred Tauby (.308, 46 SB). Pitcher Vance Page (21–8), a future Chicago Cub, had a great season while Monte Weaver, though his record was only 12–7, had a league best ERA of 1.94. The Bulls fell apart in the playoffs with second place Greensboro and lost, four games to one.

Led by league MVP Tom Wolfe (.351, 39 HR, 154 RBIs), the Bulls won the Piedmont League championship in 1930. The team finished second in the regular season with a 71–68 record, then defeated first place Henderson in the playoffs, four games to three. Wolfe was not the only offensive power

the Bulls had; his two fellow outfielders were just as impressive. Fred Tauby (.358, 25 HR, 137 RBIs, 55 SB) had his best season yet and finished with the league's second highest RBI total while Jack Lindley (.353, 37 HR, 125 RBIs) led the league with 148 runs scored. These three players combined to form the greatest outfield in the long history of the Durham Bulls (if not the entire state). Surprisingly, only Tauby ever played in the major leagues. In 24 games with the White Sox and the Phillies, he hit only .077.

In 1931, a year in which Charlotte ran away with the league title, Durham (56–72) finished fifth. Future big leaguer Gil English, the Bulls' third baseman, was the star of the team, hitting .344 with 106 RBIs. The 1932 team dropped to the league cellar, winning 54 games and losing 77. Tom Wolfe, who returned to Durham after playing the first part of the season with Raleigh, won the batting title with a .381 average. Eighteen-year-old rookie pitcher Nate Andrews, 3–6, went on to spend much of eight seasons in the big leagues.

In 1933, the Bulls became a New York Yankees farm club. It did not help the team win, however, as they finished fifth with a 65–76 record. Outfielder Ernie Koy (.328) and catcher Rip Collins (.327) were both named to the league All-Star team. Outfielder "Sunny Jim" Blakesley, in the final season of an outstanding minor league career, hit .330 in 46 games. Third baseman Merrill "Pinky" May hit .309. The father of longtime big league catcher Milt May, he spent five seasons as the Phillies' starting third baseman, three times leading the league in fielding. After his playing career, May spent 25 seasons as a minor league manager.

The Bulls were out of the Piedmont League for the 1934 and '35 seasons after the team folded due to poor attendance. In 1936, the Piedmont League's Wilmington franchise, a Cincinnati Reds farm club, moved to Durham. Again named the Bulls, the team's two biggest stars that season, first baseman Frank McCormick and pitcher Johnny Vander Meer, both went on to stardom in Cincinnati.

The 1939 Durham Bulls included: *Back:* Charles Aleno, Barney DeForge, Charles Hawley, Edwin Ignasiak, unidentified, unidentified, unidentified: *Middle:* unidentified, unidentified, unidentified, Oscar Roettger, Allen Hunt, Elmer Riddle, Pudge Powers; *Front:* Everett Hill, Van Harrington, Wayne Blackburn, Don Bird, Tom Oliver (courtesy Miles Wolff).

McCormick, named to the league All-Star team, batted .381 with 211 hits and 138 RBIs. Vander Meer (19–6) led the league in strikeouts (295) and ERA (2.65) and was named Minor League Player of the Year by *The Sporting News.* As a team, the Bulls finished the season in second place. With a 79–63 record, they advanced to the playoffs and defeated Rocky Mount in the first round, but were swept by Norfolk in the finals.

The 1937 season saw the Bulls drop to fifth place. With a 68–69 record, the team finished 20 games behind first place Asheville. Pitcher Paul Gehrman (21–13) had a great season, finishing it with Cincinnati. The next season the Bulls, 64–71, dropped even lower as they finished sixth in the league. Second baseman Wayne Blackburn (.335) and outfielders Dutch Mele (.342) and Carl "Pinky"

Jorgenson (.351) supplied much of the team's offense.

The Bulls rose to finish second in 1939. With a 75–65 record, they advanced to the playoffs but lost in the first round to Rocky Mount. Wayne Blackburn (.344) and Dutch Mele (.340) both returned and played well. Former Red Sox outfielder Tom Oliver (.274) led the team with 79 RBIs. Chuck Hawley (17–5) was the star of an otherwise weak pitching staff.

Turning in a 73–62 record in 1940, the Bulls — now an affiliate of the Brooklyn Dodgers —finished fourth. They upset Richmond's Colts in the first round of the playoffs and then took the championship by defeating Rocky Mount, four games to two. The Bulls had only average hitting that season but a good pitching staff led them to victory.

The 1942 Durham Bulls included: *L to R:* Steve Nagy, Ferrell Anderson, Emo Showfety, Richard Whit-man, Charles Welchel, Harold Haub, Lou Welaj, Bud Kimball (all of whom were preparing to join the military) (courtesy Emo Showfety).

Everett Hill (14–8) and Barney DeForge (13–5), who had a league leading 2.40 ERA, were the team's best.

The Bulls were the league's best team in 1941. Managed by Bruno Betzel, their record of 84–53 gave them the league pennant by ten games. The Bulls then took the championship by defeating first Norfolk and then Greensboro in the playoffs, dropping only one game in the process. All-Star second baseman John Burman won the batting title with a .327 average while outfielder Paul Bruno (.303) led the league with 89 RBIs. The Bulls had an outstanding pitching staff that season, led by All-Star Ed Albosta (15–5, 1.73 ERA), Jack Kraus (18–12) and Glenn Moulder (15–10). Manager Betzel, whose real name is surely the longest in baseball history (Christian Frederick Albert John Henry David Betzel), would spend three seasons at the helm of the Bulls. A former major league infielder, his minor league managerial career would span 30 years.

After the two previous seasons, 1942 was a disappointment for Bulls fans. The team

could manage no better than a fifth place, 65–70 finish. Catcher Ferrell Anderson (.319) and outfielder Emo Showfety (.290), a former Elon College star, were the team's best players.

The Bulls were the only team in the state to take the field in 1943. The other North Carolina members of the Piedmont League had dropped out due to war-time travel restrictions and an overall shortage of players. It was not a successful season for the Bulls as they finished last in the league with a 44–86 record. The team did feature two notable players: shortstop Gene Mauch (.322) and pitcher Rex Barney (4–6). Mauch spent several seasons as a player in the big leagues before becoming a manager. His big league managerial career lasted 26 seasons with stops in Philadelphia, Montreal, California and Minnesota. Rex Barney finished the 1943 season with Brooklyn and played there for six seasons. He then became a well-known radio announcer.

Though the Piedmont League continued play in 1944, Durham did not, dropping

The 1946 Durham Bulls included: *Back:* Teddy Wilson, unidentified, Hal Brown, Chuck Hastedt, John Streza, unidentified, unidentified, Tom Wright, Ralph Caldwell, unidentified; *Front:* Cotton Powell, Woody Fair, Ray Daedlow, unidentified, unidentified, Lee Mohr, Paul Crawford, Nick DeLuca, Pat Patterson (mgr.) (courtesy Cotton Powell).

out of the league due to difficulties caused by the war. The Bulls, a Red Sox farm club, were back in 1945 as a new league was formed. The Class C Carolina League included several former members of both the Piedmont and Bi-State leagues. With many baseball players still serving in the armed forces, teams had difficulty finding players. Many teams used older players who were past their prime, or high school age boys. Durham pitcher Tom Poholsky (5–3) was only 15 years old when the season began. He later pitched six seasons in the big leagues. The Bulls had a decent pitching staff that season but lacked offense, finishing in seventh place (out of eight) with a record of 59–77. Manager Pat Patterson appeared in ten games that season, ending a playing career that began in 1922. His minor league managerial and major league scouting career, however, would last until 1972, when he retired from the Montreal Expos organization.

The Bulls (80–62) improved in 1946 to finish third in the league. The team had no lack of offense that season. While the team batting average had been .240 in 1945, the 1946 Bulls set a still-standing league record with a .305 average. Outfielder Tom Wright (.380, 116 RBIs) won the batting title while fellow outfielder Woody Fair (.348, 24 HR, 161 runs, 161 RBIs, 51 doubles) had a legendary season. The Bulls' third outfielder, Teddy Wilson, hit .327 with 121 RBIs. The team also had excellent pitching as Hal "Skinny" Brown (15–5, 2.42 ERA) was one of the league's best. In the first round of playoffs, the Bulls defeated Greensboro, but as talented as the team was, they failed to win the championship, losing to Raleigh, four games to two. Wright, Brown and Wilson would all make the big leagues.

The 1947 Bulls dropped to fourth place with a 70–71 record. Manager-outfielder Willie Duke (.385, 117 RBIs, 104 runs) and first baseman Cecil "Turkey" Tyson (.349, 105 RBIs, 138 runs) both had impressive seasons and were named to the league's postseason All-Star team. The pitching staff featured Claude "Buck" Weaver, who turned in an 18–8 record. The Bulls upset Winston-Salem, four games to two, in the first round of the playoffs but lost by the same margin to Raleigh in the finals.

Willie Duke (.355) returned as the Bulls' manager in 1948. That season was the first as a member of the Detroit Tigers farm system, a relationship that would last through the 1961 season. The Bulls were not as strong as the previous seasons and finished sixth (63–79). All-Star second baseman Lawrence "Crash" Davis batted .317 and led the league with 50 doubles. The results of the 1949 season were much the same as the Bulls (70–72) again finished sixth. The team was led that season by pitcher Eddie Neville (25–10, 2.59 ERA) who surely would have won more games had he played for a better team. The Bulls' offense that season featured outfielder Carl Linhart (.311, 23 HR, 114 RBIs). The 1949 season was the first of four for manager Ace Parker. A former football All-American at Duke University, Parker spent seven seasons playing professional football and was named to that sport's Hall of Fame in 1972. Also a talented baseball player, he played for the Philadelphia Athletics in 1937 and '38. In 83 games for the Bulls in 1949, Parker hit .299.

Another sixth place finish was all the Bulls could manage in 1950. With a 73–79 record they finished 32 games behind first place Winston-Salem. Finally in 1951, Ace Parker's Bulls (84–56) improved to win another pennant. Outfielder Gordon Bragg (.340) finished with the league's second highest batting average while All-Star shortstop Hank Navarro (.306) led the league with 116 runs. Mickey McPadden (20–10, 2.93 ERA) was the ace of the pitching staff. Unfortunately for the Bulls, they were upset in the first round of the playoffs by Reidsville, four games to one.

The Bulls of 1952, led by batting champion outfielder Emil Karlick (.347, 93 RBIs, 31 SB) and pitcher Eddie Neville (17–9, 1.72 ERA), finished second with a 76–59 record.

Neville turned in one of the league's all-time great performances on August 29 of that season. He pitched all 18 innings of a scoreless game then hit a double and scored the game's only run to give his team the win. The Bulls swept Winston-Salem in the first round of the playoffs but were themselves swept in four games, by Reidsville in the finals. Manager Ace Parker left the team after the season to become the baseball coach at Duke University.

The 1953 season was not a successful one for the Bulls as they won 64 games and lost 75, finishing seventh. Despite this, Eddie Neville (21–8, 2.28) had another great season while All-Star first baseman Bill Radulovich (.349, 19 HR, 90 RBIs) won the batting title. The Bulls (70–68) improved to fourth in 1954. Led by outfielders George Bullard (.341) and Bill Hoffer (.319) and pitcher Bob Cruze (19–7), the Bulls advanced to the playoffs. They lost, however, to Fayetteville, three games to one.

The 1955 season saw another fourth place finish for the team. The Bulls qualified for the playoffs but lost to High Point–Thomasville in seven games. All-Star catcher Charlie Lau (.293, 18 HR) and pitcher Malcolm Simmons (17–9) were that season's top players. The Bulls improved to a second place, 84–69 finish in 1956 under new manager Johnny Pesky. Led by outfielder Dale Ferris (.310), first baseman Jim McManus (.308) and pitcher Bob Cruze (16–8), the team returned to the playoffs but again lost in the first round, this time to Danville.

The Bulls won another Carolina League pennant in 1957. They took the first half of a split season and finished tied for the league's best overall record at 79–61. In the playoffs with second half champ High Point–Thomasville, the Bulls prevailed in seven games. Outfielder Bubba Morton (.310, 18 HR, 82 RBIs), the Bulls' first black player, and shortstop Frank Kostro (.290), the league leader in hits (167), doubles (34) and triples (12), provided much of the team's offense. Pitcher David Reed (14–8, 2.04 ERA) led the league with 200 strikeouts.

Nineteen fifty-eight proved to be the Bulls' worst season yet. They finished in the league cellar with a 58–79 record. Fortunately, the 1959 season saw great improvement as the team rose to third place (70–60) in the league standings. Pitcher Bob Humphreys (8–2, 1.94 ERA) had a strong season. Dick McAuliffe, the league's All-Star shortstop, hit .263. He would debut with Detroit at the end of the following season. The Bulls advanced to the playoffs only to be swept by the Wilson Tobs.

The Bulls returned to the league cellar in 1960, though with an overall record of 57–78, they finished last in neither half of the split season. Their combined record, however, was the league's worst. The next season the Bulls (65–73) rose one place to fifth. They had started the season well, finishing second in the first half of the season, but stumbled in the second half. Future Detroit Tigers outfielder Gates Brown (.324, 15 HR, 33 SB) won the batting title.

In 1962, after signing a new working agreement with the expansion Houston Colt .45s, the Bulls made drastic improvements. Led by first baseman and league Player of the Year Rusty Staub (.293, 23 HR, 93 RBIs, 115 runs), they took the league pennant with an 89–51 record. Pitching ace Wally Wolf also had an outstanding season and finished the season 16–3. In a move that hurt the team, one of the Bulls' best hitters, outfielder Ron Davis (.296), received an early August promotion to Houston. Advancing to the playoffs, the Bulls swept Burlington in the first round but lost the hard fought finals to Kinston, four games to three. Rusty Staub made it to the big leagues the next season. Retiring in 1985, the six-time All-Star accumulated 2,716 hits, 1,466 RBIs and 292 home runs.

Former big leaguer Billy Goodman returned to his home state to manage the Bulls in 1963. The team had a decent season and finished second in the league's western half with a 78–65 record, but lost in a playoff with Greensboro, three games to two. Manager Goodman hit .354 for the Bulls that season,

playing in 71 games. That season's team featured the only Bulls player to date to reach the Hall of Fame. Second baseman Joe Morgan (.332, 13 HR) had a great rookie season and finished the year with Houston. He would go on to spend 22 seasons in the major leagues and was named to the All-Star team nine times. Bulls pitchers Bucky Brandon (14–6) and Tom Burgmeier (3–9) would also make it to the big leagues. Burgmeier was one of baseball's best relievers for much of his 17-year career.

Winning 54 games and losing 82, the Bulls again finished with the league's worst record in 1964. The 1965 season, however, saw the Bulls back on top as they won the league's West Division with an 83–60 record. A strong pitching staff led by Mike Daniel (10–3), Marvin Dutt (15–5) and Jim Holbrook (13–9) was the Bulls' key to success. In the playoffs they defeated Greensboro but were swept in the finals by Portsmouth, two games to none.

It was back to the cellar for the 1966 Bulls. They finished last in their division with a record of 62–76. The roller-coaster ride continued as the team was back on top in 1967. The Bulls (74–64), now a New York Mets farm team, finished that season as champs of the West Division. They advanced to the playoffs, and in an expanded format, swept both Burlington and Lynchburg. The Bulls then took the Carolina League pennant by defeating Portsmouth in the finals, two games to one. Versatile infielder Bob Heise (.298) had a good season and finished the year with the Mets, as did pitcher Danny Frisella (9–3, 1.49 ERA).

Even though the Bulls were league champs in 1967, attendance was last — only 24,210 came to see the team play. Since 1947, when 152,000 paid to see the Bulls, attendance had slowly dropped off. Raleigh was suffering from equally poor attendance so the two teams decided to merge for the 1968 season. Home games were split between Durham Athletic Park and Raleigh's Devereaux Meadow (see **Raleigh-Durham** entry).

It was 1980 before professional baseball

returned to Durham. That season the Carolina League expanded from six to eight teams and Durham was granted a franchise. Owned and operated by veteran minor league general manager Miles Wolff, the Bulls signed a player development contract with the Atlanta Braves. Decrepit Durham Athletic Park, which had been built in 1939, was renovated and play began.

The Bulls had a great return to professional baseball, winning both halves of the season in their division with identical 42–28 records. Managed by "Dirty Al" Gallagher, the Bulls had a talent-laden team. The offense featured six future big-leaguers. Speedy outfielders Albert Hall (.283, 100 SB), Milt Thompson (.290, 38 SB) and Brett Butler (.366, 36 SB) all had great seasons. First baseman Gerald Perry hit only .249 but drove in 92 runs. Shortstop Paul Zuvella hit .318 in 48 games. Two members of the Bulls' pitching staff, Joe Cowley (6–0) and Mike Smith (11–3), would also make the major leagues. Surprisingly, the team's best pitcher, reliever Ike Pettaway (11–4, 2.08 ERA, 20 saves), never did. Although they had a great team, the Bulls were swept by the Peninsula Pilots in the championship. The Bulls did, however, run away with the attendance title; they drew over 175,000 while the next closest team was Salem at 102,000.

The Bulls again led the league in attendance in 1981 but the team was not as successful on the field. Though led by outfielder Brad Komminsk (.322, 33 HR, 104 RBIs, 35 SB), the league MVP, they finished last in their division. With a record of 70–68, they were still only two games out of first. Komminsk, who had been a Braves first round draft pick, appeared to be headed for stardom in Atlanta. He made it to the major leagues for parts of eight seasons, hitting only .218 with 23 total home runs.

Playing well in 1982, the Bulls finished with the second best record in their division. They defeated Peninsula for the divisional title and advanced to face Alexandria for the league championship, only to be swept in three games. First baseman Keith Hagman

(.303) and shortstop Miguel Sosa (.288, 25 HR) were both named to the league All-Star team.

The 1983 season was a disappointing one for the Bulls. Their combined record of 59–78 left them with the third best record in their division. Pitchers Duane Ward (11–13) and Zane Smith (9–15), who both made the big leagues, were better than their records would indicate.

The Bulls won the first half of the 1984 season with a 39–31 record but dropped below .500 in the second half (29–41). They swept Peninsula in the playoff for the divisional title but lost to Lynchburg in the championship, three games to one. It was another average season for the Bulls in 1985 as they finished second in their division with a 66–74 record. The team had no real standout players that season though pitcher Paul Assenmacher (3–2) would make it to Atlanta. Outfielder Mike Yastrzemski (.270, 63 RBIs) led the weak-hitting offense.

The team improved in 1986 to 72–68, finishing above .500 but remaining in second place in their division. Three of that season's Bulls went on to stardom in Atlanta: shortstop Jeff Blauser (.286, 13 HR), second baseman Ron Gant (.277, 26 HR, 102 RBIs, 35 SB) and outfielder David Justice (.279, 12 HR), who joined the team in midseason.

The 1987 season saw the Bulls finish in the cellar of their division with a 65–75 record. Overall, their record left them seventh in the eight team league.

Three players were named to the league's postseason All-Star team, however, as second baseman Mark Lemke (.292, 20 HR), outfielder Alex Smith (.323), and pitcher Dave Miller (15–9, 155 SO) all had good seasons.

While the Bulls were playing only mediocre baseball, attendance continued to grow. In 1988, the team drew 271,650, nearly double the figure for second place Hagerstown. On the field the Bulls improved to 88–52 but still finished six games behind Kinston in their division. All-Star pitcher Kent Mercker (11–4, 2.68 ERA) had a great season before being promoted to Greenville in August, a move which hurt the Bulls. The offense featured third baseman Ken Pennington (.316) and first baseman Mike Bell (.257, 17 HR, 84 RBIs).

The Bulls played well in 1989. They won both halves of the season in their division and finished with a league best record of 84–54, earning Grady Little manager of the year honors. The Carolina League pennant eluded them, however, as they lost to Prince William, three games to one, in the championship. The Bulls won that season on the strength of their pitching. Pat Tilmon (11–4), Steve Ziem (9–0, 1.66 ERA), Jim Czajkowski (14 SV, 0.99 ERA) and Steve Avery (6–4, 1.45 ERA) were part of a staff that was the league's best with a combined ERA of 3.02. Dennis Burlingame was the most remarkable Bulls pitcher. On opening day he pitched a perfect game — believed to be the only one ever thrown on opening day in professional baseball history — and was 4–0 with an ERA of 0.50 before arm problems ended his season.

The 1990 season was not as successful as the Bulls (71–68) slipped to third in their division, 19 games behind Kinston. Pitchers Chris Czarnik (5–1, 1.15 ERA) and Preston Watson (10–6, 2.42 ERA) were two of the team's best while shortstop Mike Mordecai (.280) and outfielder Keith Mitchell (.294) led the offense. First baseman Ryan Klesko, one of the Braves' top prospects, joined the team at midseason and hit .274 with seven home runs. Attendance in Durham topped 300,000 for the first time that season, breaking the Bulls' own all-time Class A record and out-drawing all AA and most of the AAA teams.

The Bulls played better in 1991, improving their record to 79–58, but still finished with their division's third best record. Mike Mordecai (.262, 30 SB) returned and again played well as did pitcher Dennis Burlingame (11–7, 3.01 ERA), who was trying to recover from arm problems. Future Braves catcher Javy Lopez hit .245 with 11 home runs. Pitcher David Nied, whom Colorado would choose as its first pick in the expansion draft, was 8–3 with a 1.56 ERA.

Breaking even at 70–70, the Bulls turned in a second place divisional finish in 1992. Outfielder Brian Kowitz (.301, 64 RBIs) led the team in hitting while Mike Hostetler (9–3, 2.15 ERA) was the ace of the pitching staff. Outfielder Lee Heath (.277) was the league's top base stealer with 50. Highly regarded Braves shortstop prospect Chipper Jones hit .277 in 70 games before being promoted.

Again the Bulls finished second in 1993 with an even .500 record (69–69). All-Star second baseman Tony Graffanino (.275, 15 HR, 24 SB) led the team along with third baseman Dom Therrien (.300). Outfielder Pedro Swann hit .346 in 61 games before being promoted.

Though the Bulls had been scheduled to move to their new ballpark in 1994, construction delays forced them to return to Durham Athletic Park for one more season. With an overall record of 66–70, the Bulls finished the first half in last place in their division but improved to win the second half of the season. They moved on to the playoffs but lost to Winston-Salem, two games to none, in the first round. The Bulls had several talented players, including outfielder Damon Hollins (.270, 23 HR, 88 RBIs) and designated hitter Mike Warner (.321, 24 SB). Outfielder Kevin Grijak (.368) was promoted after hitting 11 home runs in the first 22 games.

Durham's new ballpark, named Durham Bulls Athletic Park, finally opened in 1995. A record crowd of over 390,000 turned out to see the Bulls play in their state-of-the-art park that season. The season was not as successful on the field as the team finished last in their division with an overall record of 63–76. First baseman Randall Simon (.264, 18 HR, 79 RBIs) and outfielder Wonderful Monds (.279, 28 SB), who hit a home run as the first Bull to bat in the new park, were leaders of the offense. Ryan Jacobs (11–6) and Matt Byrd (27 saves) led the pitching staff.

With an immensely talented ball club, Durham won the first half of the 1996 season. Outfielder Andruw Jones (.313, 17 HR, 43

RBIs), named Minor League Player of the Year by *Baseball America*, third baseman Wes Helms (.322, 13 HR, 54 RBIs), first baseman Ron Wright (.275, 20 HR, 62 RBIs) and pitcher Damian Moss (9–1, 2.25 ERA) led the team to victory. In an unprecedented move, however, Atlanta promoted all four players at midseason and severely hurt the Bulls'

chance for a league pennant. Though helped by the addition of outfielder Marc Lewis (.298) and third baseman Gabe Whatley (.331), the team dropped to third place in the second half and finished with a combined record of 73–66. In the playoff with second half champ Kinston, the Bulls were defeated two games to one.

◆ ———————— *Edenton* ———————— ◆

The professional baseball history of Edenton is a brief one. The Edenton Colonials existed for only two years as a professional team. They were a member of the Class D Virginia League in 1951 and the Class D Coastal Plain League in 1952.

For several years, the Edenton Colonials had been a successful member of the semipro Albemarle League. Its popularity led town leaders to believe Edenton might be ready for true professional baseball. After the 1950 season, the Virginia League franchise of Hopewell failed and league officials awarded the vacancy to Edenton. Local favorite William "Gashouse" Parker was hired to manage and play first base for the team. Parker had been a star player and manager for Edenton in the Albemarle League. The same ballpark the semipro team had used, Hicks Field, with a seating capacity of around 1,500, was also retained.

The 1951 team met with marginal success, going 63–55 for a third place finish. Parker, named to the league All-Star team, was the offensive leader and batted .303 (19 HR, 73 RBIs), closely followed by outfielder Archie Templeton and his .302 average. Richard Brockwell was the leading pitcher with at 18–9, while John "Monk" Raines went 16–13. The Colonials did qualify for the playoffs but lost to Elizabeth City in the first round, four games to three. Total attendance for the year was 28,528.

After the 1951 season the Virginia League

folded. Fortunately, the Colonials were able to transfer to the Coastal Plain League. The team went through three managers during the 1952 season. Pitcher Vernon Mustian, a former Wake Forest star, began as manager but resigned in late June. He was replaced by third baseman Tom Inge, who served until previous manager Gashouse Parker could be rehired. The star of the team was pitcher Monk Raines (26–5, 1.48 ERA), who tied for the league lead in wins while striking out 244 batters. Pitcher Ron White (8–3) also turned in a good season on the mound. While the Colonials had a good pitching staff, they lacked offensive power, hitting only .231 as a team. Outfielder Hillary "Mo" Evans (.283) and first baseman Claude Griffin (.265) were the team's leading hitters, supplying much of the offense.

The Colonials finished the regular season with almost the same results as the previous year. The total attendance was 24,420 and a 69 — 55 record put them in third place, 7½ games behind first place Kinston. In the playoffs, however, the Colonials swept Wilson four games to none and in the finals defeated Goldsboro, four games to one. The Coastal Plain League folded after the season, leaving Edenton as its final champion.

Hicks Field, built as a WPA project in 1939, still exists and is used by the local high school.

Hicks Field in Edenton (from the collection of the author).

◆ ——————— *Elizabeth City* ——————— ◆

The baseball history of Elizabeth City is similar to that of Edenton. The Elizabeth City Albemarles were also in existence as a professional franchise for only two years. The town, too, had fielded a successful team in the Albemarle League, one of the state's top semipro leagues.

After the 1949 season the Lawrenceville Robins of the Virginia League decided to relocate due to poor attendance. In Elizabeth City the owners found a town eager to receive them. The name was changed to Albemarles and play began in 1950 at 2,500-seat Memorial Park.

All-Star catcher and manager Paul Crawford (.312, 26 HR, 110 RBIs) had a great season and guided the 1950 team to a third place, 68–61 record, 3½ games behind first place Emporia. Outfielders Tom Inge (.273, 15 HR, 86 RBIs) and Tom Higgins (.319) also had good seasons at the plate. Pitcher Herman Dowdy (13–7) led the league in strikeouts with 176 while Tom Reeves had the best

pitching record at 18–7. The Albemarles advanced to the playoffs but lost to Petersburg, four games to two. Attendance for the year was 35,000, the league's second highest total.

The 1951 team was again managed by Paul Crawford, the league's All-Star catcher. Batting .330 with 95 RBIs, he led the team to a 67–50, second place finish, 12 games behind Colonial Heights–Petersburg. All-Star shortstop St. Pierre "Pete" Howard (.273, 92 runs) and outfielder Don Warfield (.291, 26 HR, 84 RBIs) both had good seasons. Once again Tom Reeves (15–10) and Herm Dowdy (12–6) were the team's best pitchers. In the first round of the playoffs the Albemarles defeated Edenton, four games to three. They went on to have little trouble with Colonial Heights–Petersburg in the finals, winning four games to one. The Elizabeth City Albemarles became the final champions of the Virginia League as the league shut down after the season.

In 1952, Elizabeth City tried to gain

The 1951 Elizabeth City Albemarles included: *Back:* Howard Harriman, unidentified, Don Warfield, Pete Howard, unidentified, Jack Barkenbush, Frank Socozza, Glen Lockamy; *Front:* George Wright, Herm Dowdy, Tom Reeves, Jim Curtis, Paul Crawford, unidentified, unidentified (courtesy Pete Howard).

entry into the Coastal Plain League. The league had room for only one team and the franchise was granted to Edenton, due to its closer proximity to the other towns in the league. The city tried again in 1953 to gain membership and was successful. Three days later, however, the league decided not to operate that season. It later officially disbanded.

 ——————————— *Elkin* ——————————— ◆

The town of Elkin fielded many successful teams in the textile leagues of the 1930s and '40s. In 1936, Elkin's Chatham Blanketeers won the amateur state championship. Sponsored by the mill, the team was again the state champion in 1948. They advanced all the way to the national finals before losing.

With the popularity and success of the local amateur and semipro teams, the town decided to enter professional baseball in 1949. That season the Elkin Blanketeers joined the Class D Blue Ridge League as a new franchise. That first year, managed by outfielder Wayne "Tige" Harris (.276), the team turned in a fifth place finish with a record of 62–65, 6½ games back. Harris, an Elkin native, had been a star baseball and soccer player at High Point College as well as a three-time All-Conference basketball player. All-Star outfielder Henry Brown (.296, 86 runs) led the offense, the league's weakest. Pitcher Ray Boles (12–6, 2.31 ERA) was the leader of Elkin's solid pitching staff that also included David Powers (14–8) and John Mostak (12–10, 2.17 ERA).

The Blanketeers of 1950, once again managed by Harris, finished the year with the excellent record of 82–32. This gave them the pennant, 13½ games ahead of second place Mt. Airy. Stars on the team included returning outfielder Henry Brown, who led the league in batting average (.379) and RBIs (87), and shortstop Bobby Withrow (.310), league leader in runs (104). Ray Boles was again one of the league's best pitchers as he finished the season with a 15–3 record and an ERA of 2.39. Dave Powers (16–3, 3.06 ERA), Van Fletcher (15–7) and John Pyecha (13–4)

Elkin's All-Star outfielder, Henry "Shorty" Brown (courtesy Henry Brown).

teamed with Boles to give Elkin a dominating pitching staff. Pyecha, who played basketball at Appalachian State during the school year, went on to make a brief appearance in the major leagues, as did Fletcher. They were two of only three players from the Blue Ridge League to ever do so. In the first round of the playoffs that year, the Blanketeers swept Galax three games to none. In the finals, however, Elkin was swept by the Mt. Airy Graniteers. After the 1950 season, the Blanketeers and the entire Blue Ridge League folded due to the financial difficulties caused by poor attendance.

During the 1951 season the Landis Spinners of the Class D North Carolina State League decided to relocate in search of better attendance. They chose Elkin as their new home and the move took place on July 18. Managed by former major leaguer Fred Chapman, the team, again called the Blanketeers, finished in third place with a record of 67–59. Outfielder Milton Walker was the star of the team with a .336 batting average, 104 runs scored and 89 RBIs. Chapman, playing mainly third base, batted .328 and scored 98 runs. Left-hander Charlie Morant was the team's leading pitcher at 15–7. The team qualified for the playoffs but lost to High Point–Thomasville in the first round, four games to one.

The next season, the Blanketeers, again managed by Tige Harris, finished the season with a record of 45–64. Though not talent

Wayne "Tige" Harris (center) is flanked by Henry Brown (right) and another Chatham Blanketeer teammate (courtesy Henry Brown).

laden, the team did have strong performances from veteran outfielder Henry Brown (.336, 92 runs) and catcher Burl Storie (.315). Pitcher Jack Swift (19–12) was the league leader in both strikeouts (283) and ERA (2.31). The Blanketeers' poor record was actually good enough for fourth place, qualifying them for a playoff spot. They lost, however, in the first round, four games to one, to Mooresville's Moors.

The Blanketeers disbanded with the North Carolina State League after the 1952 season.

Fayetteville

The first professional baseball team to represent the city of Fayetteville, the Highlanders of 1909, took to the field as a new member of the Class D Eastern Carolina League, replacing the defunct New Bern franchise. The team had a successful first season, finishing tied for third place with a record of 49–41, only a game and a half out of first. The stars of the Fayetteville team were pitcher Bill Luyster (11–3) and outfielder Bill Schumaker (.301), the league batting champ.

The Highlanders played well in the first half of the 1910 season — the ECL's last before failing due to financial problems — winning it with a record of 35–9. They stumbled in the second half, however, and finished last at 14–22. In a playoff with second half champ Rocky Mount to decide the pennant, the Highlanders prevailed three games to one with a ninth inning triple play, winning the deciding game by a 2–1 score. Pitcher Erskine Mayer (15–2) and outfielder J.T. Mullins (.250, 44 SB) were the stars of the team. Mayer went on to spend eight seasons in the major leagues, twice winning more than 20 games in a season. In 1919, he was a member of the infamous Chicago White Sox (though not involved in the scandal) and appeared in one game in the World Series. On August 12, 1910, Fayetteville acquired first baseman Jim Thorpe from the Rocky Mount Railroaders in a two-for-two trade. Thorpe played in 16 games for the Highlanders, batting .250, before being hit in the head by a catcher's throw while trying to steal second. He missed the season's final few games and the playoffs while in the hospital. Thorpe would go on to become one of the greatest athletes of the twentieth century, winning gold medals in the decathlon and pentathlon at the 1912 Olympics. He also made it to the major leagues in baseball and became a legend in professional football.

It was 1928 before professional baseball returned to Fayetteville. That year the Eastern Carolina League was reformed with the Highlanders as a charter member. The league was only in existence for two seasons and the Highlanders posted records of 53–60 in 1928 (fifth place) and 55–62 in 1929 (fourth place). Outfielder and manager Lee Gooch led the 1928 team with a .348 batting average while outfielder Toni Young (.328, 21 HR, 89 RBIs) was the star of the 1929 team before being traded to Wilmington in midseason. Once again the league disbanded, leaving Fayetteville without professional baseball.

In 1946, with the postwar boom in minor league baseball and Fayetteville's growth (due primarily to Ft. Bragg), city leaders decided it was time to reenter professional baseball. A new team was formed and a working agreement was signed with the Chicago Cubs. The Fayetteville Cubs joined the rather prestigious Class D Coastal Plain League when it

1909 batting champ Bill Schumaker of Fayetteville (from the collection of the author).

resumed operations that season, filling a vacancy left by Williamston's decision not to field a team. Over 3,000 people turned out for the Cubs' home opener that April at just-completed Cumberland Memorial Stadium. Though attendance remained good, the Cubs managed to finish in dead last with a record of 51–75, 23½ games out of first. The team's best hitter was right fielder Ed Musial (brother of Stan) who hit .334 and was named to the All-Coastal Plain team. Second baseman Don Anderson (.316) led the league with 50 stolen bases while outfielder Gene DeAngelis (.280, 87 RBIs, 14 HR, 29 SB) provided much of the team's power. Billy Price (4–2) and George Starrette (10–8) were the only members of the otherwise weak pitching staff to post winning records.

For the 1947 season the club made a big jump and switched to the Class B Tri-State League. Again they finished near the bottom, in seventh place, with a record of 61–78. All-Star catcher Smoky Burgess (.387, 76 RBI), on his way to spending 18 years in the big leagues, supplied most of Fayetteville's offense. The team improved the next season, however, rising to a fourth place finish at 73–71. Though they were 21 games out of first, the Cubs qualified for the playoffs. In the first round they upset Anderson, three games to one. The finals saw them have little trouble with Rock Hill, winning that series four games to one to take the championship. Third baseman Floyd Fogg (144 RBIs) and catcher Les Peden (.339, 24 HR, 98 RBIs) had great seasons for the Cubs in 1948, both earning league All-Star honors. Peden would make it to the major leagues briefly in 1953 with Washington, appearing in nine games.

Once again in 1949, Fayetteville jumped leagues, this time down to the Class D Tobacco State League. The club also changed its name to the Scotties, as they were no longer a Chicago farm club. The Scotties won 61 games and lost 76, finishing sixth in the eight team league. They began the season managed by long-time minor league legend Cecil "Zip" Payne. He left the team in mid-July, ending a playing career that began in Goldsboro in 1929. Outfielder Joe Roseberry (who also briefly served as manager) won the league batting title with an outstanding .408 average. Surprisingly, it was an extremely close race for the title as Roseberry edged Wilmington's Hargrove Davis by only .0004. Roseberry's only real help in leading the Scotties' offense came from first baseman Julian Kittrell, who hit .285 with 82 RBIs. Also proving to be one of the best pitchers on the Scotties' weak staff, Roseberry contributed a 7–7 record. The team disbanded after the season.

A new team, the Fayetteville Athletics, was formed in 1950, joining the Class B Carolina League. A farm team of the lowly Philadelphia Athletics, Fayetteville was supplied with very few talented players. Former major leaguer Mule Haas was hired as manager but was fired as the team failed to win games. The team finished the season in the cellar with a horrible record of 47–106, the exact opposite of first place Winston-Salem. The Athletics had a pitiful .228 team batting average and at one point had a league record 19-game losing streak.

The 1951 team (59–79) improved slightly, finishing in seventh place out of eight. Outfielder Mike Sichko (.315) and third baseman Jake Spruill (.295) led the league's weakest hitting offense. Pitcher Bill Harrington, who was better than his 14–14 record indicates, would later appear in parts of three seasons with the big league Athletics. Another seventh place finish was turned in by the Athletics in 1952, as they finished at 53–63. The only star of that team was pitcher Len Matarazzo. Greatly improved from his 8–13 record with the team in 1951, he went 22–8 with an ERA of 2.21. Called up to Philadelphia at the end of the season, he pitched one inning in relief, his only appearance in the major leagues.

The 1953 season saw the team, once again called the Hilanders (though with a different spelling), back in the cellar. Their 44–95 record left them 38½ games out of first. Pitcher Joe Vilk, who also played in the field, was the team's leading hitter with an average of .342 in 68 games. He was, however, 9–18 on the mound. No member of the terrible pitching staff was able to achieve a winning record. Catcher Bill Robertson (.316) was the only other real player of note as he finished fourth in the league in hitting.

The Hilanders became independent for the 1954 season, allowing them to hire players with more experience. It helped immensely as they finished with the pennant (86–51), winning 42 games more than the previous season. Veteran players such as first baseman Jim Pokel (.296, 38 HR, 103 RBIs), outfielders Jack Hussey (.322, 32 HR, 115

The 1954 Fayetteville Hilanders included: *Back:* Claude "Diz" Voiselle, Aaron Robinson, Jim Foxworth, unidentified, unidentified, Jack Hussy; *Middle:* Bill Fowler, Art Raynor, Bucky Jacobs, Harry Helmer, Jim Pokel; *Front:* Gus Montalbano, unidentified, unidentified, Bobby Lyons (courtesy Bill Fowler).

RBIs) and Bill Fowler (.270), and pitcher Diz Voiselle (12–5) were the reason for the team's newfound success. A deep and talented team, the Hilanders also had outfielder Dewey Benson (.385) and second baseman Bobby Lyons (.315, 108 runs), along with pitchers Jim Foxworth (17–7) and Al Cleary (18–6), two of the league's best. In July the team hired former New York Yankee Aaron Robinson as manager. He led the Hilanders to the championship as they defeated Durham, three games to one, in the first round of the playoffs and Burlington, four games to one, in the finals.

The Hilanders signed on as an affiliate of the Baltimore Orioles in 1955. They again played well, this time finishing third at 70–67. Several players from the previous season's championship team, including Jim Pokel

(.321), Bobby Lyons (.318), Bill Fowler (.277) and Diz Voiselle (4–3), returned but did not remain for the entire season. Returning pitchers Jim Foxworth (16–11) and Harry Helmer (15–8) had good seasons, as did newcomer outfielders Al Viotto (.309, 22 HR, 104 runs) and Joe Cristello (.303, 22 HR, 97 RBIs). Aaron Robinson was back as manager but was fired in June. He was replaced by player-manager Jack McKeon, who would later go on to manage in the majors. The Hilanders advanced to the playoffs but lost to Danville in the first round, four games to one.

The 1956 season was the last for the Fayetteville Hilanders. They finished the regular season in fourth place with a record of 78–71. In the first round of the playoffs they swept the regular season first place team, High Point–Thomasville, three games to

none. The finals saw them take the championship by defeating Danville, four games to
two. The Hilanders won on the strength of
their pitching staff that featured Lawrence
Dresen (17–10, 2.76 ERA). Four other pitchers posted wins in double figures, including
Wynn Hawkins (16–12, 2.92 ERA), who
would later pitch for Cleveland. Utility player
Don Montgomery was the team's leading hitter with an average of only .300, though
outfielders Richard Hofleit (.290, 20 HR) and
Ed Cook (.272, 28 HR, 87 RBIs), along with
veteran first baseman Jim Pokel (.267, 25
HR), did provide substantial power. Despite
their success on the field, the Hilanders were
struggling financially. During the winter,
team owners decided to drop out of the
league and disband the team.

It was to be 1987 before Fayetteville
would again be home to a minor league baseball team. That season the Fayettevile Generals of the Class A South Atlantic League took
the field as a farm team of the Detroit Tigers.
Their home was brand new J.P. Riddle Stadium, with 3,250 seats. The team had a rather
unmemorable first season, finishing fourth
in the Northern Division of the league with a
record of 65–74. Future big leaguers Milt
Cuyler (.292, 27 SB) and Phil Clark (.295, 79
RBIs), the Tigers' first round draft pick in
1986, were named to the league All-Star team.
Third baseman Torey Lovullo (.257), who
had been an All-American at UCLA, and
pitcher Mike Schwabe (1–1, 2.45 ERA) would
also make it to Detroit. The Generals drew
just over 95,000 in attendance their first season back in professional baseball.

The 1988 and '89 seasons were also
mediocre ones for the Generals. In 1988 they
finished fourth (62–73) in their division.
Shortstop Travis Fryman (.234) would go on
to star for the Tigers. The 1989 Generals
broke .500 with a record of 70–69 and a third
place divisional finish. The star of that team
was pitcher Rusty Meacham (10–3, 2.29
ERA).

The Generals improved in 1990, winning the first half of the season and finishing
with the league's second best overall record

at 82–61. In the playoffs, the Generals lost to
Charleston (W.Va.) in the first round, two
games to none. Outfielder Brian Cornelius
(.305) was the team's best offensive player
while Randy Marshall was named as the
league All-Star team's left-handed pitcher as
well as Most Outstanding Pitcher. Before
being promoted at midseason, Marshall was
13–0 with an ERA of 1.33. At Lakeland in the
Florida State League, Marshall turned in a
7–2 record, giving him the best winning percentage (.909) in all of professional baseball
that season.

Slipping to sixth place in 1991, the Generals posted a losing record of 58–79. Outfielder Jeff Goodale (.326), who was promoted in midseason, was the team's best
hitter while reliever Phil Stidham had eight
saves and an ERA of 1.60. The 1992 season
saw the Generals break the 100,000 mark in
attendance for the first time as the team improved to 74–67, tied for fourth. Ben Blom-
dahl (10–4), Kelley Rich (13–5) and Tom
Schwarber (1.53 ERA, 24 saves) led that season's outstanding pitching staff.

The Generals started slow in 1993,
finishing the first half of the season with a
record of 31–38, fourth in their division. Led
by second baseman Tim Thomas (.303) and
pitcher Brian Maxcy (12–4), the team improved in the second half, winning it with a
record of 44–28. Unfortunately, they lost the
playoff with Greensboro, two games to one.

The 1994 season proved to be an unsuccessful one for the Generals. They finished
each half of the season in sixth place and had
a combined record of 62–75. The team did
feature the league batting champion and All-
Star second baseman as Frank Catalanotto
batted .325. In 1995 the Generals finished second to Piedmont in the first half of the season
and then second to Asheville (by half a game)
in the second half. Though their combined
record of 86–55 was the best in the league,
they were not eligible for the playoffs since
they won neither half. All-Star first baseman
Daryle Ward (.284, 106 RBIs) led the offense
while the pitching staff included Jason Jordan
(10–4, 2.28 ERA) and Cam Smith (13–8). The

real star of the team, however, was reliever Brandon Reed (3–0, 0.97 ERA) who led all minor leagues with his 41 saves. He was named as the Detroit Tigers' minor league player of the year.

Under third year manager Dwight Lowry,

the Generals again played well in 1996, winning the second half of the season and finishing with a record of 76–63. Led by All-Star outfielder Gabe Kapler, they advanced to the playoffs but were swept by Delmarva in the first round.

Forest City

The Forest City Owls were a charter member of the Class D Western Carolina League in 1948. One of only three teams in the league to have a major league affiliate, the Owls signed a working agreement with the Chicago Cubs. The team finished tied with Shelby for fourth that first season with a record of 55–56. Shelby refused to break the tie with a play off and it was awarded to Forest City, allowing the Owls to advance to the playoffs. They lost, however, four games to two, to Newton-Conover. Outfielder Ned Waldrop, a native of nearby Rutherfordton, led the Owls' offense with a .343 batting average and 107 RBIs. All-Star pitcher Bill Haynes (20–12) was one of the league's best.

For the 1949 season the team became known as the Rutherford County Owls as it also represented the town of Spindale. The Owls played well and finished the regular season in third place at 64–45. They went on to take the championship, defeating Newton-Conover in the first round and Morganton, four games to one, in the finals. All-Star outfielder Ralph Dixon (.345) and first baseman Dean Padgett (.339, 108 RBIs) were the team's top hitters.

The Owls again finished in third in 1950, this time with a record of 57–53. They lost in the first round of the playoffs to Newton-Conover, four games to two.

Though improving their record to 62–48 in 1951, the Owls slipped to fifth in the league standings. Still a member of the Chicago Cubs farm system, the Owls were one of only two teams in the league affiliated with a major league team. Outfielder Bill McKenny was

the team's leading hitter with a .322 average. He drove in 82 runs and his 22 home runs were second in the league. George Long (13–2, 2.12 ERA) was the team's leading pitcher. Pitcher John Pyecha, who was 9–9 for the Owls, made it up to the Cubs in 1954 and appeared in one game.

In 1952 the Owls finished fourth and qualified for the playoffs even though they finished 46–58, 22½ games out of first. They were promptly swept in the first round by Shelby, four games to none.

The Western Carolina League disbanded after the 1952 season. Many of that league's teams, including Rutherford County, joined with teams from the also defunct North Carolina State League to form the Tar Heel League in 1953. The Owls played well in the new league and finished in second place with a record of 72–40. They also led the league in attendance with 48,812. Outfielder George Rose, who played the first half of the season with Lincolnton, was the Owls' leading hitter with a .350 batting average and 110 RBIs. First baseman–manager Boger McGimsey also had a good year, batting .299 with 73 RBIs. Former major league pitcher Kirby Higbe pitched in nine games for the Owls, going 6–2. The team's best pitcher, another former big leaguer, was Woody Rich at 11–2 with a 2.65 ERA. The Owls were upset in the first round of the playoffs by Lexington, four games to two.

The 1954 season saw the Tar Heel League begin play with only four teams (ten teams began the previous season). On June 21, league officials decided that the league could not continue. When the league disbanded the

Rutherford County Owls had a record of 24–24. Pitcher Joe Cristello was 7–2 while manager Woody Rich won three games and lost two with an ERA of 1.85.

It was 1960 before professional baseball returned to Rutherford County for one final season. That year the Western Carolina League was reformed. The Owls, owned and managed by former major leaguer Jim Poole, finished sixth in the eight team league with a record of 43–57. The team's leading hitter was first baseman Russ Buhite at .303. Pitcher Raymond Searcy won 14 games and had an ERA of 2.67. He lost 17 games, however, as he got little run support from his team. Tom Jamieson pitched well as a reliever, going 5–1. Attendance for the Owls was extremely poor at 16,167, and the franchise was moved to Belmont after the season.

Gastonia

Professional baseball first came to Gastonia in July of 1923, when the Columbia (S.C.) Comers of the Class B South Atlantic League decided to move to the town due to poor attendance. The team was unsuccessful, finishing last with a 44–96 record and disbanded after the season. Outfielder Roxy Middleton, a former Pacific Coast League star, led the team with a .307 average.

It was 1937 before professional baseball returned to Gastonia. That season, a team named the Gastonia Spinners was formed for entry in the independent Carolina League. The league was considered professional although it was not a member of the National Association. The Spinners had an unsuccessful first season as they finished last in the league with a 39–60 record. Third baseman Howard Moss, a native of Gastonia who would later appear in the major leagues, led the team in hitting with a .354 average and 20 home runs. Two other notable players on the team were outfielder Russel Mincy (.289), who would have a long, distinguished minor league career, and second baseman Lawrence "Crash" Davis (.267). A Duke University student at the time, Davis would play three seasons with the Athletics and later become a mainstay in the early years of the other Carolina League.

The Spinners returned in 1938 managed by former Charlotte Hornets star Frank Packard (.264). The team had some good talent, including former big league outfielder Frank Doljack (.324), but in June of that season a decision was made to move the team to High Point in search of better attendance. The Spinners would only last there for a week before filing bankruptcy.

On July 22 of that same season, the Shelby Cardinals of the Class D North Carolina State League, a St. Louis farm club, decided to relocate and chose Gastonia as their new home. The Gastonia Cardinals finished the season well, their overall record of 66–45 good enough for second place. They advanced to the playoffs but were swept in three games by Mooresville. First baseman–manager George Silvey (.316, 80 SB) and center fielder Gene Nafie (.353, 103 RBIs, 27 HR, 120 runs), both named to the league All-Star team, led the offense while pitchers Glenn Gardner and Richard Strage posted identical 15–10 records.

The Cardinals moved to the new Tar Heel League, also Class D, in 1939, and led by Triple Crown–winning left fielder Hooper Triplett (.391, 27 HR, 115 RBIs), they took the pennant. The team also had outstanding hitters in catcher-manager Al Unser (.370, 81 RBIs), first baseman Mike Natasin (.353, 106 RBIs), shortstop Regis Wortman (.351, 73 RBIs) and outfielder Forrest Rogers (.340, 99 runs). The pitching staff was led by Glenn Gardner (17–5). Out of this impressive lineup only Unser and Gardner ever reached the major leagues. Unser played parts of four seasons during the war with Detroit and Cincinnati, hitting only .251, while Gardner was 3–1 for the 1945 Cardinals. Gastonia finished the regular season with a 72–36 record, 10 games ahead of the second place team. Defeating Shelby in the first round of the playoffs, the Cardinals were taken to a seventh game in the finals by Statesville before prevailing.

Right fielder and manager Milt Bocek (.364, 109 RBIs, 13 HR, 98 runs) turned in a great offensive performance in 1940, winning the batting title and leading the Cardinals to a second place finish. Forrest Rogers had another good year, hitting .346 — third in the league. Ben Baumgartner (14–9) and John Herr (15–9) were the Cardinals' leading pitchers. With a 64–44 record, the team advanced to the playoffs but was swept by Hickory in the first round, three games to none. The team disbanded with the league after the season.

Baseball fans in Gastonia had to wait until 1950 to see another minor league team come to town. That season, a group of Gastonia businessmen bought the franchise in the Western Carolina League which had been located in Hendersonville and moved it to town. Named the Gastonia Browns, the team took the field at Sims Stadium. Unfortunately, they finished last in the eight team league with a 40–70 record and disbanded after the season.

Gastonia was without a team in 1951 but a new team was formed for the 1952 season. Called the Rockets, the team joined the Class B Tri-State League as a replacement for the failed Greenwood, South Carolina, team. The Rockets signed a Chicago White Sox working agreement, and had an amazing regular season. They won the league pennant — a rare feat for a new team in any league — with an 89–50 record. Outfielder Fred Leonard (.355, 105 RBIs), shortstop Alex Cosmidis (.265, 122 runs) and first baseman–manager Hal Van Pelt (.301) were all named to the league All-Star team. Zeb Eaton (16–11), Frank Skinner (9–1), Joe Karakul (14–6) and Billy Williams (12–3) combined to give the Rockets the league's strongest pitching staff.

Unfortunately for the Rockets, they were upset in the first round of the playoffs by third-place Spartanburg, three games to two. The team's attendance was nearly 95,000, second by 2,000 to the much larger city of Charlotte. Gastonia's 1950 team had drawn less than 40,000 fans.

The Rockets did not meet with the same success in 1953. No longer affiliated with the White Sox, they finished fifth in the league standings with a 66–81 record, 28½ games out of first. All-Star third baseman Jack Falls (.326, 93 RBIs, 20 HR, 94 runs), a native of Gastonia, was one of the league's best hitters and provided most of the team's offense. Though attendance was decent (69,052), the team disbanded after the season. Independent teams like the Rockets were finding it more and more difficult to make ends meet without a major league affiliate to pay player salaries.

It was again several years before Gastonia had another team. On July 6, 1959, the Columbus Pirates of the Class A South Atlantic League moved to Gastonia due to poor attendance. The team, a Pittsburgh farm club, finished the season in fourth with a 70–69 record. They qualified for the playoffs and upset Charlotte, three games to two, in the first round. The Pirates then went on to take the championship by sweeping Charleston, three games to none, in the finals. Though the team was successful and had good attendance, the franchise moved to Columbia, South Carolina.

A new team, the Gastonia Rippers, was formed in 1960 as a charter franchise in the newly reorganized Class D Western Carolina League. The independent Rippers, managed by infielder Billy Queen (.296), played poorly and finished last in the league. Team attendance was only 16,456. Jack Falls, who played almost every position at some time during the season, led the team in hitting (.318) and was named to the league All-Star team. The Rippers disbanded after the season.

Gastonia was without a team for two seasons, but in 1963 a new Pittsburgh farm team, again called the Gastonia Pirates, rejoined the Western Carolina League. The Pirates played

The Gastonia Rockets won the Tri-State League pennant in 1952 (from the collection of the author).

excellent baseball and, like the Gastonia Rockets of 1951, surprisingly finished with the league's best record as a new team. Future major leaguer Bob Oliver, playing first base, hit .281 with 84 RBIs. Outfielder Al Martinez (.297) led the league with 41 stolen bases while Jim Shellenback was the league's best pitcher with a 17–3 record and an ERA of 2.03. Unfortunately the Pirates (73–52) did not qualify for the playoffs as they did not win either half of the split season. They finished second in both halves, missing the second half title and a playoff spot by half a game.

The Pirates slipped to fifth in the league with a 60–68 record in 1964. Third baseman Murray Cook (.289) and outfielder Roy Foster (.259, 72 RBIs), who would later spend three seasons with Cleveland, were the team's best players. The Pirates of 1965 improved to third overall in the league with a 70–54 record. That team was led by future major leaguers Al Oliver (.309) and Bob Robertson (.303). Robertson led the Western Carolinas League in home runs (32) and RBIs (98) on his way to an 11-year major league career. Oliver was a seven time All-Star in 18 big league seasons and retired with a career .303 average.

An overall fourth place finish was the best the Pirates could manage in 1966. Their record of 67–57 left them 23 games out of first. Pitcher Bob Moose (9–3) had a great half season before being promoted to Raleigh. The 1967 team (61–59) improved to second overall in the league but no playoff was held since

Spartanburg won both halves of the season. Shortstop Dave Cash (.335) and outfielder John Jeter (.315) were both named to the league All-Star team. Cash went on to spend 12 seasons in the National League and was named to the All-Star team three times. Jeter, who led the WCL in home runs with 18, also spent several seasons in the majors.

Gastonia's Pirates had another mediocre season in 1968, finishing fourth in the six team league with a record of 68–55. The team did have some outstanding players, including All-Star outfielder Zelman Jack (.326, 84 runs, 24 HRs), who led the league in almost every offensive category. Pitcher Dave Warmbrod also had a good season leading the league in wins (12) and ERA (2.27). Future big league standout Richie Zisk played 53 games for Gastonia that season, hitting .281 with 13 home runs. The next year the Pirates (67–58) again finished second overall but missed the playoffs by not winning either half of the season. Catcher Milt May hit .289 on his way to a 15-year major league career.

The Pirates dropped to the league cellar in 1970 with a 55–75 record. The only notable player on the team was Dominican shortstop Frank Taveras (.260, 35 SB), who would go on to have a solid major league career. After the 1970 season the team decided to move to Monroe in search of better attendance.

After having a horrible 1971 season in Monroe, the Pirates decided to return to Gastonia in 1972. They posted a 60–70 record and finished fourth in the league. Attendance, however, which had been less than 12,000 in Monroe, rose to nearly 45,000.

Gastonia became an affiliate of the Texas Rangers in 1973. Although last in the league in attendance (18,696), the Gastonia Rangers played well. Led by future big league player and manager Mike Hargrove, who won the WCL batting title with a .351 average, the

Rangers won the first half of the season. Outfielder Doug Ault also had a big offensive year, leading the league in RBIs (88) and home runs (19). Finishing the season with an overall record of 74–54, the team advanced to the playoffs but was swept by Spartanburg, two games to none.

With a record of 84–48, the Rangers easily took the league pennant in 1974 as they won both halves of the season and finished 12 games ahead of the second place team. Pitcher Mike Bacsik (15–5) lead the league in wins while All-Star first baseman Dan Duran drove in a league leading 99 runs. Surprisingly, the Rangers' attendance was last in the league by far with only 18,977 paying to see them play. As a result, the team disbanded after the season.

Professional baseball did not return to Gastonia until 1977. That season the Gastonia Cardinals, a St. Louis farm team, reentered the Western Carolinas League. The team played surprisingly well, winning the second half of the season and finishing with the best overall record (82–57) in the league. In the playoffs the Cardinals had little trouble with Greenwood, winning three games to one and taking the league championship. Attendance was up to nearly 35,000.

The Cardinals were not as fortunate in 1978. They dropped to fifth place with a 69–71 record. The next season saw another overall fifth place finish, this time with a 65–74 record. The Cardinals actually tied for first in the first half of the season but lost a 10-inning playoff game to Greenwood. In the second half of the season the team dropped to last place. They did have some good talent as All-Star second baseman Jeff Doyle (.316, 90 runs) led the league in runs and hits while pitcher Jerry Johnson (10–6, 2.65 ERA) was the league ERA leader.

In 1980, the league (now called the South Atlantic League) split into two divisions. Gastonia played in the North and finished each half of the season with an identical 37–33 record. Second baseman Mike Wolters (.273), named to the league All-Star team, was the offensive leader of the team

and one of the league's best fielders. Relief pitcher Ralph Citarella (11–4) was the league's best pitcher, finishing the season with an ERA of 1.64. The Cardinals advanced to the playoffs but lost to Greensboro, two games to one. Attendance more than doubled in Gastonia that season, up to 90,000.

The 1981 season saw the Cardinals drop to fourth in their division with a 68–76 record. Third baseman Luis Ojeda (.304) was the offensive star of a weak-hitting team. Pitcher John Martin, though he had a record of 11–13, had an ERA of 2.12 and was called up to St. Louis. The next season was the last for Gastonia as a St. Louis farm team. The team finished fifth (and last) in their division with a record of 54–89. Outfielder Richard James led the team in hitting with a .296 average. No pitcher had a winning record.

Gastonia became a Montreal farm club in 1983 and changed its nickname to that of its parent. The team finished first in its division with an 84–59 record. Gastonia's Expos, led by All-Star second baseman Armando Moreno (.327), then brought home the league pennant by defeating Columbia, three games to two, in the playoff. The 1984 season was not as successful as the Expos finished fourth at 67–75.

Montreal dropped Gastonia from its farm system after the 1984 season. The team changed its name to the Jets and operated as the league's only independent team in 1985. A lack of talent, due to not having support from a major league team, left the Jets in the cellar with a record of 44–93. One player of note on that team was outfielder Roberto Clemente, Jr. He managed only a .186 batting average, however, playing in 37 games. For the 1986 season an agreement was signed and Gastonia joined the Detroit Tigers farm system. It was a relationship that would last only one season. Gastonia's Tigers finished fourth in their division, winning 59 games while losing 80, 30 games out of first.

Gastonia again became a Texas Rangers farm team in 1987 and would remain a part of that organization through the 1992 season. The Gastonia Rangers could manage no better than a fifth place, 58–82 finish that first season though the team did produce three future big league sluggers: outfielders Juan Gonzalez (.265, 14 HR) and Sammy Sosa (.279, 11 HR), and third baseman Dean Palmer (.215, 9 HR). In 1988, although led by league MVP Brant Alyea (.300, 25 HR, 98 RBIs), the Rangers finished with a league worst 47–90 record. Pitcher Roger Pavlik, a future Texas starter, turned in a lowly 2–12 record.

In another rare example of a team going from last one season to first the next, the Rangers dominated the league in 1989. Second baseman Jeff Frye (.313) won the batting title, first baseman Doug Cronk (.251, 22 HR) led the league in home runs while outfielder Kevin Belcher hit .296 with 14 home runs. Kyle Spencer (11–5) and Francisco Valdez (14–3) led the pitching staff. Reliever Jim Hvizda (8–2, 1.19 ERA) set a league record with 35 saves. The Rangers finished with a league best record of 92–48, 13 games ahead of second place. They were not so fortunate in the playoffs, however, as they were upset by the Augusta Pirates, three games to one.

The Rangers (82–61) again played well in 1990 and finished tied for the best record in the North Division of the league. They failed, however, to win either half of the season so were not involved to the playoffs. Pitchers Jonathan Hurst (8–1, 2.64 ERA) and Brian Romero (9–2, 1.48 ERA) were the Rangers' best players. The next season the team dropped to a fourth place divisional finish with a 69–73 record. Attendance, at

44,060, was last in the league. Third baseman David Lowery (.294) and shortstop Jon Shave (.291) led the team in hitting while future Texas reliever Matt Whiteside (3–1, 2.15 ERA) had 29 saves. Gastonia owner George Shinn, also the owner of the NBA Charlotte Hornets, recruited two Hornets players to appear in a game as a promotion for the Rangers. Dell Curry started a game at pitcher and actually played well, giving up one run in three innings while striking out four. Hornets guard Muggsy Bogues played second base and struck out in two trips to the plate.

The 1992 season was the last for the Gastonia Rangers. Managed by former big leaguer Walt Williams, the team finished last in their division. Texas' highly regarded shortstop prospect Benji Gil hit .274 with 26 stolen bases. At a time when attendance figures were growing for most minor league teams in the state, Gastonia dropped to less than 33,000. Due to this, the franchise was sold and moved to Hickory.

Professional baseball returned to Gastonia briefly in 1995 when the newly formed independent Atlantic Coast League placed a team, named the Gaston King Cougars, in the city. The four team league (the other three were in South Carolina) lasted only 15 games before suspending operations. Constant rainouts, poor attendance and a lack of financing led to the league's demise. Unfortunately for Gastonia, they appeared to have actually had a good team and were in first with a 12–3 record when the league shut down.

Goldsboro

The professional baseball history of Goldsboro goes back to 1908, when the Goldsboro Athletic Association was formed with A. W. Edgerton as its president. The association solicited donations from local businesses and residents in order to bring professional baseball to Goldsboro. They were successful and the Goldsboro Giants became

a charter member of the Class D Eastern Carolina League that season. The league, though it folded before the season was complete in 1908, existed through 1910 and Goldsboro was a member all three years. The Giants played at Goldsboro Athletic Park, sometimes seeing crowds of up to 1,200, but probably the average crowd was around 400.

The team turned in records of 29–28, 43–46 and 38–42. Their best finish was third place in the inaugural season of 1908. The 1909 season saw pitcher Harry Otis, who appeared in five games for Cleveland that September, lead the league with 19 victories. In 1910, second baseman Curly Brown (.294), who went on to play for the St. Louis Browns, won the batting title.

After the demise of the Eastern Carolina League, Goldsboro was without baseball until 1928. That year a new Eastern Carolina League was organized and the Goldsboro Manufacturers became a charter member. The team finished in second place with a record of 66–48 and went on to win a playoff with Wilmington, four games to three. The Manufacturers were led to the championship by outfielder Charles Hamel (.361, 81 RBIs), league leader in runs with 101, and pitcher Ralph Carver (17–1).

The next season the Goldsboro team changed its name to the Goldbugs. They again finished the season in second place, with a record of 68–50, but did not participate in the playoff since they failed to win either half of a split season. Goldbug pitcher Edward Heller (17–7, 2.37 ERA) led the league in both wins and ERA. Pitcher Kemp Wicker, 5–5 for the Goldbugs, went on to pitch in the big leagues for the Yankees and the Dodgers. Playing in the first season of a career that would span 20, minor league legend Cecil "Zip" Payne batted .280 for the 1929 Goldbugs.

After the 1929 season the Eastern Carolina League dissolved once again and Goldsboro was without baseball. In 1935, Goldsboro joined the semipro Coastal Plain League as an expansion team. The name Goldbugs was revived and play commenced. For two seasons the team played in the league, finishing near the bottom of the standings each time. One noteworthy player from those seasons was outfielder James "Buster" Maynard. He went on to spend parts of four seasons with the New York Giants.

In 1937, the Coastal Plain League gained entry into the National Association and became a professional Class D circuit. The Goldbugs began that season playing well but a lack of hitting soon caught up with them. Pitcher Owen "Ace" Elliot (18–7) led the league in wins that year and was named to the All-Coastal Plain team, but it was not enough to help the otherwise weak team. The Goldbugs finished sixth in the eight team league with a record of 47–51.

The Goldbugs again finished in sixth place for the 1938 season, posting a record of 47–65. Several teams in the league were guilty of player eligibility violations that season and the Goldbugs were awarded victories by forfeiture, giving them a final record of 55–57 in the revised standings. It did not, however, affect their position in the league standings. Third baseman Doyt Morris was the leader of the team, batting .324 in 71 games while catcher Jesse "Buck" Overton (.275) was named to the league All-Star team. In August of 1938, Goldsboro became the first league member to install lights for night games.

The following year the Goldbugs, managed by Goldsboro native and former Washington first baseman Mule Shirley, improved greatly and finished second with a record of 69–54. Unfortunately, they lost in the first round of the playoffs to the Williamston Martins, four games to one. Outfielders Sandy Peele (.335) and Claude Capps (.308) were the stars of the 1939 team. Pitcher Ed Chapman (15–4, 2.34 ERA) was among the league's best that season. Along with Capps, catcher Buck Overton (.299) was again named to the All-Coastal Plain team.

Another respectable finish was turned in by the Goldbugs in 1940. They finished in third place, winning 66 games and losing 58. Like the previous season they lost in the first round of the playoffs, four games to one, this time to Tarboro. First baseman Nick Iarossi (.326, 84 runs, 70 RBIs) and second baseman Hilliard Pawlak (.324, 86 runs, 55 RBIs) were the team's offensive leaders. Third baseman Mack Arnette, who also served as manager, hit .289 with 70 RBIs. Ed Chapman (13–8) had another good

Goldsboro, third baseman–manager Mack Arnette in 1940 (courtesy Mack Arnette).

season on the mound but the ace of the pitching staff proved to be Walt Wilson with his 21–4 record.

The Goldbugs of 1941 slipped in the standings to a fifth place finish with a record of 58–61, 30 games behind first place Wilson. Goldbug pitcher Julio Acosta (17–17, 3.10 ERA) led the league with 199 strikeouts that season. Outfielder Harry Clifton was second in the league batting race with a .359 average and was the only Goldbug named to the All-Star team. Other contributors to the offense included catcher Sandy Peele (.291) and outfielder Sylvester Sturges (.284). Overall, the Goldbugs had talent but they lacked depth.

Play in the Coastal Plain League was suspended after the 1941 season due to the outbreak of World War II and the subsequent player shortage. Two members of the 1941 Goldsboro team — outfielder Sylvester Sturges and pitcher Fred Yeske — would give their lives in the service of their country.

The Goldbugs returned when league play resumed in 1946. Managed by pitcher

Bill Herring, the Goldbugs signed a working agreement with the New Orleans Pelicans of the AA Southern Association. The Pelicans' manager that season happened to be Wayne County native Johnny Peacock, recently retired from a big league playing career. He arranged the working agreement to help his hometown Goldbugs find quality players.

That first year back, Goldsboro finished in fourth place (64–60) and qualified for the playoffs. They lost, however, in the first round to eventual champion Rocky Mount, four games to one. Bill Herring had a great season with a 21–6 pitching record, but like all pitchers in the league was overshadowed by Bill Kennedy's performance with Rocky Mount. Herring also played in the field, hitting .287, fourth best average on the team. The team's best hitters that season were outfielder Wally Schroeder (.324) and shortstop David Lingle (.316).

The Goldbugs of 1947, again led by pitcher-manager Bill Herring, finished the season with a record of 72–67. This left them in fifth place, 6½ games behind first place Wilson. Herring (14–11) also led the league that season in ERA with an impressive 1.79 — his 11 losses indicating that he probably received little in the way of run support. Wally Schroeder had another good season, hitting .335 with 88 RBIs and 26 stolen bases, as did David Lingle, who hit .283 and stole 38 bases. First baseman Jack Hussey contributed to the team with his .317 batting average and 84 RBIs. His 14 home runs accounted for nearly two-thirds of the team's lowly total of 23.

For the 1948 season, the Goldbugs signed a working agreement with the Buffalo Bisons of the AAA International League. Bill Herring was at the helm once again that season and the team finished third with a record of 79–61. In the first round of the playoffs they lost to Kinston in seven games, with the deciding game going 11 innings before the Goldbugs fell 4–3. First baseman Jack Hussey (.367, 135 RBIs, 129 runs, 29 HR), was one of the league's dominant hitters that season,

The 1948 Goldsboro Goldbugs included: *Back:* Ed Worley, unidentified, Frank Robinson, Tom Simpson, Jim Faircloth, Jack Hussey, unidentified, Joe Nessing, unidentified, unidentified; *Front:* Clyde Whitener, Francis Whitehart, Merle Blackwell, unidentified, Bill Herring, Adam "Benny" Bengoechea, Warren Schroeder, unidentified (courtesy Gene Summerlin).

while Wally Schroeder (.359, 92 runs) again had a great year. Outfielder Clyde Whitener (.355), third baseman Merle Blackwell (.278, 100 RBIs) and catcher Ted Jones (.306) also made great contributions to the Goldbugs' talented offense. Bill Herring's reputation as the Coastal Plain League's greatest pitcher grew as he turned in a 19–7 record with a league-leading ERA of 2.60.

In 1949, the Goldbugs, who had changed their working agreement to Sumter of the Class B Tri-State League, finished the season at an even .500. Their record of 68–68 left them in fifth place. The star of the team that year was league batting champ Clyde Whitener, who hit .355 and stole 47 bases. Unfortunately, the Goldbug offense proved to be only a two-man show as Whitener's only real support came from third baseman Leo Katkaveck (.286, 95 RBIs). Veteran second baseman and manager Steve Mizerak (.294)

was hitting well but was suspended for the remainder of the season in July for hitting an umpire. The pitching staff featured strikeout champ Bob Mangum (20–14, 248 SO), with support from Terry Pollack (12–6) and Joe Alusik (10–5).

In 1950, ownership of the team was taken over by the St. Louis Cardinals and the nickname of the Goldsboro team was changed to that of its new parent club. It did not help them win, though, as they finished the season in last place (56–83). Their poor finish was probably due to the fact that the parent Cardinals sent too many inexperienced players. Attendance was also last in the league at 35,719, less than half of what it had been the previous year. The only real standouts on the team that season were outfielder Bill Johnson (.300, 18 HR, 86 RBIs) and first baseman Bill Smith (.261, 92 RBIs), who led the league in home

Raleigh	AB	R	H	Goldsboro	AB	R	H
Lockamy,2b	2	3	1	Salyer,2b	3	1	1
Holliday,lf	6	2	2	Lingle,rf	2	1	1
JimMills,cf	5	3	4	Boucher,rf	2	0	0
D.Baxter,1b	5	0	1	Marcheg.,lf	1	0	0
Bass,rf	5	0	1	Schroedr,lf	1	0	0
Parrott,rf	1	0	0	Hallow,1b	4	0	0
Jordan,3b	4	0	0	Phipps,c	2	0	0
Fogle,ss	4	1	1	Russ,c	2	0	1
JoeMills,ss	1	0	0	Cupka,cf	3	1	1
J. Baxter,c	5	2	2	Bullock,3b	2	0	0
Grocki,p	1	0	0	Rose,3b	2	0	0
xSullivan	1	0	0	Heath,ss	2	0	0
Hardee,p	1	0	0	Davis,ss	1	1	1
				Plant,p	1	0	0
				Taylor,p	1	0	0
				yHodges	1	0	0
				Faircloth,p	1	0	0
TOTALS	41	11	12	TOTALS	34	4	5

x-flied out for Grocki in 5th
y-on by error for Taylor in 7th
Raleigh................040 130 102—11
Goldsboro.............000 200 200—4

Fortunately for the sport of boxing, Rocky Marciano (whose real name was Rocco Marchegiano) gave up dreams of becoming a baseball player after a brief tryout with Goldsboro in 1947. The above box score is from an April 9 preseason game with Raleigh of the Carolina League.

runs with 24. Catcher Bill Wilhelm (.143 in 46 games) would later go to become the head baseball coach at Clemson University, a capacity in which he would serve for 36 years (1958–93), winning 1,161 games.

The Cardinals were back in 1951 and, thanks to the addition of a few veteran ballplayers, actually played rather well. Manager George Ferrell led the team to a third place finish with a record of 70–55. Third baseman Gerry Thomas (.343, 175 hits) had an outstanding season, winning the league batting title. Outfielder Clyde Whitener (.323, 79 RBIs) returned to Goldsboro and played well as did fellow outfielder Granville "Shamrock" Denning (.341, 88 RBIs), who had been the previous season's batting champ

in the Tobacco State League. Second baseman Billy Bevill (.261, 92 runs), who had played at New Bern the past two seasons, led the league in stolen bases for the third straight year with 52. Bobby Slaybaugh (17–10, 2.33 ERA) was the ace of the pitching staff and led the league in strikeouts with 223. Slaybaugh later lost an eye to a line drive during St. Louis spring training, ending a promising career. Despite their talented team, the 1951 Goldsboro Cardinals lost to New Bern in the playoffs, four games to two.

In 1952, the Goldsboro team changed its name to the Jets in reference to the planes at Seymour Johnson Air Force Base. Ownership of the team was transferred back to a local group but a working agreement was kept with St. Louis. The team was managed that season by former Kinston manager Wes Livengood and finished the year 63–59, good enough for fourth place and a playoff berth. In the first round of the playoffs, the Jets upset Kinston in seven games. They weren't as successful in the finals as they lost to Edenton, four games to one. Center fielder Tom Leonard (.375) won the batting title, and proved to be the Coastal Plain League's last batting champ. Other than Leonard, the Jets were a weak-hitting team that produced a total of just 21 home runs. The Jets' RBI leader managed a total of only 42. Goldsboro's strength came from a pitching staff led by John Perry (16–7, 1.90 ERA) and Haywood Watts (12–6, 2.16 ERA).

The 1952 season proved to be the final one for professional baseball in Goldsboro as the Coastal Plain League suspended operations in February of 1953. In 1954, Municipal Stadium, built in 1940 and home to many of Goldsboro's professional teams, was damaged by Hurricane Hazel. Declared unsafe, it was eventually torn down. It is now the site of Goldsboro Middle School.

Granite Falls

The Granite Falls Graniteers joined the Class D Western Carolina League in 1951. The town had fielded several very successful teams at the semipro textile league level and town leaders believed that the same success could be found at the professional level. They were wrong. The team, which changed its name to the Rocks (a very suitable name), lost 96 games and won only 14. The Rocks finished 57 games behind first place Morganton. At one point during the season they lost 33 consecutive games and went on to win only one game in their last 60.

The Rocks' .127 winning percentage displaced the Cleveland Spiders of 1899 (20–134, .129 winning percentage) as the worst team in professional baseball history. Official paying attendance was also horrific at only 11,500 for the season.

No player from the Rocks went on to the major leagues, though Charlie Bowles, the first of five different Rocks managers, had pitched for the Philadelphia Athletics briefly during the war. Bowles played a few innings with the Rocks before resigning in frustration on May 9. Johnny Hollar, who had played football at Appalachian State and later for the Washington Redskins and Detroit Lions of the National Football League, played in 10 games at catcher for the Rocks, batting .194.

On August 25, 1951, the Granite Falls Rocks did something that no other team in North Carolina had ever done: They hired three black players. Russell Shuford, a catcher, Gene Abernathy, an outfielder, and pitcher Christopher Rankin were hired by team president and part owner Fin German to help finish out the season for the Rocks. The next day he hired two more black players: pitcher Boney Fleming, who had played for the negro Asheville Blues, and catcher Bill Smith. All five men played for the Rocks in the final days of the season; however, all official records have been lost due to the official scorer from Granite Falls failing to send in the box scores for the team's final 16 games to the record keepers. This was apparently due to a loss of interest. Because of this these five men never received the recognition they deserve.

The Granite Falls ballpark is still in existence, though much changed. In 1951 it also served as the high school football field so it had the unusual dimensions of 325 feet down the left field line, 360 to center and 420 feet to the right field fence. The park is now known as M.S. Deal Stadium, in honor of a member of the 1951 Rocks who became a teacher and coach in the town.

Greensboro

Greensboro's professional baseball roots go back to 1902. That summer the city fielded a team, named the Farmers, in the Class C North Carolina League. The league failed to finish the season and disbanded on July 12. At that time Greensboro was in fourth place out of the six teams with a 20–28 record.

The next attempt to bring professional baseball to Greensboro was made in 1905. A new Farmers team was organized to play in the Class D Virginia–North Carolina League. Again the league disbanded early, at which time the Farmers were in last place with a record of 36–47.

The city was without a team until 1908. That season a new team known as the Greensboro Champs joined the Class D Carolina Association, a league made up of three teams from South Carolina and three from North Carolina. Managed by first baseman James McKevitt (.248), Greensboro took the league pennant with a record of 51–38. Walt Hammersley (22–8) was the league's winningest pitcher. The team repeated as league champions in 1909. Led by pitcher R.C. Walters (25–12), the Champs posted a record of 65–44. Rookie pitcher Jesse "Rube" Eldridge, in the first season of a more than 20-year minor league career, contributed a 3–1 record. The 1910 season proved to be a disappointment for the team, however, as they dropped all the way to the league cellar with a 46–64 record.

For the 1911 season the Greensboro team became known as the Patriots, a name that would be used by most of the city's baseball teams until 1958. The team played well and finished second to Charlotte with a 66–43 record. Rube Eldridge had a great season on the mound, turning in a 25–13 record with an ERA of 2.43. Outfielder Walt Rickard (.315) scored a league-leading 105 runs, while Frank Doyle, the team's manager and second baseman, hit .288. The Patriots slipped back to fifth place in 1912, going 51–59 for the sea-

son. They did feature the league batting champion, however, as catcher Ralph Stuart hit .326. Rube Eldridge, even though his ERA was 2.22, led the league in losses with 19. Apparently receiving little run support from his team, he won only 13.

The league changed its name to the North Carolina State League in 1913 after all of the South Carolina teams had been replaced by ones from North Carolina. Greensboro's Patriots did not have a good season as their record of 46–69 left them in last place, 20 games out of first. The 1914 season was much the same as the Patriots won 47 games and lost 67, managing to climb to fifth in the league. It was back to the cellar for the Patriots in 1915. The team finished with their worst record yet: 46–71. Rising only one place in the league standings in 1916, the Patriots posted a 45–67 record for another dismal finish. The league began the 1917 season but disbanded on May 30, primarily due to World War I. At that time the Patriots' record stood at 20–17.

The city was without professional baseball for two seasons. In 1920 the Class D Piedmont League was formed and Greensboro's Patriots became a charter member. Managed by shortstop Charlie Carroll, the Patriots (69–51) had a great season. They won the first half of the season and then took the league pennant by defeating Raleigh in the playoffs, four games to three. It was a well-balanced team with both good pitching and hitting. First baseman Lloyd Smith (.327) and outfielder Alex Danielly (.300) led the offense. The pitchers were led by Roy Sadler (19–9), Carl Ray (15–7) and Garland Braxton (14–14). Braxton, a native of Snow Camp, North Carolina, made it to the big leagues the following season, where he would spend the next ten years.

The Patriots repeated as league champs in 1921. Though their record of 64–58 was the third best in the league, they won the first half of the season and advanced to the playoff. The Patriots had little trouble with second half champ High Point, winning four games to one. First baseman Lloyd Smith (.404) had another great season and won the batting title. The offense also included outfielders Alex Danielly (.312) and George Moorefield (.327, 17 HR). The Patriots' best pitcher was E.H. Ferris (20–9).

The 1922 season was an unsuccessful one as the Patriots finished fourth in the six team league with a 60–65 record. They improved the next year, winning the first half of the season. Their combined record of 66–56 was the league's second best. The Patriots played second half champ Danville in the playoffs but were swept in four games. Pitcher D.F. Crews (22–10) was the star of an otherwise weak pitching staff. The talented offense was led by outfielders Francis Shay (.335), Dave Harris (.313) and Jim Conley (.305). First baseman Molly Cox hit .310 with 16 home runs.

Led by Charlie Carroll (.285) for a fifth season, the Patriots of 1924 finished fourth with a 61–59 record. Outfielder Dave Harris (.347, 27 HR, 98 RBIs) was the star of the team. He spent the next season in the big leagues with the Boston Braves. The Patriots had another average season in 1925, finishing in a distant third place with a 61–63 record. Though they had good hitting, a lack of pitching doomed the team. First baseman Molly Cox was the standout with a .308 batting average, 19 home runs and a league leading 108 RBIs.

Cox (.287, 22 HR, 89 RBIs) teamed with third baseman Dave Barbee (.372, 29 HR, 85 RBIs) to lead Greensboro to the pennant in 1926. The Patriots, under manager Lee Gooch (.306), won the first half of the season and their record of 86–60 was the league's best. In the playoffs they easily handled Durham, taking the series four games to one. Dave Barbee, a native of Greensboro, finished the season with the Philadelphia Athletics. Pitcher Rube Eldridge, who had last played for the Patriots in 1912, returned to the team and finished with a 13–11 record.

Greensboro's franchise was moved to Rocky Mount in 1927, leaving the city without baseball that season. The Patriots returned in 1928 and, led by veteran manager Charlie Carroll, played well enough to finish third with a 76–56 record. That team featured a powerful offense led by Molly Cox (.342, 19 HR, 100 RBIs), outfielder Hobart Brummitt (.397, 22 HR, 112 RBIs) and catcher Jack Brandon (.296, 15 HR, 87 RBIs). Outfielder Carr Smith joined the team during the second half of the season and hit .370. Pitcher Frank Barnes won 15 games and lost 11 while veteran D.F. Crews turned in an 11–6 record.

The Patriots (85–51) finished second to Durham in 1929. The offense had many of the same players from the previous season, including Molly Cox (.354, 33 HR, 108 RBIs) and Hobart Brummitt (.316, 99 RBIs). The star of the team, however, was outfielder Henry Parrish (.344, 45 HR, 124 RBIs). Pitcher Jim Turner led the league with a 25–9 record. The Patriots faced Durham in the playoffs and defeated them to take the championship, four games to one.

The 1930 season saw the Patriots finish with an average 70–71 record, good enough for third place. Outfielder Clay Hopper (.355, 23 HR, 121 RBIs) was the star of the team. Hopper went on to manage in the minor leagues for 25 seasons. In 1946 he became a part of baseball history when he managed the Montreal Royals, a team that featured Jackie Robinson. North Carolina native Everett Booe, whose professional baseball career had begun in 1910, finished his career with the Patriots. A former Federal League player, Booe hit .313 in 26 games. The Patriots' shortstop that season had what has to be one of the most unusual baseball names in the country: Lyllo Lymperopoulos.

Charlotte dominated the 1931 season, and the Patriots, even though much improved at 81–56, again finished third. Before the season, Greensboro had become part of baseball's first farm system: that of Branch Rickey's St. Louis Cardinals. A future Cardinal star (later with the Giants and Yankees)

named Johnny Mize had a good season with the '31 Patriots, hitting .337 with 64 RBIs. When he retired after a 15-year major league career his batting average stood at .312 with 359 home runs and 1,337 runs batted in. Mize is now enshrined in the Hall of Fame.

In 1932, the Patriots improved to win the first half of the season and finished with an overall record of 73–59. In the playoffs with second half champ Charlotte, the Patriots prevailed, taking the pennant in seven games. It was a well-balanced team with that usually elusive combination of good hitting and pitching. Fritz Ostermueller (21–9) and Ted Kleinhans (21–8) led the pitchers while the offense featured first baseman Neil Caldwell (.354, 14 HR, 114 RBIs) and shortstop Benny Borgmann (.321, 122 runs, 51 stolen bases). Borgmann later became a minor league manager in leagues as high as the International and Pacific Coast. Surprisingly, baseball is not the sport in which he is best known. For four seasons Borgmann led the professional American Basketball League in scoring and is now enshrined in the Naismith Basketball Hall of Fame.

The Piedmont League pennant came back to Greensboro in 1933. Managed by former St. Louis pitcher Eddie Dyer, the Patriots won both halves of the season with a combined record of 90–48. Second baseman Jim Bucher (.369, 25 HR, 118 RBIs) was the league's best offensive player, missing the Triple Crown by one RBI. Johnny Mize (.360, 22 HR, 104 RBIs) was back with the Patriots and continued to improve. Shortstop Jimmy Brown, who would join Mize in St. Louis, hit .289 and scored 117 runs. Leading the pitching staff were three 20-game winners: Johnnie Chambers (23–8), Virgil Brown (22–8) and Dykes Potter (20–7).

The Patriots fell to last place in 1934. Their record of 56–81 left them 32 games out of first. The only players of note on the team

were first baseman Larry Barton (.283, 23 HR, 97 RBIs) and pitcher Nate Andrews (7–10). Andrews went on to spend several seasons in the big leagues. Forty-five-year-old pitcher Rube Eldridge appeared in his final game that season. A complete game victory, the win was his 285th in the minor leagues without ever having appeared in majors. After that season, the Cardinals decided to move the team to Asheville.

Greensboro was without a professional team for six seasons until a new Boston Red Sox farm club team was formed in 1941. It was a decent season for Greensboro's Red Sox; they finished third with a record of 71–66. They advanced to face Portsmouth in the playoffs and won the series, four games to two. The finals were not as kind to the Red Sox as they were swept by Durham. First baseman Herb Scheffler (.300, 78 RBIs) was named to the league All-Star team.

The next season was much more successful for the Red Sox as they went home with the league pennant. Managed by former major league star outfielder Heinie Manush (now in the Hall of Fame), they finished the regular season at 78–53, tied for first with Portsmouth. Sweeping Charlotte in the first round of the playoffs, the Red Sox were matched against Portsmouth in the finals. They took the championship by winning four games to Portsmouth's two. While lacking offense, Greensboro's team featured an outstanding pitching staff that season. Joe Ostrowski (21–8, 1.69 ERA) was the league's best pitcher. He was supported by Adam Gluchoski (15–8), Roger Wright (15–10) and Bill Elbert (11–5). Due to the war the team was disbanded after the season.

With the end of the war in sight in the spring of 1945, a new league began play. Dubbed the Carolina League, it was to include many of the former North Carolina members of the Piedmont and Bi-State

Opposite: (top) A streetcar displays a banner announcing that day's scheduled game for the 1909 Greensboro Champs (middle), who lived up to their name that season as champions of the Carolina Association. The Champs played their home games at Cone Park (bottom) (courtesy Greensboro Historical Museum).

Eighteen-year-old Greensboro outfielder Johnny Mize in 1931 (courtesy Greensboro Historical Museum Archives).

leagues. Greensboro, an independent team, became a charter member of this new Class C league. It was not a successful season for this new Patriots team: they finished dead last in the eight team league with a 53–83 record. A team made up primarily of inexperienced teenagers (due to the large number of players in the military), the Patriots set a still-standing Carolina League record of 479 errors.

The 1946 season saw a completely different Greensboro team. The Patriots finished the season at 85–57, winning the pennant by five games. All three starting outfielders — Don Butzer, Tige Harris and Bob Falk — hit over .300 while pitchers Bernie Keating (18–7) and Bill Plummer (17–5) were among the best in the league. Unfortunately for the Patriots, they were upset in the playoffs by the Durham Bulls, four games to two.

The Patriots' 1947 season was not a memorable one as their record of 65–75 put them in fifth place. Greensboro native and former Elon College star Emo Showfety (.328, 26 HR, 121 RBIs) powered the offense after being purchased from Burlington and was named as the league's All-Star right fielder. Outfielder Don Butzer (.317, 118 runs), shortstop Matty Topkins (.305, 80 RBIs) and third baseman "Sheepy" Lamb (.264, 32 SB, 15 3B) also played well. In a tragic note, Patriots pitcher Woody Crowson was killed in a bus accident as the team returned from a game in Martinsville (Va.) on August 14, 1947. The results of the 1948 season were even worse; the Patriots were back in the league cellar with a horrible 49–93 record. Emo Showfety (.337, 19 HR, 105 RBIs) had another great season but it wasn't enough to help the lowly Patriots. Showfety had his best season yet in 1949, hitting .347 with 35 home runs and 120 RBIs. His offense and the pitching of Luis Arroyo (21–10) helped the Patriots improve to fifth that season with a record 72–73.

The Patriots (78–74) were again fifth in the 1950 league standings. Second baseman Fred Vaughn (.320) led the league with 27 home runs while pitcher Woody Rich (16–9) had a league best 2.41 ERA. In 1951 Greensboro joined a major league farm system for the first time in its Carolina League history as the team signed a working agreement with the Chicago Cubs. For the third straight season the Patriots finished fifth. Their 67–73 record left them 17 games out of first. Outfielders Malcolm McKeithan (.335) and John Mitchell (.316) had good seasons, as did pitcher George Erath (18–10).

For two more seasons the Patriots would finish fifth. The 1952 team posted a 70–64 record while the 1953 team broke even at 70–70. The 1953 Patriots, now a Red Sox farm team, featured All-Star shortstop Don Buddin (.300, 25 HR), the league RBI leader with 123. He went on to spend five seasons as Boston's starting shortstop. Pitcher Duane Wilson's 2.21 ERA was the league's best but his record of only 13–12 would indicate a lack of run support from his own team.

The 1954 Greensboro Patriots finished third in the Carolina League with a 79–59 record (from the collection of the author).

Finally, in 1954, the Patriots improved beyond fifth place as they finished third with 79–59 record. Catcher Guy Morton (.348, 32 HR, 120 RBIs), the league MVP, won the batting title and led the league in RBIs. He received a late season call-up to Boston and had one at-bat as a pinch hitter. It proved to be his only big league appearance. John Patula (12–7, 1.58 ERA) and left-hander Ed Mayer (17–8) were the Patriots' best pitchers that season. The team advanced to the playoffs but lost to Burlington in the first round, three games to two.

Dropping back into mediocrity in 1955, the Patriots finished sixth, posting a 66–72 record. The team had some good hitters, including utilityman Joe LaMonica (.312), the league leader in runs (111) and stolen bases (34), but the pitching staff lacked talent. The 1956 season was only slightly better as the team finished at 75–79, improving to fifth. First baseman George Contratto led the team

in hitting with a .319 average while third baseman Doug Hubacek (.280) provided power with his 24 home runs and 119 RBIs. The highlight of that season came on August 30 when pitcher Ken McBride (9–7, 2.64 ERA) no-hit Fayetteville. He went on to spend several seasons in the big leagues, appearing in the 1963 All-Star game.

With a record of 76–64 in 1957, the Patriots rose to third place. They failed to qualify for the playoffs as they won neither half of the split season. Relief pitcher Bill Lore (13–3, 1.31 ERA) and starters Charles Smith (14–11) and Bill Monbouquette (11–6) combined to give the Patriots a strong pitching staff. The offense, however, only hit for a combined .238 average.

Greensboro became a farm club of the New York Yankees in 1958. Also called the Yankees, Greensboro played well. Led by All-Star first baseman Jim Johnston (.284, 79 RBIs), they posted a record of 75–64, good enough for third place. In the playoffs the Yankees defeated High Point–Thomasville, two games to one, but lost to Burlington in the finals by the same margin. The 1959 Greensboro Yankees (54–76) were relegated to fifth place by a lack of good pitching. They did have decent hitting as outfielder Don Lock (.283) led the league in home runs (30), RBIs (122) and runs (102). He went on to spend several years with the Senators and Phillies. Outfielder Tom Tresh (.281), who was promoted to Class A during the season, became the 1962 American League Rookie of the Year with New York.

All-Star shortstop Phil Linz (.320) — the league batting champ — and a strong pitching staff that included Jim Bouton and Jack Cullen helped Greensboro win the 1960 Carolina League pennant. The Yankees (84–55) won the first half of the season and easily defeated second half champ Burlington, four games to one, in the playoff. Attendance jumped from 39,408 in 1959 to a league leading 97,594 in 1960.

The Yankees had an average season in 1961. Managed by former big league infielder Wayne Terwilliger, they finished third at 70–68. First baseman Chuck Reidell (.275, 28 HR, 100 RBIs) and shortstop Ron Retton (.291, 114 runs, 35 SB) were named to the All-Star team. Retton is the father of gold medal winning Olympic gymnast Mary Lou Retton. The 1962 Greensboro Yankees slipped to sixth place. Their 65–75 record left them 24 games out of first. One of the stars of that team was pitcher Mel Stottlemyre (17–9, 2.50 ERA). He became one of the American League's best pitchers in the late 1960s with New York.

The Greensboro Yankees returned to winning form in 1963. They easily won the West Division of the divided league with an 85–59 record. It was a well-balanced team with both hitting and pitching. The offense was paced by second baseman Roy White (.309) — league leader in runs with 117 — and outfielder Curt Blefary (.289, 25 HR). White would go on to spend 15 seasons with the big league Yankees. The pitching staff featured Ted Dillard (11–5, 2.21 ERA) and Jim Hors-

ford (12–4, 1.41 ERA). In the playoffs the Yankees survived a challenge from Durham, three games to two. They were not so fortunate in the final with East Division champ Wilson — the Yankees lost, two games to one.

In 1964, the Yankees (76–61) played well but finished second in the West Division to Winston-Salem. In the divisional playoff they were swept in two games by that same Winston-Salem team. Outfielder Steve Whitaker (.303, 27 HR, 100 RBIs) powered the offense while Ted Dillard (12–5) had another good season on the mound for Greensboro. The results of the 1965 season were much the same as the Yankees (79–65) again finished second in their division, this time to Durham. They were then defeated in the playoff by Durham, two games to one. Greensboro's stars that season were shortstop Bobby Murcer (.322, 16 HR, 90 RBIs) and pitcher Fritz Peterson (11–1, 1.50 ERA). Murcer, named the Carolina League MVP, received a September call-up to New York and became a star. Named to five All-Star teams, Murcer spent 17 seasons in the big leagues. Peterson also made it to New York and was a 20-game winner in 1970.

The 1966 season was a forgettable one for the Greensboro Yankees as they finished at 64–76, fifth in their division. The team had no offense as evidenced by the pitching record of Bill Burbach. Though his record was 3–14, his ERA was an excellent 2.19. The Yankees' team batting average was only .208. The 1967 Yankees finished in the same place in the league standings with a 66–72 record. Pitcher Gary Jones (15–9, 2.42 ERA) tied for the league lead in wins. Nineteen-year-old first baseman Frank Tepedino (.222) began the season in New York but was sent back down for more experience. He would make it back to the big league Yankees in 1969.

The New York Yankees switched their player development contract to Kinston for the 1968 season. Greensboro signed on with the Houston Astros and changed its name to that of its parent. The new affiliation did nothing to help the Greensboro Astros win as they finished the season at 61–79, fourth in their division. In a new playoff format that included eight teams, the Astros were amazingly included but lost their one game playoff with High Point–Thomasville. First baseman John Mayberry hit .329 in 43 games with the Greensboro Astros before moving up to AAA. He would finish the season in Houston. Greensboro dropped out of the Carolina League following the season.

Minor league baseball finally returned to Greensboro in 1979. Rather than rejoin the Carolina League, team owners opted for the Class A Western Carolinas League. Named the Hornets, the team was a huge success as far as attendance went. Their total of 165, 596 was almost triple that of the next closest team. On the field, the Hornets — a Cincinnati farm club — had an unmemorable season as they finished 12 games out of first with a 65–71 record. All-Star pitcher Jeff Lahti (7–2, 13 SV, 2.84 ERA) would make it to the big leagues for a few seasons.

In 1980 the Hornets returned to dominate the league (now called the South Atlantic League). They won both halves of the season in their division and had an overall record of 82–57. In the first round of the playoffs, the Hornets defeated Gastonia, two games to one. The finals saw them take the pennant by sweeping Charleston in three games. Again a New York Yankees farm club, the Hornets featured several future big league stars. Possibly destined for Cooperstown, Don Mattingly (.358, 105 RBIs) won the league batting title. Other future big leaguers included Otis Nixon (.278, 67 SB, 124 runs), Greg Gagne (.270) and Rex Hudler (.227 in 20 games). Designated hitter Matt Winters (.320, 20 HR) finished second in the league in batting while Byron Ballard (17–6) was one of the league's best pitchers. Attendance for the Hornets grew to over 250,000, more than double the second place team.

The 1981 season proved to be even more dominant for the Hornets. With a 98–43 record, they won their division by 24½ games. They then took the pennant by defeating Greenwood's Pirates, three games to two. Hornet third baseman Jeff Reynolds (.306, 26 HR, 103 RBIs) tied for league MVP honors. Other Hornet stars included outfielder Matt Winters (.300, 16 HR) and infielder Greg Gagne (.297), both returnees from the previous season. The pitching staff was led by Martin Mason (11–2, 2.73 ERA) and Kelly Scott (16–6, 2.98 ERA).

The Hornets won their third consecutive South Atlantic League pennant in 1982. Finishing the season at 96–45, they advanced to face South Division champ Florence in the playoffs. The Hornets prevailed, three games to two. The pitching staff featured outstanding performances by David Szymczak (14–2) and Mark Shiflett (14–5, 2.42 ERA). Matt Winters (.325, 20 HR, 93 RBIs) was back for a third season and led the team in hitting. Though he only made the major leagues for only 42 games in 1989, Winters was a star for several seasons in Japan.

Coming back down to earth in 1983, the Hornets finished second in their division with a 73–71 record. Since they won neither half of the season they were not involved in the playoffs. Outfielder Stan Javier (.311, 77 RBIs, 33 SB), a future big leaguer, was the star of that team. The 1984 Hornets won the first half of the season and finished with a division best 75–69 record. They were defeated, however, in the playoffs with second half champ Asheville, two games to one. Outfielder Brad Winkler (.298) made the league All-Star team.

In 1985, the Hornets (74–63) became a Red Sox farm club. They started slowly but recovered to win the second half of the season. The Hornets then swept first half champ Sumter in the divisional playoff but came up short in the finals, losing to Florence, three games to two. Pat Jelks, named as the All-Star team's designated hitter, hit .301 with 18 home runs and 87 RBIs while second baseman Alan Ashkinazy (.255, 53 SB) scored a league leading 115 runs

Though they played well in 1986, the Hornets finished third in a season dominated by Asheville. Their decent 75–63 record left them 14 games behind the Tourists. The 1987 season was a dismal one for the Hornets as they finished with a league worst record of 55–85.

They did still manage to lead the league in attendance with over 166,000. Two future major leaguers — third baseman Scott Cooper (.251) and pitcher Curt Schilling (8–15) — were members of the team though neither played particularly well.

The Hornets, now part of the Reds organization, were back on top of their division in 1988. Winning the second half of the season, the Hornets posted a record of 79–60. They were upset in the playoffs, however, by first half champ Spartanburg, two games to none. Third baseman Brian Lane (.282) and catcher Eddie Taubensee (.258) were named to the league All-Star team. Steve Hester (12–5) and Joe Turek (10–3) led the pitching staff.

Though their record of 78–60 in 1989 was almost identical to the previous season's, the Hornets finished second to Gastonia by 13 games. First baseman Mike Mulvaney (.266, 19 HR, 112 RBIs) was the star of the team and the league's Most Valuable Player. Others standouts included shortstop Reggie Sanders (.288), and pitchers Victor Garcia (10–1) and Mo Sanford (12–6).

It was back to the divisional cellar for the 1990 Hornets. Again a Yankees affiliate, the team finished with a 59–85 record. Pitcher Sterling Hitchcock (12–12) led the league with 171 strikeouts while Jeff Hoffman (8–3) had a league best ERA of 1.47. The 1991 season saw the team improve to second place, though their record of 73–68 still left them 18 games behind Charleston (W.Va.). All-Star catcher Kiki Hernandez led the team in hitting with a .332 average and 78 RBIs. Attendance was first in the league that season at 191,048.

The 1992 season was an average one for Greensboro. The Hornets' record of 74–67 was the fourth best in their division. Future Yankees star Andy Pettitte (10–4, 2.20 ERA) had a good season, as did outfielder Lew Hill (.313).

Led by shortstop Derek Jeter (.295, 71 RBIs), outfielder Matt Luke (.286, 21 HR, 91 RBIs), first baseman Nick Delvecchio (.270, 21 HR, 80 RBIs) and pitcher Ryan Karp (13–1, 1.81 ERA), all of whom were named to the league All-Star team, the 1993 Hornets won the first half of the season. Finishing with the best record in their division (85–56), the team defeated Fayetteville in the playoffs. They lost the championship, however, to Savannah, two games to one.

In 1994, the team changed its name to the Greensboro Bats. It was an average season for the team, which finished at 71–69, with the exception of the performance of outfielder Ruben Rivera. Named the league's Most Valuable Player, Rivera hit .288 with 28 home runs, 81 RBIs and 36 stolen bases. The Bats did have a couple of other standouts, including pitchers Chris Cumberland (14–5) and Dan Rios (17 saves, 0.87 ERA).

Again in 1995, the Bats had an average season as they finished with a 70–70 record, sixth in their division. The team's only real star was reliever Chris Corn, who saved 24 games and had an ERA of 1.76. First baseman Brian Buchanan, the Yankees' number one draft pick in 1994 out of the University of Virginia, hit .302 in 23 games before severely injuring his ankle. The 1996 season was an even worse one for the team as they dropped to 56–86, their record placing them 13th in the 14-team league.

◆ ——————— *Greenville* ——————— ◆

Greenville's first professional baseball team, the Tobacconists (or Tobs), began play in 1928 as a member of the new Class D Eastern Carolina League. The league was only in existence for two seasons and Greenville was

a member both years. The 1928 season saw the Tobs finish in last place with a record of 43–71. Pitcher Louis "Bobo" Newsom, who would spend 20 seasons in the big leagues, split the season between Greenville and Wilmington

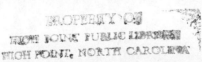

and achieved a record of 15–6. The next year was not much better as the Tobs, posting a record of 45–68, finished fifth out of the six teams. The league and the team folded after the 1929 season.

Baseball returned to Greenville on a semipro level in 1934 as the town entered a team in the newly formed Coastal Plain League. The Greenville Greenies played well on that level, winning the championship that first year. For the 1937 season the Coastal Plain League became a true professional league and was designated Class D. The Greenies had a losing season that first year as professionals, finishing in seventh place (out of eight) with a record of 40–58. The team was lacking in every way as the leading hitters were center fielder Uriah "Swamp" Norwood and third baseman–manager Roland "Bo" Farley, who each had an average of only .271. Farley also served as the baseball coach at Greenville's East Carolina State Teachers College. No pitcher on the team was able to achieve a winning record. Pitcher Fred Caligiuri (8–15) improved to appear in 18 games for the Philadelphia Athletics in 1941 and '42.

The Greenies had another poor season in 1938 as they again finished seventh, winning 45 games and losing 68. The league standings were revised, however, in early August due to many teams using ineligible players. This resulted in forfeits and general confusion as to the league standings. The Greenies, not guilty of infractions, were granted 20 victories, giving them a record of 41–38 at that time. The team played well for the remainder of the season and finished at 64–47, the fifth best record in the revised standings. The star of the team that season was pitcher Don King, who was named to the All–Coastal Plain team with his 16–6 record. The Greenies' best hitters were outfielder John Heavener (.333) and second baseman Harry Christopher (.307), neither of whom spent the entire season with the team. Manager Rube Wilson, a midseason replacement, hit .349 in 39 games at first base. Catcher Vinnie Smith (.238) would

later make it to the Pittsburgh Pirates for a few games and eventually become a National League umpire.

The 1939 season saw the Greenies improve dramatically. Playing in brand new Guy Smith Stadium, they won 75 games while losing 47, finishing in first place by 6½ games. Outfielders Ed Black (.329, 153 hits) and Alex Daniels (.337) had great seasons and were two of the best hitters in the league. Shortstop Clarence "Gracie" Allen (.296, 88 runs) was named to the league All-Star team. Lefty Don King was again the ace of the pitching staff as he posted a 20–7 record and led the league with an incredible ERA of 1.25. Fred Caligiuri returned for a third season with the team, pitching well with an 8–0 record. Unfortunately for the Greenies, they were upset in the first round of the playoffs, four games to two, by Kinston, the regular season fourth place team. Greenville's manager, Rube Wilson, was named league manager of the year.

The next season the Greenies were back near the league cellar. They finished in seventh place at 53–71, 23 games out of first. Fred Caligiuri was back for his fourth season with the team and was one of the best pitchers in the league. His 20–6 record and 2.17 ERA earned him a spot on the All–Coastal Plain League Team (the only Greenie so named). Outfielder Bennie Crowe (.307) and manager Rube Wilson (.297, 14 HR) were the leaders of the otherwise weak-hitting offense.

In 1941, the Greenies finished even farther out of first place (23½ games), yet their 64–54 record was good enough for second place (Wilson dominated the league that season with a record of 87–30). The talented team featured several outstanding players, including outfielder Charlie Scagg (.327, 84 RBIs), manager–first baseman Rube Wilson (.325, 81 RBIs), third baseman Harry Jenkins (.322, 93 RBIs), and pitcher Joe Long (16–4, 2.32 ERA). The Greenies defeated New Bern in the first round of the playoffs, four games to two, but lost in the finals to the powerful Wilson Tobs by the same margin. (Charlie Scagg's real name was Amerigo

Scagliarini, under which he had played at Mayodan in 1939.)

The Coastal Plain League suspended play after the 1941 season due to the war. The Greenies returned when league play resumed in 1946. That season's good hitting team was led by shortstop Ray Carlson (.334, 32 SB) and left fielder Vern Blackwell (.313, 114 RBIs), both named to the All–Coastal Plain team. With a lack of pitching, however, sixth place was the best the Greenies could manage as they finished the season with a 58–67 record.

The 1947 season saw the Greenies return to the cellar. Their 58–82 record left them 21 games out of first. The Greenies also finished last in the league in attendance, drawing 66,316 fans (four teams in the league drew over 100,000, with Wilson leading the league with 138,548 in paid attendance). Outfielder Willard Mauney (.354, 94 RBIs) managed to have a great season despite playing for a last place team.

The next season, 1948, was much the same: The Greenies finished in last place (50–89) and were again last in attendance (60,938). Outfielders Bob Cohen (.333, 94 RBIs), Wiley Nash (.288, 85 RBIs) and Willard Mauney (.344 in 59 games) all played well but were not enough to make up for the team's shortcomings. Pitcher Luis Arroyo had potential beyond his 9–13 record and went on to an eight year major league career.

Finally in 1949 the Greenies posted a winning record. They finished at 71–67, good enough for fourth place and a playoff berth. Player-manager Fred "Pappy" Williams (.335, 122 RBIs) led the Greenies to the Coastal Plain League championship as they upset

Rocky Mount, four games to two, in the first round and Kinston by the same margin in the finals. Other standouts on the team included shortstop John Tepedino (.319, 47 SB) and outfielder Willard Mauney (.299, 101 RBIs, 49 SB). Other than former Wake Forest star Vernon Mustian (7–4, 3.17 ERA), the Greenie pitching staff was merely average.

For their final two seasons—1950 and '51—the owners of the Greenville team changed its name to the Robins. The winning ways of 1949 did not return in 1950. Managed by former big league pitcher Randy Heflin, the Robins slipped to a sixth place finish, winning 67 games and losing 70. Catcher John Baktis (.301, 12 HR) led that team's offense with help from base-stealing threats John Tepedino (.280, 40 SB) and Paul Strausser (.272, 47 SB). The solid pitching staff suffered from a lack of run support and manager Heflin's 13–13 record was the best among the starters. The 1951 season was a brief one for the Robins as they withdrew from the league (along with Tarboro) on June 6. At that time their record stood at 10–24 and attendance had been averaging only around 350 per game. The Greenville Robins suffered the same fate as many other lower level minor league teams in North Carolina — and the entire nation — in the early 1950s. The entire Coastal Plain League would fold after the 1952 season due to financial difficulties caused by a loss of interest by the fans.

Guy Smith Stadium, home of Greenville teams from 1939 to 1951, still exists. Built in 1939 as a WPA project, the park is still well-maintained.

◆ —— *Henderson* —— ◆

In 1929, Henderson was awarded a new franchise in the Class C Piedmont League. Lassiter Field was given a total renovation and play commenced. The team was given the unusual name of the Bunnies. Not the

type of ferocious animal usually associated with the names of sports teams, the Bunnies were actually named for manager Bunn Hearn. Hearn had been a major league pitcher and had played for and or managed several teams in North Carolina. That first year the Bunnies didn't meet with much success as they finished the season with a 54–85 record, 32½ games out of first. Pitcher Leo Townsend, who had played briefly in the majors, was the team's leading pitcher at 21–16. The offensive star of the Bunnies was left fielder John Jones who produced a .327 batting average, 31 home runs and 75 RBIs.

Before the 1930 season the team name was changed, after the departure of Bunn Hearn, to the Gamecocks. New second baseman–manager, Jimmy Teague (.335), led the team to a complete turnaround. Leo Townsend returned and had another good year at 18–13, and five starting players — led by John Jones (.345, 28 HRs, 124 RBIs) — batted at least .300. Maybe giving the team a more fearsome name worked, for the Gamecocks won the league pennant

with a 78–63 record. They did, however, lose to Durham, four games to three, in the playoffs.

The Gamecocks returned for the 1931 season but their winning ways did not. They finished in seventh place, 47 games out of first, winning 51 games and losing 82. Pitcher Jesse Petty, having just finished a seven year major league career the previous season, posted a record of 13–14. Manager Jimmy Teague (.336) returned and had a good season, supported by outfielder Hobart Brummit (.340) and third baseman Mack Arnette (.306). Outfielder Cecil "Zip" Payne joined the team in midseason and hit .240, a poor performance for someone whose career batting average would be .334 when he retired in 1949.

The team disbanded during the winter due to low attendance and its franchise was taken over by Wilmington. Professional baseball has never returned to Henderson.

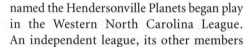

Hendersonville

In July of 1909, a professional team named the Hendersonville Planets began play in the Western North Carolina League. An independent league, its other members consisted of Asheville, Waynesville and Canton. After approximately 40 games, and only a few days before it was scheduled to end, the league disbanded due to financial problems.

It was nearly 40 years before professional baseball returned to the town. In 1948, the Class D Western Carolina League was formed with the Hendersonville Skylarks as a charter member. The team would last only two seasons and finish in the cellar both times. The 1948 team turned in a record of 36–70, 31 games out of first. Attendance was also last with 35,768. The team had good hitting, led by manager-catcher Charlie Munday (.352), outfielder Bruce Reynolds (.306, 92 runs) and first baseman Joe Plick (.303, 15 HR), but no pitcher on the staff came close to having a winning record.

The Skylarks of 1949 had another poor season, posting a record of 29–78, 42½ games behind first place Newton-Conover. The team, managed first by Rube Wilson and then Ray Hunt, again had good hitting but absolutely no pitching. Third baseman Mack Hatfield (.302) and outfielder Bruce Reynolds (.290) both had good seasons.

The team's best hitter, however, proved to be outfielder Mal Stevens (.373, 59 RBIs), who was purchased from Richmond of the Piedmont League in mid–June. Another of the Skylarks' top offensive threats, first baseman Joe Plick, was lost for the season after only a few games when he broke his leg in a collision at home plate. Once again attendance was last in the league with only 21,235 paying to see the Skylarks' home games at the Western North Carolina Fairgrounds.

The team was sold to a group from Gastonia after the 1949 season and moved there.

The 1948 Hendersonville Skylarks included: *Back:* Charlie Munday, Ebb Williams, Pete Hendershot, Vern "Dusty" Rhodes, Burl Gilbert, Perry, Norman "Slim" Ayers; *Front:* Fred Witek, Eddie Lowe, Ingleses, Tommy Holcombe, Lester Bangs, William "Burrhead" Whitten, Ray Miller, Joe Plick (courtesy Joe Plick).

◆ ——————— *Hickory* ——————— ◆

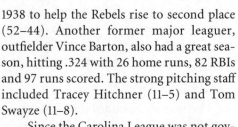

Professional baseball was first played in Hickory in 1936. That season a team, named the Hickory Rebels, took to the field in the independent Carolina league. Since it was not a member of minor league baseball's National Assocation, it was declared an "outlaw" league. That first season was not successful as the team finished fifth out of the league's eight teams at 48–49.

The Rebels improved to third in 1937 with a 55–44 record. First baseman Pete Susko (.354, 20 HR, 86 runs), who had spent the 1934 season in the big leagues with Washington, led the team in hitting. Outfielder Henry "Prince" Oana hit .337 with 17 home runs. A native of Hawaii, Oana had been a star in the Pacific Coast League before appearing in a few major league games with the Phillies in 1934. He would later switch to pitcher and return to the big leagues with Detroit in 1943.

Pete Susko (.342, 60 RBIs) returned in

1938 to help the Rebels rise to second place (52–44). Another former major leaguer, outfielder Vince Barton, also had a great season, hitting .324 with 26 home runs, 82 RBIs and 97 runs scored. The strong pitching staff included Tracey Hitchner (11–5) and Tom Swayze (11–8).

Since the Carolina League was not governed by the National Association, teams could pay whatever salaries they could afford. The high salaries necessary to keep the teams competitive were the reason that quite a few former major leaguers appeared in the league. Ultimately, the league ran into financial troubles which, along with threats from the National Association to ban any player that appeared in the league, led to its demise after the 1938 season,

In 1939 the Rebels joined the newly formed Class D Tar Heel League and were members of that league for both seasons it was in existence. In 1939, Hickory finished fifth out of six teams with a record of 48–62. Right fielder Norman James had a great season for that team, hitting .348 with 105 RBIs, as did left-handed pitcher Bill Skinner (14–15, 212 SO). Both were named to the league All-Star team.

The next season the Rebels fared better, posting a record of 54–52. Their third place finish qualified them for the playoffs, where they swept Gastonia in the first round, three games to none (only four teams in the league managed to finish the season as Newton-Conover and Shelby dropped out July 19). In the finals the Rebels lost to Statesville, four games to one. First baseman Woody Traylor (.316), who tied for the league home run lead with 16, was the team's best hitter. The league folded after the season.

A member of the 1940 Hickory team that caused a great deal of controversy was Edwin "Alabama" Pitts. In 1935, Pitts had been paroled from New York's Sing Sing prison. His attempts to play organized baseball were met with much resistance until Commissioner Landis ruled in his favor. Pitts, an outfielder, played well for Hickory, hitting .302 in 64 games. He was killed the next summer in a knife fight at a Valdese, North Carolina, bar.

Hickory was without a minor league team in 1941 but in 1942 the town was granted a franchise in the North Carolina State League. The team name was kept and the Rebels played one season before league play was suspended due to the war. That season was a memorable one for the Rebels — not for their winning but for their losing. Their 18–80 record gave them a winning percentage of only .184, the third worst in North Carolina's minor league history. Only teams from Granite Falls in 1951 (14–96, .127) and Rocky Mount in 1980 (24–114, .174) have been worse. Manager Bud Shaney (8–9, 2.92 ERA) would doubtless have won more games had the Rebels had an offense.

The Rebels were back in 1945 as N.C. State League play resumed. The team showed no similarities to the 1942 Rebels as they finished at 80–34, winning the pennant by 11½ games. Outfielder Phil Alotta (.322) drove in 109 while shortstop John Allen (.325) scored an impressive 140 runs. Pitcher Frank Hidalgo won 20 games and lost only six. Unfortunately for the Rebels, they were upset in the first round of the playoffs by the Landis Millers.

The 1946 season saw the Rebels slip to sixth place (out of eight) with a record of 55–56. The most notable player on that team was pitcher Dick Stoll (14–9). The Rebels improved somewhat in 1947 to 61–49, good enough for third place. They were defeated, however, in the first round of the playoffs by regular season and eventual playoff champion Mooresville. First baseman Charlie Knight (.366, 107 runs, 14 3B) and outfielder Jim Thomas (.355, 31 HR, 131 RBIs, 101 runs) both had outstanding seasons. Knight led the league in runs scored, bases on balls and triples. Thomas led in RBIs and hits, and tied with Mooresville's Norman Small in home runs. Miller Shealy led the Rebels' pitching staff with a 16–6 record.

The Rebels posted an identical 61–49 record in 1948 and again finished third. This time they won in the first round of the playoffs but lost in seven games to Statesville in the finals. Outfielders Owen Linn (.330, 80 RBIs, 107 runs) and Otis Stephens (.328, 32 HR, 105 RBIs) were the stars of the team.

The Rebels dropped down to seventh place in 1949, 40 games out of first, at 50–74. Owen Linn remained with the team and was again the leading hitter with a .321 average and 110 RBIs. The downward slide continued in 1950 as the Rebels finished in the cellar with a record of 38–73. The bright spots in an otherwise dismal season were player-manager D.C. "Pud" Miller (29 HR, 92 RBIs), who led the league with a .369 batting average, and pitcher John Shofer (19–13), the league strikeout king with 276.

Pud Miller turned the team around in 1951, partly due to his own offensive efforts, and the Rebels finished in second place, winning 72 games and losing 54. Miller won the Triple Crown that season as he led the league in batting average (.425), RBIs (136) and

Otis Stephens hit 32 home runs and drove in 105 for Hickory in 1948 (courtesy Otis Stephens).

home runs (40). His batting average was the highest in all of professional baseball that season. Miller's fellow outfielder, Norman Small, also had an impressive year. He hit .340, with 127 RBIs and 37 home runs, second in the league to Miller in both home runs and RBIs. Pitcher Ray Boles (23–5) was the league leader in wins. Once again the Rebels had trouble in the playoffs, losing to Statesville in the first round, four games to none.

For the 1952 season the Rebels switched to the Western Carolina League, also Class D. They finished in last place out of the five teams that completed the season, posting a record of 28–79. Norman Small began the season as manager but was released when the team failed to win games. His replacement, Eddie Yount, could do no better and was eventually replaced by Charlie Bowles. Pud Miller had left the Rebels for a job managing Owensboro of the KITTY League but left that team in midseason. He returned to Hickory

for the final 44 games of the season and hit .331. Attendance for the Rebels was poor at 14,729, last in the league and down from a league-leading high of 53,662 the previous season. That season was to be the only one in the Western Carolina League as the league folded after the season.

The old Tar Heel League was reincarnated in 1953 with Hickory as a member. The Rebels finished seventh out of the eight teams that finished the season (10 had begun), at 46–66. First baseman Giles Setzer (.358, 72 RBIs) led the team in hitting while Monk Raines (12–5) was the best pitcher on an otherwise weak staff. The 1954 season began as a promising one for the Rebels. Unfortunately, the league folded on June 21 with the Rebels in first place, leaving them with a final record of 34–18. At the time of the league's demise, outfielder Mike Yaremchuk was leading it in batting average (.376), hits (74) and RBIs (45).

Hickory was without professional baseball until 1960, when the Rebels were reborn as members of the also resurrected Western Carolina League. The Rebels' record of 53–44 was good enough for third place. Their attendance, however, was next to last (seventh) at only 14,503. The team was led by player-manager Joe Abernethy (.319) and third baseman Ken Free (.311). Pitcher Danny Hayling had a great year, posting a 22–9 record with an ERA of 2.00 and hitting .367 in 109 at-bats. He set still-standing league records for wins and complete games (24). In the first round of the playoffs the Rebels managed to beat regular season champion Lexington, two games to one. They fell short in the finals, losing to Salisbury, three games to two. The team folded after the season due to the lack of fan interest.

For the next 32 seasons, Hickory was without a professional baseball team. In 1993, minor league baseball returned to the town with a bang. The Hickory Crawdads of the Class A South Atlantic League took to the field at brand new $5 million L.P. Frans Stadium. The Crawdads, part of the Chicago White Sox farm system, were not successful on the field as they finished at 52–88, 13th in the 14-member league. As a team they only hit for a .224 average. The successes of the Crawdads came in attendance. They set a league attendance record of 283,727, averaging nearly 4,000 fans per home game. The Crawdads were also wildly successful in marketing. Of all the minor league teams in the country, they were third in merchandise sales behind only the Carolina Mudcats and the Durham Bulls.

In 1994, the Crawdads played well and won the second half of the season in the northern division of their league. With an overall record of 86–54 — the league's second best — they advanced to the playoffs. There, unfortunately, the Crawdads were swept by first half champ Hagerstown, two games to none. Crawdads first baseman Harold Williams (.303, 24 HR, 104 RBIs, 99 runs) was probably the league's best player that season, leading it in runs, hits, total bases, and runs batted in. He was named to the All-Star team along with manager Fred Kendall. Rich Pratt was the ace of the team's pitching staff with his 11–6 record and 2.02 ERA.

For the Crawdads, 1995 was a season spent in the cellar. They finished last in their division in both halves and their combined record of 49–89 was the league's worst. Despite the performance on the field, the Crawdads maintained their impressive attendance figures as they drew 258,022 to L.P. Frans Stadium.

The first half of the 1996 season saw continued poor play as the lowly Crawdads finished with a 16–53 record. They did improve in the second half, however, playing better than .500 ball with a 39–32 record, second in their division. All-Star third baseman Carlos Lee (.313, 70 RBIs), along with catcher Josh Paul (.327) and first baseman Pete Pryor (.307) — two midseason additions to the team — were the Crawdads' best hitters. Relief pitcher Chad Bradford (0.90 ERA, 18 SV) also had an outstanding season.

High Point

High Point's first professional baseball team was the High Point Furniture Makers of 1920, members of the Class D Piedmont League. The Furniture Makers were a charter franchise in the new league and finished the season in third place with an even .500 record of 57–57. Left-handed pitcher Rube Eldridge posted a 13–6 record with an ERA of 1.36 before being sold to Columbus of the American Association. Shortstop Earl Bitting (.319) and second baseman W. Waldron (.318) led the team in hitting.

The next year the league moved up a level to Class C. The Furniture Makers played well, winning the second half of a split season, with an overall record of 65–55. Rube Eldridge, who won 15 games but lost 19, returned to the team but Tom Day was the team's best pitcher with a 14–2 record. First baseman Jim Holt (.342, 35 2B) led the league in home runs with 26 while shortstop and manager Herb "Dummy" Murphy (.316, 23 HR) also contributed to the offense. The Furniture Makers faced Greensboro in the playoffs but lost, four games to one.

The 1922 season saw the Furniture Makers win the first half of the season and go on to have the best record in the league at 70–55. They lost to Durham, however, in a hard fought playoff series, four games to three. Outfielder Al Smith led the league with a .366 batting average while Rube Eldridge (26–9, 2.76 ERA) was the league's winningest pitcher.

For the 1923 season the team changed its name to the Pointers. Rube Eldridge again pitched well, finishing the season with a 20–10 record. Third baseman John Kane (.355, 16 HR, 189 hits), along with outfielders Loren Thrasher (.343, 15 HR) and W.L. Irby (.343, 105 runs), led the team's offense. Though they had some talented players, the Pointers were not deep and finished third in a close race, winning 65 games and losing 59.

The Pointers of 1924 just missed winning the pennant. Their record of 71–50 left them only 1½ games behind Durham. The team's offensive attack was by outfielding brothers Loren and George Thrasher. Loren hit .349 and scored a league leading 93 runs while George hit .323 with 21 home runs and 101 RBIs. Catcher Arnold Townsend (.354, 27 HR, 102 RBIs) also had a great season, leading the league in both RBIs and home runs.

The 1925 season was a short one for the Pointers. The team moved to Danville (Va.) on June 18, hoping for better attendance.

The Pointers returned in 1926 and played well, finishing in second place with a record of 85–61. They missed the playoffs, however, as they failed to win either half of a split season. That season was the first of the Danny Boone years. Boone was probably the best hitter in the history of the league. In 1926, he led the league in every major offensive category except home runs; his 28 homers were one short of the 29 of Greensboro's Dave Barbee. Playing first base, Boone batted .399 with 214 hits, 112 runs, and 117 RBIs. Boone was not the only star of the team that season as pitcher Ray Phelps (27–8, 151 SO) was the league's best.

For the 1927 season, Danny Boone was hired as player-manager. The Pointers didn't fare well and finished the season in fifth, 22 games back, at 62–82. Outfielder Moose Clabaugh, who had played part of the 1926 season with Brooklyn, led the league with a .363 batting average and 187 hits. Danny Boone hit .342 with 71 runs and 57 RBIs (an off year for him). Rookie catcher Cliff Bolton batted .286 in 28 games. Pitcher Rube Eldridge returned to the Pointers after two seasons with other teams in the league. His record of 15–12 gave him an overall record of 97–66 in six seasons with High Point.

In 1928, Boone had the best year of his career. In fact, his stats (.419, 131 RBIs, 38 HR, 40 2B, 11 3B, 196 hits, and 123 runs) would probably put his season as one of the best in the history of professional baseball.

Boone led the Pointers to a 83–52 record and a tie for first place. They lost in the playoffs, however, to Winston-Salem, four games to three. Overshadowed by Boone, Cliff Bolton returned and had a great season, batting .403 with 81 RBIs. He would reach the major leagues in 1931. Another player, first baseman Ed Lundeen (.412) also hit over .400 in 59 games. It is doubtful that there is another team in baseball history with three players, each with at least 200 at-bats, to hit over .400. As a team the Pointers hit an incredible .331. Outfielders Jimmy Williams (.355, 97 RBIs) and Jete Long (.341, 84 RBIs), second baseman Jim Stewart (.324) and shortstop Hod Ford (.316, 89 RBIs), all hit well over .300 and would have been the stars of any other team.

The Pointers slipped down to fourth place in 1929 as they finished at 67–72, 19½ games behind first place Durham. Once again Danny Boone had an impressive year (.372 BA, 46 HR, 191 hits, 125 RBIs, 116 runs). Nineteen-year-old rookie pitcher Bucky Walters posted a 5–6 record. The next season he switched to the infield and in 1931 debuted in the major leagues as a third baseman. Walters went back to pitching in 1934 and became one of the National League's best while playing for the Phillies and the Reds. He was named to the All-Star team six times and won the 1939 National League MVP award with a 27–11 record and an ERA of 2.29.

Despite the efforts of player-manager Danny Boone (.385, 25 HR, 113 RBIs, 124 runs) and outfielder Clay Parrish (.372, 20 HR, 100 RBIs), the Pointers finished the 1930 season in the cellar with a record of 64–76. The team's weakness was its pitching staff. Though it featured one of the league's best, Richard Durham (22–13), no other pitcher could manage a winning record.

The Pointers played even more poorly in 1931. Once again they finished in the cellar with a horrible record of 39–91, 57½ games behind first place Charlotte. It was also to be the last season for Danny Boone. Boone began the season as player-manager but left midway through the season and signed with York of the New York–Pennsylvania League. In his 73 games in High Point, Boone batted .388 with 20 home runs and 76 RBIs. Goldie Holt, in the middle of a minor league playing career that lasted more than 20 seasons, played third and outfield for the Pointers, batting .284. Holt's total baseball career spanned 50 years as a minor league player and manager, as well as major league coach and scout. He retired as a scout for the Dodgers in 1973 at age 71.

The Piedmont League jumped to Class B for the 1932 season. It was a short season for the Pointers as they withdrew from the league (along with Asheville) on July 7 due to financial problems caused by the Depression. At the time of their withdrawal the team had a record of 33–39. Outfielder Parker Perry was having a great season and signed on with Wilmington when the team failed.

He finished with a combined .339 average and 110 RBIs. On August 20 of that season the Piedmont League returned to High Point as the Winston-Salem club relocated to town. That team finished in third place with a combined record of 69–62. Outfielder Hank Leiber (.362, 103 RBIs) and pitcher Al Smith (17–8), who would both go on to long big league careers, led that team.

The move from Winston-Salem proved to be only temporary for the team as they returned there the next season. The next professional team to move to High Point was the Gastonia franchise in the independent Carolina League in 1938. Named the Spinners, the team only played four or five games in High Point before declaring bankruptcy. After that short-lived venture, High Point would be left without professional baseball for the next nine seasons.

High Point–Thomasville

In 1948, the cities of High Point and Thomasville joined together to field a team in the Class D North Carolina State League. Each city appointed members to a board of directors that oversaw operations of the team. The team, named the Hi-Toms, played at Finch Field, the former home of the Thomasville Tommies. Situated between the two cities, the ballpark seated at that time about 2,900 under a covered grandstand.

The Hi-Toms had a good season that first year. Managed by Jimmy Gruzdis, they finished the regular season in first place, with a record of 67–43. Gruzdis, who played first base and in the outfield, led the league in batting with a .388 average while pitcher Al Jarlett was the league's best with a 27–4 record. Former major league catcher and High Point native Cliff Bolton, at age 41, batted .417 in 50 games. Even though the team lost in the first round of the playoffs to Hickory (four games to three), it had been a very successful first season. The Hi-Toms were

first in the league in attendance with 100,227, over 30,000 more than second place Statesville.

Jimmy Gruzdis again led the Hi-Toms to a first place finish in 1949, their record of 90–34 giving them the pennant by 18 games. Cliff Bolton, now 42, won the league batting title with a .399 average while driving in 105 runs. Other Hi-Toms leaders were shortstop Clarence Williams (.343, 133 runs) and pitchers Lynn Southworth (21–1, 3.14 ERA) and Ron Schuettenberg (19–4). Southworth's winning percentage (.955) still ranks as second best in the history of professional baseball. Future Hall of Famer Eddie Mathews joined the team in midseason at age 17 and took over third base. In 63 games he hit .363 with 17 home runs. The team went on to win the league championship by defeating Landis in the first round of the playoffs and then Lexington, by a margin of four games to three, in the finals.

In 1950, the Hi-Toms slipped to a fourth place finish but their record of 61–50 did qualify them for the last playoff spot. In the

Inside the press box at Finch Field, home of the Hi-Toms, early 1950s (courtesy High Point Museum Archives).

seasons. Cliff Bolton, despite his age, still played excellent baseball, batting .323 in 85 games.

The 1952 season was the last for the North Carolina State League. Once again, Jimmy Gruzdis led the Hi-Toms to the pennant as they won 74 games and lost 33. The team's offensive leaders were second baseman Charlie Levene and outfielder John Lybrand, both of whom hit .356. The Hi-Toms also had a talented pitching staff led by Bill Zonner (16–7) and John Zavada (16–5). It is doubtful that any other team in baseball history has had two starting pitchers whose last names began with the letter Z. In the playoffs, the team was swept by Salisbury in an upset, four games to none. Attendance, which had been over 52,000 in 1951, dropped to 17,345 despite the Hi-Toms' first place finish.

first round, the Hi-Toms defeated the regular season second place team, Mooresville, four games to two. They took Landis to a seventh game in the finals before losing, four games to three. Cliff Bolton hit .347 in 80 games that season but the real star of the team was third baseman John Lybrand, who hit .334 with 101 RBIs. Al Jarlett (18–10) was the team's best pitcher and had a league-leading ERA of 2.63.

The Hi-Toms, who signed a working agreement with the Boston Red Sox, were back on top of the 1951 league standings with a 90–36 record. The team went on to win the league championship, dropping only one game in the playoffs. They beat Elkin, four games to one, in the first round and then swept Statesville in the finals. Third baseman John Lybrand led the team with a .380 batting average, 114 RBIs, and 103 runs while outfielders Gene Stephens (.337, 112 RBIs, 118 runs) and Tom Umphlett (.310, 79 RBIs) also provided offense. Pitchers Tom Brewer (19–3), who would go on to win 91 games for Boston, and Arvid Hamilton (18–4) had outstanding

In 1953, with the demise of the North Carolina State League, the Hi-Toms joined the newly formed Tar Heel League. Also a Class D circuit, the league was made up of mainly former members of the Western Carolina and North Carolina State leagues. The season was short for the Hi-Toms, as they withdrew from the league (along with Statesville) on June 11 due to poor attendance. At the time of their withdrawal the Hi-Toms' record stood at 13–28.

The Hi-Toms returned in 1954, taking a big jump upward to join the Class B Carolina League. The Raleigh franchise had decided to move and chose High Point–Thomasville as its new home. A member of the Cincinnati Reds farm system, the team did not play particularly well and finished in sixth place with a record of 66–73. Outfielder Noah Goode (.335, 17 HR) led the team in hitting while veteran pitcher Woody Rich, in his eighteenth professional baseball season, turned in a 13–6 record. Attendance was good at 65,403.

The 1956 High Point–Thomasville Hi-Toms included: *Back:* George Erath (bus. mgr.), Nelvin Cooper, Gail Thomas, Woody Rich, Bud Cooke, Amiel "Lefty" Solomon, Haven Schmidt, Jack Taylor, Gus Carmichael, Fred Harrington, Austin Kerns (groundskeeper); *Front:* Mike Goocy, Bo Bossard, Rene Solis, Bill Ford, Bert Haas (mgr.), Orlando Pena, Curt Flood, Karl Keuhl, Charlie Brown (courtesy High Point Museum Archives).

The Hi-Toms of 1955 played well and took the league pennant with an 80–58 record. The team was led by an excellent pitching staff that included All-Stars Woody Rich (19–4) and Jack Taylor (17–11, 1.78 ERA). The offense featured outfielder and Carolina League Player of the Year Danny Morejon (.324, 86 RBIs). The talented Hi-Toms struggled in the first round of the playoffs before defeating Durham in a seventh game. In the finals they were upset by Danville, four games to two.

The 1956 season saw the Hi-Toms finish once again in first place. Led by Carolina League Player of the Year and future big league star Curt Flood (.340, 133 runs, 190 hits, 29 HR, 128 RBIs) and manager-outfielder Bert Haas (.326), the team posted a record of 91–63. All-Star pitcher Jack Taylor (22–12) had another great season for the team and led the league in wins while future big league reliever Orlando Pena won 19. Thirty-nine-year-old Woody Rich won 17 and lost 12. As

with the previous year, the favored Hi-Toms were upset in the playoffs, this time in the first round by Fayetteville, three games to none.

For the 1957 season, the Carolina League declared a split season. The Hi-Toms, now a Philadelphia Phillies farm club, were the winners of the second half and had an overall record of 79–61. In the playoffs they faced first half winner Durham, but unfortunately for the Hi-Toms, they lost the league championship to the Bulls, four games to three. For the third consecutive season, the Hi-Toms were led by the Carolina League Player of the Year, as outfielder Fred Van Dusen hit .310 with 25 home runs and 93 RBIs. The offense that season also included outfielder Eddie Logan (.327, 104 runs), who won the league batting title, and All-Star second baseman Billy Ford (.290, 20 HRs, 85 RBIs). Jack Taylor (17–15) was again the team's best pitcher, leading the league with 24 complete games. Pitcher Dallas Green (12–9) went on to both play for and manage the Phillies.

Guided by future major league manager Frank Lucchesi for a second season in 1958, the Hi-Toms played well and finished in second place at 76–63. Led by All-Star outfielder Jacke Davis (.302, 25 HR, 88 RBIs)—who was named as the league's Rookie of the Year—and veteran pitcher Jack Taylor (19–9), the team advanced to face Greensboro in the playoffs but lost, two games to one. Outfielder Tony Curry also had an outstanding year, leading the league in runs (106) and hits (168) to go with a .293 batting average and 20 home runs. Both Curry and Davis went on to play briefly with the Phillies.

The Phillies dropped their affiliation with the Hi-Toms after the 1958 season. Unable to find support from another major league team, they were forced to disband, leaving High Point and Thomasville without professional baseball. The Hi-Toms finally returned to the Carolina League in 1968 as a co-op team. Even without the full support of a major league team, they played decent baseball. Managed by Jack McKeon, the Hi-Toms finished the season in second place in the league's Western Division with a record of 69–71. They did not drop a single game in the playoffs, defeating Greensboro, Lynchburg and Raleigh-Durham in the finals to claim the league championship. Hi-Tom first baseman Tony Solaita, a native of American Samoa, was named Player of the Year, hitting .302 with 49 home runs, 122 RBIs, and 106 runs.

For the 1969 season the team signed a player development contract with the Kansas City Royals and changed their name to that of their parent team. The High Point–Thomasville Royals finished the season and a long tradition of minor league baseball in the two cities with a record of 69–74, fourth in the Western Division. Other than Ken Huebner winning the batting title (.324), it was not a memorable season. Pitcher Monty Montgomery (4–6), a native of Albemarle, North Carolina, went on to spend parts of two seasons with Kansas City. Pitcher Jim Rooker had an impressive two games with the team; he pitched two complete games, striking out 27 and giving up no runs. He was immediately promoted to Omaha, and after two games there, he was on to Kansas City. After the season Kansas City dropped its affiliation with the High Point–Thomasville team. Unable to secure a relationship with another major league team, the two towns were again left without baseball. All other attempts to bring minor league baseball back to the area since have been unsuccessful. Due to the present rule that all minor league teams must be 35 miles apart, and High Point's proximity to Greensboro and Winston-Salem, the High Point–Thomasville area will probably never have another minor league team.

The home of the Hi-Toms, Finch Field, was built in 1935 between High Point and Thomasville. It was also the home of the Thomasville Tommies from 1937 to 1942 and from 1945 to 1947. Though the grandstand burned in 1983, a smaller 1,000 seat facility was rebuilt and the ballpark is still used for high school and American Legion games (see also **Thomasville** entry).

Kannapolis

Textile mill teams from the town of Kannapolis competed in the area's semipro leagues long before professional baseball came to the area. In 1936, several of the textile towns of the area—Kannapolis included—joined together to form a professional baseball league. Named the Carolina League, it was not a member of minor league baseball's National Association and therefore considered to be an "outlaw" league. Named the Towelers, after the main product of the town's textile mill, the Kannapolis team finished in third that first season at 59–40.

The next season, the Towelers won the

league pennant with a 57–42 record. Short-stop Marvin Watts (.320, 85 RBIs) and outfielder Vince Barton (.320, 27 HR, 77 RBIs) were the team's top hitters. Barton, a Canadian, had spent the 1931 and '32 seasons with the Chicago Cubs.

In 1938, the Towelers finished with a record of 49–47, placing third in the league. They did, however, win the playoff championship. Outfielder Eric Tipton (.375, 76 RBIs), who had been a star football player at Duke University, won the league batting title. He made it to the major leagues the following season. Other Toweler standouts included outfielder Glenn "Razz" Miller (.324) and pitcher Jimmie White (13–9), the league strikeout leader with 147. First baseman Jake Daniel, who had appeared in a few games with the Brooklyn Dodgers the previous season, hit .241 with 10 home runs. The Carolina League disbanded after that season due in part to financial difficulties caused by the league's unrestricted salaries. There was also pressure from the National Association, which threatened to declare ineligible all players who participated in the league.

Kannapolis, along with nearby Concord, joined the Class D North Carolina State League in 1939, filling vacancies left by the departure of two other teams. The Towelers finished 46–65, 26 games behind first place Mooresville. Over 60 different players made appearances for the Towelers that year but only a few remained with the team for the entire season. Outfielder Dan Amaral (.419, 31 RBIs) and third baseman E.C. Culbreth (.416) were two of the top hitters in the league though each only spent about a month with the Towelers. Outfielder Red Bennett, in the final season of a long career that included two short stays in the majors, batted .317 in 17 games.

The 1940 season saw the Towelers improve dramatically as they took the league pennant with a record of 67–45, two games ahead of the second place Salisbury Giants. Pitcher Jimmie White (16–9) led the league with an ERA of 1.85 and had a no-hit game against Thomasville on August 30 while left-hander Jack Whitney turned in a 12–3 record. All-Star right fielder Bill Carrier was the team's offensive leader, hitting .356 with 97 RBIs. The Towelers were not very fortunate in the playoffs, as they were shut out three games to none in the first round by the Lexington Indians.

In 1941, the Towelers turned in an impressive record of 70–30, giving them the pennant by eight games. Several Kannapolis players had outstanding seasons, including Jimmie White (20–5, 2.79 ERA), again one of the dominant pitchers in the league, leading in both wins and strikeouts (192). Outfielder Lewis "Stinky" Davis (.285) led the league in runs with 102 while Bill Carrier (.334), again an All-Star, was the leader in RBIs with 88. The Towelers once again lost in the first round of the playoffs as the Mooresville Moors beat them three games to one. In December of 1941, the Towelers franchise was sold to a group from Hickory for a sum of $1,066, leaving the town without professional baseball.

Professional baseball finally returned to Kannapolis in 1995. The franchise which had been the Spartanburg (S.C.) Phillies of the Class A South Atlantic League relocated to Kannapolis and became the Piedmont Phillies. The new 4,500 seat Fieldcrest Cannon Stadium, which remained under construction for the entire season, became the home of the Phillies. Led by South Atlantic League Manager of the Year Roy Majtyka, the Phillies finished first in the first half of the season in the Northern Division. Overall the team had the league's second best record at 82–58. Left-hander Larry Wimberly, named the league's most outstanding pitcher, posted a 10–3 record with a 2.67 ERA. Other members of the outstanding pitching staff included Rich Hunter (10–2) and Silvio Censale (10–6). The offense was powered by first baseman Adam Milan, who hit .294 with 10 home runs and 64 RBIs.

For the 1996 season the team changed its name to the Piedmont Boll Weevils in an attempt to gain its own identity and to cash in on the lucrative souvenir market. On the field it was an average season for the team as they finished with a 72–66 record, sixth best in the 14-team league. Shortstop Mark Raynor led the team in hitting with a .304 average.

 ——————— *Kinston* ———————

Kinston's first entry into professional baseball was as a member of the Class D Eastern Carolina League of 1908. The team did not finish the season and withdrew from the league on July 8 with a record of 6–12. The entire league folded on August 19 without finishing the season.

It was 1925 before another team called Kinston home. This time it was the Kinston Eagles of the Class B Virginia League. The league's Petersburg team had folded after the previous season due to poor attendance and the franchise was granted to Kinston. The Eagles finished last that season with a 52–80 record, mainly due to poor pitching. Relief pitcher Frank Lucas was the only pitcher to have a winning record, at 5–1. The team did have some good offensive players, especially in the outfield. Left fielder J.E. Meeks (.327, 72 RBIs), center fielder Pat Wright (.320, 57 RBIs) and right fielder Art Hauger (.350, 102 RBIs, 183 hits) were the team's best hitters. Hauger, who was 32 years old that season, had appeared in the major leagues when he was only 19, getting one hit in 18 at-bats for Cleveland. He never made it back but had a long, distinguished minor league career.

The Eagles of 1926 rose out of the cellar, barely, as they finished in fifth, 15½ games out of first, with a record of 69–83. Art Hauger had another good year (.316, 95 RBIs) and 36-year-old Ben Spencer (.335, 67 RBIs) excelled in left field. Like Hauger, Spencer had appeared briefly in the major leagues (1913) but never made it back. Catcher Rick Ferrell, a future big league All-Star, batted .265 while playing part time. Elected to the Hall of Fame in 1984, the Greensboro native played 18 seasons with Washington, the Boston Red Sox and the St. Louis Browns. Pitcher Al Shealy, 18–16 for the Eagles, would

go on to pitch for the 1928 World Series champion New York Yankees.

Kinston dropped back to last place in 1927 as the Eagles' record of 56–75 left them 21½ games out of first. Once again, a lack of pitching handicapped the team despite good offensive players. Art Hauger (.303) was back and took over as manager. Outfielders George Rhinehardt (.332) and Jack Rice (.319) also had good seasons. Third baseman Art Reinholz (.318) would make it to the Cleveland Indians for two games late in 1928.

After the 1927 season the Eagles dropped out of the Virginia League. Hoping they would be more competitive in a lower level league, the team joined the new Class D Eastern Carolina League in 1928. That first season in the new league the Eagles finished fourth (out of six) with a record of 55–59. The next season the team was back in the cellar, 23½ games out of first, with a record of 46–71. Clarence Roper, the Eagles' shortstop and manager, did win the batting title in 1929, however, with a .368 average. The league folded after the 1929 season and again Kinston was left without baseball.

The Kinston Eagles joined the semipro Coastal Plain League in 1934. With teams made up mainly of college players, the league was highly regarded across the country as a showcase for college talent. The 1934 and '35 teams were managed by former major leaguer Bunn Hearn, who also served as the head baseball coach at the University of North Carolina. He guided the Eagles to the league championship in 1935. Charlie "King Kong" Keller played for Kinston in 1936 and dominated the league, batting an incredible .468, with 20 home runs and 93 RBIs. He went on to become a feared slugger and All-Star for the New York Yankees in the 1940s. His outfield mate at Kinston, former Duke football star Eric Tipton, also went on to a decent major league career.

The Eagles became truly professional once again in 1937 as the league voted to join the National Association. Despite a working agreement with the St. Louis Cardinals, it was not a good year for the team, as they finished last with a record of 32–65. The offensive stars of the team were catcher Joe Schultz (.335), and outfielders John Wyrostek (.332) and Carden Gillenwater (.301). All three went on to the major leagues. Schultz would later manage the Seattle Pilots for their one and only season of 1969. The team had good talent but not a single pitcher posted a winning record.

The team improved in 1938, posting a 60–50 record, good enough for fourth place. The use of ineligible players by some teams led the league to revise the standings during the season. Kinston, not guilty of infractions, gained six victories by forfeit and finished with a record of 64–45 in the revised standings. Either way, the Eagles had the league's fourth best record. Center fielder John Wyrostek (.332, 83 RBIs) returned and led the league in hits with 149. He was named to the league All-Star team along with utility-man Sid Stringfellow (.242). The Eagles' improvement was due to a good pitching staff that included Eddie Hurley (15–5), Henry Muhlenbein (13–8) and Cliff Wentz (12–10), who led the league with 179 strikeouts. The team qualified for the playoffs but was swept by New Bern in the first round.

Another fourth place finish was turned in by the Eagles in 1939. Winning 65 games and losing 58, the Eagles went to the playoffs. They defeated Greenville in the first round but lost to Williamston in the finals, four games to one. Pitcher Bill Herring (22–11, 1.97 ERA), who would become a legend in the Coastal Plain League, managed the team for much of the season and was one of the league's top pitchers. Outfielder Earl Hahn (.318) and first baseman Doyt Morris (.317, 80 RBIs) were the Eagles' best hitters, with help from outfielder Roy Kennedy (.280).

Versatile Sid Stringfellow, the only Eagle named to the All-Star team, hit .272 and took a turn on the mound, achieving a 14–9 record. Though he hit only .257 for the Eagles, outfielder Gene Hermanski made it to the big leagues for much of nine seasons.

Once again in 1940, with a record of 63–60, the Eagles finished in fourth. Brothers Louis (11–4) and Bill Zinser (17–9), natives of New York, were the team's best pitchers and among the best in the league. (Bill would later appear in two big league games for Washington in 1944.) Right fielder Roy Kennedy (.333, 103 runs) led the Eagles in hitting, closely followed by shortstop Louis Russo (.330, 86 RBIs). Advancing to the playoffs, the Eagles won a hard fought seven game series with Wilson but lost to Tarboro in the finals, four games to two.

The 1941 season saw the Eagles finish in the cellar with a 42–77 record, 43½ games behind first place Wilson. Though they had some talented players, the team was in constant financial trouble. Charles Metelski (.318) and outfielder-manager Arthur "Cowboy" McHenry (.308) were among the players sent back to the Eagles' parent club, the Portsmouth Cubs of the Piedmont League, in an effort to save money. The only member of the Eagles to be named to the All-Star team, third baseman Bill Upchurch (.310), did manage to stay with the team for the entire season. The team and the league suspended operations before the beginning of the next season due to the war.

After a four year hiatus, Coastal Plain League play resumed in 1946. The Eagles returned and played well, finishing in second with a 67–56 record. In the playoffs, the Eagles lost a close seven game series to Wilson. Outfielders Bob Cohen (.332) and Uriah Norwood (.304) were Kinston's leading hitters, while Tom Bankston (21–8) and Sam McLawhorn (16–9) were the aces of the pitching staff.

Managed by second baseman Steve Collins in 1947, the Eagles again finished second with a record of 74–65. Collins hit .353 and drove in 91 runs while returning outfielder

Bob Cohen hit .342 and drove in 92. Short-stop Frank Tepedino (.340, 30 SB) also had a great year but the star of the team was pitcher Sam McLawhorn. With a record of 26–12, an ERA of 2.32 and 238 strikeouts, McLawhorn had an outstanding season. The Eagles went on to win the postseason championship by defeating Tarboro in the first round and Wilson in the finals, both by four-game-to-two margins.

Steve Collins (.311, 90 RBIs) again led the Eagles to a second place (80–59) finish in 1948. An all-around good team, the Eagles featured the bats of first baseman Jud Deaton (.369), third baseman Emil Peters (.325, 89 RBIs, 102 runs) and catcher Matt Pliszka (.317). Fred "Pappy" Williams — the Eagles' most power-ful slugger — was released in early August due to reported problems between himself and manager Collins. He was then signed by Rocky Mount, where he played 27 games, and for the season had the impressive statistics of a .364 batting average, 24 home runs, 134 RBIs and 122 runs scored. The star of the pitching staff was again Sam McLawhorn (14–6), though injuries cut his season short. The Ea-gles advanced to beat Goldsboro in the first round of the playoffs but lost to Tarboro, four games to one, in the finals.

The 1949 season marked the first for Grainger Stadium, the home of baseball in Kinston to this day. The wooden grandstand of Grainger Park was torn down and a new one of concrete and steel was erected on the same site. The 1949 Eagles turned in a second place finish for the fourth year in a row. The team had some talented players, namely pitchers Claude "Diz" Voiselle (20–10) and Ray Keys (10–3). Veteran Harry Soufas led the offense with a .315 average with help from Ray Rosenwinkle (.285, 82 RBIs). Third year manager Steve Collins had a disap-pointing season at the plate and finished with an average of only .232. Again the Eagles failed to win the championship, falling in the final round of the playoffs to Greenville, four games to two. They were first in the league in attendance, however, drawing nearly 89,000 paying fans.

For the 1950 season, the Eagles signed a working agreement with the Boston Red Sox. The team had an average season and dropped to fourth place (70–68), still qualifying for the playoffs. They swept Roanoke Rapids in the first round but were swept themselves in the finals by New Bern. Shortstop and future big leaguer Ken Aspromonte (.295) led the overall weak offense while the pitching staff featured the league's best pitcher, Leo Groeschen (18–7, 1.74 ERA). Two midseason additions to the team — pitcher Alex Zych (10–3) and 18-year-old outfielder Neil Chris-ley (.287) — made valuable contributions.

Managed by pitcher Wes Livengood in 1951, the Eagles won the pennant with a record of 79–47. Again an independent franchise, the team was able to pursue the best players they could afford rather than rely on inexperienced players provided by a major league affiliate. The Eagles put together a strong pitching staff that featured Alex Zych (22–9) — the league leader in wins — with support from Walt Wil-son (16–9) and manager Livengood (12–3, 1.60 ERA). Surprisingly, the offense was rather weak with third baseman Jim Horton (.319, 103 runs) and outfielder Bob Horan (.276, 93 RBIs) the most productive hitters. Unfortu-nately for the Eagles, they were upset in the first round of the playoffs, four games to two, by the Wilson Tobs, the regular season fourth place team. Though the team played well, fan interest dropped. Attendance was down to 41,516, less than half of what it had been two years earlier.

The 1952 season was the last for the Coastal Plain League. The Eagles, now a De-troit Tigers farm club, proved to be its last pennant winners as they posted a record of 76–47. Player-manager Wayne Blackburn hit .350 (second in the league), scoring 91 runs and stealing 33 bases. Left-handed pitcher Gene Host was the league's best with a 26–7 record and an ERA of 1.81. Other notable team members included outfielders Eddie Davis (.297) and Dale Ferris (.272). Ferris also took an occasional turn on the mound and turned in a 4–0 record with an ERA of 2.16. As with the previous season the Eagles were upset in the first round of the playoffs, this time by Goldsboro.

Grainger Stadium sat empty for three seasons until 1956, when the Burlington franchise of the Class B Carolina League relocated to Kinston and changed its name to the Eagles. A Pittsburgh farm club, the team did not play well; their record of 66–87 left them in seventh place, ahead of only Winston-Salem. Outfielder Carl Long (.291, 18 HR, 111 RBIs) — named to the league All-Star team — and pitcher Jim Duffalo (16–8, 2.94 ERA) were that season's best players.

The Eagles, who had signed a new working agreement with Washington, began the season in 1957 but financial difficulties caused the team to move to Wilson on May 11. It would be 1962 before a Carolina League team returned to Kinston. Sticking with the traditional name of Eagles, the new team signed a working agreement with the Pittsburgh Pirates. A phenomenal success, the Eagles finished second in the league standings with a record of 83–57. In attendance they were first drawing over 141,000 spectators, twice as many as the next team, regular season champ Durham. Raleigh, a much larger city than Kinston, drew only 29,552 to see its games. Led by pitchers Steve Blass (17–3, 1.97 ERA) and Frank Bork (19–7, 2.00 ERA), the Eagles went on to win the championship, defeating Winston-Salem in the playoffs and then Durham in the finals. The series with Durham was an exciting one with the Eagles winning the seventh game 3–2.

The Eagles again played well in 1963. They finished first in the Eastern bracket of the now split league with a record of 77–66. Attendance was again first by a huge margin. Outfielder Don Bosch won the batting title with a .332 average, scoring 108 runs and stealing 32 bases, while future New York Yankee shortstop Gene Michael hit .304. Catcher Jim Price was named league Player of the Year, batting .311 with 109 RBIs and 19 home runs. He went on to spend five seasons as a backup catcher for the Detroit Tigers. Unfortunately for the Eagles, they were swept in the first round of the playoffs by Wilson.

Once again winning the Eastern bracket of the league (79–59) in 1964, the Eagles advanced to the playoffs only to be swept again in the first round, this time by Portsmouth. They were hurt by the promotion of their best pitcher, Gary Waslewski (12–1, 1.64 ERA), to Asheville of the Southern League.

The Eagles slipped to third in the East and missed the playoffs in 1965. The team was led by two players who would go on to the major leagues: pitcher Dock Ellis (14–8, 1.98 ERA) and first baseman Mike Derrick (.289, 28 HR, 103 RBIs), both of whom were named to the league All-Star team. Ellis would have a long major league career, winning 138 games over 12 seasons. Derrick would reach the majors for only 24 games with the Boston Red Sox in 1970.

The Atlanta Braves became Kinston's parent team in 1966. Managed by former major league All-Star Andy Pafko, the Eagles finished back on top of the East. The Braves supplied the team with good talent, including pitcher George Stone (8–2, 2.25 ERA), shortstop Al Cambero (115 runs) and outfielder Barry Morgan (104 RBIs), the league leader with 28 home runs. Pitcher Ron Reed was 5–2 for the Eagles on his way to a 19-year big league career. The Eagles' troubles in the playoffs continued as they were swept by Rocky Mount.

The 1967 and '68 seasons were bad ones for the Kinston Eagles. They finished last with records of 60–75 and 62–75. Kinston did have the league batting champ — third baseman Van Kelly (.323) — in 1967. He and first baseman Hal Breeden (.305) made it to the majors for short periods. Pitcher Carl Morton (10–9), had been an outfielder for the Eagles in 1966. After hitting only .227 he switched positions and eventually pitched eight seasons in the majors. In 1968 the Eagles, now a New York Yankees farm team, had outfielder Ron Blomberg (.251). He went on to become the American League's first designated hitter in 1973. All-Star shortstop Frank Baker (.248) would also make it to New York.

In 1969, the Eagles improved to a third

place finish in the Eastern half of the Carolina League. Led by All-Star shortstop Mario Guerrero (.282), outfielder Rusty Torres (.270, 96 runs) and pitcher Bruce Olson (13–6), the Eagles advanced to the extended playoffs. They lost however, to Raleigh-Durham, two games to none. Torres and Guerrero both went on to have average big league careers.

The 1970 season (72–65, fourth place) was not very memorable for Kinston. The next season was much better. The Eagles won the first half of the season and finished with a record of 83–52. Third baseman Otto Velez (.310, 16 HR) and outfielders Wayne Nordhagen (.294, 76 RBIs) and Charlie Spikes (.270, 22 HR) led the team. All three went on to solid major league careers. The Eagle pitching staff featured another future big leaguer: George "Doc" Medich. Joining the team in midseason while on vacation from medical school, Medich won seven games and lost four while striking out 72 batters in 74 innings. Pitcher Don Schroeder also had a good season on the mound, leading the league in strikeouts with 176. Despite the talented team, the Eagles' string of bad luck in the playoffs continued as they were swept by second half champ Peninsula.

Kinston's last year affiliated with the New York Yankees came in 1972. The team had a mediocre season, finishing 6 games out of first, with a record of 73–64. Pitcher Dave Pagan (14–9) was the team's most notable player, leading the league in strikeouts (192) and ERA (2.53). After the season New York dropped its affiliation with the Eagles, forcing the team to operate as a co-op in 1973. Outfielder Terry Whitfield, on his way to a ten year big league career, was named league Player of the Year. He batted .335, hit 18 home runs and drove in 91 runs. Two other future big leaguers — pitchers Tippy Martinez (13–8) and Ron Guidry (7–6) — were on the team. Martinez became an excellent reliever and Guidry was one of the best pitchers in baseball in the late 1970s. Despite all of their talent, the Eagles posted a record of 68–69 in 1973, leaving them in fourth place.

Kinston secured a player development contract with the Montreal Expos in 1974. For the first time the Kinston team would have a name other than the Eagles as they took the name of their parent team. The Kinston Expos had little talent and finished last in the league with a horrible record of 38–93. After that season the financially troubled Kinston franchise, which had also finished last in the league in attendance, dropped out of the Carolina League.

A new Kinston team, again named the Eagles, was formed in 1978 and rejoined the Carolina League. They played as an independent team and met with little success, finishing fifth at 57–77. The team linked up with the Toronto Blue Jays for the 1979 season. Catcher Pat Kelly won the batting title with a .309 average and second baseman Eduardo Dennis (.307) was just behind him. Both were named to the league All-Star team. Kelly would have a major league career that lasted for only three games with Toronto in 1980. Outfielder Jesse Barfield (.264) would have a much longer career, becoming a powerful slugger with the Blue Jays and Yankees. Kinston finished fourth in the league that season with a record of 67–69.

The Kinston teams of the early 1980s met with little success. The 1980 team was third in the once-again split league with an even record of 69–69. Pitcher Mark Eichorn (14–10, 2.90 ERA) went to become a solid big league reliever. In 1981 the team improved slightly to 72–68, again finishing third. Tony Fernandez played shortstop for Kinston in 1980 (.278) and 1981 (.318) on his way to becoming a big league All-Star.

The team changed its name to that of its parent Blue Jays in 1982. They improved their record to 76–59 but remained in third place in the Southern half of the Carolina League. A member of the 1982 Kinston team was Jay Schroeder (.218, 15 HR). He gave up baseball and went on to become a star quarterback in the NFL with the Washington Redskins and Los Angeles Raiders. Even though they posted a losing record of 62–76, the Blue Jays rose to second place in 1983.

The 1979 Kinston Eagles included: *Back:* Mike Lebo, Pat Kelly, Ed Ricks, Mike Darr, Jay Robertson, Jesse Flores, Kem Wright, Keith Walker; *Middle:* Duane Larson (mgr.), Dave Buckley, Jesse Barfield, Bob Silverman, Tom Dejak, Rafael Santana, Mike Coyne, Kirby Patterson, (trainer); *Front:* Eddie Dennis, Benjie Perez, Al Castillo, Ralph "Rocket" Wheeler, Willie Ereu, Pedro Hernandez (courtesy Kinston Indians).

That team featured future big league star Fred McGriff (.243, 21 HR).

The team showed signs of improving in 1984 as they finished only two games out of first with a record of 71–69. Future Detroit Tigers slugger Cecil Fielder (19 HR, 49 RBIs) spent half of a season in Kinston in 1984 before being promoted to AA. The losing continued in 1985, however, as the Blue Jays finished at 64–73. They did improve enough late in the season to win the second half of the Southern Division. Facing Winston-Salem in the playoffs, the Blue Jays lost, two games to none. Leading members of that season's team included outfielder Glenallen Hill (.210, 20 HR, 42 SB), second baseman Nelson Liriano (.288) and first baseman Pat Borders (.261, 60 RBIs).

Kinston's relationship with Toronto ended after the 1985 season. Forced to operate as an independent, the Eagles (as they were renamed) sank to last in the Southern half of the league at 60–76. They did have a few talented players, including All-Star designated hitter Gene Gentile (.267, 26 HR, 85 RBIs) and pitcher Martin Reed (16–6). In 1987 Kinston signed a player development contract with the Cleveland Indians and so changed their name. Managed by former major leaguer Mike Hargrove, the team made a dramatic turnaround that season and finished first in their division with a record of 75–65. Third baseman Casey Webster (.318, 20 HR, 111 RBIs) — the league MVP — and pitcher Andy Ghelfi (12–6) were the stars of the team. Advancing to the playoffs, the Indians defeated Winston-Salem in the first round but lost to Salem, three games to one, in the finals. Those wins were the first by a Kinston team in the postseason since they won the Carolina League pennant in 1962. Since that season Kinston teams had been 0–14 in the playoffs.

Kinston finally won the pennant in 1988. The Indians won both halves of the season in the Southern Division with records of 45–25 and 43–27. They went on to defeat Lynchburg, three games to two, for the league title.

Left to right: Kinston catcher Jesse Levis, outfielder Nolan Lane and first baseman Marc Tepper in 1980 (courtesy the Kinston Indians).

Less than two months into the season, the Indians suspended outfielder Joey (now known as Albert) Belle. Belle (.301, 8 HR) had left the team, saying the game was no longer fun. He returned to baseball (but not Kinston) by the end of the season and went on to become a star player for Cleveland. Kinston had an excellent pitching staff that combined for a team ERA of 3.10. It included Kevin Bearse (10–8, 22 saves, 1.31 ERA), John Githens (11–6), Todd Gonzales (11–5) and Steve Olin (5–2, 8 saves). All-Star utilityman Mike Twardoski (.322, 87 RBIs) led the offense.

The Indians of 1989 had good talent but could not keep up with the Durham Bulls, who won both halves of the season. Led by pitchers Charles Nagy (8–4) and Jeff Mutis (7–3), Kinston finished second in their division with a 76–60 record.

The next season was a much better one as the Indians won both halves and had a combined record of 88–47. All-Star outfielder Ken Ramos won the batting title with a .345 average. Catcher Jesse Levis, a former star at the University of North Carolina, batted .296, as did first baseman Jim Orsag. Cleveland's first round draft pick that season, shortstop Tim Costo, made his debut with Kinston and hit .316 in 56 games. Pitchers Jerry DiPoto and Todd Gonzales were both

11–4. Despite all of this talent the Indians lost to Northern Division champion Frederick in the playoffs, three games to two. Kinston held a 5–0 lead in the deciding game but Frederick came back and won 7–5 (the Indians' best relief pitcher had been promoted to AA). That season Kinston topped 100,000 in attendance for the first time since 1964.

Kinston was more successful in the playoffs of 1991, as they swept Lynchburg to take the pennant in three games. The Indians had won both halves of the season with a combined record of 89–49. The team was led by pitchers Curtis Leskanic (15–8, 2.79 ERA) and Mike Soper, who tied the minor league record with his 41 saves. Kinston's All-Star outfielder Tracy Sanders (.266) led the league in home runs with 18.

The Indians dropped to third in their division in 1992 with a record of 65–71. Pitchers Alan Embree (10–5) and Chad Ogea (13–3) had great first halves and were promoted at midseason. The offense was led by outfielder Manny Ramirez (.278) and first baseman Herbert Perry (.278, 19 HR, 77 RBIs).

In 1993, the Indians played well and won the first half of the season in their division, turning in a combined 71–67 record. They lost to Winston-Salem in the playoffs, however, two games to one. The team included All-Star pitchers Julian Tavarez (11–5, 2.42 ERA) and Ian Doyle (5–1, 23 SV). Outfielder Marc Marini (.300), led the league with 34 doubles.

The 1994 season was a disappointment for Kinston baseball fans as the Indians dropped to last in their division at 60–78. Pitcher Daron Kirkreit (8–7, 2.68 ERA) was considered one of the league's top prospects.

The 1995 Kinston team proved to be one of the most talented in recent Carolina League history. Led by first baseman and league MVP Richie Sexson (.306, 22 HR, 85 RBIs) along with league Pitcher of the Year Bartolo Colon (13–3, 1.96 ERA), the Indians won both halves of the season in their division, finishing 81–56. They went on to take the league pennant by sweeping Wilmington (Del.) in the playoffs, three games to none. Second baseman Ricky Gutierrez (.262, 43 SB) and outfielder James Betszold (.268, 25 HR) joined Sexson and Colon on the league All-Star team.

The Indians again played well in 1996, winning the second half of the season and posting a combined record of 76–62. The team again featured the league batting champ, as All-Star first baseman Sean Casey hit .331.

The pitching staff featured two of the league's best as Noe Najera (12–2, 2.70 ERA), was named as the league's Pitcher of the Year and David Caldwell (13–9) led the league in wins. The playoffs that season were interrupted by Hurricane Fran, which caused serious damage to Grainger Stadium. The final two games of the first round with the Durham Bulls had to be played in Winston-Salem as Durham's ballpark was without power. Kinston prevailed and advanced to face Wilmington, with the entire championship series having to be played in Delaware. The Indians lost the series three games to one. The Indians drew 145,493 fans in 1996, most likely the all-time record for minor league baseball in Kinston.

Landis

When a new North Carolina State League was formed in 1937, the Landis Senators became a charter member of the Class D circuit. The Senators played fairly well in their first year, winning 60 games and losing 51. Their third place finish qualified them for the playoffs, but they lost in the first round to Mooresville, three games to one. Outfielders Dewey Miller (.324) and Charles Whitaker (.318, 93 RBIs) led the offense while Marvin Ferrell (12–4) and Ed Black (11–5) were the team's best pitchers.

The Senators of 1938 did not fare as well. They finished in dead last with a record of 41–71, 34½ games out of first. Outfielder Dewey Miller (.315, 71 RBIs) was the best hitter to spend the entire season with the team. Reid Gowan (7–3) and Harold Burck (16–13) were the most successful members of the otherwise very weak pitching staff.

The 1939 season was just as bad (37–74), with another last place finish. Third baseman Bill Barnes led the team in hitting with a .305 average while Rufe Gentry, who would later play for the Detroit Tigers, was the ace of the pitching staff with a 12–6 record. Legendary

veteran Jim Poole (.269) joined the team in midseason and took over first base, but even he could not help the team win.

The team changed its name to the Dodgers in 1940 after signing a working agreement with Brooklyn, but the losing continued. The team finished seventh at 49–63, rising just one place out of the cellar. Bill Barnes had another good season, though, hitting .326 and leading the league with 14 triples and 47 stolen bases. Longtime minor league player and manager Blackie Carter finished his baseball career with Landis that season, serving as manager and playing in a few games.

In 1941 the team changed its name back to the Senators as they again became independent. It proved to be their worst season yet as they posted a record of 29–71, finishing in seventh, one game ahead of lowly Cooleemee. Pitcher Reid Gowan was probably the team's best player. Though he had an ERA of 2.56, his won-lost record was only 9–6. He probably would have won more of his games had the Senators not had the league's worst team batting average (.247). Gowan was also the team's best hitter with a .368 average in 41 games. Very few members of the Senators spent the entire season with the team. Two of the team's best hitters, second baseman George Motto (.322) and third baseman Bill Barnes (.305), each spent only part of the season in Landis before being sold or traded to other league members.

The next season the team changed its name again, this time to the Millers. They made vast improvements, finishing in fourth place with their first winning season since 1937. Outfielder Nesbit Wilson, in the third season of a minor league career that would last through 1960, batted .312 and hit a league leading 40 doubles. Bob Ennis (12–7, 2.90 ERA) and Jim Hopper (15–9) led the pitching staff. With their record of 59–39 the Millers advanced to the playoffs. In the first round they beat a strong Mooresville club, three games to none. In the finals the Millers took Thomasville to a seventh game before losing.

The league shut down due to the war for the 1943 and '44 seasons. When the war appeared to be winding down the N.C. State League resumed play for the 1945 season. The Millers played good baseball, finishing in third place with 65 wins and 46 losses. Pitching ace Jim Blackwell (14–3), outfielder Glenn Mullinax (.338) and third baseman Felix "Weenie" Stirewalt (.356) led the team. In the first round of the playoffs the Millers defeated Hickory, four games to three. They then went on to take the league championship, beating Lexington, four games to two, in the finals.

The 1946 season saw the winning ways continue. A record of 62–50 put the Millers in second place. They lost, however, a hard fought seven game playoff series to Mooresville. Catcher George Bradshaw (.326) and outfielder Jim Miller (.314) were the top hitters that season. Bradshaw also took a turn on the mound, compiling a 13–6 record with a 2.75 ERA. Veteran pitcher Reid Gowan (13–9, 2.83 ERA) also had a solid season.

The 1947 team, managed by veteran catcher Ginger Watts (.270), slipped to sixth place in the league standings with a record of 51–60. The Spinners did, however, feature the league batting champ as All-Star outfielder Jim Miller hit .402. The team had a few other talented players, including shortstop George Wright (.321) and pitcher Ed Beaumier (16–10), but overall they lacked depth. Attendance was last in the league that season with only 22,596 spectators paying to see the Millers' home games. This led to financial difficulties and the relocation of the franchise to Albemarle after the season.

Landis was without professional baseball for the 1948 season but in 1949 the former Landis franchise was moved back to the town from Albemarle. Renamed the Spinners, the team signed a working agreement with the Atlanta Crackers of the Southern League, who supplied the team with playing manager Fred Chapman, a native of nearby Kannapolis. The Spinners did well that first year back in the league, winning 69 games and losing 53 for a third place finish. Manager Chapman (.366, 122 RBIs), who had played parts of three seasons with the Philadelphia Athletics before the war, tied for the league lead within 169 hits. Shortstop Bob Deese (.323), who tied for the league lead with 12 triples, was the Spinners' second best hitter. The pitching staff had several talented members, including Francis Killian (9–3, 2.42 ERA), Jim Hopper (17–8) and Bob Palmer (14–6). In the playoffs the Spinners lost in the first round to High Point-Thomasville, four games to one.

The Spinners of 1950, again led by third baseman and manager Fred Chapman (.354, 83 RBIs), finished in third place. Outfielder Owen Linn (.334, 21 HR, 110 RBIs) provided much of the team's power while pitcher Charlie Moore (20–9) led the league in wins. The Spinners beat Salisbury, four games to two, in the playoffs and went on to take their second league championship by defeating High Point–Thomasville in the finals, four games to three. Attendance for the team was up to nearly 32,000 but was still low compared to some of the other towns in the league.

The 1951 season was the last for minor league baseball in Landis.

Due to poor attendance, team owners decided to move the team to Elkin on July 18. The team played well, finishing in third place, but the fans had lost interest.

♦ ── *Leaksville-Spray-Draper* ── ♦

The first professional baseball team to represent the three small Rockingham County towns of Leaksville, Spray and Draper was the aptly named Triplets in 1934. The team was a charter franchise in the Class D Bi-State League, a league made up of three North Carolina and three Virginia teams. The Triplets were not very successful that first season and finished fifth at 32–44. Third baseman Woody Williams (.398), league leader with 86 runs scored, had a great season on his way to a short major league career. He returned to the Triplets in 1935, hitting .337 and again leading the league as he scored 111 runs. The team played much better that season, finishing with a league best record of 71–44. Unfortunately, they failed to win either half of a split season so were not eligible for the playoffs. Manager-outfielder Blackie Carter (.356, 98 runs), who played for eight different minor league teams in the state, won the home run title with 30.

Managed by former big league catcher Clyde Sukeforth, the 1936 Triplets won the first half of the season. They were not as strong in the second half and finished with the league's third best overall record (65–51). In the playoffs, the Triplets lost out to second half champ Bassett, four games to two. Joe McCabe (.363, 111 RBIs) and Cyril Kalback (.346, 100 runs) led the offensive attack that season with help from manager Sukeforth, who hit .365 playing part-time. The team's best hitter, outfielder George Cisar (.377, 69 RBIs), played only 67 games with the team before being sold to the Brooklyn Dodgers.

In 1937, the Triplets signed a working agreement with Wilkes-Barre of the Class A New York–Penn League. Apparently, the relationship supplied little in the way of talent to the Triplets, as they spent both the seasons of 1937 and '38 in the league cellar. The '37 Triplets record of 41–73 left them 27½ games out of first. They did have a few talented players, including outfielder George Scantling (.319, 23 HR) and pitcher John Ragar (13–15), who also played in the field. A better pitcher than his record would indicate, Ragar was also the team's leading hitter with a .364 average. The Triplets of '38, even worse than the previous season's team, finished 40½ games back with a 37–82 record.

The team improved in 1939 to finish second in the league with a record of 67–48. In the first round of the playoffs the Triplets beat Martinsville but they lost in the finals to Danville, four games to two. The team had two outstanding players that season who became minor league stars: second baseman Jimmy Gruzdis (.368, 145 runs, 46 SB) and outfielder Cecil "Zip" Payne (.389, 126 RBIs, 110 runs). Both had long, distinguished minor league careers but neither made the big leagues. Pitcher Forrest Thompson, who spent the 1948 and '49 seasons in the majors, was 7–3 for the Triplets.

The Triplets (56–63) dropped to a sixth place finish in 1940. Zip Payne (.316, 100 RBIs) was again with the team and had another good season. The team's offense also included third baseman Emmitt Johnson (.357) and outfielder Jim Milner (.337, 80 RBIs). Clyde Teague was the Triplets' best pitcher with his 16–8 record. Payne returned in 1941, hitting .357 with 75 RBIs to lead the team to the pennant and a 64–46 finish. Pitcher Charlie Cuellar (16–7) tied for the league lead in wins while striking out 182. Catcher Harry Land hit .303 with 86 RBIs and manager Wes Ferrell, recently retired from a long major league career, played outfield and hit .351 with 114 RBIs. Third baseman Joe Frazier (.309) would spend four seasons as a player in the major leagues and then return to manage the New York Mets in 1976 and '77. Despite their talent, the Triplets were upset in the playoffs by Danville, four games to one.

The 1942 season was the last for the Bi-State League and the Triplets finished fifth, winning 57 games and losing 66. In his

The 1941 Leaksville-Spray-Draper Triplets included: *Back:* Vinnie Fernandez, Lynwood "Hank" Tillotson, unidentified, Harold Scalpini, Al Letrick, Ken Rhyne, unidentified, Joe Frazier, unidentified; *Front:* Cecil "Zip" Payne, Cotton Powell, Harry Land, Charlie Cuellar, unidentified (courtesy Harry Land).

fourth season with the team Zip Payne hit .301 and drove in 64 runs. Charlie Cuellar (22–6) returned and was the league's dominant pitcher, leading the circuit in wins, strikeouts (204) and ERA (1.67). Cuellar was one of the best minor league pitchers of the 1940s, winning 209 games and losing only 123 in his career. He finally reached the majors at age 32, appearing in two games as a reliever for the 1950 Chicago White Sox.

The Class C Carolina League was formed in 1945 from the remnants of the Bi-State League, with the L-S-D Triplets as a charter member. They finished that season at 66–70, fifth in the eight team league. Talented Bill Bustle was the team's best all-around player. Named to the league All-Star team, he batted .286 and as a left-handed pitcher was 16–7 with a 2.81 ERA. The next season the Triplets finished last at 57–85.

Outfielder W.L. Hobson was the only offensive star of the team, as he hit .350 and drove in 126 runs. All-Star pitcher Frank Paulin, league leader in both strikeouts (220) and wins (19), pitched a still standing league record 303 innings and 31 complete games. He would doubtless, have won more games had he played for a better team.

The Triplets were not much better in 1947—their last season in the Carolina League—as they finished seventh at 59–82. Former major league third baseman Bill Nagel (.290, 30 HR, 128 RBIs) played much of the season with Leaksville but was sold to Raleigh after 85 games. Second baseman Joe Trotta (.317) and shortstop Walter "Teapot" Frye (.308) were the Triplets' best hitters, while Tal Abernathy (14–12, 3.18 ERA) was the top pitcher. The team suffered financially and, announcing it was $8,600 in debt,

Leaksville team bus with driver Rabbit Martin, 1941 (courtesy Harry Land).

decided to fold during the season. The league stepped in, however, and helped the Triplets complete the season. They folded for good after the season.

A new team was formed in 1948 for membership in the Class D Blue Ridge League. Unfortunately, team owner Ed Weingarten was banned from baseball for life for involve-ment in the gambling scandal at Reidsville. He was forced to sell the franchise to a group from Abingdon, Virginia, and the team was moved to that town. That season was the last for minor league baseball in Leaksville, Spray and Draper. In 1967 the three towns merged to form the town of Eden.

 Lenoir

Lenoir is another of the many towns that played in the semipro textile leagues before ever fielding a professional team. In 1937 a team was formed for entry into the professional Carolina League. This league was considered an "outlaw league" by orga-nized baseball since it was not a member of the National Association. Named the Lenoir Finishers, the team finished fifth that first season with a 42–54 record. They im-proved to 60–39 in 1938 to win the league pennant. First baseman and manager Bobby Hipps, a well-traveled minor league veteran, led the team in hitting with a .361 average.

George Boutwell (17–4) was the league's top pitcher.

The Carolina League ceased operations after the 1938 season, and in 1939 Lenoir be-came a charter member of the Class D Tar Heel League. Home games were played at 3,000 seat Lenoir Athletic Park. The park had a very short left field (260 feet), a 410-foot cen-ter field and a long right field (385 feet). The team, named the Indians, played well in their first season, finishing at 61–46 in second place. They were swept, however, in the first round of the playoffs by Statesville. First baseman Birch Douglass was the team's offensive leader that season, hitting .365 with 21 home runs and scoring a league leading 127 runs. Catcher Marvin Felderman (.314), who was named to the league All-Star team, had a good season, as did pitcher Witt "Lefty" Guise (15–7).

For the 1940 season the team changed its name to the Reds after joining the Cincinnati farm system. They had an average season, winning 53 games and losing 55. Finishing in fourth place, the Reds qualified for the playoffs but lost once again in the first round to Statesville, three games to two. Catcher Ray Rice (.329) and center fielder Frank Shone (.303, 16 HR) were both named to the league All-Star team.

The Tar Heel League (in its first incarnation) disbanded after the 1940 season. Lenoir was without professional baseball until 1946, when the Salem (Va.) Friends of the Class D Blue Ridge League decided to relocate. Team owner Stanley Radke decided to move the team because Salem couldn't furnish lights for night games. The Friends moved to Lenoir and, since they had a working agreement with Boston, changed their name to the Red Sox. They played their first game in town on June 25 at 2,500 seat Lenoir High School Park.

The Red Sox dominated the small four team Blue Ridge League. They finished the season with a record of 71–35, taking the pennant by 11 games. Outfielder Eddie Wayne (.403, 77 RBIs) won the batting title, while third baseman Richard Kalal (.308) led in runs with 127. Shortstop-manager Noel Casbier hit .333 with 97 RBIs. Pitchers Ed Wallace (13–4), Richard Cooper (10–5) and Don Roode (14–5) gave the Red Sox the league's best staff.

The winning ways of the Lenoir Red Sox left them in 1947. The team nearly reversed its record of the previous year, finishing in last place at 43–73. Manager Noel Casbier, who played shortstop as well as pitcher, led the team as he again hit for a .333 average. His 12 home runs led the league. Outfielder Nick Ciani (.324) also had a good season at the plate. No pitcher, including manager Casbier (4–5), had a winning record. For some reason it was decided that all four league members should be involved in the

playoffs that season. Lenoir upset Mt. Airy in the first round and nearly won the league championship as they took first place Galax to a seventh game in the finals before losing.

After the 1947 season the Red Sox left the Blue Ridge League and joined the new Class D Western Carolina League. It was a league made up of teams located closer to Lenoir and all of them were in North Carolina (two of the four members of the Blue Ridge League had been in Virginia). The first two years in the new league were not successful ones for the Lenoir team on the field. The 1948 season saw the Red Sox finish seventh (out of eight teams). That team was led by outfielder Carl Schardt (.347) and first baseman Ralph Satterfield (.346). In 1949, the team, which had signed a working agreement with the New York Giants (yet surprisingly kept the name Red Sox), improved slightly to finish fifth. All-Star shortstop Noel Casbier (.343, 21 HR, 109 RBIs) led the team in hitting. Financially, the team did much better in the new league. Attendance rose from 25,592 in 1947 to 38,710 in 1948 to 43,660 in 1949.

In 1950, the Red Sox, managed by former big league pitcher Claude Jonnard for a third season, improved greatly. The team finished half a game out of first with a 60–47 record. In the first round of the playoffs they defeated Marion, four games to three, and went on to beat Newton-Conover, also in seven games, in the finals to take the league championship. Outfielder Bob Featherstone, who led the league with 27 home runs, and third baseman Tom Marino were named to the league All-Star team.

The 1951 season was the last one for professional baseball in Lenoir. The Red Sox slipped all the way down to a seventh place finish (40–70, 31 games back). Outfielder Bob Featherstone batted .348 and scored 94 runs to lead the team. Pitcher Okey Flowers (12–11) was better than his record would indicate. Attendance dropped drastically that season to only 17,736, down from 42,996 the previous year. Loss of interest by the fans and poor playing by the team spelled the end for the Lenoir Red Sox as they dropped out of the league and disbanded.

Lexington

The Davidson County town of Lexington got its first professional baseball team in 1936. That season the Forest City franchise of the independent Carolina League decided to relocate after a month of play, choosing Lexington as their new home. The Lexington Indians played poorly and finished in a distant sixth place with a record of 37–61. The team's only real standout was pitcher Bill Strickland. At midseason, the only time from which statistics are available, he had a record of 8–3. The following season Strickland would appear in nine games for the St. Louis Browns. The Indians disbanded after the season.

In 1937, a new Lexington Indians team was organized by local businessmen A.C. Fite and Edgar Timberlake to become a charter member of the Class D North Carolina State League. The Indians signed a working agreement with the Williamsport Grays of the Class A New York–Penn League, themselves a farm team of the Philadelphia Athletics. This was a relationship that would last for four years. That first season in the league was not very successful, as the Indians finished sixth out of the eight teams with a 50–59 record. Outfielder Bill Carrier, however, did win the league batting title with a .388 average while pitcher Wilbur Reeser (12–9) led the league with 177 strikeouts. With a 17–2 record, Les McCrabb was the team's best pitcher. He would make it up to the Philadelphia A's in 1939.

The Indians played the 1936 and '37 seasons at 2,000 seat Wennonah Field, which had previously been the home to the textile league teams of Wennonah Cotton Mills. After the 1937 season the mill offered to donate the park to the city if a new stadium would be built. The city agreed and worked out a deal with the WPA. The new Holt-Moffitt Field (named after the owners of the cotton mill) seated 3,000 and was ready shortly after the beginning of the 1938 season. The ballpark's dimensions in 1938 were 324 feet to left, 378 to center, and 314 to right. Holt-Moffitt would be the home to all Lexington teams thereafter.

Led by pitcher Wilbur Reeser (15–9) and left fielder Harry Leonard (.344) — both of whom were named to the league All-Star team — the Indians improved to third place in 1938 with a 66–46 record. Bill Carrier returned and played well in half a season with the team, hitting .380 with 14 home runs. The Indians qualified for the playoffs but lost to Davidson County neighbor and archrival Thomasville, three games to none.

The 1939 team finished second with a record identical to the previous season. Outfielder Gus Juskey (.328) led the team in hitting while pitcher Paige Dennis, who split the season with Thomasville, posted a combined 17–10 record. Again the Indians lost to Thomasville in the playoffs, though it was closer this time, three games to two.

In 1940 the Indians won what would prove to be the only league championship for a Lexington team. They finished the regular season in third place at 64–48. Advancing to the playoffs, the Indians swept Kannapolis in the first round, and in the finals defeated Mooresville, four games to one. Outfielder Roy Pinkston, who began the season with Landis before coming over to Lexington, won the batting title, hitting .383. Other members of the strong offense included outfielder Borden Helms (.336) and All-Star shortstop-manager Lester Smith (.315). First baseman Stan Lujack (.227) never met with the same successes on the athletic field that his younger brother Johnny enjoyed. Johnny would win the 1947 Heisman Trophy while quarterback of Notre Dame's football team. After winning the championship the Indians went on to play a series with the Statesville Owls, champions of the Tar Heel League. The Owls prevailed in that series, however, four games to two.

The 1941 Indians dropped back to sixth

Lexington's Bill Carrier (back row, third from left) won the 1937 North Carolina's State League batting title with a .388 average (courtesy Betty Fite).

in the league standings. Their 47–53 record left them 23 games out of first. Roy Pinkston (.323)—who led the league with his 13 triples—and pitcher Norman Shope (13–5) were the team's standouts that season. The team improved only slightly the next season to a fifth place, 55–44 record. Outfielders Phil Morris (.353) and Roy Pinkston (.350) led the team in hitting while former major leaguer Baxter "Buck" Jordan, the team's manager, hit .321. After that season the North Carolina State League suspended operations due to the war.

The league resumed play in 1945, one of only four Class D leagues to operate that season. The new Lexington team, now called the A's, was owned and operated by the Philadelphia Athletics. Led by outfielder and league batting champ Homer Lee Cox (.367), the team played well and finished second. Cox, who had been a star for Guilford College, played for several teams in the league and later served three terms as Davidson County Sheriff. A's catcher Guy Clodfelter (.355) finished

third in batting while Bill Miller (14–5) was one of the league's best pitchers. The team took its 69–46 record into the playoffs to face Salisbury in the first round. Lexington prevailed, four games to one, but lost to Landis, four games to two, in the finals.

Nineteen forty-six saw Lexington finish last in the league with a 34–75 record. Pitcher Ray Lindsay (9–4, 2.29 ERA, 105 SO) had a great first half of the season before being sold to Martinsville of the Carolina League. Seventeen-year-old first baseman Lou Limmer, who would eventually reach the big leagues, hit .313 in 40 games. The team improved to fourth place in 1947 with a 54–56 record. Lou Limmer returned and had another good season, hitting .326 with 24 home runs and 95 RBIs, while manager Homer Lee Cox hit .340 as a part-time catcher. The A's defeated Salisbury in seven games in the first round of the playoffs but lost to Mooresville, also in seven games, in the finals.

Lexington, renamed the Indians, finished

The 1940 Lexington Indians included: *Back:* L.C. "Buck" Kelly, Roy Pinkston, Ray Ross, Reid Gowan, Fremont Connor, Wilbur Reeser, Ramon Couto; *Front:* Paul Gassoway, George Saab, Robert "Buck" Glover, A.C. Fite (owner), Lester Smith (mgr.), Stan Hoyniski, Walter Posey, Borden "Goose" Helms (courtesy Betty Fite).

fourth in the league in both 1948 and 1949. The 1948 team, at 59–50, lost in the first round of the playoffs to Statesville, four games to one. Second baseman Gray Hampton finished second in the league in batting with a .374 average. The 1949 team, led by pitchers Plaskie McCree (13–6, 2.19 ERA) and Harold Wood (18–12, 2.65 ERA), turned in a 60–64 record. The Indians swept Mooresville in the first round of the playoffs but lost in the finals, four games to three, to High Point–Thomasville.

The team, with its name changed back to the A's, slipped to sixth place in 1950 with a 49–62 record. Outfielder Bill Stewart, who would make a brief appearance with the big league Athletics, hit .348 in 64 games, followed by Gray Hampton (19 HR) at .331. Plaskie McCree again pitched well, achieving an 18–9 record despite playing for a team with a losing record.

Once again named the Indians in 1951, and still with a Philadelphia Athletics work-

ing agreement, the team had an average season. They finished with a fifth place, 61–65 record, missing the playoffs by one game. Outfielder Miles Carter (.344) and second baseman Gray Hampton (.321), who managed the team for part of the season, were that team's leading hitters. Pitcher Plaskie McCree was again one of the league's best at 20–10, walking only 62 batters in 280 innings.

The 1952 season, the last for the North Carolina State League, saw Lexington play poorly and finish last at 30–77. Plaskie McCree was responsible for more than half of the team's wins with his record of 16–9. That season also marked the last for catcher Cliff Bolton as he finished out his 25 year baseball career playing with the Indians. The 45-year-old Bolton, who had played in 335 major league games, hit .344 in 27 games for Lexington.

With the demise of the Western Carolina and North Carolina State leagues after the 1952 season, several members of those leagues decided to form a new league. That led to the creation of the Tar Heel League — also Class D — with the Lexington Indians a charter member. Managed by second baseman Alex Monchak (.232), the Indians finished the regular season in fourth place with a 59–54 record. In the first round of the playoffs the team beat Rutherford County, four games to two. They then took the championship, upsetting Marion in the finals, also by a four-games-to-two margin. The team was led by a good pitching staff which included William Forgay (10–7, 2.76 ERA), Ralph Poole (15–9, 3.10 ERA) and George Burrell (10–6). First baseman Don Stafford (.374, 19 HR, 124 RBIs), who began the season with the High Point–Thomasville team and joined the Indians when that team failed, won the batting title and led the league in RBIs.

Despite the success on the field, the team disbanded after the season due to financial difficulties. The entire league, down to only four teams out of the ten that started the 1953 season, disbanded in June of 1954.

When a new Western Carolina League was formed in 1960, Lexington joined. The independent team, again called the Indians, had a great season and finished first, winning 70 games and losing only 29. Outfielder Herby Burnette (.343) and outfielder-catcher Robert Cannon (.311, 71 RBIs) provided much of the offense for the team. Pitchers Bill Bethea (11–3, 1.35 ERA), the league ERA leader, and James Harrell (13–4, 2.50 ERA) both had outstanding seasons. Unfortunately for the Indians, they were upset in the playoffs by Hickory.

The next season the team finished third. Advancing to the playoffs with their 51–53 record, the Indians upset Statesville in the first round but lost to Shelby, two games to one, in the finals. Outfielder Ron Henson finished second in the league in batting with a .346 average. Other than Henson, however, the team had little offense. A decent pitching staff, led by Gary Bodenheimer (7–7)

and George Warfford (9–11) got poor run support.

Lexington did not field a team in the Western Carolinas League in 1962 but returned in 1963. That team, managed by longtime St. Louis Cardinal pitcher Max Lanier, was a San Francisco Giants farm club. Taking the name of their parent team, the Lexington Giants had an average season, finishing fourth at 64–60. Shortstop Cesar Gutierrez (.320), third in league batting, had a short major league career as a utility outfielder with the Giants and Tigers. Nineteen-year-old outfielder Bob Taylor (.293) made it to San Francisco for part of the 1970 season.

Max Lanier was back at the helm in 1964 and led the improved team to a third place, 71–54 finish. That team lacked in hitting but had a good pitching staff led by Rich Licklider (16–6, 1.52 ERA), Herm Alvarez (13–8, 2.24 ERA) and Dick Bosman (8–5, 3.21 ERA). Bosman made it to the major leagues in 1966 and stayed there for 11 seasons, pitching for several American League teams.

Again managed by Lanier in 1965, the Giants finished fourth at 62–54, seven games out of first. Pitcher Mike Corkins (11–9) went on to pitch several seasons for San Diego after the Padres drafted him from the Giants in the 1968 expansion draft. The next season Lexington dropped to the league cellar, 52½ games out of first, as they won only 37 games and lost 86. Shortstop Chris Arnold (.255) would go on to spend six seasons as a utility infielder with San Francisco.

The 1967 season was the last for minor league baseball in Lexington. That season's team switched affiliations to the Atlanta Braves, also changing its name to the Braves. They finished fourth in the five team league with a 55–63 record. First baseman Paul Tenebrous (.311, 16 HR, 83 RBIs) and catcher Walter Czopczyc (.309) — both named as league All-Stars along with shortstop Udell Chambers (.325) — were among the league's best players.

Lincolnton

The Lincolnton Cardinals were one of the eight original members of the Western Carolina League when it was formed in 1948. The Cardinals played well that first year and took home the league pennant with a record of 69–41. In the playoffs they beat Morganton, four games to two, and then edged Newton-Conover, four games to three, in the finals. The Cardinals had an outstanding offense and batted .307 as a team. Outfielder and manager Russell "Red" Mincy, who joined the team at midseason, hit .323. The team's leading hitter, shortstop Junior Dodgin (.367), teamed with his outfielder brother Jim (.291) to provide much of the team's offense.

In 1949, the Cardinals finished the season with a record identical to that of the previous year, though this time it was good enough only for second place. All-Star first baseman and manager Carl Miller was the dominant offensive player in the league that season. He led the league in batting average (.404), runs (125), hits (159) and home runs (22). Other members of the strong offense included All-Star second baseman Bus Huffstetler (.333, 104 RBIs) and shortstop Junior Dodgin (.318, 71 RBIs). The team's top pitchers were Harold Abernathy (8–2), Warren Richards (10–4) and Sam Jones (16–7). The Cardinals wound up losing to Morganton that year in the playoffs, four games to three.

Fifth place was the best the Cardinals could do in 1950 with a 49–61 record. They improved to 67–45 in 1951, good enough for third place. All-Star shortstop Bob Peters finished third in the league in batting that season at .373, while stealing 41 bases and scoring 105 runs. Third baseman and manager Bobby Beal, also named an All-Star, hit .336. The pitching staff featured two 20-game winners, William Roland (20–7) and Rogelio Perez (20–8). Like the 1949 playoffs, the Cardinals again lost to Morganton, four games to three.

Lincolnton was back on top in 1952, the final season of the Western Carolina League. Led by manager Bobby Beal, they took the pennant by finishing half a game ahead of Shelby with a record of 72–39. Third baseman Carroll Wright (155 hits) and outfielder George Rose (107 RBIs) were both named to the league All-Star team. In the playoffs they easily defeated Marion, four games to one. In the finals, however, the Cardinals lost to Shelby in seven games.

After the 1952 season, both the Western Carolina and the North Carolina State leagues disbanded. Many of the former members of these two leagues joined together to form the new Tar Heel League (still Class D). The Lincolnton Cardinals were one such franchise. Professional baseball was declining in the smaller towns of North Carolina by 1953. Season attendance was down for Lincolnton, from 66,766 in 1949 to 48,711 in 1950 and to 30,503 in 1952 (and this was for a first place team). Attendance for the 1953 Cardinals was a dismal 6,941 by midseason so the owners decided to move the team to Statesville on July 12. The franchise lasted only the rest of that season before disbanding.

Lumberton

Lumberton joined the year-old Class D Tobacco State League as a new franchise in 1947. A member of the Chicago Cubs farm system, they named themselves after their parent team. Former big league pitcher Red Lucas served as manager that first season as the team began play at Armory Field. Led by first baseman Elzer Marx (.315, 100 RBIs, 122 runs) and pitchers Bob Spicer (16–7) and Doug Lorman (16–6) the Cubs' first season

1949 Lumberton Auctioneers (courtesy Cecil Tyson).

was a good one. They finished the regular season in second place with a record of 71–49. In the first round of the playoffs they easily defeated Dunn-Erwin, four games to one. In the finals, the Cubs, though leading the series three games to none, lost to Sanford, four games to three. All of the Cubs playoff games that season that fell on a Sunday had to be played in Red Springs since Sunday baseball was not allowed in Lumberton.

The 1948 season was not as successful for the Lumberton Cubs. Managed by outfielder Charlie Jamin (.281), they finished the year in seventh place, 25 games out of first, with a 55–81 record. First baseman Dean Padgett (.310, 16 HR, 115 RBIs, 105 runs) provided most of the Cubs' offense.

In 1949 the Lumberton team changed its name to the Auctioneers, though they remained a part of the Chicago Cubs organization. The Auks, as they were often called, won 75 games that year and lost 61, finishing in third place. They qualified for the playoffs but lost to Dunn-Erwin, four games to one, in the first round. First baseman Cecil "Turkey"

Tyson (.318) and All-Star outfielder Bill Bohlender (.305, 88 RBIs, 101 runs) were the team's leading hitters, while lefty Gordon McDonald (15–6, 2.95 ERA) and August Vierra (14–7) led the pitching staff. Attendance for 1949 was first in the league, as the team drew 60,038 fans.

The Auctioneers of 1950 were an outstanding team. Led by first baseman–manager John Streza (.320, 111 RBIs), they finished the season in first with a record of 92–43. All-Star shortstop Mike Milosevich (.314, 14 HR, 121 RBIs) led the league in both home runs and RBIs while second baseman Pierre Ethier (.300, 43 SB, 135 BB) led in runs with 146. Unfortunately for the Auks, they were upset in the first round of the playoffs, four games to two, by fourth place Rockingham.

Attendance was down all across the league in 1950. It dropped to less than 43,000 for the Auctioneers that year although they did lead the league. Due to this loss of interest, which caused financial difficulties for many of the teams, the league decided to fold after the season.

Marion

The Marion Marauders were a charter franchise in the Class D Western Carolina League in 1948. To accommodate the team, bleachers and box seats were added to the high school athletic field, increasing seating capacity to around 3,500. The Marauders were managed in their inaugural season by longtime major league pitcher Wes Ferrell, a native of Greensboro. Playing in the outfield, Ferrell proved to be quite an outstanding hitter as he led the league in batting with a .425 average. He was supported by All-Star second baseman Harold Holt (.366) and first baseman Charlie Ferguson (.320, 20 HR, 99 RBIs). Ernest Brown was the top pitcher at 14–8. Though they had several talented players, the Marauders lacked depth and finished in only sixth place (out of eight) that first season at 49–54.

The Marauders finished much the same in 1949, in sixth place with a record of 40–62. All-Star outfielder Tom Cumby (.347, 80 RBIs) was the team leader. The 1950 season saw the team post a winning record for the first time as they finished at 56–54, good enough for fourth place. Player–manager Red Mincy (.421, 104 RBIs, 98 runs, 161 hits) had an outstanding season, winning the league batting title. The Marauders qualified for the playoffs but lost in the first round to Lenoir, four games to three.

The 1951 team, again managed by Red Mincy, posted another winning record (58–52), but slipped in the standings to sixth place. Mincy (.353, 66 RBIs) and fellow outfielders Jack Netcher (.352) and Jack Triplett (.348, 103 runs, 27 SB) were the team's offensive leaders. Hoyt Clegg was the leading pitcher at 11–3. The next season a nearly identical record (58–50) put the Marauders in third place. They lost in the first round of the playoffs, however, to Lincolnton, four games to one.

After the 1952 season the Western Carolina League folded, so for the 1953 season Marion joined the newly formed Tar Heel League. The Marauders dominated the new league, winning the pennant with a record of 74–35. The team had several outstanding players, including pitcher Jack Swift (30–7, 2.54 ERA, 321 SOs) and outfielder Carl Miller (.333, 129 runs, 21 HRs). Manager Bob Beal hit .314 while playing second base. In the first round of the playoffs the Marauders defeated Shelby, four games to two. They were upset in the finals, however, by Lexington, the regular season fourth place team, four games to two.

The Tarheel League began play in 1954 with only four teams. Financial difficulties soon caught up with the remaining teams and the league folded on June 21. Managed by catcher Bob Knoke (.319), the Marauders had a record of 26–26 when they disbanded. That partial season proved to be the last for professional baseball in Marion.

Mayodan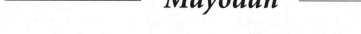

The textile mill town of Mayodan was an original member of the Class D Bi-State League when it entered professional baseball in 1934. The Mayodan Senators, as they were called, did not do well in their professional baseball debut. The team, which had a working agreement with Louisville of the American Association, finished last in the league of six with a record of 29–45. Outfielders Cecil Payne (.375, 32 2B) and Eddie Weston (.333, 26 HR) did play well, however, and managed to be among the league leaders.

The 1953 Marion Marauders included: *Back:* James Mendenhall, Fred Parnell, Dwight Feimster, Curt Ballentine, Jack Swift, unidentified, Joe Hornacek, Bill Collins; *Front:* Carl Miller, Richard Hendricks, Robert Van Tarleton, James Smiley, Bob Barker, Bob Thomas, Bobby Beal (courtesy David Beal).

They had fairly impressive numbers considering the team only played 74 games. Cecil "Zip" Payne went on to play five seasons with Mayodan. Over that time period his batting average was .368. He would play 17 seasons in the minors (14 of them in North Carolina) without ever reaching the major leagues.

In 1935 the Mayodan team changed its name to the Mills. All-Star outfielder Zip Payne had one of his best seasons ever, hitting .386, but he lost the batting title to Ralph Hodgin of Fieldale by .001. First baseman and manager Phil Lundeen hit .308. The team improved slightly from the previous year, their record of 51–63 putting them in fifth place out of eight teams, 19½ games back.

The 1936 team, with its name changed to the Orphans, finished in the league cellar, winning 35 games and losing 83. Manager Phil Lundeen (.371, 84 RBIs), who finished second in the league in batting, was the team's best player.

The 1937 season saw a complete turnaround. The Senators, having changed back to their original name, signed a working agreement with the Charlotte Hornets of the Piedmont League, a team owned by the Washington Senators. The team played well and finished in a tie atop the Bi-State League with a record of 69–46. First baseman Doug Wheeler led the league in batting (.359) and runs scored (111) while fellow All-Star Zip Payne (.351, 85 RBIs, 102 runs) was the league leader in hits with 167. The deep and talented pitching staff featured ace Jesse Plummer (21–9) along with Jim Fogleman (13–4) and Claude Weaver (10–4). Overall the Senators had a great year, with the exception of losing to the Martinsville Manufacturers, three games to two, in the playoffs.

The team, with its name changed to the Millers, again played well in 1938. They finished in second place, winning 73 games and losing 46. The Millers were swept in the playoffs, however, by the Danville Leafs. Manager and All-Star third baseman Harry Daughtry, along with outfielders Eddie Weston and Zip Payne (.353, 97 RBIs), were the team leaders.

In 1939, the team signed a working agreement with the Philadelphia Phillies. It was an unsuccessful season on the field, however, as the Millers dropped to a fifth place finish with a record of 58–57, 12½ games out of first. Outfielder Amerigo Scagliarini (.333, 91 RBIs, 27 HR) led the league in home runs, while future major leaguer Frank "Lefty" Hoerst (8–9) led the league in ERA with 2.82. Hoerst debuted in the majors the next year with the Phillies and pitched in 98 games for them over parts of five seasons. Two other Mayodan players — pitcher Gene Lambert (13–2) and outfielder Paul Busby (.354) — would also appear in a few games for the Phillies, while second baseman Steve Shemo (.272) spent parts of the 1944 and '45 seasons with the Braves. Manager William "Chick" Outen, who hit .411 in 39 games, had spent the 1933 season as the backup catcher for the Brooklyn Dodgers.

The Millers finished the season at 53–66 in 1940, good enough only to avoid the cellar and finish seventh. The league batting title was won by Mayodan's All-Star outfielder Dan Amaral (.387, 23 HR, 86 RBIs), while fellow outfielder Alex Johnson (.357, 17 HR) led the league in runs with 119. The team's talented offense also included first baseman Robert Bond (.350), outfielder Dewey Miller (.320, 87 RBIs) and second baseman Steve Shemo (.291). Though the Senators had a wealth of good hitters, they lacked pitching.

The final season for professional baseball in Mayodan came in 1941. It was not even to be a complete season as the Millers withdrew from the league on July 18. An attempt had been made to move the team to Reidsville at the end of June that year and the Millers actually played four games at Lucky Strike Park in Reidsville to test the market. On July 3, the team owners turned over control of the team to league officials. It appeared that the team would stay in Reidsville and the July 3 game was actually played with the team's name officially changed to the Reidsville Luckies. On July 5, the owners from Mayodan decided to keep the team and brought it back . The Millers' subsequent 15 game losing streak caused a loss of interest and the team owners called it quits for good on July 18. At that time the Millers' record stood at 25–47. Outfielder Eddie Weston (.392) was leading the league in hitting and first baseman–manager Taylor Sanford was batting .353 when the team disbanded.

The Mayodan Ball Park was located on 5th Avenue, a few blocks northwest of the mill (formerly Washington Mills, now a division of Tultex). A baseball field still exists on the site but nothing remains of the old park. The original grandstand was located in what today is center field.

 Monroe

Monroe got its first professional baseball team in 1969 when the Statesville Indians of the Class A Western Carolinas League decided to relocate in midseason due to poor attendance. The move took place on June 20, and the name Indians was retained as they were a Cleveland farm club. The team was managed that year by Pinky May (former Philadelphia Phillies third baseman) and finished with a mediocre record of 61— 63, eight games out of first. Attendance of 27,570

was last in the league. Outfielder Cecil Rankhorn (.299, 32 stolen bases) played well, as did pitcher Mike Biko (11–5, 3.07 ERA), one of the best in the league. The Indians disbanded after the season and Monroe was without baseball for the 1970 season.

In 1971 the Monroe Pirates, an affiliate of the Pittsburgh Pirates, entered the Western Carolina League as a new franchise. The team, managed by Tom Saffell, finished in dead last, 40 games out of first, with a record of 44–77. Attendance was last with a dismal 11,587 for the season, over 2,000 less than the next-to-last-place team. Playing in 31 games, outfielder Tony Armas hit .227 with one home run. He would hit 251 home runs in a 14-year major league career.

Monroe had an even bigger future major league star in outfielder Dave Parker. In 71 games for Monroe, Parker hit .358 with 11 home runs. When he retired in 1991 after 19 big league seasons, Parker had hit 339 home runs and driven in 1,493 runs. He also won two batting titles and finished with a lifetime .290 batting average.

The Monroe Pirates, due to financial difficulties brought on by the team's extremely low attendance, disbanded after the season.

◆ ——————— *Mooresville* ——————— ◆

Mooresville had a long history of semi-pro and textile league baseball before it ever fielded a truly professional team. Mooresville Cotton Mills, the foundation of the whole town, had sponsored teams as far back as 1919 to provide entertainment for mill workers. The Mooresville Baseball Park, located on Broad Street — just across the railroad tracks from the mill — was built and lighted by the mill. The park had a medium sized grandstand and seated around 2,500. Semipro teams played in such leagues as the Border Belt League and the Carolina Textile League.

In 1936 the Mooresville Moors, as all Mooresville teams were called (Moor brand Turkish towels were the main product of the cotton mill), joined the newly formed Carolina League, which was a professional league but not a member of the National Association. The team had begun the season in Salisbury but moved to Mooresville after only a month. Former major leaguer Jim Poole managed the team and played first base. The only statistics available from that year are from midseason. At that time Poole was hitting .399 with 13 home runs and 54 RBIs. Outfielders Eddie Yount (.416) and Norman Small (.315, 10 HR) would both become longtime minor league stars. The team finished seventh in the eight team league with a record of 35–64.

Many players from organized baseball jumped their contracts and came to play for more money with the teams in the Carolina League. Judge Bramham, president of the National Association, cracked down on players doing this, putting them on the ineligible list. His actions made it harder for outlaw leagues to get players. This, plus the growing popularity of minor league baseball led many towns — Mooresville included — to want legitimate teams. These were the main reasons behind the formation of the Class D North Carolina State League, in 1937.

The Mooresville Moors became a charter franchise in the North Carolina State League in 1937. Again led by player-manager Jim Poole, former Philadelphia Athletic, the Moors had an outstanding season. They finished the season 12 games ahead of the second place team, taking the league's inaugural pennant with a record of 74–35. Pitcher Joe Rucidio (20–5) led the team and the league in wins while manager Poole played first base and hit .344 with 83 RBIs. The Moors defeated Landis, three games to one, in the first round of the playoffs and went on to beat Thomasville, three games to two, in the finals to also take the postseason championship. Outfielder Norman Small (.392, 12 HR) played 35 games in Mooresville before being sold to the Cincinnati Reds and assigned to their Durham team. He would later return to play a total of 11 seasons with the Moors.

In 1938, the Moors slipped to third place in the regular season standings, finishing at 59–53, 16½ games behind first place Thomasville. Advancing to the playoffs, the Moors

The 1937 Mooresville Moors included: *Back:* Richard Robinson, Jim Poole, Leonard White, Joe Rucido, Clyde Teague, Trip Sigmon, Pres. C.F. Clark; *Front:* Wallace Godwin, Charlie Robinson, Johnny Hicks, Luther Whitlock, Paul Blair, Selby Keller, Charlie Frye (courtesy Norman Small).

swept Gastonia, three games to none, in the first round. In the finals against Thomasville, the series was tied at three games when play was suspended by the league president due to fan violence in Thomasville. All-Star third baseman Bob White (.335) was the star of the team that season. He was supported by outfielder Paul Blair (.313, 83 RBIs) and a strong pitching staff that featured John Lisk (14–8, 2.58 ERA) and Clyde Teague (13–7, 2.69 ERA).

The Moors took their second league pennant in 1939 as they posted a record of 71–38. Led by All-Star outfielder Bill Carrier (.349, 92 RBIs) and second baseman Garland Lawing (.343), Mooresville's team batting average was a remarkable .307. Pitchers Richard "Lefty" Robinson (23–6, 2.45 ERA) and Clyde Teague (21–8, 2.63 ERA) were two of the league's best. In the playoffs, the Moors beat Concord in the first round and went on to defeat Thomasville in the finals by a margin of four games to one.

The 1940 season saw the Moors slip to a fourth place finish, winning 60 games and losing 51. Norman Small (.346), returning to the team after a two-and-a-half-year absence, provided much of the team's offensive power as he hit 25 home runs, scored 95 runs and drove in 115. He led the league in all three categories. The Moors qualified for the playoffs and swept Salisbury in the first round. They lost in the finals to Lexington, four games to one.

The Moors improved one place in the standings to finish in third in 1941 with a 57–43 record. Norman Small (.332, 18 HR) led the team in hitting, closely followed by catcher-manager Ginger Watts (.331). Lefty Robinson (16–5, 2.54 ERA) and Harry Jordan (15–9) were two of the league's most successful pitchers. In the playoffs the Moors won in the first round, defeating Kannapolis, but lost in the finals to Salisbury, four games to three.

The next season the team tied for second, at 61–39. They lost in the first round of the playoffs to Landis, three games to none. Norman Small was once again the Moors' best offensive player, leading the league in three categories: hits (144), RBIs (107) and home runs (32) to go along with his batting average of .376. Eighteen-year-old knuckleball pitcher Hoyt Wilhelm, a native of nearby Huntersville, posted a 10–3 record for the Moors. He would make the major leagues in 1952 and have a career that would eventually lead to his enshrinement in Cooperstown.

The North Carolina State League was inactive for the 1943 and '44 seasons due to the war. When league play resumed in 1945, the Mooresville Moors returned. The Moors had previously been an independent team operated by Mooresville Cotton Mills but in 1945 signed a one year working agreement with the Boston Braves. The team turned in its worst finish yet — sixth place — with a record of 51–61. The season was not a memorable one with the exception of pitcher Forrest Thompson. Thompson, a native of Mooresville, dominated the league. He led the league with 24 wins, 278 strikeouts and an ERA of 2.13. He went on to spend much of the 1948 and '49 seasons with Washington in the American League.

The Moors of 1946 improved their record to 57–52, good enough for fourth place. Norman Small (.348) returned from military service and led the league in runs (100), doubles (31) and home runs (18). He also took over as manager of the team in mid–July when manager and second baseman Bob Crow was suspended from baseball for a year after a fight with an umpire during a game at Hickory. Also returning from the military was pitcher Hoyt Wilhelm (21–8). The Moors defeated Landis in seven games in the first round of the playoffs and went on to take the championship by beating Concord, four games to two, in the finals.

The Moors returned to their prewar form in 1947, taking the league pennant. Player-manager Norman Small (.359, 102 RBIs) led the team to a 68–43 record, himself hitting 31 home runs in the process. Fellow outfielder Ross Morrow also had a great season, hitting .377 with 21 home runs and 119 RBIs. In his final season with Mooresville before advancing, knuckleballer Hoyt Wilhelm (20–7) led the league in wins. Tom Mc-Call (19–9, 2.71 ERA) and Dave Jolly (14–7) teamed with Wilhelm to give the Moors the league's best pitching staff. In the first round of the playoffs that season, the Moors beat Hickory, four games to three. The finals also went a full seven games before the Moors prevailed over Lexington, winning their second consecutive league championship.

The 1948 season was not as successful for the Moors. They finished in fifth place, at 57–52. Once again, outfielder-manager Norman Small led the league in RBIs (130) and home runs (33) while batting .357. In 1949 the Moors were back near the top, finishing in second place with a record of 72–52. Norman Small (.344) led the league in home runs for the sixth time with 41 and RBIs for the fourth time with 152. New manager Jim Mills, who played third base as well as in the outfield, finished second in league hitting with a .386 average. The outstanding pitching staff was led by Elwood Bringle (21–4, 3.43 ERA) and Charlie Cudd (17–7, 3.34 ERA). The team advanced to the playoffs but was swept in the first round by Lexington, four games to none.

With a record of 64–47, the Moors finished second in 1950. As with the previous season, they lost in the first round of the playoffs, this time to High Point–Thomasville, four games to two. Prolific slugger Norman Small (.294, 104 RBIs) led the league in home runs for a seventh time with 32. Manager Jim Mills batted .338 and scored 100 runs while Jimmy Foxworth (19–11, 2.71 ERA), a former High Point College star, was one of the league's best pitchers.

The 1951 season was the worst in the history of the team. Seventh place, with a record of 55–71, was the best the Moors could manage. Pitcher Forrest Thompson was back with his hometown team but only had a 5–5 record. Third baseman Fred Daniels, who

The 1947 Mooresville Moors included: *Back:* Red Lane, Ike Isenhour, Norman Small, Carl Wray, Ross Morrow,; *Middle:* Martin Pollio, Eddie Walczak, Brooks Harrington, Buddy Milito, Ray Walczak, Gene Deal; Front: Lefty Jetum, Tom McCall, Dave Jolley, Earl Sorrels, Dewey Hoyt, Hoyt Wilhelm (a future Hall of Famer) (courtesy Norman Small).

had played for the Philadelphia Phillies in 1945, led the team with a batting average of .359, driving in 97 runs and scoring 91.

In the 1952 season the Moors made a complete turnaround, led by the offense of Fred Daniels (.342, 69 RBIs) and player-manager Jim Mills (.347, 74 RBIs). They finished the regular season 70–39, rising to second place. In the first round of the playoffs the Moors beat Elkin, four games to one. The finals saw them defeat Salisbury in seven games to take the league championship. It was a fitting end to the league that the Moors should be its final champion, just as they had been the first. The North Carolina State League was dissolved after the season.

In 1953, the Moors played their final season as a professional baseball team. That year the team joined to the new Class D

Tar Heel League. They finished the season in fifth place at 58–55, missing the playoffs by one game. The Moors had a good offense led by outfielder-manager Jim Mills (.322) and fellow outfielder Wade Martin (.319, 105 runs). Third baseman Fred Daniels also contributed with his .294 average. Norman Small returned to the Moors after playing the previous two seasons with Hickory and Raleigh. Batting .340 with 14 home runs and 87 RBIs, Small retired after the season at age 39. With attendance at less than 20,000 — half of what it had been in the peak years of 1947 and '48 — it became financially impossible for the team to continue. The Moors withdrew from the league and disbanded after the season.

The Mooresville Moors were the most successful team in the history of the North

Carolina State League, if not the most successful team ever in the state. In their 14 years in that league they won three pennants, three postseason championships and went to the playoffs every year but three.

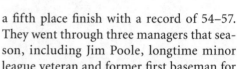

Morganton

The Morganton Aggies were a charter franchise when the Class D Western Carolina League began play in 1948. They finished that first season in third place and qualified for the playoffs with a record of 54–53. They lost, however, to league champion Lincolnton in the first round, four games to one. Pitcher Boger McGimsey (who managed the Aggies for the final part of the season) won 12 games and led the league in ERA with 2.76. When he wasn't on the mound McGimsey played first base and led the team in hitting with a .355 average.

As a whole, the Aggies were the league's best hitting team with an impressive .308 average. First baseman–outfielder Spencer Robbins (.342, 26 HR, 108 RBIs) was the team's power hitter, supported by outfielders Jack Harvey (.321) and Elmer Roberts (.314). Rookie shortstop Johnny Temple hit .316 in 59 games. He would go on to be a four time All-Star in a 13-year major league career.

The Aggies were the league's most successful team at the ticket window as they led in attendance with 65,791.

The 1949 team, managed by Sam Bell, improved its record to 58–49 but finished in fourth place. In the playoffs the club defeated Lincolnton in the first round but lost to Rutherford County, four games to one, in the finals. Pitcher Lelon Jaynes (19–7) led the league in wins and strikeouts (202), while first baseman Boger McGimsey (.369) led with 118 RBIs. Also the team's second best pitcher, McGimsey turned in an 8–2 record. Returning outfielder Elmer Roberts (.319, 80 RBIs) was named to the league All-Star team.

The 1950 season saw the Aggies turn in a fifth place finish with a record of 54–57. They went through three managers that season, including Jim Poole, longtime minor league veteran and former first baseman for the Philadelphia Athletics.

The Aggies had their best season in 1951. Led by player-manager George Bradshaw (.350, 20 HR, 90 RBIs), they took the league pennant with a record of 71–39. Pitcher Pete Treece (25–10, 264 SO) led the league in wins and strikeouts, while outfielder Bordie Waddle (.369, 107 RBIs) was the league leader in home runs with 24. In the first round of the playoffs, the Aggies came out on top after the Lincolnton Cardinals pushed them to a seventh game. Unfortunately for the Aggies, they lost the finals in another seven game series to the Shelby Farmers.

League attendance had been dropping almost every year. The 1952 season saw only six teams take to the field, down from eight the previous year.

The Morganton Aggies, managed first by George Bradshaw and then by Pete Treece, failed to finish that season. They withdrew from the league on August 3 due to financial difficulties resulting from poor attendance, finishing with a record of 41–51. The entire league disbanded at season's end.

A week after the team broke up, former catcher and manager George Bradshaw made his big league debut with the Washington Senators. He played in ten games for the Senators that year, his only one in the majors.

Mt. Airy

Professional baseball first came to the town of Mt. Airy in 1934. That year the Mt. Airy Graniteers took to the field in the Class D Bi-State League, a league that had previously operated as semipro for several seasons. The Graniteers, who had a working agreement with the Cincinnati Reds, posted a record of 34–42, finishing fourth in the six team league. Though they had a good offense, led by outfielder Ray Cote (.353), the team lacked reliable pitching.

The following season the team changed its name to that of its parent Cincinnati Reds. They improved in the league standings with a 66–47 record, finishing fourth out of eight teams. Outfielder Ray Cote (.323), shortstop Len Kahny (.295), pitcher Cy Honeycutt (21–8) and manager Mickey Shader were all named to the league All-Star team. The Reds of 1936 did not do as well; they finished at 53–63, 22½ games back and in sixth place. Ray Cote (.321) was again named an All-Star while fellow outfielder Gene Handley led the league in batting with an average of .403. Promoted to Durham at the end of the season, Handley later went on to play two seasons with the Philadelphia Athletics.

For the next three seasons the Reds continued to fare poorly in league play. They posted records of 52–61 in 1937 and 49–69 in 1938, with fifth and sixth place finishes. All-Star outfielder Maury Jungman (.329) led the 1937 team.

The 1937 season was also the first for night baseball in Mt. Airy as lights were installed at 1,500 seat Riverside Park. In 1938, the team changed its name back to the Graniteers as it again became independent.

The Graniteers again played poorly and dropped to last place in 1939 with their 42–70 record. Outfielders Eddie Weston (.341, 15 HR, 77 RBIs) and George Baker (.319, 81 RBIs) were that season's stars. Manager Guy Lacy, who hit .261 in 35 games, was near the end of a minor league playing and managing career that had begun in 1916.

Finally in 1940 the team showed improvement. They posted a record of 63–56, good enough for third place. Outfielder Tony Mazurek (.329), catcher Frank Warren (.300) and second baseman Woody Bottoms (.376) were some of the Graniteers' more talented players. Manager Walter Novak (.222), who also played shortstop, was named to the league All-Star team. The Graniteers qualified for the playoffs but lost in the first round to Bassett, four games to one.

The Graniteers of 1941 wound up back in the cellar with a record of 42–70, despite the efforts of All-Star pitcher Roy Boles (10–4). Returning player Woody Bottoms (.334), who had switched to shortstop, and third baseman Henry Corriggio (.315) led the team in hitting. The Graniteers' poor play led to low attendance and resulting financial difficulties. The team disbanded after the season.

After the war, baseball returned to Mt. Airy. Judge Edward Bivins, a former Duke University and Asheville Tourists player, led a group of local fans and bought a franchise in the newly formed Class D Blue Ridge League. The name Graniteers was resurrected and play commenced in 1946. The team finished in second place in the four team league, winning 59 games while losing 45. The Graniteers featured two former major leaguers: first baseman Eddie Morgan and pitcher Chubby Dean, a Mt. Airy native. Morgan (.391, 16 HR, 127 RBIs), who also served as the team's manager, was traded to Galax after 76 games and finished as the league leader in hits, RBIs, and home runs. Dean was 12–7 as a pitcher but, also playing in the outfield, he hit .419 in 53 games.

Over the next four years the Graniteers played consistently well. In 1947 they finished in second place with a record of 72–52. Multiposition-playing Sam Moir (.339), All-Star third baseman Ed Cousins (.328) and second baseman Francis Essic (.308, 82 RBIs) gave the Graniteers a strong offense.

Mt. Airy catcher Mike Brelich in 1949 (courtesy Worth Cuthbertson).

Jack Holt (100 RBIs) and second baseman Francis Essic both hit .318. Despite playing well, the team was last in the league in attendance, averaging less than 300 spectators per game.

The team continued its winning ways in 1949. The Graniteers took the league pennant in a tightly contested race with a record of 68–58. They were upset, however, in the first round of the playoffs by Wytheville, four games to two. Pitcher Pete Treece (21–8, 3.01 ERA) again dominated the league, striking out 229 batters. The team also had a potent offense led by All-Star outfielder Jack Holt (.312, 94 RBIs), first baseman Charlie Hope (.317) and outfielder Dub Akens (.314). Attendance more than doubled for the 1949 season, up to 36,230.

The 1950 season was the last for the Blue Ridge League and for the Graniteers. They played well and posted a regular season record of 71–48, leaving them in second place. The team was managed by the legendary Cecil "Zip" Payne for most of the season before he was replaced on August 12 by Joe Roseberry. A truly talented ballplayer, Roseberry was the team's leading hitter with a .320 average. Besides playing the outfield, he also pitched, achieving a 7–4 record. Returning outfielder Jack Holt had another good season, hitting .302, while Richard Wasco (11–4) was the team's best pitcher. In the playoffs the Graniteers beat Radford, three games to one, and went on to sweep the Elkin Blanketeers in four games to take the final league championship.

Chubby Dean returned to the team and took over as manager. Playing first base, he hit .319. With Pete Treece (20–12, 234 SO), Jack Williams (16–7) and former big leaguer Bob Bowman (17–4), the team also had the league's best pitching staff.

The 1948 season saw the Graniteers win their first championship. Led by shortstop-manager Noel Casbier (.378), the team finished the regular season in fourth place with a 65–58 record. The Graniteers advanced to defeat North Wilkesboro in the first round of the playoffs, three games to one, and Galax in the finals, four games to three. Casbier, who also posted a 3–4 record as a pitcher, won the league batting title. Outfielder Dub Akins finished second with a .352 average, while fellow outfielder

Attendance figures were down all across the Blue Ridge League in 1950 and the Graniteers drew only 16,306. Due to the resulting financial difficulties, the league decided to fold after the season.

◆ ——————— *New Bern* ——————— ◆

New Bern first entered professional baseball in the summer of 1902 when the New Bern Truckers joined the Class C North Carolina League. The league failed to finish

the season and disbanded on July 15. At that time the Truckers were in second place with a record of 26–22.

New Bern's next professional team was

founded in 1908 for play in the Class D Eastern Carolina League. The team only played 21 games, however, before disbanding on July 4 with a record of 5–16.

In 1934 the New Bern Bears became a charter member of the semipro Coastal Plain League. Consisting largely of college players, the league existed for three seasons before team owners decided to make it truly professional (Class D) by joining the National Association. The Bears became professional along with the league for the 1937 season. For several years in the late 1930s and early '40s, the Bears had an ownership group unique to all of baseball: the New Bern Fire Department.

In their first season as a professional team, the Bears — who signed a working agreement with Macon of the Class A South Atlantic League — finished the season in fourth place at 48–45. They qualified for the playoffs but lost to Snow Hill in the first round, three games to two. Outfielders Glenn Mullinax (.333, 17 HR, 71 RBIs) and Worlise Knowles (.295, 73 RBIs) led the team in hitting and were both named to the league All-Star team. Bull Hamons (14–8) was the best member of the average pitching staff.

The 1938 season saw the Bears finish the regular season with a record of 63–49 and the league pennant. Alfred Anderson (.368, 101 runs), Bill Harper (.322, 84 RBIs), Les Burge (.348, 22 home runs) and Worlise Knowles (.341) led the Bears' powerful offense. The pitching staff featured Len Berry (12–4) and Bull Hamons (14–7). The team went on to win the championship by sweeping both Kinston in the first round and Snow Hill in the finals.

The Bears slipped to fifth place in 1939 with a record of 62–59 and did not qualify for the playoffs. All-Star center fielder Uriah Norwood did win the batting title, however, with a .336 average, and Len Berry (18–8) was again one of the league's best pitchers. The 1940 team fell even further to sixth place, winning 58 games and losing 67. Third baseman Floyd Harper (.284) was named to the All–Coastal Plain team while Berry won 17 games and lost 8.

The next season the Bears improved to a third place finish at 61–57. Despite the offense of All-Star outfielder Dowd Averette (.313, 99 RBIs), first baseman Lyle Thompson (.330, 111 RBIs) and Claude Swiggett (.331, 93 runs), the team lost to Greenville, four games to two, in the first round of the playoffs.

The Coastal Plain League suspended play before the start of the 1942 season due to the war. The Bears returned when league play resumed in 1946 but did not play well and finished seventh with a record of 57–68. All-Star first baseman Vern Shetler led the league in batting with a .362 average while hitting 20 home runs and driving in 95. Adel White was the Bears' best pitcher at 13–7. Legendary minor league slugger Ken Guettler, who would hit 62 home runs for Shreveport (La.) in 1956, hit only three for New Bern in 47 games while batting .246.

In 1947, the team posted a 73–66 record, good enough for fourth place. In the first round of the playoffs the Bears lost to Wilson, four games to one. All-Star first baseman Harry Soufas (.342) had an excellent season, leading the league in RBIs (122) and home runs (25). Outfielder Sal "Zippy" Zunno led the league in runs with 133 and in stolen bases with 70.

The Bears of 1948 finished fifth, winning 69 games and losing 70. Harry Soufas was again one of the league's best players, hitting .343 while driving in 135 runs. Dennis Gaskins (20–13) and Ellaire Baldwin (20–14) were responsible for more than half of the Bears' wins. Eighteen-year-old pitcher Ernie Sawyer (10–7) pitched an 11-inning, no-hit, 1-to-0 victory over Rocky Mount on June 18 of that season.

The 1949 team, managed by pitcher Bull Hamons, improved to third place in the league standings with a 73–66 record. The Bears started the season well but suffered when their two best hitters — first baseman Jake Daniel (.344) and outfielder Jim Burns (.312) — were sold to Burlington of the Carolina League. Shortstop Billy Bevill (.276, 104 runs) set the all-time stolen base record

Base stealer extraordinaire, Billy Bevill of New Bern (courtesy Billy Bevill).

for the Coastal Plain League that season with 92. Pitcher William Padgett (22–13, 1.97 ERA) was one of the league's best, winning 22 games. The team lost in the first round of the playoffs to Kinston, four games to two.

The next season the Bears, managed by catcher Harry Land (.247), finished third with a record of 71–67. They went on to defeat Rocky Mount, four games to two, in the first round of the playoffs. The Bears then took the championship with a four game sweep of the Kinston Eagles in the finals. Shortstop Billy Bevill (.259, 100 runs) again

led the league with 87 stolen bases and Harry Soufas (.342, 117 RBIs, 95 runs) — playing his final season before retirement — led the league in walks (113) and finished second in batting average. Other contributors to the offense included outfielder Eddie Christoff (.317) and second baseman John Cornwell (.302, 105 runs). Outfielder Larry Quartararo was purchased from Roanoke Rapids late in the season to help with the pennant drive and was an important part of the team in the playoffs.

The Bears took their second consecutive league championship in 1951. Again led by Harry Land, they finished the regular season in second place at 72–54. They defeated Goldsboro, four games to two, in the first round of the playoffs, and Wilson, four games to three, in the finals. First baseman Gene Stewart (.316, 87 RBIs) and third baseman Frank Tepedino (.312, 100 runs) led the team's offense with help from second baseman John Russo (.300) and outfielder Walt McJunkin (.286, 94 RBIs). The pitching staff featured the league's best as New Bern native Veston "Bunky" Stewart (15–2, 1.16 ERA) and Larry Dempsey (20–10) both had outstanding seasons. Stewart went on to spend parts of five seasons with Washington.

The 1952 season was the last for the Bears and for the Coastal Plain League. George Scott, who had owned the Bears for several seasons, sold the team to local developer Mark Skinner after the 1951 season. The team, which had few veterans and was made up mainly of local players, played poorly in their final season and finished last with a record of 40–83. No pitcher posted a winning record. Larry Dempsey (13–14, 1.81 ERA, including seven games with Wilson) returned and pitched well but received little support from the Bears' offense. He was sold to the Wilson Tobs in mid–August in an effort to raise money. Shortstop Billy Bevill (.275) returned to the Bears and stole 69 bases, second in the league, while manager Steve Collins, who took over on July 15, hit .293 in 31 games.

Kafer Park, home of the Bears of the

The 1951 New Bern Bears included: *Back:* Marshall Gemberling, Gene Stewart, Graham Stilley, Duke Marino, Walt McJunkin, Russ Wheeler; *Middle:* Red Benton, Harry Stark, Harry Land (mgr.), V. Conner, Joe Russo; *Front:* Bob Dempsey, Buster Mathews, Kemp Haywood, Jake Farrell, Ed Egelure (courtesy Harry Land).

Coastal Plain League, still exists as a baseball field. The grandstand and all traces of the old park were torn down, however, in the late 1950s. In its Coastal Plain days the field had dimensions of 290 feet down the right field line, 360 to left field and 400 to center. Home runs to left and center would often land on the roof of the National Guard Armory, which was just beyond the outfield wall.

Newton-Conover

When the Class D North Carolina State League was formed in 1937, a team representing the neighboring Catawba County towns of Newton and Conover was organized as a charter member. The Newton-Conover Twins, as they were called, had a poor first season and finished in last place with a 36–73 record. That season's team would be one of only two representing the two towns to sign a major league working agreement, as they joined up with the Cleveland Indians. Outfielder Jim Layton (.326) and pitcher Ray Lindsay (11–7) were that season's best players.

With a 46–66 finish, the team rose to sixth place in 1938. The Twins had several good hitters, including shortstop Clarence Allen (.391 in 38 games) and third baseman Mack Arnette (.330 in 29 games), but none were with the team for the entire season. Pitcher Fremont Connor (15–9) was one of the league's best.

In 1939, the Twins switched to the new Tar Heel League, also a Class D circuit made up of Western Piedmont towns. Unfortunately for the Twins, they finished the season in the cellar, 34½ games out of first, with a

Left: First baseman Joe Plick of Newton-Conover in 1951 (courtesy Joe Plick). *Right:* Catcher-manager Eddie Yount of Newton-Conover led the Western Carolina League in nearly all offensive categories in 1948 (courtesy Joe Plick).

record of 36–69. Pitcher Ralph Fox (17–11) was responsible for nearly half of the team's victories. Also playing in the outfield when not on the mound, he batted .342, leading the team. The Twins of 1940 did not even finish the season, dropping out along with Shelby on July 19. At the time of the team's withdrawal, outfielder Mike Skaff was leading the league with a .370 batting average. The entire league folded after that season.

Professional baseball returned to Newton-Conover in 1948 when the Twins joined the new Class D Western Carolina League. The Twins played well that season, finishing in second place with a record of 67–43. Catcher and manager Eddie Yount, a Newton native who had played briefly in the major leagues, led the league in nearly all offensive categories: 139 runs, 169 hits, 140 RBIs, 43 home runs. His .420 batting average was second only to the .425 of Marion's Wes Ferrell. Pitcher Ray Lindsay also dominated the league as he turned in a 21–9 performance with 255 strikeouts. The Twins went on to beat Forest City in the first round of the playoffs, four games to two, but lost the finals to Lincolnton in seven games.

The Twins, again managed by Eddie

Yount, played well in 1949 and '50, winning the pennant both seasons with records of 72–36 and 69–41, respectively. They were upset, however, in the first round of the 1949 playoffs by Rutherford County, four games to two. Yount (.324, 109 runs)—named as the league's All-Star catcher—and pitchers Ray Lindsay (17–11) and Bill Greene (17–6) were the stars of that team. In the 1950 playoffs, the Twins won in the first round, defeating Rutherford County, four games to two, but lost in the finals to Lenoir, four games to three.

In 1951 the Twins posted a 63–48 record, good enough for fourth place and a playoff berth, but lost to eventual champion Shelby in the first round, four games to two. First baseman Don Stafford led the team with a .372 batting average while manager Eddie Yount hit .305 in 51 games. Norman Reinhardt was the team's leading pitcher at 17–10. Ray Lindsay, one of the best pitchers in Class D ball during the 1940s, was 4–1 for the Twins at the end of an outstanding minor league career. Lindsay was an excellent control pitcher, walking only 490 batters in 298 games. After spending 11 seasons in the minors (ten of them in North Carolina and four of those with Newton-Conover), he retired with a 154–98 record, an ERA of 2.97 and 1,904 strikeouts.

The 1951 season saw attendance decline all across the league. Newton-Conover drew only 31,625 fans in 1951, down from a league leading 82,481 just two years earlier. Due to financial troubles the Twins disbanded after the 1951 season, followed a year later by the entire league.

In 1960 the Western Carolina League was reborn and professional baseball returned to Newton and Conover as a new Twins team was formed. Led by first baseman Richard Schmidt (.333, 14 triples) and All-Star pitcher and manager John Isaac (16–9, 1.60 ERA, 177 SO), the team finished below .500 (47–52) but qualified for the playoffs with a fourth place finish. They lost, however, to Salisbury, two games to one, in the first round. The Twins managed to draw only 16,052 fans that season. The 1961 season saw the Twins, who had signed a working agreement with the Milwaukee Braves, finish in the cellar with a record of 36–58. Other than third baseman Willie Hayes (.304) and outfielder Ernesto Mesa (.301), each of whom only spent half a season with the team, the Twins had no real standouts.

The final season for professional baseball in the two towns came in 1962. The Twins, once again independent, finished that year at 42–57, third in the league, which had shrunken to only four members. Outfielder and manager Henry Nichols (.305) established a still-standing record for the lowest league leading RBI total, as he drove in only 66. Though he was only with the team for part of the season, left-hander John Isaac (10–4) pitched well. Attendance dropped even lower that season as the team drew only a dismal 10,452. Unable to financially continue, the team folded after the season.

North Wilkesboro

The North Wilkesboro Flashers, who played at Memorial Park Field, were admitted to the Class D Blue Ridge League as a new franchise in 1948. The Flashers—named after manager Henry "Flash" Loman—did well that first year. Led by third baseman Doug Shores (.335, 93 RBIs) and pitcher Sam

Gibson (19–9), the team finished 72–54, good enough for second place. The Flashers were also second in attendance, drawing 36,575. They qualified for the playoffs but lost in the first round to Mt. Airy, three games to one. Pitcher Paul Pryor (4–6) never made it to the major leagues as a player, but

Top: North Wilkesboro's Memorial Park, home of the Flashers (courtesy Worth Cuthbertson). *Left:* Henry "Flash" Loman, manager of the North Wilkesboro Flashers (courtesy Worth Cuthbertson).

1948 squad, recalled a run-in one game with the men in blue.

> One game, I got into an argument with the umpire. I can't remember what I said but it must have been pretty bad because he threw me out of the game and fined me fifteen dollars.
> I had to pay the fine before the next day's game or I couldn't suit up. So that morning I went down to the bank and withdrew the money, all in pennies. Just before the game started I went out and set the bag of pennies on home plate. The crowd loved it and went wild.

The Flashers of 1949 went through three managers and finished an even .500 at 62–62. Led by pitchers Bill Weston (8–2) and James Rhoades (11–6) along with All-Star third baseman Doug Shores (.315, 68 RBIs), the team finished fourth, five games behind first place Mt. Airy. In the playoffs, the Flashers beat Galax four games to two. They then took the championship, defeating Wytheville four games to one in the finals.

The 1950 season did not turn out as well for the Flashers. Managed by Bernard Loman and then later by his brother Flash, the team finished in last place with a record of 40–78,

for 21 seasons (1961–81) he was one of the National League's best umpires. He worked several All-Star games and league championship series as well as the 1967, 1973 and 1980 World Series.

Worth Cuthbertson, a pitcher on that

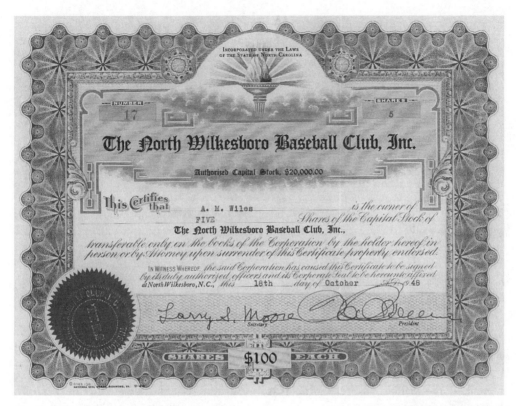

Many teams sold stock to the public to raise money. This is the certificate A.M. Wiles received for purchasing five shares of the North Wilkesboro Baseball Club, Inc. (from the collection of the author).

44 games out of first. They did, however, lead the league in attendance drawing 23,118 spectators. This was still much less than the team's high attendance figure of over 36,000 in 1948. Pitcher Gary Thornburg (10–4) was the league ERA leader with 2.27. Much of what little offense the team had that season was provided by catcher Robert Wright (.326, 74 RBIs).

The Flashers disbanded after the 1950 season as did the entire Blue Ridge League due to poor attendance.

 Raleigh

The 1901 Raleigh Red Birds became the first professional team to represent the city when they joined the Virginia–North Carolina League, probably the state's first truly professional league. The Red Birds finished the first half of the season in fourth (29–28) but won the shortened second half (the season was brought to a premature end after several teams dropped out). The team played a playoff series with first half champ Wilmington and took the championship by winning all four games. Raleigh second baseman Jake Atz would go on to spend parts of four seasons as a utility infielder in the big leagues, but his greatest baseball success came as a minor league manager. For 27 seasons, Atz managed in the southern minors. His Fort Worth Panthers teams of 1920–25, winners of six consecutive Texas League pennants, are considered to be some of the greatest minor league teams ever.

In 1902, a new Raleigh Red Birds team was organized for membership in the newly formed Class C North Carolina League. The league did not finish the season and disbanded on July 15. At that time the Red Birds were in third place with a record of 35–27.

It was 1908 before another attempt was made to bring professional baseball to the capital city. That season a team, again named the Red Birds, became a charter member of the Class D Eastern Carolina League. Not a strong team, the Red Birds finished the season in fourth place with a record of 23–36. (This was actually last place since two league members failed to finish the season.) The Red Birds, managed by outfielder Richard Crozier (.225), improved to 49–41 in 1909 and tied for third. Pitcher Brandon posted a 14–7 record.

The 1910 season was not a successful one as the Red Birds dropped to last place with their 38–45 record. Outfielder Pete Clemens (.260), who led the league with 74 hits, was named to the league All-Star team. The league disbanded after the season.

In 1913, professional baseball returned to Raleigh when a team was entered in the Class D North Carolina State League. Using the name Capitals for the first time, the team had a decent season and finished third with a 60–53 record. Catcher and manager Earle Mack, whose father Connie owned the Philadelphia Athletics, batted .287 while pitcher Jerry Belanger was 12–4.

Again managed by Earle Mack (.244) in 1914, the Capitals (52–68) slipped to fourth place. They improved the following season to third place with a record of 63–57. Pitcher Elmer Myers (29–10, 268 SO), the league's best, was responsible for nearly half of the team's victories. He finished that season with the Philadelphia Athletics and remained in the big leagues through 1922.

The Capitals finished the 1916 season in the league cellar. Despite the efforts of former big league outfielder Duke Duncan (.336), a native of nearby Clayton, the team finished at only 39–71. The 1917 season also began poorly, and the team (8–20) dropped out of the league on May 18 due to poor attendance and financial difficulties. The entire league shut down shortly thereafter due to the United States' entry into World War I.

The demise of the North Carolina State League left Raleigh without professional baseball for two seasons. In 1920 the Class D Piedmont League was formed and Raleigh entered a franchise. The Raleigh Nats, as they were called, played well and won the second half of that first season. The team finished with an overall 67–53 record and faced first half champ Greensboro in the playoffs. They lost there, however, four games to three. The Nats were led offensively that season by left fielder Joe Munson (.304, 38 SB, 88 runs) while pitchers W.H. Allen (18–10, 205 SO) and Bill Hughes (19–13, 1.76 ERA) were among the best in the league.

The next season Raleigh (now the Red Birds) finished the season with the best record in the league at 68–52. They failed, however, to win either half of the season so they did not participate in the playoffs. Pitcher Bill Hughes (26–7) returned to the team and was the league's dominant pitcher. W.H. Allen (19–14) also had a good season as a returning player and left fielder Hoke Floyd (.312 BA) led the league with 102 runs scored. Bill Hughes was called up to Pittsburgh in September and pitched two innings in one game. He would play another 18 seasons in the minor leagues but would never make it back to the big leagues. Raleigh's part-time catcher in 1921, Roy Spencer (.336), was more successful; he spent most of 12 seasons in the majors.

Becoming known as the Raleigh Capitals in 1922, the team had an unsuccessful season. With 60 wins and 66 losses, they finished fifth in the six team league. Two notable players from that team were outfielder Hoke Floyd (.365, 84 runs), who lost the batting title by one percentage point, and pitcher Grier "Skipper" Friday (22–14). The results of the 1923 season were not much different as a 57–67 record again left the Capitals in fifth place. That team was led by the impressive performance of outfielder

Carr Smith (.418, 24 HR, 137 RBIs, 107 runs, 25 triples). A native of Kernersville, Smith led the Piedmont League in almost every offensive category that season. He finished the year with Washington in the American League.

The Capitals sank to the cellar in 1924. Their record of 47–74 left them 25 games behind first place Durham. The 1925 and '26 seasons were no better as the team turned in records of 57–69 and 57–86, respectively. It wasn't until the 1927 season that the Capitals posted a winning record. Led by outfielder Odie Strain (.345, 103 RBIs), first baseman Ed Lundeen (.309, 88 RBIs) and pitcher Bob Moger (23–14), the team started strong and won the first half of the season. They slumped in the second half and finished with the league's fourth best record at 77–70. In the playoffs with second half champion Salisbury-Spencer, the Capitals lost the series, three games to two.

The 1928 season saw the losing ways return. The Capitals finished fifth with a 56–74 record, 24 games out of first. Outfielder Bill Bankston (.271) finished a long minor league career with Raleigh that season. He retired after 15 minor league seasons (and 11 games with Philadelphia in 1915) with a career .322 batting average. The only other noteworthy player on that team was shortstop Greg Mulleavy (.302, 15 triples) who became the Chicago White Sox starting shortstop for much of the 1930 season. Due to the team's poor quality of play and resulting low attendance, the Capitals folded after the season.

The Capitals returned in 1930 after a one year absence from the league. The team still met with little success and finished fifth with a 68–72 record. Veteran third baseman Rasty Walters, for many seasons a star with Wilson of the Virginia League, hit .313 in his last full season in baseball. The Capitals' best player that season was first baseman Hank Greenberg (.314, 19 HR, 93 RBIs). He was called up to the Detroit Tigers at the end of the season, thus beginning a 13-year major league career that would ultimately end with his enshrinement in the Baseball Hall of Fame.

Cigarette card of a Raleigh player, circa 1910 (from the collection of the author).

The Capitals of 1931 made great improvements, finishing second to Charlotte with a record of 86–50. They then faced Charlotte in a playoff but lost, four games to two. Pitcher Rip Sewell (17–7), who became a star for the Pittsburgh Pirates, led the outstanding pitching staff, supported by Frank Coleman (14–5, 173 strikeouts) and Hal Briggs (14–4). The offense was led by outfielder Odie Strain (.343, 93 RBIs) and shortstop Flea Clifton (.301).

The 1932 season was Raleigh's last in the Piedmont League. The Capitals' 63–70 record

Raleigh shortstop Cotton Bagwell receiving an award for most popular player in 1946 (courtesy Mahlon "Cotton" Bagwell).

left them fourth in the league standings. It was a mediocre team led by pitcher DeWitt Perry (15–12), outfielder Harry Smith (.363, 198 hits) and first baseman R. Stevenson (.294, 12 HR, 94 RBIs). The team disbanded after the season, leaving Raleigh without professional baseball for what would prove to be 12 seasons. This is surprising since during this period minor league baseball began to flourish in many much smaller towns of the state.

It was 1945 before Raleigh became home to another professional team. That season a new Raleigh Capitals team was formed as a charter member of the Class C Carolina League. It was a good first season for the Caps as they finished second in the league standings with a 78–60 record. Led by pitch-

ers Roy Pinyoun (21–10) and Charlie Timm (17–10, 2.36 ERA) the team advanced to the playoffs. They defeated Burlington, four games to three, but lost to Danville in the finals, four games to one.

The Capitals again finished second in 1946, although tied with Durham at 80–62. They were an all-around excellent team with strong performances once again from Roy Pinyoun (19–12) and Charlie Timm (16–10). The offense was led by outfielders Jim Mills (.318) and Emo Showfety (.343), catcher Harry Sullivan (.303) and second baseman Glen Lockamy (.320). The Capitals knocked off Burlington, four games to two, in the first round of the playoffs and then took the league championship, defeating Durham by the same margin.

The team members were much the same in 1947, as were the results. The Capitals finished third with an 81–60 record and then went on to take their second consecutive league championship by again defeating Burlington and then Durham, four games to two. All-Star catcher Harry Sullivan (.391, 109 RBIs, 200 hits) won the batting title with what has proved to be the highest average in league history. Returning players Dave Baxter (.308, 20 HR, 117 RBIs), Glen Lockamy (.302, 115 runs) and Charlie Timm (10–4) all again played well.

In 1948, the Capitals finally won a league pennant. Their 84–58 record put them three games ahead of second place Martinsville. Unfortunately, they were upset by Burlington, four games to two, in the playoffs. Player-manager Glen Lockamy hit .328 while All-Star pitcher Al Henencheck (22–9, 2.24 ERA) was one of the best in the league.

The Capitals dropped back to third place in 1949 with a 76–68 record. They went to sweep Winston-Salem in the playoffs but lost to Burlington, four games to three, in a hard-fought finals. The Caps had a good pitching staff that season which included Charlie Miller (18–11, 2.91 ERA), and Eugene Kelly (16–11, 2.96 ERA) but they lacked a strong offense. Second baseman Crash Davis led the team with a .296 average, followed by All-Star third baseman Don Siegert (.292, 22 HR, 102 RBIs, 106 runs).

The 1950 season was not a good one for the Raleigh Capitals; they finished seventh in the eight team league with a 55–97 record. Attendance, which had been 125,000 just two seasons before, dropped to less than 53,000. Managed by Hall of Famer Joe "Ducky" Medwick, the Capitals made great improvements in 1951 and finished with a 78–62 record, good enough for third place. Attendance also rose to nearly 81,000. Third baseman Joe Tedesco (.299, 115 RBIs, 97 runs) and outfielders Ted Browning (.298) and Bill Fowler (.297, 95 runs) provided much of the team's offense, while Diz Voiselle led the pitching staff with a 14–4 record. Medwick played part-time in the outfield and hit .285 with 33 RBIs. Unfortunately for the Capitals, they were swept in the first round of the playoffs by Winston-Salem.

While most of the teams in the league were signing major league working agreements, Raleigh remained independent in 1952. This gave the team more freedom to sign veteran players rather than rely on young prospects supplied by a major league affiliate. Manager Herb Brett signed several well-known veterans, including outfielders Norman Small (.270, 12 HR) and Don MacLean (.312). Small was purchased from Hickory and MacLean from Burlington. The Capitals had a great season and finished with a 79–57 record and the league pennant. They were not so fortunate in the playoffs as Reidsville — the league's other independent team — swept the Caps in the first round, three games to none.

Manager Herb Brett again led the Capitals to the pennant in 1953. The talented Caps were led on the field by pitchers Ben Rossman (20–5, 2.45 ERA) and Diz Voiselle (13–3, 2.51 ERA) and All-Star outfielder Jack Hussey (.292, 29 HR, 112 RBIs), the league home run leader. Once again, Ralph Hodgin's Reidsville Luckies defeated the Caps in the first round of the playoffs, this time three games to two.

After the 1953 season the Caps franchise

was moved to High Point–Thomasville, and many of the players were sold to Fayetteville. Raleigh was left without a team until 1958, when a new Capitals team was organized. Managed by Len Okrie, the Caps signed a working agreement with the Boston Red Sox. The best the team could manage that first season back in the league was a sixth place, 63–73, finish. Catcher Bob Tillman (.292, 18 HR) made it to the Red Sox in 1962 and spent a few seasons as their starting catcher. Pitcher Tracy Stallard (9–6) spent parts of seven seasons in the big leagues and is most famous for giving up Roger Maris' 61st home run in 1961.

The Red Sox provided the Caps with an abundance of talent in 1959. The outstanding pitching staff was led by All-Stars Bill Spanswick (15–4, 2.49 ERA) and Warren Hodgdon (13–5). Third baseman Tom Agosta (.314) and outfielder George Lewis (.302) had good seasons at the plate. All of these performances pale in comparison to that of a rookie second baseman named Carl Yastrzemski. Yastrzemski, named the league MVP, dominated league pitching, hitting .377 with 170 hits, 15 home runs and 100 RBIs. The Caps, at 78–52, won the pennant by six games. In the playoffs, they swept Winston-Salem but were then swept themselves in four games by Wilson in the finals.

The 1960 Caps had a decent season and finished with the league's third best record: 70–65. They failed to win either half of a split season so were not involved in the playoffs. Pitcher Dick Radatz (9–4) went on to become a two-time All-Star reliever with Boston. Attendance dropped to around 30,000, considerably less than that of teams from the smaller cities of Burlington and Wilson.

For the 1961 season the Capitals became an affiliate of the expansion New York Mets, a year before the Mets actually took to the field. The Caps had little talent and slipped to the cellar with a 58–80 record, 24½ games out of first. Recently retired big leaguer and North Carolina native Enos Slaughter (.341 in 42 games) was hired as manager to give the team experienced leadership. It did not help, apparently.

The 1952 Raleigh Capitals included: *Back:* Al Ronay, Bobby Pearson, Al Henencheck, Ben Rossman, Mike Kash, Crash Davis, Al Cleary, George Hallow, Herb Brett (mgr.); *Front:* Ken Raddant, Bucky Jacobs, unidentified, Norman Small, unidentified, Beny Cavaliere, Sid Varney, Don MacLean (courtesy Lawrence "Crash" Davis).

Raleigh switched its working agreement to the Washington Senators for the 1962 season. The Caps, again given little talent to work with, returned to the league cellar. Their record of 56–84 left them 33 games out of first, an even worse finish than the previous season. They did have talented shortstop Ed Brinkman (.324), who, promoted to the big league club in midseason, would spend 15 seasons as one of the best fielders in the major leagues.

Again switching working agreements in 1963, Raleigh rejoined the Mets farm system. For the first time since the early 1920s, the Raleigh team was known as something other than the Capitals, as they took the name of their parent club. It proved to be another dismal year for baseball in Raleigh as the Mets finished last in the league with a 62–82 record. One of the only standouts on the team was All-Star pitcher Sherman "Roadblock" Jones. A former big leaguer, Jones was trying to recover from arm problems. He turned in a 12–6 record and led the league with a 2.10 ERA.

In 1964 the team yet again switched major league affiliates, this time to the St. Louis Cardinals. Raleigh's team, which also became the Cardinals, showed some improvement from the past few seasons teams as they finished third in the West Division of the league with a 76–62 record. Pitcher Don Hagen (16–7) led the league in wins and strikeouts (202) while outfielder Ed Chasteen (.257, 28 HR, 90 RBIs) led in home runs. All-Star third baseman Coco Laboy (.340, 24 HR), who would spend several seasons with Montreal, was the team's leading hitter. Nineteen sixty-five saw Raleigh's Cards slip back to fourth in the West. Their 64–79 record left them 19 games out of first. Pitcher Mike Torrez, who was 4–8 for the Cards, went on to win 185 games in the majors.

Raleigh became a Pittsburgh farm club in 1966. Again taking the name of their parent club, Raleigh's Pirates managed a third place West finish with a record of 71–66. First baseman Al Oliver (.299) and catcher Manny Sanguillen (.328), both destined to be stars for Pittsburgh, led the team. Finally in 1967, the talent laden Raleigh team returned to first place. With outstanding performances from shortstop Don Money (.310, 86 RBIs), who was named league Player of the Year, infielder Rich Hebner (.336), first baseman Al Oliver (.297), third baseman Duncan Campbell (.331) and pitchers Harold Clem (15–3, 1.64 ERA) and Gene Garber (8–6, 1.89 ERA), the team won the league's East Division with a 77–65 record. Unfortunately, they were swept by the fourth place Portsmouth

Tides in the first round of the playoffs, two games to none.

After the 1967 season, Pittsburgh dropped its affiliation with Raleigh. Meanwhile, the Durham Bulls, a Mets farm club, had been suffering from poor attendance. A new team, called the Raleigh-Durham Mets, was formed to represent both cities (see below).

◆ ——— *Raleigh-Durham* ——— ◆

For the 1968 season Raleigh and Durham joined together to form the Raleigh-Durham Mets. After the 1967 season the Pittsburgh Pirates had dropped their player development contract with Raleigh. The Durham Bulls, a New York Mets affiliate, decided to merge with Raleigh to form the new team. Attendance had been very poor in Durham and team owners hoped having some home games in Raleigh would boost revenues. Home games were split between Devereaux Meadow in Raleigh and Durham Athletic Park.

The team played well in their first season, winning the Eastern Division of the Carolina League with a record of 83–56. Led by pitchers Charlie Hudson (16–7, 2.22 ERA), Jim Bibby (7–7) and Jon Matlack (13–6), the team advanced to the championship round of the playoffs before losing to the surprising High Point–Thomasville Hi-Toms. Offensively, the team was led by first baseman Mike Jorgenson (.315), shortstop Ted Martinez (.330) and outfielder Leroy Stanton (.266, 27 SB). Jorgenson would go on to spend 17 seasons in the big leagues while Martinez and Stanton would both play nine. Matlack and Bibby both became star pitchers in the majors. Outfielder Ken Singleton, later a three-time All-Star while with the Baltimore Orioles, appeared in 26 games with Raleigh-Durham before being promoted.

For 1969, the Raleigh-Durham team became the Phillies, reflecting their new affili-

ation with the major league Phillies. League All-Stars Greg Luzinski and Sammy Parilla were the power behind the team. First baseman Luzinski (.289) led the league in home runs (31) and RBIs (92). Outfielder Parilla wasn't far behind, batting .383 with 28 home runs and 85 RBIs. Both were called up to Philadelphia in 1970 but their careers took different paths. Parilla played in only 11 big league games, batting .125, while Luzinski played 15 years, was a four time All-Star and finished with 307 career home runs and 1,128 RBIs. Catcher Bob Boone, who joined Raleigh-Durham in midseason, also had a distinguished major league career, playing 19 seasons and establishing himself as one of the best defensive catchers ever. The Phillies' best pitcher was John Penn (15–9), league leader in strikeouts with 183. All of this talent led Raleigh-Durham to a second place regular season finish in the league's Eastern Division with a record of 79–62. They advanced to the playoffs (which involved eight of the league's ten teams) and dispatched both Kinston and Peninsula. They went on to take the league pennant, defeating Burlington, two games to one, in the finals.

Philadelphia transferred its player development contract to the Peninsula team in the Carolina League in 1970. Raleigh-Durham was unable to sign a contract with another major league team and was forced to operate as a co-op. The team was renamed the Triangles. Cliff Johnson, the Triangles' catcher, was the league's best offensive player and was named Player of the Year. He hit .332 with 27 home runs and 91 RBIs before being promoted to AAA in early August. The Triangles played well despite its co-op status and mediocre talent (other than Johnson); they finished with the league's second best overall record at 77–63. They did not qualify for the playoffs since the league had switched back to a split season, with the winners of the two halves playing each other for the championship.

The 1971 season was the last for a joint Raleigh-Durham team. The Triangles again operated as a co-op and finished seventh in the eight team league with a record of 56–80, 27 games out of first. The star of the team was pitcher Jerry Bell (8–1, 1.77 ERA) who only appeared in ten games before being called up to the Milwaukee Brewers. In an interesting side note, the Triangles, suffering poor attendance, announced late in the season that they were prepared to sign a woman player. If she had been signed, Jackie Jackson would have been the first woman to play professional baseball on a team with men. Instead, the Triangles were discouraged by the league and withdrew their offer to Jackson. Unable to secure major league support and with poor attendance, the Triangles withdrew from the league and disbanded after the season.

The 1971 season was the last for minor league baseball in Raleigh. With the present rule that teams must be 35 miles apart, it doesn't appear that a team will again call Raleigh home. When team owner Steve Bryant decided to move his Mudcats to the area in 1991, the Wake County town of Zebulon was the closest to Durham he could locate the team. Nineteen seventy-one was also the last season for Devereaux Meadow, the ballpark with perhaps the best name of all the state's ballparks. It was torn down in the late 1970s, and the site is now a parking lot for city buses.

◆ —————— *Red Springs* —————— ◆

The Red Springs Red Robins, a farm club of the Philadelphia Athletics, were a new franchise in the year-old Class D Tobacco State League in 1947 as it expanded from six to eight teams. The Red Robins, under manager Red Norris, did not fare well that first year as they finished in seventh place at 47–78. First baseman Joe Mangini and second baseman Gus Rogers, who both hit an even .300, were that season's best players. Attendance was last in the league by far with only 21,000.

Red Norris turned the team around in 1948, leading them to third place with a record of 75–62. Returning first baseman Joe Mangini, named to the league All-Star team, was the offensive leader, batting .302 with 113 RBIs. He also hit an amazing 24 triples to go with his 38 doubles. The Robins had a strong pitching staff that season, led by Harold Wood (17–9) and Al Burch (18–9). Burch also batted .354, playing part-time in the field. In the playoffs the Robins prevailed over Wilmington, four games to three, and then easily upset regular season champion Sanford, four games to one, to take the championship. This was the first of two championships for Red Springs, as Red Norris again led them to victory in 1949. That season the team won 76 games and lost 59 to finish the regular season in second place. They defeated Sanford, four games to two, in the playoffs and went on to take the championship from Dunn-Erwin, four games to two. Outfielder Bob Doak (.313) led the team in hitting but their real strength was the pitching staff. With Allen Pfeiffer (12–8, 2.38 ERA), Wallace Carpenter (10–5) and Billy Harrington (17–11), the Robins had a great staff.

In 1950, the team — still affiliated with the Philadelphia Athletics — was renamed the Red Springs–Laurinburg Red Robins (some games were played in Laurinburg). They were managed that season by first baseman Ducky Detweiler (.342, 95 RBIs), who had played briefly in the major leagues. Detweiler related a humorous incident from that season:

I remember a night in Smithfield, there was a fence sign that advertised Smithfield Hams in right center field. Anyone hitting a ball over that sign would receive a ham. Well, I hit a home run over that sign and I was presented on the field my ham: a live half-grown pig!! I still laugh when I think of it. After the game a man offered me fifty dollars for the pig, and of course, I took it.

Later in the year I hit a home run over a jeweler's sign in Laurinburg and I won a watch. I picked one out for my wife who was home in Maryland with our newborn baby girl.

Other than Detweiler and outfielder Al Parnell (.311, 80 RBIs), the team was of average talent. One of the Tobacco State League's greatest hitters, outfielder Hargrove Davis (.362), joined the team but was only around for 38 games. The Robins finished that season in third place at 68–61 and advanced to the playoffs, but were swept by Sanford in four games.

The Tobacco State League folded after the 1950 season and left Red Springs (and Laurinburg) without professional baseball.

Pro baseball in the small towns of North Carolina practically died out in the 1950s, and it appeared it would never return to Red Springs. However, in 1969 that changed. That year Matt Boykin, owner–general manager of the Wilson Tobs of the Class A Carolina League, decided to move his team due to years of poor attendance. He chose Red Springs even though it had a population of only around 4,000, making it the smallest town in the entire country to host a minor league baseball team. The team became the Red Springs Twins after signing a player development contract with the Minnesota Twins. The move was basically an experiment to see if smaller towns could support teams since owners were struggling even in the larger towns of the state. The Twins were successful as a business; attendance was up to 40,332 — twice what it had been in Wilson. On the field, however, the Twins did not fare as well, finishing the season in last place at 57–84. The only real players of note on the team were utility infielder Dan Monzon (.228) and shortstop Eric Soderholm (.294). Monzon would later spend two seasons in Minnesota, while Soderholm — who only appeared in 20 games with Red Springs before being promoted to Charlotte — would spend nine seasons in the big leagues.

The Twins had great support from the community but in the end it was decided that the town was too small and the team disbanded.

Reidsville

The Reidsville Luckies, named for the Lucky Strike cigarettes produced by Reidsville's American Tobacco Company, joined the Class D Bi-State League in 1935, the second year of that league's existence. As with most new teams, they did not fare very well. The Luckies finished in last place with a record of 38–76, 32½ games out of first. All-Star center fielder Ralph Hodgin, who won

the batting title with a .387 average, was sold to Fieldale in midseason.

The next two seasons were mediocre ones for the Luckies. In 1936 their record of 54–61 was good enough for fifth place in the eight team league. All-Star second baseman Howard Briggs (.345) and outfielder Herb Leary (.330, 27 HR, 93 RBIs) led the team. The 1937 Luckies, who had secured a working

Big league pitcher and Greensboro native Wes Ferrell held out on reporting to the Red Sox in 1934. While waiting for better terms from the team, he was hired by American Tobacco to pitch a couple of games for the semipro Luckies. *Back:* Wes Ferrell, Nap Lufty, John Briggs, Sherman Hoggard, Flop Beaver, Pat Brady, Pat Griffin, Howard Lamberth; *Front:* Willie Wagoner, Howard Briggs, Al Shaw, Marvin Coker, Van Howard, G.C. Deviney (mgr.); bat boy: James Deviney (courtesy Sherman Hoggard).

agreement with the Brooklyn Dodgers, finished in sixth, at 51–65. Other than returning outfielder Herb Leary (.316)—league leader with 29 home runs—it was an unmemorable team.

The 1938 Luckies improved to a third place finish, only 6½ games out of first, with a record of 71–48. The Luckies had the dominant offensive player in the league as All-Star outfielder Ray Scantling led the league in home runs (33), RBIs (147), and runs (130). First baseman and manager Jim Poole hit .326 with 94 RBIs and 97 runs scored. The team qualified for the playoffs but lost in the first round, three games to two, to the Bassett Furnituremakers.

The next season the Luckies dropped back to sixth place with their 48–65 record. Shortstop and league All-Star Dick Culler, who would spend several seasons in the big leagues, led the team in hitting with a .347 average. He was followed closely by outfielder Stan Platek (.341, 21 HR, 107 RBIs),

who was second in the league in both home runs and runs batted in. The 1940 season was an even worse one for the again independent team as they finished in the league cellar with a 43–75 record, 30½ games back. Second baseman Jimmy Gruzdis (.369, 85 RBIs), who took over as manager during the season, played well and was the only member of the Luckies named to the All-Star team. Catcher Harry Land (.310) and first baseman Gene Kessler (.299, 19 HR) also contributed to the offense, but the team lacked pitching. The Luckies were sold to a group from Leaksville and moved there after the season.

It was 1947 before Reidsville fielded another professional team. That year a franchise was entered into the year-old Class B Tri-State League and the name Luckies was resurrected. Managed by former Cincinnati Reds outfielder Lee Gamble, the team played at Kiker Stadium. It was not a successful return to baseball as the Luckies finished last, 42 games back, with a record of 45–92. The

Luckies were also last in the league in attendance with 59,403 (four teams in the league drew well over 100,000).

For the 1948 season the Luckies jumped to the Class C Carolina League. The team finished seventh in the eight team league, winning 57 games and losing 85, though official attendance figures were up considerably to 71,509. Luckies left-handed pitcher Lewis Hester was named the league's Player of the Year after posting a record of 25–13. Much of the team's offense was produced by outfielder Dick Sipek (who had spent the 1945 season with the Cincinnati Reds) with his .318 batting average.

The Luckies were involved in a gambling scandal in May of 1948. Pitcher-manager Barney DeForge was offered $300 to make sure his team lost a game to Winston-Salem by at least three runs. DeForge placed himself in the game in the eighth inning with his team down by two runs. He gave up three more runs and his team lost by five. Several days later, word of the thrown game leaked out and DeForge confessed. He was banned from baseball for life by the president of the National Association. DeForge was succeeded as manager by another pitcher, Tal Abernathy, who had played for the Philadelphia Athletics during the war. Abernathy was himself later replaced as manager by Bill Nagel, another former big leaguer.

The Carolina League changed classifications to Class B in 1949, a move that Reidsville voted against though they remained in the league. The higher classification allowed for greater salaries, placing financial strain on the smaller league members. The Luckies, who signed a working agreement with the St. Louis Browns, turned in a seventh place (63–80) finish for the second consecutive year. Reidsville first baseman Leo "Muscle" Shoals, named league MVP, had one of the most impressive seasons in the history of minor league baseball in the state. He batted .359, scored 131 runs, drove in 137 and hit 55 home runs. His home run total still stands as the league record. Dick Sipek hit .321 in his second season with the Luckies while fellow

outfielder Jim Miller hit .319. All-Star pitcher Mike Forline was one of the league's best with his record of 19–9.

Again an independent franchise, the 1950 Luckies improved to fourth place and qualified for the playoffs. Manager Herb Brett, who had pitched briefly for the Chicago Cubs in the 1920s, led the team to an 82–72 record. First baseman Bill Nagel (.290, 19 HR, 85 RBIs) and pitcher Joe Micich (18–8) were among the team's best players. The Luckies advanced to the playoffs but lost in the first round to the very talented Winston-Salem Cards, three games to two.

Herb Brett was back as manager in 1951 and the team again finished in fourth, eight games out of first, at 78–62. Pitcher Mike Forline (21–8) led the league in wins while outfielder Carl Miller (.311, 114 RBIs) tied for the league lead in home runs with 28. Dick Sipek, in his fourth season with the Luckies, was the team's leading hitter with a .322 average. All three players were named to the league's postseason All-Star team. In the first round of the playoffs the Luckies upset first place Durham, four games to one. They lost in the finals, however, again to Winston-Salem, four games to one.

In 1952, the Reidsville Luckies won their one and only league championship. The team, managed by former major leaguer Ralph Hodgin, finished the regular season in fourth place (74–64) and was led by outfielder Joe Pancoe (.304, 19 HR, and 85 RBIs) and pitcher Mike Forline (18–11). Manager Hodgin, who had played for Reidsville as a rookie in 1935, played in the outfield and hit .282. Advancing to the playoffs, the Luckies were impressive, sweeping Raleigh in the first round and Durham — four games to none — in the finals.

The Luckies of 1953 again finished in fourth place. Outfielder Ralph Hodgin was back as manager and led the team to a 73–66 record. Hodgin batted .303, first baseman Jack Sanford hit .324 and outfielder Jack Mitchell hit .316 as leaders of the offense. Mitchell, named to the All-Star team, was also the league stolen base king with 52. Joe

Reidsville's Crash Davis (second from left) and Bill Nagel are flanked by two unidentified teammates in 1950 (courtesy Lawrence "Crash" Davis).

Micich (17–11, 23 complete games) was the ace of an otherwise weak pitching staff. That season's playoffs saw the Luckies defeat Raleigh in the first round but lose to Danville in the finals, four games to two.

The 1954 Luckies dropped to a seventh place finish, winning 56 games while losing 83. The team suffered from both poor hitting and pitching. No starting pitcher had a winning record and only center fielder Bill Evans (.307) hit above the .300 mark. Pitcher Mike Forline (5–6, 3.32 ERA) played his final season, finishing his career with a Carolina League record of 89 wins. Attendance for the Luckies dropped to 28,321, a dismal last in the league.

What would prove to be Reidsville's last professional baseball team took to the field in 1955. For the first time since 1949, the team affiliated itself with a major league team, the Philadelphia Phillies. The Reidsville Phillies finished their one and only season in fifth place with a record of 68–70, missing the playoffs by a game.

Catcher Ellsworth Dean led the team in hitting with a .311 average, followed by second baseman Bill Dougan at .304. First baseman Ken Menkel started the season with a bang and was hitting .313 with 10 home runs in 40 games before being promoted. His replacement, John Moskus (.288), also had power as he hit 21 home runs and drove in 87. Once again, the Luckies were doomed by poor pitching. Despite an increase in attendance to over 38,000, the team was moved to Wilson before the start of the next season.

◆ ──────── *Roanoke Rapids* ──────── ◆

Professional baseball came to Roanoke Rapids in 1947, when the vacated Fayetteville franchise in the Class D Coastal Plain League was granted to the town. Simmons Park, which was located at the intersection of Jefferson and East 11th streets, was renovated and lights were added to get ready for the arrival of the team. Named the Blue Jays, the team had an unsuccessful debut season; they finished seventh in the eight team league with a 60–80 record. Managed by former big league infielder Stu Martin, a North Carolina native, the team struggled but had a few talented players. Martin hit .305 playing third base, while outfielder Merle Blackwell hit .303 and drove in 90 runs. Glenn Titus was the team's best pitcher, posting an 18–9 record. The real star of the team, however, was first baseman Val Gonzalez (.329, 62 RBIs), who joined the team in midseason. Even though the Jays didn't fare well on the field that season they had exceptional support from local fans. Attendance was nearly 116,000, second in the league.

Stu Martin returned as manager in 1948 but during spring training he was struck in the head with a pitch thrown by Ed "Whitey" Ford of the Norfolk Tars. He missed the first six weeks of the season while recovering. Val Gonzalez also returned to the Jays in 1948 and proceeded to win the batting title with an average of .383. Hitting 24 home runs, driving in 104 runs and scoring 103, Gonzalez's batting mark established the all-time record for the league. Other contributors to the offense included outfielder Herb May (.325, 94 RBIs) and catcher John Pavlich (.316). Despite having good hitters, a lack of pitching doomed the Jays (54–86), as they again finished in seventh place.

The 1949 season was another poor one for the Roanoke Rapids Blue Jays. The team went through several dozen players in search of a winning combination but it was not to be found as they turned in their third con-secutive seventh place finish. With a 60–78 record, the Jays finished 18½ games out of first. Second baseman Milt Bolick managed to have a good season as he hit .308 with 90 RBIs. Val Gonzalez returned to the Jays in midseason and hit .309 but he alone could not turn the team around.

In 1950, however, things did turn around for the Jays. They finished the year in first place with a record of 80–58, seven games ahead of second place Rocky Mount. Pitcher Alton Brown (28–11, 2.38 ERA), league MVP, led the league in both wins and strikeouts (204) while outfielder Warriner Bass (.302) led the league in RBIs with 148. Pitcher J.D. Thorne (17–6) had a good season on the mound as well as at the plate, hitting .321 in 40 games. Third baseman Leo Katkaveck also made a great contribution to the team, hitting .290 with 105 RBIs. The Jays were unsuccessful in the playoffs, however, as they were upset in the first round by fourth place Kinston, four games to none. Alton Brown later went on to pitch in a few games for the Washington Senators.

For the 1951 season, the Jays signed a working agreement with the Washington Senators, thereby removing some of the financial burden from the team. It didn't help the team on the field, as the Jays couldn't equal the success of the previous season, dropping to fifth place with a 59–66 record. Outfielder John Garrison led the team, batting .323 with 94 RBIs, while manager Morris "Smut" Aderholt, who played at first base and in the outfield, hit .315. Andy Turowski (.280), who could play either second or third base, stole 51 bases, second in the league. Alex Zukowski (16–12, 3.51 ERA) was the best member of the weak pitching staff.

The Senators sent longtime major league pitcher Pete Appleton to manage the Jays in 1952. The team's talent was thin (as it was in most of the Senators farm system), unfortunately, and the best the Jays could

Roanoke Rapids manager Walt McJunkin (left) with New Bern manager Harry Land and Coastal Plain League umpires, 1950 (courtesy Harry Land).

manage was another fifth place finish (63–61). The team did feature two outstanding players, as third baseman Bill Wollet (.311) led the league in hits (155) and stolen bases (78) and rookie pitcher Ted Abernathy (20–13, 1.69 ERA)—on his way to a long major league career—led in strikeouts with 293. Other contributing players on the team included outfielder Mike Garone (.288, 60 RBIs) and pitcher Charles Steinmetz (14–12).

Attendance had been declining all across the league. The Jays drew only 36,830 in 1952, less than a third of what they had drawn five seasons before. Obviously this loss of interest by the fans led to financial difficulties and the Coastal Plain League decided to suspend operations just before the 1953 season. Though it was originally meant to be only a one-year hiatus, the league never resumed play, leaving Roanoke Rapids without professional baseball.

♦ ———————— *Rockingham* ———————— ♦

Rockingham's entry into professional baseball lasted for only one year. The Rockingham Eagles took the field for their only season in 1950 as a member of the Class D Tobacco State League. It was a very successful year, however. The Eagles, managed first by Jack Bell and later by first baseman Cecil "Turkey" Tyson (.315, 77 RBIs), finished the regular season with a record of only 63–69,

27½ games out of first. It was good enough, however, for fourth place and a spot in the playoffs. In the first round the Eagles upset Lumberton (the regular season first place team), four games to two. In the finals they defeated Sanford, four games to three in a series that went the full seven games. Outfielder Bill Duffy (.289, 99 runs) teamed with Tyson to provide much of the team's offense.

Outfielder Willie Duke, finishing out a long, distinguished minor league career, batted .348 in 38 games for the Eagles after coming over from the Carolina League.

Though it had been a successful year, professional baseball never returned to Rockingham. The team had drawn nearly 32,000 in attendance (third in the league) but the Tobacco State League had financial difficulties and decided to shut down after the season.

◆ ——— *Rocky Mount* ——— ◆

The Railroaders of 1909 were the first professional team to represent Rocky Mount. As members of the Class D Eastern Carolina League, the team finished last among the six teams that first season with a record of 33–56. They improved the next year (41–43) and won the second half of the split season but lost in the playoffs to first half champ Fayetteville. The 1910 season proved to be the last for the league as it disbanded that fall.

One of the greatest athletes in American sports history played for Rocky Mount in 1909 and 1910. Jim Thorpe, who would go on to star in the 1912 Olympics and play professional football and major league baseball, was an outfielder and pitcher for Rocky Mount. While with Rocky Mount, Thorpe was an average hitter, batting around .250. He excelled in baserunning, however, and was a good pitcher, going 9–10 in 1909 and 10–10 in 1910. Unfortunately, it was his play in Rocky Mount (and later Fayetteville) that led to his Olympic medals being stripped once it was discovered he had played professional sports. The medals were not returned to his family until long after his death. Thorpe actually did nothing different than many other college players at that time. Many played professional baseball in the summers under an alias so that their amateur standings would not be jeopardized. Thorpe just happened to use his real name.

In 1915 the Class C Virginia League expanded and a franchise was granted to Rocky Mount. The Carolinians, as the team was known, were successful in their first season and won the pennant with a record of 74–48. They went on to take the postseason championship, winning a playoff with Portsmouth, four games to one. The team had several outstanding players, including pitchers Al Leake (14–5) and Buck O'Brien (19–12) and league home run champ Carl Gray (.300, 15 HR), who played left field. O'Brien had played from 1911 to 1913 with the Boston Red Sox. After that season, Rocky Mount played a series with the Asheville Tourists, champions of the North Carolina State League. The Carolinians again prevailed, four games to two.

For the 1916 season the team became known as the Tar Heels. They played well in the first part of the season but could not hold on and finished third, winning 61 and losing 60. Pitcher Abe Applegate posted an 18–10 record while Clarence Teague (14–14) led the league in strikeouts with 205.

Due to World War I, the league's 1917 season was cancelled on May 17. At that time Rocky Mount had a 6–9 record. The Virginia League returned the next season but Rocky Mount did not reenter until 1920, a season in which the league moved up to Class B. The Tar Heels could only manage a fifth place finish with their record of 53–66. Outfielder Frank Walker batted .369 but was called up to the Philadelphia Athletics in midseason. Manager Al Bridwell, who had played 11 seasons in the majors, hit .300 for the Tar Heels.

The Tar Heels' record of 77–57 was a great improvement in 1921 and the team finished third. They actually won the first half of the season but were disqualified in the standings due to getting caught paying salaries in excess of league limits. Because of this they were not allowed to participate in the postseason playoff. Frank Walker was back with the team and batted .355. The best offensive player on the team, however, was outfielder Ben Spencer, who hit .361 with 194 hits, 153 runs and 50 doubles.

The Tar Heels of 1922, managed by outfielder Frank Walker (.314), finished in fourth at 60–61. The team was led by shortstop Bill Narleski (.346, 86 RBIs, 15 HR) and first baseman Harry Swacina (.310, 88 RBIs, 13 HR). Narleski was on his way up, reaching the majors in 1929 for a two year stay, while Swacina was on his way down, having already played a few seasons in the big leagues.

Again led by Frank Walker (.367, 126 runs) in 1923, the Tar Heels finished in third place with a 63–59 record. Ben Spencer had another good year for the team, hitting .369 with 77 RBIs. Mark Webb (21–13) and Jake Hehl (19–17) were the leading pitchers. Frank Walker (.370) had another great season in 1924 as he won the batting title while again leading the team to a third place finish (74–62). He also led the league in runs scored with 117 and stolen bases with 50. Cecil Duff (23–11) and Ken Ash (17–14, 2.39 ERA) were the league's top pitchers.

Rocky Mount slipped to a fifth place finish in 1925. Twenty-five games out of first, the team won 53 and lost 79. Catchers Sid Womack (.332) and Jim Hamby (.302), who each spent half a season with the team, and center fielder Jack Reis (.304, 10 HR) were the leading hitters. Jake Hehl won 12 games but lost 19, though no member of the weak pitching staff posted a winning record. The team disbanded after the season.

The city was without professional baseball in 1926. In 1927, Rocky Mount took over Greensboro's place in the Class C Piedmont League with the new team becoming known as the Buccaneers. Outfielder Otis Cashion was one of the best players in the league, batting .335 with 102 RBIs and scoring a league leading 113 runs. Thirty-seven-year-old outfielder and manager Lee Gooch, who had played briefly in the major leagues ten years earlier, also had a good season, batting .320 with 90 RBIs. The best pitchers were Herb

May (22–11) and Bob Gufford (19–9). Overall it was an outstanding team, finishing with a league best record of 84–60. They failed to qualify for the playoffs, however, as they finished second (to two different teams) in both halves of the season.

The next season a new Eastern Carolina League (also Class D) was formed and Rocky Mount joined. The league was to last only two years. The Buccaneers finished third, at 55–56, in 1928. In 1929, however, the team won the second half of the season and finished with the league's best overall record (69–47). Led by pitcher Eddie Alsobrook (17–6) and outfielders Alta Cohen (.300), and Sam Fayonsky (.280, 94 runs, 100 BB, 46 SB), the Buccaneers went on to take the pennant, defeating Wilmington, four games to two, in the playoffs. The team and the league disbanded after the season due to financial difficulties.

It was 1936 before professional baseball returned to Rocky Mount. That season the Boston Red Sox moved their Piedmont League farm club from Charlotte to Rocky Mount. The Rocky Mount Red Sox, as they were named, had several powerful hitters, including right fielder Mike Christoff (.319, 36 HR, 135 RBIs) and third baseman Harl Maggert (.339, 30 HR, 119 RBIs). The other outfielders, Stan Spence (.315) and Emile "Red" Barnes (.309), also had good seasons. Of these four, only Christoff, though he had the best season, never played in the major leagues. Maggert made it to Boston for part of a season in 1938, while Spence became a four time All-Star with Washington. Barnes had already played several seasons in the majors and was finishing out his career in the minors. Thirty-seven-year-old shortstop George "Specs" Toporcer (.277), who also served as manager, had played much of eight seasons with the St. Louis Cardinals, beginning in 1921. Charlie Wagner, at 20–14, was the team's leading pitcher. He made it to Boston in 1938 and played parts of six seasons for the Red Sox. Despite all of Rocky Mount's talent the team could only manage a fourth place finish, winning 74 games and losing 69.

The 1937 team slipped even farther in the standings, to sixth place, with a record of 67–75. First baseman Paul Campbell, who would spend parts of six seasons in the majors, was the leading hitter (.309, 71 RBIs) and Andy Karl, who would also reach the big leagues, was the leading pitcher at 12–9. Outfielder Bob Daughters (.260) had one of the shortest major league careers in history. In April of 1937, Daughters had made the Boston team. He would appear in one game as a pinch runner, scoring a run but never batting or playing in the field. Sent to Rocky Mount to play the rest of the season, Daughters never made it back to the big leagues.

Managed by Herb Brett, the Rocky Mount Red Sox improved to third place in 1938. Led by catcher George Lacy (.314, 32 HR, 107 RBIs), the team posted a record of 70–64. They qualified for the playoffs and made it to the finals before losing to Charlotte, four games to one. The results of the 1939 season were not much different. The team finished third (70–67) and again made it to the playoff finals before losing, four games to two, to Asheville. The leaders of the 1939 team were third baseman Tom Reed (.279, 29 HR, 107 RBIs) and pitcher Charlie Pescod (15–10).

In 1940, Rocky Mount once again finished in third place, this time with a record of 75–61. As with the two previous seasons, the team advanced to the playoff finals before losing to the Durham Bulls, four games to two. The Red Sox were managed that season by future Hall of Famer Heinie Manush. Playing part-time in the outfield, Manush batted .280 with 16 RBIs. Rocky Mount's star player was shortstop Johnny Pesky. Named to the league All-Star team, Pesky led in hits with 187 and batted .325 on his way to becoming a standout with Boston. Earl Johnson was the team's leading pitcher at 12–6, even though he had been promoted to Boston in July. He went on to an eight year major league career, winning 40 games mainly as a reliever. Bill Voiselle (6–4, 2.61 ERA) would spend nine seasons in the big leagues, most of them with the Giants. A

total of ten players from Rocky Mount's 1940 team (including Manush) played at least a few games in the majors.

After the 1940 season, Rocky Mount lost its Piedmont League franchise when Boston transferred the team to Greensboro. When the Coastal Plain League franchise in Snow Hill announced that they could financially no longer continue to play, a group of Rocky Mount businessmen took action. Led by former big leaguer Frank Walker, who had played for and managed Rocky Mount in the early 1920s, the group purchased the team for $2,400 and renamed it the Leafs. In their first season — 1941— the Leafs finished at an even 59–59, good enough for fourth place. First baseman Tommy Kurst (.308, 26 HR, 105 RBIs) was the team's offensive leader, while Bill Kennedy (10–6, 2.23 ERA) had a good season on the mound. The Leafs qualified for the playoffs but lost in the first round to Wilson, four games to two.

The Coastal Plain League suspended operations before the start of the 1942 season due to the war, but Rocky Mount wanted to continue play. Renamed the Rocks, the team (along with the Wilson team) joined the Class D Bi-State League. Managed by George Ferrell (.314, 22 HR, 105 RBIs), the Rocks finished third in the six team league with a record of 63–60. Center fielder Harry Soufas (.316, 100 runs), who led the league with 29 home runs, was named as the league's Most Valuable Player. The Rocks beat Wilson in the first round of the playoffs and went on to take the league pennant by defeating Sanford, four games to one. Third baseman Bobby Thomson (.241), who played in 29 games for the Rocks, would achieve baseball immortality with the New York Giants in 1951 when he hit his pennant winning home run off Brooklyn's Ralph Branca.

Without a team for three seasons, Rocky Mount rejoined the Coastal Plain League when it resumed play in 1946. Player-manager Harry Soufas (.320) led the team to the pennant as they finished the regular season in first with a record of 74–51. They then went on to beat Goldsboro, four games to one, in the first round of the playoffs and Kinston, four games to two, in the finals. In addition to Soufas, the Rocks also had excellent hitters Dave Fowler (.325, 15 HR) and Quentin Martin (.312, 20 HR). Catcher Charlie Munday (.283, 83 RBIs) won the league home run title with 22. The real star of the Rocky Mount team, however, was left-handed pitcher Bill Kennedy. Kennedy turned in one of the most dominant pitching performances in the history of baseball, winning 28 games and losing only three with an amazing ERA of 1.03. He pitched 280 innings and 28 complete games. Winning his last 17 games, Kennedy went on to win all four games in the playoffs. The most incredible of his feats, however, was striking out 456 batters. No one has even come close to this total since. In a game against Goldsboro on June 24, Kennedy struck out 24 batters. Another game against Tarboro saw him strike out 22.

Kennedy made it to the major leagues in 1948 but his big-league career was much less spectacular than his season in Rocky Mount. He pitched for five teams over eight seasons, mainly as a reliever. Finishing his career with a 15–28 record and a 4.73 ERA, Kennedy struck out a total of only 256 big-league batters.

Managed by catcher Charlie Munday in 1947, the Rocky Mount Leafs finished a disappointing sixth with their 60–80 record. The team had some talent but lacked depth. Outfielder Herb May (.343, 24 HR, 113 RBIs) was one of the league's best hitters. Outfielder Eddie Musial (.315) and first baseman Curt Ballentine (.297) also contributed to the Leafs' offense. Veteran minor leaguer Al Jarlett (22–11) was the star of the otherwise lackluster pitching staff.

The 1948 team, led by first baseman-manager Cecil "Turkey" Tyson (.291), improved to fourth. Outfielder Quentin "Pepper" Martin (.366) had a great year for the Leafs, driving in 133 runs and setting the all-time Coastal Plain League record for hits with 207. Catcher Dave Fowler (.331, 114 RBIs) also set an all-time league record by scoring 138 runs, as did outfielder John Hanley (.304, 116 RBIs) with his 35 home runs.

Red Benton (28–10), who would later serve as the mayor of the city of Wilson, tied the league record for wins. Left-hander Harry Helmer (26–10) led the league in strikeouts with 268, the fourth highest total in league history. Despite all of this great talent, the Leafs lost to first place Tarboro in the first round of the playoffs, four games to two.

Rocky Mount was back on top in 1949. They posted a 79–60 record to win the pennant by four-and-a-half games over second place Kinston. Pepper Martin (.302), who began the season as manager before being replaced by pitcher Red Benton, had another great year, hitting 27 home runs with 119 RBIs. Benton again pitched well, turning in a 13–6 record on the mound. Third baseman Bob "Babe" Johnson (.292, 19 HR, 92 RBIs) and outfielder John Hanley (.340, 21 HR) also contributed greatly to the Leafs' offense. In the playoffs, the Leafs were upset in the first round by Greenville, four games to two.

Pitcher Red Benton (14–9) remained manager in 1950 and led the team to a second place, 73–65 finish. Pepper Martin had another impressive year as he won the batting title with a .351 average and led the league with 171 hits. As with the two previous seasons, Rocky Mount lost in the first round of the playoffs, this time to New Bern. By the 1950 season attendance all across the league was really starting to drop off. Rocky Mount drew over 100,000 fans in 1947 but only 62,000 in 1950.

The 1951 season saw the Leafs drop to sixth place (and last since two teams dropped out of the league during the season) with a record of 39–86. All-Star catcher Dave Fowler (.299, 83 RBIs) and outfielder Felix Frazier (.287, 18 HR, 86 RBIs) were two of the team's top players. Attendance dropped dramatically down to less than 28,000 for the season.

Another sixth place finish (out of eight teams this time) was the best the Leafs could manage in 1952, their record of 59–63 leaving them 16½ games out of first. Left-hander Rodney Heath led all pitchers with an ERA of 1.27 to go along with his 12–2 record. All-Star second baseman Oscar Barham (.265)

The 1951 Rocky Mount Leafs included: *Back:* Vanis Williamson, "Eskimo" Bill Tompkins, Gilbert Miller, Bill Rushich, Mel Mannino, Bill Fowler, Bill Anders; *Middle:* Earle Bruckner. Quentin "Pepper" Martin, Art Hoch, manager Red Benton, Robert "Babe" Johnson, Art Freiberger; *Front:* Joe Kopatch, Jim Reges, George Griffin, Ben "Streeter" Tugwell, Wade Martin, Pete King (courtesy Bill Fowler).

and shortstop Wade Martin (.263) led the offense. After that season the Coastal Plain League disbanded, leaving Rocky Mount without professional baseball.

It was to be 1962 before Rocky Mount was able to join another league. That season the city was granted a franchise in the Class B Carolina League. The team, again called the Leafs, was affiliated with the Cincinnati Reds. Walter "Buck" Leonard, a native of Rocky Mount and former Negro League star (who was later elected to the Hall of Fame), was hired as the team's vice president and unofficial batting instructor.

The Reds supplied the Leafs with good talent, especially hitting. Future major league stars Tony Perez and Cesar Tovar had Carolina League All-Star seasons in Rocky Mount. Perez batted .292 with 18 home runs, while Tovar won the batting title with a .329 average, tied for the league lead in runs (115)

and hits (168) and stole 56 bases. Outfielder Bert Barth, though he never made the major leagues, also had a great season for the Leafs. He batted .286 and led the league with 33 home runs and 136 RBIs. While the team had great hitters, it was lacking in pitching. The Leafs finished the season in seventh place with a record of 60–80.

For the 1963 season the Carolina League — now classified A in the new system — split into East and West halves. Rocky Mount was placed in the East along with Wilson, Kinston and the two Virginia teams, Portsmouth and Peninsula. The Leafs finished third in that division with an even 72–72 record. All-Star pitcher Gerry Merz led the league with 17 wins, while the offense was powered by outfielder Joe Wilson (.299, 26 HR, 106 RBIs). Future major league star Lee May, playing first base, batted .263 with 18 home runs.

The Rocky Mount Leafs became an

affiliate of the Washington Senators in 1964. The team did not play well and finished fourth in the East Division with a record of 61–77. Catcher Jim French (.270) would make it to Washington and spend several seasons as the Senators' reserve backstop.

The team switched its major league affiliation again for the 1965 season, this time to the Detroit Tigers. The Leafs met with little Carolina League success as they finished last in the East with a 68–82 record. Pitcher Jack DiLauro (12–7) would later spend the 1969 season as a reliever for the Mets. The team improved in 1966, finishing second in the East with a record of 72–63. They went on to win the pennant by sweeping both Kinston and Winston-Salem in the playoffs. The Leafs were led by future major league pitchers Dick Drago (15–9, 1.79 ERA) and Jim Rooker (12–5, 2.05 ERA). Catcher Jim Leyland batted .243 for the Leafs and though he would never make the major leagues as a player, he made it as a manager. That season the Leafs accomplished a feat that has never been matched in all of baseball history. In Greensboro, on May 15, Rocky Mount pitchers Dick Drago and Darrell Clark pitched no-hitters in both games of a doubleheader.

In a tight 1967 race, the Leafs finished third, three games behind Raleigh in the Eastern Division with a 74–68 record. The team then lost to Raleigh in a one game, first round playoff. Left-handed pitcher Jon Warden tied for the league lead in wins, posting a 15–11 record. In 1968, the Leafs slipped to 70–70, fifth in the East. The 1969 season saw the team make a complete turnaround : they finished first in the East with an 82–62 record. They were upset, however, in the first round of the playoffs by Peninsula, two games to none. Outfielder Elliott Maddox, who spent part of 1968 and all of 1969 with the Leafs, went on to an 11-year big league career. All-Star catcher Tim Hosley (27 HR) made it to Detroit the following year and spent nine seasons in the big leagues as a backup.

The Leafs of 1970, managed by longtime big league pitcher Max Lanier, dropped back

to a fifth place finish with a 70–68 record. Danny Bootchek (13–8) was the team's leading pitcher and the league leader with an ERA of 1.92. The 1971 team, managed by Len Okrie — another former major league player and coach — also finished in fifth. The Leafs' 65–69 record left them 17½ games out of first. Outfielder Marv Lane was named to the league All-Star team. The next season was even worse. The team's 49–88 record left them in last place, 30 games back. Attendance dropped to an all-time low that season with only 21,242 paying to see the Leafs play.

Attendance increased slightly in 1973 as the team played better baseball, finishing third in the league with a 75–65 record. The team was now known as the Phillies, borrowing the name of their new major league parent. Catcher Bill Nahorodny (.262) and shortstop Greg Pryor (.301) both went on to average major league careers. Pitcher Roy Thomas (15–8) also made it to the big leagues after leading the Carolina League in wins, strikeouts (193), and ERA (2.24).

Rocky Mount dropped back to fourth in 1974 after finishing at 73–66, 14 games out of first. All-Star shortstop Todd Cruz, who hit only .193, would make it to the big leagues. The Phillies played much better in 1975, winning both halves of a split season and taking the pennant with a record of 91–51. Third baseman Jim Morrison, on his way to a long major league career, was the team's offensive leader, hitting .288 and leading the league in home runs (20) and runs scored (98). Pitcher Warren Brusstar also made it to the majors after tying teammate Oliver Bell for the league lead in wins with 14. Despite winning the pennant, Rocky Mount dropped out of the Carolina League after the 1975 season due mainly to poor attendance.

Rocky Mount was readmitted to the Carolina League in 1980 as an independent team. Looking back, it was probably a big mistake on the part of the league. The Pines, as the team was called, finished with a record of only 24–114, worst in the history of the Carolina League and second only to Granite

Falls as the worst in the history of professional baseball in the state. The plan had been to stock the team with players from a baseball school in Florida owned by Pines owner Lou Haneles. The quantity and quality of available players was grossly underestimated by Haneles and his manager Mal Fichman. The Pines always had a shortage of players and those who did play were not up to Carolina League standards. After the disastrous season came to an end, the league voted to revoke the team's membership, probably ending forever Rocky Mount's minor league baseball history.

Rutherford County *see* Forest City

◆ ─────── *Salisbury* ─────── ◆

With the demise of the Salisbury-Spencer Colonials after the 1929 season, the town of Salisbury was without professional baseball until 1936. That season a new team, also called the Colonials, joined the independent Carolina League. The league was considered professional since players were paid, though it was not a member of minor league baseball's governing body, the National Association. The league was basically a professional version of the semipro Carolina Textile League of 1935, of which Salisbury had been a member. The 1936 season was a short one for the Colonials as they moved to Mooresville during the first month of the season in search of better attendance.

A new team, the Salisbury Bees, was formed in 1937 to participate in the newly created Class D North Carolina State League. Home games were played at Catawba College's Newman Park, which had been built in 1932. A Boston Bees farm club, Salisbury (57–55) had a mediocre first season and finished fifth in the eight team league. Outfielder Blackie Carter (.325) was the team's leading hitter as well as its manager. Fellow outfielder Mike Skaff hit .308 with 76 RBIs while John Seasoltz (13–9) was the leading pitcher.

Salisbury again finished fifth in both 1938 and 1939. The 1938 team, again managed by Blackie Carter (.302), posted a record of 51–60. Outfielder Claude Wilborn (.321, 90 RBIs) led in hitting while Bruno Perzan (8–3) and John Threlfall (14–7) were the Bees' best pitchers. The 1939 team, now named the Giants after signing a working agreement with the New York Giants, broke .500 and finished at 56–54. The star of that team was right fielder Borden Helms (.325, 44 SB, 100 runs), the only Salisbury player named as a league All-Star.

The 1940 Giants, still a New York farm club, improved to second place with a 64–46 record. First baseman Mike Schemer (.365) had a great year and was named to the league All-Star team. He made it up to the big league Giants for part of the 1945 season. Outfielder Norbert Barker (.315, 101 RBIs) was the team's leading run producer, while pitchers George Joseph (10–8, 2.68 ERA) and John Tansey (12–7, 2.98 ERA) were first and second in the league in earned run average. Though the team was talented, they were swept in the first round of the playoffs by Mooresville.

The next season Salisbury's Giants were more successful, winning the league championship. Again finishing the regular season in second place (62–38), they defeated Thomasville, three games to two, in the playoff's first round. The Giants then took the championship from Mooresville in a hard fought series, four games to three. All-Star third baseman Hal Harrigan won the batting title with a .359 average, also leading the league with 26 home runs. He was supported by shortstop Roy Nichols (.326) and pitchers Howard DeMartini (17–7, 2.31 ERA) and Ken Brondell (16–6).

The Giants of 1942 showed little resemblance to the championship winning team of 1941. They finished seventh, 35 games out of first, with a record of 29–69. Only outfielder Leander Morrison (.307) and second baseman Les Anderson (.306) stood out on a team that lacked both pitching and hitting. After that season the league suspended play due to World War II.

The league and the team resumed play in 1945. Owned and operated by the Pittsburgh Pirates, the Salisbury team adopted the name of their parent club. Salisbury's Pirates had an average season and finished at 59–55, good enough for fourth place. Led by outfielder Steve Lesigonich (.344) and a pitching staff that featured Marino Fasano (12–6, 2.33 ERA) and George Cramer (16–8), the Pirates advanced to the playoffs. There they lost to Lexington in the first round, four games to one.

The 1946 Pirates, winning 58 games and losing 54, dropped to fifth place. With an amazingly low team batting average of .211, only a good pitching staff, led by Stan Fain (11–3, 1.54 ERA), kept the team out of the cellar. They improved to second the next season with a record of 63–47. Third baseman Hal Harrigan returned and led the team with a .322 average, driving in 90 runs and hitting 24 home runs. The strong pitching staff included Jim Hechinger (12–5), Ray Kalkowski (15–5) and Craig Bennett (10–4). Advancing to the playoffs, the Pirates lost to Lexington in seven games. Attendance for the Pirates, at just over 60,000, was the best in the league that season.

Sixth place was all the 1948 Pirates could manage as they posted a record of 51–53, 13 games out of first. Hal Harrigan (.344, 102 RBIs), again the star of the team, tied for the league in home runs with 33. The team dropped even farther in 1949, all the way to the league cellar, with a 49–73 record. Outfielder John Paszek was the star of that team, hitting .297 with 19 home runs and 85 RBIs.

Finally in 1950, Salisbury's Pirates won the pennant, a dramatic turnaround from the previous season. Managed by George Detore, the team included first baseman George Hott (.338, 86 runs) and pitchers Reid Lemly (15–7) and Joe Gorski (11–6). With a record of 68–44, the Pirates advanced to the playoffs. There they were upset by Landis, however, four games to two.

Amazingly, the Pirates were back in the cellar in 1951; the team finished the season at 41–85, 49 games out of first. The offensive leader of the team was third baseman Bill Cayavec (.302, 21 HR, 98 runs). Ron Necciai, who would be a pitching sensation with Burlington the next season, was 4–9 for Salisbury. He also hit .364 in the 20 games he played. No pitcher on the team had a winning record. Attendance dropped by nearly 50,000 that season, down to only 14,964.

Salisbury fielded a good team in 1952, the North Carolina State League's final season. The Pirates finished third in the regular season with a record of 64–43 and then swept regular season champion Hi-Toms in the first round of the playoffs, four games to none. In the finals they took Mooresville to a seventh game before losing. Several Pirate players had outstanding seasons. First baseman Don Stafford won the batting title with an impressive .408 average and second baseman Henry Hampton finished second, hitting .358. Outfielder Glenn Eury (.298) won the home run title with 27 while pitcher Roy Mathews (20–8) led the league in wins.

After the 1952 season, the league folded due to poor attendance. Salisbury had not suffered as much as the other teams in the league; their 1952 attendance figures were nearly twice that of every other team in the league. Some members of the league — including Salisbury — joined with former members of the also defunct Western Carolina league to form the Tar Heel League in 1953. The Salisbury Rocots, which had signed a working agreement with the Boston Red Sox, finished last in the league with a 44–67 record. Infielders John Burns (.346) and John Smith (.332, 97 runs) led the team in hitting. Future major league pitcher Eli Grba was 7–11 for the Rocots and batted .333. The team disbanded after the season.

Salisbury was without baseball until the Western Carolina League was reformed in 1960. The Salisbury Braves, a Milwaukee farm team, entered the new league as a charter franchise. They played well, finishing the regular season in second place at 65–35. The Braves then went on to take the championship by defeating Newton-Conover in the first round and Hickory, three games to two, in the finals. All-Star second baseman Jack Turney (.362) won the batting title while third baseman Paul Roberts (.283, 23 HR, 91 RBIs) led the league in RBIs and home runs. Jimmy Basinger (12–7, 1.90 ERA) and George Schneider (7–3) were the team's leading pitchers.

Managed by Alex Cosmidis, the Salisbury Braves, a farm club of the expansion Houston Colt .45s, again played well in 1961. Their record of 64–38 was the best in the league. First baseman and league MVP Aaron Pointer had an impressive season, winning the batting title with a .402 average and leading the league in runs (117), hits (129), and stolen bases (42). He never met with the same success in the major leagues, batting only .208 in 40 games with Houston. Third baseman Tommy Murray (.290) was the league RBI leader with 83. Salisbury's leading pitchers were Richard Aird (8–4) and Marvin Dutt (9–1, 2.74 ERA). The Braves advanced to the playoffs but were upset in the first round by fourth place Shelby, two games to none.

In 1962, the Braves, now a Mets affiliate, finished second in the four team league with a 52–44 record. Outfielder Carmen Iannacone led that year's team in batting with a .342 average, while Tommy Addington was the team's best pitcher with a 7–3 record. No playoffs were held that season as Statesville had won both halves of the season.

For the 1963 season, Salisbury became a member of the Los Angeles Dodgers farm system. Salisbury's Dodgers played well, winning the second half of the season and turning in a 73–53 record. They lost, however, in the playoffs to Greenville, two games to none. Pitcher Jack Billingham (9–6, 3.49 ERA) went on to have a long major league career and was a starter for Cincinnati's Big Red Machine in 1975 and '76.

The Dodgers were not denied the pennant in 1964. They finished with a league best record of 77–51 and went on to defeat Rock Hill in the playoffs, two games to one. Second baseman Richard Schmidt, named as the league's Most Valuable Player, won the batting title with a .306 average and scored a league leading 86 runs. Outfielder Bill Parlier, though he played in only 61 games, led the league with 20 home runs. The pitching staff was led by John Purdin (14–3), who received a September call-up to Los Angeles.

Salisbury again switched major league affiliations in 1965, this time to Houston. Renamed the Astros, the team again finished with the league's best record at 70–48, winning the first half of the season. Outfielder Ed Moxey (.345) won the batting title. Eighteen-year-old shortstop Fred Stanley, who played half of the season with Salisbury and hit .241, would spend 14 years as a big league utility infielder. Outfielder Bob Watson (.285) would become a star with Houston and later serve as general manager of the New York Yankees. Unfortunately for the Astros, they lost in the playoffs to Rock Hill, two games to none. The next season, the Astros slipped down to sixth in the eight team league with a 44–77 record. Attendance was last in the league at 23,737 and the team disbanded after the season. Outfielder Danny Walton (.329, 20 HR, 80 RBIs) would go on to spend several seasons in the big leagues.

Salisbury was without a team for the 1967 season but a new team — the Salisbury Senators — was formed in 1968 and rejoined the WCL. A Washington farm club, the team played poorly and finished last in the league with a 34–87 record. The only notable player

Dick Loughridge, Tom Murray, league MVP Aaron Pointer and Fred White were members of the 1961 Salisbury Braves (courtesy Alex Cosmidis).

on the team was pitcher Mike Thompson (7–13, 4.27 ERA). Thompson led the league in strikeouts and innings pitched but also in losses, walks and hits. He eventually recovered from his control problems enough to pitch a few seasons in the majors. The team, which proved to be the last for Salisbury, disbanded after the season due to poor attendance.

 ——————— *Salisbury-Spencer* ———————

Professional baseball first appeared in the towns of Salisbury and Spencer in 1905. That summer a team representing the two joined with Charlotte, Greensboro and Danville (Va.) to form the Class D Virginia–North Carolina League. On July 17, however, the team, named the Twins, decided to relocate to Winston-Salem, probably in search of better attendance.

The next professional team to represent the two towns — the Salisbury-Spencer Colonials — entered the Class C Piedmont League in 1925 as an expansion franchise. The Colonials, who played at 3,000-seat Colonial Park, were admitted to the league to fill a void left by the withdrawal of the Danville Tobacconists. The team was not very successful that first year as they finished in last place with a record of 54–69. Otis Cashion (.324) of the Colonials did manage to lead the league in home runs with 25. Second baseman Gale Staley, the team's leading hitter with a .351 average, finished the season with the Chicago Cubs. Baxter "Buck" Jordan, a native of Cooleemee, North Carolina, hit .287 with the Colonials that season. He would spend much of ten seasons in the majors, mainly with the Boston Braves, retiring with a lifetime .299 average.

The 1926 team improved to a fourth place finish and a record of 69–75. Buck Jordan returned at shortstop and hit .328, while first baseman Ed Marshall hit .311. Herm Holshauser was the team's leading pitcher at 14–12. The next season, however, proved to be the best one for the Colonials. With an offense powered by outfielders Leroy "Cowboy" Jones (.396, 63 RBIs) and George Whiteman (.320, 102 RBIs) the 1927 team finished 83–62, champions of the second half of the season. In the playoffs they faced first half champion Raleigh and defeated them, three games to two, to take the pennant. Pitchers Jim Richardson (23–11) and Bob

Huffman (16–3) led the team to victory. Outfielder Johnny Gill, who hit .295 in 29 games, finished the next season with the Cleveland Indians.

In 1928 the Colonials slipped to a fourth place finish; at 61–74, they were 22 games behind first place Winston-Salem. Leroy Jones had another great year, hitting .386 with 23 home runs, 100 RBIs, 105 runs scored and a league leading 47 doubles. Other than Jones and player-manager George Whiteman (.299, 83 RBIs), the team lacked offense. The Colonials of 1929 continued the slide and wound up in the cellar, 37½ games back, with a record of 48–89. Shortstop Ike Kahdot hit .319 and Leroy Jones — in his third year with the team — hit .357 with 12 home runs. Art Jones (6–4) was the only pitcher on the team with a winning record. He went on to have a major league career that lasted exactly one inning, with Brooklyn in 1932. After the season the team withdrew from the league and disbanded due to poor attendance. It would be eight years before professional baseball returned to Salisbury, though that team would not be shared with Spencer.

◆ ——————— *Sanford* ——————— ◆

The Sanford Spinners joined the Class D Bi-State League as a new franchise in 1941. Three teams had dropped out of the league and Sanford was invited to join to give the league an even six teams. It was a very successful first year for the Spinners. They finished the season in fourth place with a record of 58–54 and qualified for the playoffs. In the first round, the Spinners upset Martinsville, four games to three. They went on to take the championship by defeating the Danville-Schoolfield Leafs, four games to two. Pitcher Dave Odom (16–9), who went on to pitch in 22 games for the Boston Braves in 1943, led the league in strikeouts with 190. Outfielder Neb Stewart (.307, 14 HR) was the best hitter to spend the entire season with the

team. That season marked the first in a Sanford uniform for outfielder Orville "Hank" Nesselrode. In 49 games he hit 320.

In 1942 the Spinners again played well, finishing in second place with a 62–59 record. First baseman Bill Gardner (.317, 76 RBIs) provided much of the team's offense and led the league with 30 stolen bases. Outfielder Conklyn Merriwether (.301) was also one of the Spinner's best pitchers as he won ten games and lost five. Ray Boles led the team with a 14–5 pitching record. The Spinners advanced to the playoffs that season, defeating Burlington in the first round but losing to Rocky Mount in the finals, four games to one. The team disbanded after that season — as did the entire league — due to the war.

Sanford's Hank Nesselrode (right) and manager Gaither Riley in 1946 (courtesy Gaither Riley).

The 1946 Sanford Spinners included: *Back:* Hank Nesselrode, Dave Odom, George Bortz, Howard Auman, Bill Stone, Bob Pugh, Bob Wicker; *Front:* Phalti Shoffner, Joe Nessing Jimmy Guinn, Jim Gales, Ned Butcher, Zeb Harrington (mgr.), Carl Powell, Joe Trentalange (courtesy Zeb "Dan" Harrington).

In 1946 the Spinners reorganized as a member of the new Class D Tobacco State League and professional baseball returned to Sanford's 2,500-seat Temple Park. The team had a great regular season (71–48) and finished in first place. They were upset, however in the first round of the playoffs by Angier–Fuquay Springs. Outfielder Hank Nesselrode returned to the team after four years of military service and batted .354, leading the league in home runs (30) and RBIs (150). He would lead the league in these categories for three seasons. From 1946 through 1948, Nesselrode was the dominant offensive player in the league, yet he remained in Class D baseball. Shortstop Joe Nessing, the league's best fielder at that position, also had a good season, hitting .314. Bill Stone (16–8) was the Spinners' leading pitcher.

The Spinners of 1947 turned in an impressive performance, finishing 12½ games ahead of second place Lumberton with a record of 86–39. Hank Nesselrode hit .352 with 32 home runs and 166 RBIs, while fellow outfielder Jim Wilson led the league in batting average (.385), runs (133) and hits (205). Second baseman Jim Guinn (.334, 42 SB, 131 runs) joined Nesselrode and Wilson

on the All-Star team. Pitcher Bill Stone had another great season at 18–7, while John McFadden (15–5) was the league leader with an ERA of 2.44. In the playoffs the Spinners defeated Wilmington, four games to three, and went on to beat Lumberton in seven games to take the championship.

Sanford again dominated the Tobacco State League in 1948. Nesselrode (.362, 27 HRs, 159 RBIs) and Wilson (.350, 145 runs, 212 hits) again led the team to the pennant, as they finished at 80–56. The Spinners' strong pitching staff featured three of the league's best that season: John McFadden (20–9, 3.02 ERA), Hoyt Clegg (15–6) and Clarence Salter (17–7). They easily defeated Smithfield-Selma in the first round of the playoffs, four games to one. In the finals, however, the Spinners were upset by Red Springs, also four games to one.

The Spinners slipped to fourth place in 1949, winning 71 games and losing 62. They qualified for the playoffs but lost, four games to two, to Red Springs. The loss of Hank Nesselrode, who retired after the 1948 season, was felt. The team's offense, led by outfielder Ziggy Sklowdowski (.305), lacked in power. The pitching staff, however, was excellent and featured Hoyt Clegg (19–9, 2.57 ERA), Sam Gibson (17–9) and Clayton Andrews (11–8, 2.68 ERA).

The 1950 season was the last for the Tobacco State League. The Spinners, under outstanding manager Zeb Harrington for the sixth year, finished the season 1½ games out of first with a record of 90–44. They were led by pitchers Hoyt Clegg (24 wins), Richard Causey (148 SOs) and Clayton Andrews

(2.63 ERA), all league leaders. The offense featured first baseman Herb May (.340, 93 RBIs). In the first round of the playoffs the Spinners swept Red Springs. They lost the finals, however, to Rockingham, a team that they had finished 26 games ahead of in the regular season, by a margin of four games to three. That season proved to be the final one for professional baseball in Sanford.

 ———————————— *Shelby* ————————————

The town of Shelby, in which textile league ball had been played for years, first entered the world of professional baseball in 1936. A team representing the town was formed for entry in the independent Carolina League. Though not a member of the National Association — minor league baseball's governing body — the league was truly professional as it paid unlimited salaries. Named the Shelby Cee Cees (after Cleveland Cloth, the team's sponsor), the team had several outstanding hitters but lacked pitching. The only statistics available are from midseason and at that time Shelby first baseman "Cricket" Weathers was second in the league in hitting with a .427 average. Catcher Coyt "Red" Murray was hitting .389, while outfielder "Rags" Suddeth (.342, 12 HR) had driven in 49 runs. The team did not last much past midseason, however, as financial difficulties forced them to drop out of the league on August 1.

In 1937, a new Shelby team was formed. A charter member of the Class D North Carolina State League, the team was owned and operated by the St. Louis Cardinals. Shelby's Cardinals finished fourth in the league that season, posting a 55–52 record. Talented players included catcher Floyd Beal (.279, 107 RBIs, 21 HR), shortstop Frank "Creepy" Crespi (.314, 87 RBIs), and second baseman Jack Angle (.310, 109 runs). Led by first baseman–manager George Silvey (.273, 15 3B, 56

SB), the league leader in triples and stolen bases, the team advanced to the playoffs. The Cardinals defeated Thomasville in the first round but lost in the finals to Mooresville, four games to three.

The Cardinals returned in 1938 and played well. However, the team decided to move to Gastonia on July 22, hoping for better attendance.

A new team named the Shelby Nationals was formed for the 1939 season. The team, a Washington farm club, was a charter member of the new Tar Heel League, also a Class D circuit. The Nationals finished the season 22½ games out of first with a 50–59 record, good enough for fourth place and a playoff berth. They lost there, however, to Gastonia, three games to one. The team was led that season by the outstanding play of All-Star second baseman Jim Guinn (.371, 69 RBIs, 84 runs), second in the league in batting.

The team returned in 1940 but their name was changed to the Colonels. They played poorly and on July 19 they dropped out of the league, as did the Newton-Conover club. At the time of their demise, the Colonels had a record of 16–54. Outfielder Danny Gardella (.252) played 37 games for the Colonels before going to Williamston in the Coastal Plain League. He went on to spend the 1944 and '45 seasons with the New York Giants.

It was 1946 before another professional

team was formed. That season the Shelby Cubs, a Chicago farm club, joined the new Class B Tri-State League. This was an ambitious move up from the Class D leagues previous Shelby teams had competed in. The Cubs (59–81) were not very successful that season and finished 34 games out of first, tied for fourth place. After winning a one game playoff with Anderson to decide fourth place, the Cubs advanced to the playoffs and were defeated by Charlotte, four games to two. The team disbanded after the season. Two players from that season's team would go on to reach Chicago. Shortstop Roy Smalley, who hit only .219 in 30 games for Shelby, would spend ten seasons in the big leagues. Outfielder Hal Jeffcoat (.294, 15 HR, 74 RBIs) later played 12 seasons for the Chicago Cubs, first in the outfield and then later as a pitcher.

Moving back to Class D ball in 1948, Shelby formed another team and joined the new Western Carolina League. Called the Farmers, the team finished in fifth place with a 54–55 record. Pitcher Boyce Stone (16–9, 3.19 ERA) and All-Star outfielder Len Morrison (.316, 99 RBIs), who led the league in bases on balls with 105, were the team's best players. The next season, the Farmers played poorly and dropped to seventh in the eight team league with 40 wins and 68 losses. Manager and outfielder Walt Dixon, who took over at midseason, hit .368 with 61 RBIs in 70 games.

The team again finished seventh in 1950, posting a 47–63 record. Manager Walt Dixon was again the star of the team, batting .363 with 118 RBIs and 25 home runs. Pitcher Carl Brown lead the league in strikeouts with 236.

Finally in 1951 the Farmers improved. Led by the outstanding play of outfielders Henry Miller (.387, 106 RBIs, 15 HR) — the league batting champ — and Eddie Bass (.386, 157 RBIs, 18 HR), the team finished the regular season in second place. With a 67–44 record and a team batting average of .304, the Farmers advanced to the playoffs. They defeated Newton-Conover in the first round and went on to take the championship, prevailing over Morganton in seven

games. Other Shelby Farmers with standout seasons were first baseman Charlie Ballard (.365, 137 runs) and pitcher Jose Nakamura (17–6, 3.28 ERA).

The Farmers had another successful season in 1952. They again finished second in the regular season, this time with a 71–39 record. Sweeping Rutherford County in the first round of the playoffs, the Farmers took the championship by defeating Lincolnton, four games to three, in the finals. Charlie Ballard, again at first base for the Farmers, won the batting title with a .352 average, while outfielder Russell "Red" Mincy hit .336 with 85 RBIs. Pitcher Joe Sheppard was the best in the league, leading in wins (24) and ERA (2.31).

The Western Carolina League disbanded after the 1952 season and several of its former members — Shelby included — became charter members of the new Tar Heel League in 1953. The team, changing its name to the Shelby Clippers, finished third in the league standings with a 60–49 record. Charlie Ballard hit .332 with 95 RBIs and Red Mincy — near the end of a long, outstanding minor league career — hit .349 and drove in 101 runs. Pitcher Jose Nakamura (19–11) led the league with a 2.40 ERA. That season also saw the debut of an 18-year-old rookie pitcher named George Brunet. Brunet was 1–0 in seven games with Shelby. He went on to spend 32 seasons in professional baseball as a player. In the major leagues off and on from 1956 to 1971, Brunet moved to the Mexican leagues in 1973 and remained there until retirement in 1985. He holds the career record for minor league strikeouts with 3,175, the first 17 of those coming as a Shelby Clipper. Despite the Clippers' talent that season, they lost in the first round of the playoffs to Marion, four games to two.

The Tar Heel League began play in 1954 with only four teams, making it the smallest league in organized baseball. On June 21, the Shelby team decided to quit the league due to financial difficulties. The league could not continue and was forced to disband. At the time of their demise the Shelby Clippers had a record of 16–32, last in the league.

Shelby was without professional base-ball until 1960, when the Western Carolina League was resurrected. Named the Colonels, the team posted a 42–53 record that season, leaving them in fifth place. Outfielder Lanier Robinson (.347) finished second in league batting, while Don Bridges (11–8, 2.10 ERA) was the team's best pitcher. Manager Teddy Wilson, who had spent three seasons in the big leagues, hit .382 in 49 games. Though the entire league suffered from poor attendance, Shelby was particularly bad. Only 14,103 spectators came to see the Colonels play.

The 1961 team signed a working agree-ment with the Pittsburgh Pirates, and im-proved slightly to finish fourth with a 51–55 record. Surprisingly, the Colonels swept first place Salisbury in the playoffs, two games to none. They then took the league pennant by defeating Lexington, two games to one. Outfielder Benny Von Cannon (.302) led the team in batting, while Phil Andress (13–5, 3.24 ERA) was the Colonels' best pitcher.

The WCL shrank to four teams in 1962 with Shelby (40–59) finishing last. The team had little offense as leading hitter (of those qualified for the batting title) first baseman Frank Petrellis hit only .275. Petrellis did tie for the league lead in home runs with the amazingly low total of nine. Benny Von Can-non (.302) had the same batting average as the previous season but played in only 32 games. The team was also weak in pitching, as no starting pitcher had a record above .500.

The 1963 season saw the Colonels sign a working agreement with the New York Yan-kees. It did not help the team win, though, as they finished last in the now eight team league with a 48–74 record. The team batting average was a lowly .224, while the team ERA was also last at 4.48. Future big league pitcher George Culver's 1.71 ERA earned him a promotion after only nine games. The team's best hitter, outfielder Steve Whitaker (.293, 11 HR), was promoted after 45 games. The next season, the Shelby Yankees saw slight improvement as they finished sixth with a 59–68 record. Fritz Peterson was the team's best pitcher, posting a 10–7 record

with a 2.73 ERA. He also played in the field and hit .345 in 55 games. Peterson went on to win 133 games in an 11-year big league ca-reer, most of them with the Yankees.

In 1965 the team signed a working agreement with the Kansas City Athletics and changed its name to the Rebels. Man-aged by Wes Ferrell for part of the season, the team still did not meet with much success and finished sixth, winning 55 games and losing 68. Eighteen-year-old outfielder Gene Tenace hit .183 in 32 games. In his 15-year major league career, Tenace would play on four World Series champion teams (Oakland 1972–74; St. Louis 1982) and was named World Series MVP in 1972. Financial difficul-ties caused by poor attendance (22,876; last in the league) led to the disbanding of the Shelby Rebels after the 1965 season.

It was 1969 before Shelby fielded an-other team. That season the Shelby Senators, a Washington farm team, reentered the Western Carolinas League. The team started out slowly but improved to win the second half of the season, finishing with the fourth best overall record in the league at 61–63. Pitcher Jimmy Blackmon (15–5) led the league in wins while Gary Carter turned in an 8–2 record. Outfielder John Wockenfuss, who hit .325 in 39 games, went on to spend 12 years in the major leagues. In the playoffs with first half champ Greenwood, the Sena-tors lost, two games to one. The team dis-banded after the season.

With the demise of the Senators, Shelby was again left without baseball, this time until 1977. The Shelby Reds, a Cincinnati farm team, were formed that season and they rejoined the WCL. The Reds finished 22 games out of first that season with a 60–79 record. Pitcher Bruce Berenyi, who led the league with a 2.30 ERA, would go on to pitch for Cincinnati and the N.Y. Mets in the early 1980s. The Reds were much improved the next season as they finished second with a 75–64 record. However, the Greenwood Braves won both halves of the season so no playoff was held. Outfielder Ty Waller, catcher Steve Christmas and pitcher Paul

Gibson were named to the league All-Star team and would all appear in the major leagues.

Shelby became a Pittsburgh farm team in 1979 and the team changed its name to the Pirates. They finished in the league cellar, 20 games out of first, with a 56–78 record. Last in the league in both team batting and pitching, the only real standout on the team was first baseman Eddie Vargas (.282), the league home run champ with 31.

In 1980, the WCL became the South Atlantic League and the Shelby Pirates were placed in the North Division of the league. The team again played poorly and finished last in that division at 58–80. Attendance was dismal as only 15,393 paid to see the Pirates play. By comparison, Greensboro led the league in attendance with over 255,000.

Attendance did increase considerably the next season — up to 51,324 — though the team still finished in the league cellar with a 59–83 record. The Shelby Mets, now a New York Mets farm team, were led that season by All-Star first baseman Larry Pittman (.247, 19 HR, 69 RBIs). Future major league star Lenny Dykstra spent part of the season with Shelby and hit .261 in 48 games.

The Mets improved greatly in 1982, finishing second in the North Division at 77–63, but Greensboro won both halves of the season so no divisional playoff was held. Had Shelby been in the South Division they would have finished first. Outfielder Lenny Dykstra was back and had a good season, hitting .291, scoring 95 runs and stealing 77 bases. Fellow outfielders Mark Carreon (.329, 120 runs) and John Christenson (.334, 97 RBIs, 22 HR, 100 runs) had great seasons and finished second and third in the league in batting. Both made the big leagues. Once again, Shelby had a problem with poor attendance as only 11,784 came to see the Mets play in 1982. After the season the team moved to Columbia, South Carolina. Minor league baseball has not returned to Shelby.

Smithfield-Selma

The Smithfield Leafs were formed in 1946 and became a charter member of the Class D Tobacco State League. Playing at Legion Park, the Leafs finished that first season with a record of 58–62, putting them in third place. They qualified for the playoffs but lost in the first round to Clinton, four games to one. Outfielders Dick Woodard (.336, 98 RBIs) and Leo Niezgoda (.333) — the league leader in hits with 173 — were the team's best hitters. Hearn Robinson (14–9) and Alton Bird (12–8) led the pitching staff.

In 1947 the team officially changed its name to the Smithfield-Selma Leafs. They had a terrible season and finished in last place, 40 games back, with a record of 46–79. The Leafs had a good offense that season but lacked reliable pitching. The team's top hitters were outfielders Dick Woodard (.381 in 69 games), Leonard Bernstein (.324), and Preston Carroll (.329). Shortstop Pete Howard hit .304, stole 59 bases and was named to the league All-Star team. Catcher Sam Narron, who had appeared briefly in the big leagues, batted .385 in 27 games with the Leafs. Henry Koch (7–3) was the only pitcher on the team with a winning record.

The Leafs of 1948 did substantially better than the previous year, finishing in fourth place with a record of 73–65. They lost in the playoffs to Sanford, however, four games to one. The Leafs began that season managed by Sam Narron (.317 in 49 games), but he was replaced by Virgil Payne (.301, 71 RBIs) on June 1. Payne was capable of playing most positions and was named to the All-Star team as a utilityman. Dick Woodard (.399 in 36 games) was having another great season before being sold to Burlington of the Carolina League. Outfielders Preston Carroll (.323)

Smithfield outfielder Joe Eonta (left) and shortstop Pete Howard in 1946 (courtesy Pete Howard).

Smithfield-Selma outfielder Joe Eonta getting married at home plate in 1947 (courtesy Pete Howard).

and Joe Eonta (.301) turned in strong performances, while pitcher Aaron Osofsky (24–5, 2.76 ERA) led the league in wins that season.

The next season was another average one for the Leafs. They finished in fifth place with a record of 70–65 and missed qualifying for the playoffs. Virgil Payne began that season as manager but was replaced by pitcher Claude Weaver, who in turn was replaced by catcher Paul Kluk on June 9.

Amazingly, the Leafs had three players to hit .400 or better, though outfielder Joe Parise (.416 in 101 ABs) and manager Paul Kluk (.412 in 148 ABs) both lacked enough at-bats to qualify for the batting title. Outfielder Dick Woodard (.400, 113 RBIs, 106 runs) returned to the team and finished third in the league batting race. Amby Foote (18–12, 3.24)

and Carl Barham (12–5) were the Leafs' best pitchers.

The 1950 season was the last for the Tobacco State League. Attendance fell off dramatically for every team in the league and for this reason the Smithfield-Selma Leafs, who had drawn only 19,000 fans, withdrew from the league after the August 16 game. They had played 111 games and had a record of 49–62.

The Leafs' star player was again outfielder Dick Woodard. He drove in 79 runs, drew 104 bases on balls and batted .351, third best average in the league. Manager and first baseman Marvin Lorenz (.301, 91 RBIs), who signed on with Clinton for the final two weeks of the season, was named to the league All-Star team.

Snow Hill

The Snow Hill Billies were a member of the Coastal Plain League for seven years — from the league's founding in 1934 as a semi-pro circuit and from 1937 through 1940 when the league was a Class D member of the National Association. Owned by prominent local businessman and farmer Josiah Exum, the Billies had a working agreement with the New York Yankees by way of Norfolk of the Piedmont League.

That first year as true professionals the Billies played great baseball, winning the regular season pennant with a record of 62–36. In the playoffs they beat New Bern, three games to two, and then took the championship, defeating Tarboro, four games to one.

The stars of the team that season were pitcher Emil Zak (16–3) and outfielder Dwight Wall (.279), league leader in runs with 88. Future major leaguer Aaron Robinson, who had also played at Snow Hill in the semipro days, played third base and led the Billies with a .372 batting average, 85 RBIs and 130 hits. Manager D.C. "Peahead" Walker was also the Elon College football coach and would later coach at Wake Forest. Another notable player on the team was shortstop Walter Rabb (.242), who went on to become head baseball coach at UNC.

The Billies fell to third place for the 1938 season (although they were only one game back) with a record of 61–49. They won in the first round of the playoffs, defeating Tarboro, four games to two, but were swept in the finals by New Bern. Pitcher Allen Gettel, in his first year of pro baseball, went 16–7 on his way to pitching in 184 major league games over seven seasons. Third baseman Tony

Maisano was the team's leading offensive player, batting .354 with 16 home runs and 78 RBIs. Returning shortstop Walter Rabb hit .309.

Despite having the league's two leading sluggers — catcher Joe Bistroff (.291, 32 HR, 108 RBIs) — and first baseman Harry Soufas (.338, 30 HR, 104 RBIs), the Billies finished in only seventh place (56–64) in 1939. Though they had a good offense — which also included All-Star third baseman Tony Maisano (.303) — the team lacked a solid pitching staff.

The 1940 season saw the Billies improve only slightly, as they finished in fifth at 62–64. Shortstop Walter Rabb (.270, league leading 428 assists), in his fourth season with the Billies, made the All–Coastal Plain team, as did catcher Norm McCaskill (.272). First baseman L.D. Burdette (.341) was the team's leading hitter, while manager and outfielder Dwight Wall hit .298. The team's best pitchers were Bill Moran (15–9) and Virgil Taylor (17–12).

After the 1940 season the Snow Hill franchise was sold to a group from Rocky Mount, leaving the town without professional baseball.

Snow Hill has the distinction of being the smallest town in North Carolina (and probably the entire nation) to ever have a professional baseball team: In 1940 the population was just over 900. The ballpark, which no longer exists, was located near the downtown area beside Contentnea Creek. It was small — seating perhaps 1,500–2,000 people — with a covered grandstand and bleachers down both sides. The dimensions were approximately 330 feet down each line and 390–400 feet to center with a "skinned" infield.

Spindale *see* Forest City

The 1937 Snow Hill Billies included: *Back:* John "Whack" Hyder, George Hruska, Joe Bertram, Joe "Jabber" Joyce; *Middle:* Gene "White Tie" McCann (Yankees scout), Emil Zak, Walter Latham, Dwight Wall, D.C. "Peahead" Walker; *Front:* Aaron Robinson, Harry Soufas, Horace Mewborn, Walter Rabb, Joe Bistroff (courtesy Walter Rabb).

◆ ——————— *Statesville* ——————— ◆

Statesville's organized baseball history goes back to the summer of 1900. The minor leagues were just beginning to take hold in the South and baseball enthusiasts decided to start a league in North Carolina. The North Carolina Baseball Association was formed and made up of teams from Charlotte, Durham, Raleigh, Tarboro, Wilmington and Statesville. The short-lived league, which probably could be classified as only semiprofessional, lasted only from June 26 to August 4.

Nearly four decades later, in 1939, the town's first truly professional team, the Statesville Owls, was a charter member of the Class D Tar Heel League. Overall they were an average ball club though they did have some good talent, including leading hitter

Leon Thompson (.331) in the outfield and All-Star shortstop Joe Zanolli (.289, 40 SB). The Owls finished third in the league with a 56–51 record. Qualifying for the playoffs, they swept Lenoir in the first round. They lost in the finals to Gastonia, however, four games to three.

The next season, the Owls played outstanding ball and took the pennant by eight games with a record of 73–37. Led by talented pitchers Herman Drefs (17–5), Walter Lentz (11–3), Price Ferguson (14–3) and Rene DeSorcy (14–6), the Owls went on to take the championship by defeating Lenoir and then Hickory in the playoffs. Surprisingly, no member of the talented pitching staff ever reached the big leagues. The team's offense was led by outfielder Jim Miller (.340, 85 RBIs) and first baseman–manager Clarence McCrone (.269, 14 HR). The Tar Heel League, due to financial difficulties, disbanded after the season, leaving Statesville without baseball for the 1941 season.

A new Owls team was formed in 1942 as a member of the Class D North Carolina State League. The team finished sixth in the eight team league with a 48–51 record. Playing in the Owls' outfield that season was former University of Tennessee All-American football player Beattie Feathers (.296). Feathers spent seven seasons in the NFL, playing minor league baseball in the summers. After retiring from both sports as a player, he went on to coach football at North Carolina State from 1944 to 1951. Another Statesville outfielder that season, rookie George "Teddy" Wilson (.335), went on to play three seasons in the majors. Minor league legend Jim Poole — the Owls' manager and first baseman — hit .322.

North Carolina State League play was suspended after the 1942 season due to the war. When league play resumed in 1945, Statesville remained a member. A farm club of the Chicago Cubs, the team (also named the Cubs) finished fifth in the eight team league, posting a 53–58 record. Outfielder Frank Schmidt (.363, 30 SB), second in the league in batting, was the star of that team. The Cubs were even less successful in 1946 as they finished seventh, 35 games out of first, with a 41–69 record. Pitcher Gene Sylvester, though he was only with the team for half of the season, compiled a 7–3 record with an ERA of 1.41.

Renamed the Owls in 1947, the again independent team dropped to the league cellar with a 40–71 record. The 1948 season saw the team do a dramatic turnaround as the Owls finished the regular season in second place with a 63–47 record. What the team lacked in offense (they finished last in the league in team batting with a .258 average), they made up for with an outstanding pitching staff. Frank Smith (20–5) and Bill Miller (13–5) were both named to the league All-Star team. In the playoffs the Owls easily defeated Lexington, four games to one. In a hard fought seven game final series with Hickory, the Owls prevailed to take the championship.

In 1949, the Owls dropped to fifth in the league standings. With a 53–71 record, the team finished 37 games behind the first place Hi-Toms. The Owls did have some outstanding players, as catcher George Bradshaw (.342) tied for the league lead in hits with 169 while pitcher Ernie Johnson (6–7) turned in a league leading ERA of 2.04. Pitcher Frank Smith (16–16) was again named an All-Star.

Though improved, the Owls again finished in fifth place in 1950. In a close league race, the Owls' record of 59–53 left them nine games out of first. First baseman Ken Rhyne (.356, 32 HR, 119 RBIs) was one of the best players in the league, leading in RBIs and tying for the lead in home runs and hits. Second baseman Fred Daniels (.347) and pitcher Ernie Johnson (20–8) joined Rhyne on the league All-Star team. Manager and catcher George Bradshaw hit .321.

The Owls finished fourth in 1951 with a 62–64 record, 28 games behind the league dominating Hi-Toms. Ken Rhyne began the season as player-manager but was replaced on June 1 by third baseman Len Cross. Cross (.325, 103 RBIs, 33 HR, 101 runs) was the Owls' best player that season and the only one on the team to hit better than .300. Ernie Johnson (15–10) was again the team's best pitcher, leading the league with 223 strikeouts. The Owls qualified for the playoffs and swept Hickory in the first round but were swept themselves by High Point–Thomasville in the finals.

In 1952, the last season for the North Carolina State League, the Statesville Owls finished fifth out of the six teams remaining in the league. With a record of 41–68, the Owls were 34 games out of first. The team's only real standout was third baseman Owen Linn, who hit .315 with 17 home runs. Attendance was down to 16,913 from a high of nearly 70,000 for the championship team of 1948.

A new Statesville team, named the Blues, joined the new Tar Heel League in 1953. Managed by former Philadelphia Athletic Fred Chapman (.280), who played second base, the team started poorly. On June 11, the Blues (along with the Hi-Toms) withdrew from the league due to financial difficulties. On July 12, the owners of the team in Lincolnton, also in the Tar Heel League, decided to move to Statesville in search of better attendance.

Renamed the Statesville Sports, the team had little success and finished fifth with an overall record of 47–64. Second baseman Howard Henkle (.315) and outfielder-catcher Jim Harrison (.316) were that team's offensive leaders. The team disbanded after the season.

Statesville was without professional baseball until 1960. That year the Western Carolina League was reformed and Statesville — again called the Owls — joined as a charter member. Seventh place was the best the team could manage, turning in a 38–62 record. Versatile Gail Thomas (.335, 56 RBIs), who played shortstop and second base as well as pitcher, was the team's leading hitter. As a pitcher he posted a 3–2 record, appearing in 13 games.

In 1961 the team improved greatly and won the first half of the season, finishing with the league's second best record, 63–39. The Owls, led by manager Teddy Wilson, had both good hitting and pitching. The offense was led by catcher Jack Hiatt (.325, 69 RBIs) and outfielder Dick Simpson (.294, 15 HR). Utility player Gail Thomas (.283) was probably again the team's most valuable player. Besides playing almost every position, he was also the ace of the pitching staff, winning 12 and losing 5 with a 3.29 ERA. All-Star pitcher George Conrad (11–7, 3.21 ERA) led the league with 172 strikeouts. Despite their talent, the Owls were swept in the playoffs by Lexington.

The Owls dominated the league (now down to four teams) in 1962. They won both halves of the season and took the pennant with a record of 62–36, nine games ahead of the closest team. First baseman and league MVP Charles Truesdell won the batting title with a .344 average, while left-handers Robert Kenny (16–5, 2.12 ERA) and Nick De-Matteis (12–6, 2.37 ERA) were the league's top two pitchers.

The league returned to eight members in 1963. The Owls, one of only two league teams without a major league affiliation, dropped to seventh place with a 52–73 finish. The only bright spot in the season was pitcher Mike Szemplenski (14–10, 2.72 ERA), who struck out a still standing league record of 313 batters.

Statesville signed a working agreement with the Houston Colt .45s in 1964, changing their name to the Statesville Colts, but the team again finished seventh in the league with a record of 52–70. Shortstop Jose Herrera (.295) led the team in batting and eventually made it to Houston, as did first baseman Larry Howard (.240). The Colts disbanded after the season.

Statesville was without a team in 1965 but a new team — a Detroit Tigers farm club — came to town in 1966. Like the two previous teams to represent the town, the Statesville Tigers finished in seventh place. Their record of 42–81 left them 47 games out of first. In 1967, the Tigers improved to fourth, winning 59 games and losing 62. Outfielder Harvey Yancey (.295, 40 stolen bases) was the team's leading hitter, while Joe Brauer led the pitching staff with a 17–7 record. Attendance for the Tigers was last in the league at 17,473, forcing the team to disband after the season.

With the demise of the Tigers, Statesville was again left without a team, but in 1969, a new team — the Statesville Indians — was organized. A Cleveland farm club, the Indians met with the same low attendance their predecessors had faced. The Indians had a 31–31 record on June 16, the end of the first half of the season. On June 20, the team was moved to Monroe in hopes of better attendance. Statesville has been without professional baseball since.

Tarboro

In the summer of 1900, the city of Tarboro fielded a team in what was one of the first organized leagues in the state: the North Carolina Baseball Association. The league was only semiprofessional but it was an important step for organizing baseball in the state. The Tarboro team, composed of college players, won the championship of that short-lived league with a record of 16–8.

In the middle of the 1901 season the Newport News Shipbuilders of the Virginia–North Carolina League — a true professional team — relocated to Tarboro and became known as the Tarheels. That team, managed by Win Clark, was one of only four to finish the season. Ultimately, the league was plagued by financial problems and disputes amongst the teams, forcing it to disband after the season.

It was 19 years before professional baseball returned to Tarboro. Again a Virginia team relocated in midseason and lasted only the rest of that season before disbanding. On August 2, 1921, the Petersburg Trunkmakers of the Class B Virginia League decided to relocate. They chose Tarboro as their new home and became the Tarboro Tarbabies. The team finished last in the league with a record of 46–88, 32 games out of first. The team did have some talented players, including second baseman–manager Ambrose McConnell (.326) and first baseman Andy McMahon (.305), but a lack of pitching doomed the team. During the league's winter meetings that December the team decided to drop out.

High level baseball returned to Tarboro in 1934 as a team was organized to join the semipro Coastal Plain League. For three seasons Tarboro fielded quality semipro teams made up of some of the best college athletes of the day. The 1936 team was managed by former major leaguer Bunn Hearn and was named the Bunnies in his honor.

When the Coastal Plain League became a truly professional Class D circuit in 1937, the Tarboro Combs (for Edgecombe County) became a charter franchise. In midseason, the team changed its name to the Serpents to honor player-manager Fred "Snake" Henry. The team enjoyed a decent year, finishing in third place with a record of 53–42. The Serpents' biggest offensive threat that season was outfielder George Rimmer, who hit .326. Manager Henry also had a good season at the plate, hitting .291 with 59 RBIs. The solid pitching staff was led by Eddie Malone (10–4) and Bernard Mooney (17–10). In the first round of the playoffs the Serpents swept Williamston in three games. They lost to Snow Hill in the finals, however, four games to one.

Another notable member of the 1937 Serpents was catcher Jim Tatum. A former star football player at the University of North Carolina, Tatum joined the team in midseason and hit .311. He later served as the head football coach at the University of Oklahoma before moving on to the University of Maryland, leading that team to the national championship in 1953. He returned to his alma mater in 1956 to assume head coaching duties and hopefully restore the team to national prominence. Tatum's life and promising career were cut tragically short when he died from a rare disease, Rocky Mountain Spotted Fever, in 1959 at age 45.

The 1938 season was also a good one for Tarboro. Again managed by Snake Henry (.260) the Serpents finished at 60–47, half a game behind first place New Bern. The team's best pitcher, Bernard Mooney (19–7), led the league in wins and also proved he could hit, compiling a .333 batting average. A future New York Giant, center fielder Buster Maynard batted .329 with 18 home runs. Future Cleveland Indian Clarence "Soup" Campbell batted .314 and was named to the All–Coastal Plain team as a left fielder. Unfortunately for the Serpents, they lost in the first round of the playoffs to Snow Hill, four games to two.

The next year the team name was changed to the Tars with the departure of Snake Henry, the team's former namesake. At midseason, however, it was changed again, this time to the Goobers, when a new group bought the team. They had a terrible year and finished in last place, 44 games out of first, with a record of 34–90. At one point the team lost 27 games in a row. Outfielder Harold Lee was the team's only notable player and received honorable mention on the league All-Star team with his .326 batting average.

The 1940 season saw a complete turnaround for the Tarboro Cubs (as they had changed their name again). The Cubs, with a record of 72–51, finished the regular season in second place. Center fielder Arthur "Cowboy" McHenry (.354, 79 RBIs) and second baseman Hank Schenz (.328, 109 RBIs) led the team. Both were named to the All–Coastal Plain team. Schenz went on to play parts of six seasons in the major leagues. In the playoffs the Cubs defeated Goldsboro in the first round and then Kinston in the finals, four games to two, to claim the championship.

For the 1941 season the team became the Tarboro Orioles, as the name was changed once again. The 1940 season must have been a fluke, for in 1941 the team again played poorly. The Orioles won 42 games and lost 72, finishing in seventh, just one game ahead of last place Kinston. First baseman Ed Sudol (.311, 63 RBIs) had a good season, though he would never reach the major leagues as a player. Instead he turned to umpiring and spent 21 seasons (from 1957 to 1977) as a National League umpire.

League play was suspended from 1942 to 1945 due to the war. When it appeared that Coastal Plain League would return for the 1946 season, Tarboro had a problem: The wooden grandstand at Bryan Park, the home of baseball in Tarboro for many years, had burned in December of 1945. A sum of $10,000 was raised and a new ballpark, con-

structed of concrete and steel, was built on the same site. Renamed Nash Memorial Park, the grandstand had not been completed at the beginning of the season but play got underway nonetheless.

Tarboro's 1946 entry in the league, again called the Tars, had a working agreement with the Durham Bulls of the Carolina League. They had a mediocre season, and, with a record of 61–65, finished in fifth place. The Tars seemed to have undergone a constant reshuffling of players as only third baseman Bill Lucas (.293) and outfielder Johnny Moore (.288) played at least 100 out of the 126 games in the season. Dick Becker was the team's leading hitter that season with an average of .347 in 55 games. Pitchers Nathan Saxon (16–6) and Tony Polink (16–10) both won 16 games while longtime minor league star Al Jarlett was 4–1 in nine games with the Tars.

The Tars improved in 1947. Led by outstanding pitcher Eddie Neville (28–9, 2.31 ERA) and batting champ Roy Kennedy (.381, 65 SB), the Tars finished in third place, winning 74 games and losing 66. The strong offense also included the talents of outfielder Ray Komenecky (.310, 18 HR, 94 RBIs) and catcher Ralph Caldwell (.288, 21 HR, 101 RBIs). Other than Neville, unfortunately, the team's pitching staff was only average. The Tars advanced to the playoffs but lost to Kinston in the first round, four games to two.

In 1948, the Tars, now a Philadelphia Athletics farm club, won it all under returning manager Bull Hamons. They won the regular season pennant with a record of 87–53, 6½ games ahead of second place Kinston. In the playoffs the Tars defeated Rocky Mount in the first round and then Kinston in the finals, four games to one, to win the Coastal Plain League championship. Bill See (25–6) and Eddie Neville (15–4) were the dominant pitchers in the league while outfielder Ray Komenecky (.366), led the league in RBIs with 137. As a team, Tarboro hit an amazing .306 with first baseman Jake Daniel (.367, 110 RBIs, 117 BB) the team leader. Catcher Ralph Caldwell, father of

Top: The 1948 Tarboro Tars included: *Back:* Bull Hamons, Ralph Caldwell, Jake Richards, Tommy Pritchard, Jake Daniel, Ray Urban, Ken Andrewsh, Stan Russell, Ed Smith; *Front:* Bill See, Eddie Neville, Eddie Luszcynski, Jimmy Townes, Ray Komanecky, Steve Markos, Ray Dietrich, Bob Stapenhorst (courtesy Janet Neville). *Right:* Ralph Caldwell drove in 206 runs for Tarboro in the 1947-48 seasons (courtesy Janet Neville).

longtime big league pitcher Mike Caldwell, hit .296 and drove in 105 runs.

Tarboro became the Athletics in 1949 as they adopted the name of their parent team. They were not as fortunate in league play as the previous season's team had been. Despite the talents of pitcher Vince Gohl (21–4, 1.27 ERA) and third baseman Dallas Orff (.294, 32 SB, 112 walks), the Athletics finished in sixth place with an even .500 record of 68–68.

The Athletics continued their slide toward the cellar in 1950, posting a record of 67–71 and finishing in seventh place. Returning third baseman Dallas Orff (.287, 32 SB)—who led the league in runs with 110—and pitcher George Atzert (16–8) were the only real standouts on an otherwise average team.

On June 4, 1951, the Greenville Robins withdrew from the Coastal Plain League. This caused a dilemma for the league in that it was left with an odd number of teams. It was decided that one team would have to dropped. The Philadelphia Athletics had already made it clear that they were considering dropping Tarboro as an affiliate due to financial losses in that town. Since Tarboro appeared to be the most unstable of the remaining league teams, they were voted out of the league at a meeting on June 6. At that time the team had played only 35 games. Only four days before the Athletics had made Coastal Plain League history (and had the biggest inning in all of professional baseball for the season) when they scored 24 runs in one inning in a game against Wilson. Twenty-five men batted before the first out was made. Shortstop Bill Carr equaled a league record with eight total bases in the inning when he hit two doubles and a home run in addition to walking. Tarboro won the game, 31–4.

The 1952 season proved to be the last for professional baseball in Tarboro. A new team was formed that year and the name Tars was resurrected. That last team was not very successful and finished in seventh place with a record of 49–71. Outfielders Sam Stell (.308, 77 RBIs) and Cecil Fogleman (.279, 101 runs, 53 SB) had good seasons and were the stars of the team. Robert Kunze (12–10, 4.27 ERA) was the only pitcher on the team with a winning record. Attendance had dropped for Tarboro every year since 1947, which saw 75,281 fans pay to see games, and the 1952 Tars drew only 28,439 people to see the 60 home games they played. The entire Coastal Plain League had suffered poor attendance and the league disbanded before the start of the 1953 season.

Nash Memorial Park still stands on the corner of Panola and Johnston streets and is used for high school games.

◆ ——— *Thomasville* ——— ◆

The Thomasville Chairmakers were original members of the Class D North Carolina State League in 1937. They had a successful first season, finishing second with a 63–48 record. The team advanced to the playoffs but lost to fourth place Shelby, three games to two. Catcher-manager Jimmy Maus (.317), outfielder Roy Pinkston (.330), second baseman Darr Shealy (.304) and pitcher Paige Dennis (13–3, 1.96 ERA) were all named to the league All-Star team.

Thomasville, called the Orioles in 1938, dominated the league. Again managed by catcher Jimmy Maus (.282), a former UNC star, the team finished first in the league by nine games with a 75–36 record. The three best players in the league — second baseman Darr Shealy (.357, 114 RBIs), right fielder Roy Pinkston (.356, 110 RBIs) and pitcher Paige Dennis (28–2, 1.33 ERA, 220 SO) — were members of the Orioles. Shealy beat out Pinkston for the league batting title on the final day of the season. Dennis turned in one of the great all time minor league pitching performances, second in the state's history only to Bill Kennedy of the 1946 Rocky Mount Leafs. His winning percentage (.933) puts his season among the ten best in the history of professional baseball. Ray Lindsay (19–9, 247 SO) and Bill Miller (16–6) also had a great seasons on the mound, while shortstop Vann Harrington (.338) and outfielder Jim Canty (.331) added to the offense. The Orioles went on to sweep Lexington in the first round of the playoffs, and advanced to face Mooresville in the finals. The championship was never decided. The final game was canceled by the league president due to fan violence in Thomasville with the series tied at three games each.

With another name change in 1939 — this time to the Tommies — the team had an average season. Their 58–52 record left them in fourth place. They again took Lexington in the first round of the playoffs, this time three games to two. The Tommies lost to Mooresville, however, in the finals, four games to one.

The stars of the team were batting champion and first baseman Ted Mueller (.391) and pitcher Ray Lindsay (22–10, 1.89 ERA, 237 SOs), the league's strikeout and ERA leader.

For the 1940 season, the Tommies signed a working agreement with Wilkes-Barre of the Class A Eastern League. Ray Lindsay again dominated the league but the Tommies did not, as they finished in sixth place with a 56–54 record. Lindsay (20–11, 1.93 ERA), the league strikeout leader with 269, was responsible for more than a third of the team's wins. Outfielders Herb Leary (.356) and Jim Burns (.325), along with second baseman Mel Dry (.319), led the offense.

Improving in 1941, the Tommies turned in a fourth place, 56–44 finish. They advanced to the playoffs but lost to Salisbury in the first round, three games to two. With a .340 average, outfielder Dan Amaral led the team in hitting. Ray Lindsay returned to Thomasville for a fourth season and by his standards had an off year at 17–13. In his four seasons with the team he had a combined record of 78–43, striking out 942 batters. Lindsay walked only 202 batters in the same period, an amazingly low total compared to the number of strikeouts.

The Tommies (61–39) finished the 1942 season with the league's second best record. Outfielder Jimmy Gruzdis accomplished a feat equaled by only one other professional player (Hickory's Pud Miller in 1951) in North Carolina's baseball history: Hitting .418, he finished the season with the highest batting average in all of organized baseball. Besides having the league's best hitter, the Tommies also had the best pitcher. Woody Crowson led the league with an ERA of 1.60 and posted a record of 17–7. The Tommies had little trouble with Concord in the first round of the playoffs and went on to take the championship by defeating Landis, four games to three.

The North Carolina State League shut down for the 1943 and '44 seasons due to the war. League play resumed in 1945 with Thomasville again a member. The team became a Brooklyn farm club and adopted the Dodgers name. They did not have a success-ful season and finished seventh with a 40–72 record, 39 games out of first. Outfielder Fred Leonard was the team's best hitter with a .343 average.

Led by shortstop Walter Fiala (.352), the league batting champ, the Dodgers improved to a third place 58–52 finish in 1946. They advanced to the playoffs but were swept by Concord in the first round. The 1947 season proved to be mediocre as the team finished fifth with a record of 54–56. Outfielders Fred Leonard (.366, 116 RBIs) and Guy Prater (.317) led the decent offense but the team had little in the way of a pitching staff.

Beginning in 1948, Thomasville joined with neighboring High Point to form the High Point–Thomasville Hi-Toms (see **High Point–Thomasville** entry). The Hi-Toms dropped out of the Carolina League after the 1958 season, leaving both cities without professional baseball.

In 1965, a new team calling Thomasville home was formed to be a new member of the Class A Western Carolinas League. The team represented only Thomasville, even though they played at Finch Field, former home of the Hi-Toms, and even called themselves the Hi-Toms. The Hi-Toms (73–52), a Minnesota Twins farm club, played well their first season and finished with the league's second best record. Attendance (71,256) was also second and double that of most of the league members.

The Hi-Toms of 1966 had a similar season on the field, finishing third with a record of 71–52. Attendance, however, declined dramatically down to 30,940. Third baseman Luis Lagunas (.311, 35 HR, 106 RBIs) was the star of the team, leading the league in home runs and RBIs. Pitcher Dick Woodson (6–5) later spent a few seasons with Minnesota. The Hi-Toms disbanded after the season.

The High Point–Thomasville Hi-Toms were resurrected in 1968 and played two seasons before folding (see **High Point–Thomasville** entry). Minor league baseball has not been played in the two cities since. Finch Field still exists, though the original grandstand burned in the early 1980s. A smaller grandstand was built to replace it.

Valdese

Though the town of Valdese never fielded a team that was a member of "organized" baseball, it did have professional baseball for three seasons. After having played several years in various textile leagues, town leaders decided to organize a team to join the new Carolina League in 1936. The league was truly professional in that it allowed unlimited salaries for players but it was not a member of the National Association, minor league baseball's governing body. The Valdese Textiles, as they were called, played well in that first season and finished 55–43, the league's fourth best record. They advanced to the playoffs where they eliminated Charlotte and then went on to take the league championship by defeating Concord, four games to two. The only statistics available from that year are from midseason. At that time Textiles outfielder

Pick Biggerstaff was leading the team in hitting with a .381 average. First baseman Claude Capps was hitting .354 with 40 RBIs, while pitcher Buzz Phillips — who had appeared in 14 games for the 1930 Philadelphia Phillies — had compiled a 6–2 record.

The Textiles returned in 1937 and finished at an even 49–49, again fourth in the six team league. Returning players Claude Capps — who won the league batting title with a .387 average — and Pick Biggerstaff (.341) were again the leaders of the offense. Catcher Coyt "Red" Murray (.364) also played well in half a season with the team. The pitching staff featured the league's best as Ernest "Red" Evans won 13 and lost 6.

The 1938 season was the last for the outlaw Carolina League and for professional baseball in Valdese. Due to its size, the town could not support the team with the attendance

The Valdese Textiles were champions of the Carolina League in 1936 (courtesy Mack Arnette).

necessary to pay the high salaries for good players. Though the team was playing well, they were forced to declare bankruptcy in early August. Outfielder Sam Scaling (.345) and third baseman Mack Arnette (.337) were the Textiles' leading hitters. Catcher Cliff Bolton, recently retired from the major leagues, appeared in several games for the Textiles, hitting .333.

Warsaw

The Warsaw Red Sox were members of the Class D Tobacco State League for two years, 1947 and 1948. The franchise had originally been located in Angier but a group of Warsaw businessmen bought the team after the 1946 season and moved it.

The 1947 team was managed by first baseman Jim Milner (.316, 101 RBIs) and finished the year with a fifth place 59–64 record, 26 games out of first. Shortstop Ford Jordan (.333, 116 runs) was the team's leading hitter, followed by Milner and catcher Ted Jones (.315). Outfielders Otis Stephens (.299, 93 RBIs) and Andrew Scrobola (.296) also made great contributions to the offense. Pitcher Jim Faircloth (17–6) was one of the league's best while Carl Johnson (13–10) led in strikeouts with 225.

The 1948 team began the season managed by North Carolina native and former big league pitcher Sam Gibson, but he was later replaced by Verne Blackwell. Playing part-time first base, Blackwell hit .313 in 41 games. Second baseman Charlie Hutchins (.308, 86 RBIs) and outfielders Andrew Scrobola (.307, 84 runs) and Tom McGhee (.254, 17 HR, 72 RBIs) led the team's offense. Left-hander John Dopkin (17–8) was the leading pitcher on the decent staff. The Red Sox finished the year in fifth place with a mediocre record of 71–67, ten games out of first.

In attendance, the Red Sox had drawn average. In 1947 the figure was 36,865 and in 1948 the team drew 32,482. Just like the team's performance on the field, this was fifth best both seasons.

Though not a financial failure, the team couldn't afford to hire the kind of talent necessary to win. Because of this, team owners decided to sell the franchise to a group from Fayetteville.

Whiteville

The town of Whiteville has the distinction of having the shortest professional baseball history in North Carolina. In the middle of the 1950 baseball season the Dunn-Erwin Twins decided to fold due to poor attendance. Whiteville car dealer Paul Williamson led a group that bought the team and moved it to that town. The Red Comets of the semipro Border Belt League had been very popular in Whiteville and town leaders jumped at the chance to bring true profes-

sional baseball to town. Legion Memorial Field became the new home of the team and the team name was changed to the Tobacconists, a name also being used by Wilson at the time.

Play began June 16 under manager Jim Staton, and at season's end the team had a combined record of 39–92, putting them in last place, 51 games out of first. Whiteville did have a star player, however. Outfielder Granville "Shamrock" Denning led the league in batting with a .374 average and in hits with 176. He also drove in 95 runs, scored 87, and walked 98 times. Third baseman Henry Miller also had a good season, batting .321 with 80 RBIs, but the highlight of his season had to be accomplishing the rare feat of turning an unassisted triple play. Attendance did increase after the move to Whiteville and the team finished with 20,839. This actually put them ahead of second place Sanford, a much bigger town.

With the demise of the Tobacco State League after that season, professional baseball never returned to Whiteville.

Williamston

The Williamston Martins were formed in 1935 as a member of the semipro Coastal Plain League. D.C. "Peahead" Walker, the football coach at Elon College, was hired as the team's first manager. The Martins finished an even 35–35 in their first season but improved to a first place, 45–25 record in 1936. The Martins played their home games at Taylor Field, located behind Williamston High School (now a junior high), a ballpark that seated around 2,000 and measured 290 feet to left, 320 to center and 340 to right.

The Martins became a truly professional Class D team in 1937 when the league voted to join the National Association. They were fortunate enough to be one of only two teams in the league to acquire a major league working agreement as they signed on with the St. Louis Browns. Managed by Art Hauger, who had played for Cleveland in 1912, the Martins finished the regular season in second place with a 55–41 record. They advanced to the playoffs but lost in the first round to Tarboro, three games to none. The Martins' strength that season was their pitching staff, which included Jim Rollins (15–6)—league leader in strikeouts with 202—and left-hander Larry Wade (12–8). Shortstop Howard Earp (.295), named to the league All-Star team, was the Martins' leading hitter. First baseman Chuck Stevens (.288, 51 RBIs) eventually made it to St. Louis, where he spent parts of three seasons with the Browns.

The Martins of 1938 finished with an even record of 56–56, leaving them in fifth place, seven games back. Shortstop Howard Earp (.330) made the All–Coastal Plain team for a second year, while outfielder Ace Villepique hit .317. Harry "Red" Swain was the team's best pitcher at 16–9. Larry Wade finished with a 12–8 record, the same as the previous season.

The 1939 season was the Martins' best. With a 65–57 record they finished in third place. Qualifying for the playoffs, they dfeated Goldsboro, four games to one, in the first round. In the finals the Martins easily handled Kinston, taking the league champonship, four games to one. Harry Swain (22–7, 2.34 ERA) was again the star of the team, leading the league with 186 strikeouts and tying for the league lead in wins. Suprisingly, the offense had no real stars and no player hit over .300. Ace Villepique (.299, 87 RBIs) was back with the team for a third season and led the Martins in hitting, followed by outfielder George Rimmer (.291) and shortstop Howard Earp (.284).

Nineteen forty saw the Martins do a complete turnaround. The finished in last place with a dismal 47–78 record, 29½ games out of first. Harry Swain (14–18, 2.90 ERA) did lead the league again with 215 strikeouts, but he received little offensive support from his team. Swain, who was named manager of the team in May when the Martins' first one resigned, also played in the field, batting .263 with 15 home runs. This was probably due to necessity rather than choice as the Martins' offense was extremely weak, with

The 1939 Williamston Martins, Coastal Plain League champions, included: *Back:* unidentified, Pap Diem, Ace Villepique, unidentified, owner J. Eason Lilley, Gene Albritton, Dick Cherry, Red Swain; *Front:* Solly Meyers, Walt Sminski, Howard Earp, Red O'Malley, unidentified, Larry Wade, George Rimmer; *Batboys:* Laurence Lilley, John Lilley (courtesy Laurence Lilley).

the exception of first baseman Lister Rock, who led the team with a .337 batting average and 80 RBIs. His batting average was far above any other player on the team except outfielder Leon Thompson (.327), who was only with the team for 76 games. Attendance was extremely poor that season and at one point night games were discontinued in order to save money.

The 1941 team did not fare much better than the previous season's team and finished in sixth place (out of eight teams) with a record of 56–61. The Martins were 31 games out of first but league champion Wilson was so good that year that even second place Greenville was 23½ back. Pitcher Pete Kunis (17–8, 2.51 ERA) was named to the league All-Star team that season, as were outfielder-manager Frank Rodgers (.290, 16 HR, 84 RBIs) and catcher Charlie Wilcox (.311). First baseman Chester Sparr (.306) also played well. Outfielder Danny Gardella (.299 in 38 games), who joined the team after being released by Wilson, would later play a couple of seasons in the big leagues. In 1946

he was one of several players to be lured to the Mexican League by high salaries. The commissioner promptly banned them from returning to the major leagues since they had broken contracts. Gardella, who wanted to return, decided to sue and took the case to federal court, where he actually won. A settlement was reached out of court. It would be the biggest challenge to baseball's reserve clause and the major leagues' dominating control of both major and minor league players until Curt Flood sued for free agency in 1972.

The Coastal Plain League shut down operations due to the war in December of 1941. The owner of the Martins had already announced, however, that the team would not be back regardless. Attendance had been poor and with the departure of Ayden and Snow Hill, Williamston was left the smallest town in the league and unable to compete financially.

Wilmington

Wilmington fielded a team in the 1901 Virginia–North Carolina League, the first professional league in the state. The team, named the Giants, won the first half of the split season with a 35–23 record. The second half, won by Raleigh, was prematurely ended when the Virginia members of the league dropped out. Wilmington, which finished with an overall record of 58–46, faced Raleigh in a playoff for the championship but lost all four games that were played.

The league was reorganized the following season with just North Carolina teams. Named the North Carolina League, it was designated Class C by the newly formed National Association, minor league baseball's governing body. Named the Sea Gulls (though sometimes called the Sailors), Wilmington's franchise played at Hilton Park. After suffering from financial difficulties, the team withdrew from the league in early July. At that time their record stood at 10–46, last in the league.

Wilmington was without a professional team for the next five seasons. In 1908 the Class D Eastern Carolina League was formed and the town entered a team. The Wilmington Sailors finished second in the financially troubled league with a record of 35–21. The league began as six teams but two withdrew in mid–July. Wilmington faced Wilson in a playoff for the championship but bad weather led to the series being canceled with the Sailors leading, two games to one.

The league was reorganized the next season and a 90-game schedule was adopted. Wilmington, managed by former major league outfielder Steve Brodie (.255), finished in third place at 50–40, half a game behind Wilson. Brodie, who was in the next to last season of a professional baseball career that began in 1887, would later serve as baseball coach at the U.S. Naval Academy. The 1910 season proved to be the last for that incarnation of the Eastern Carolina League. The Sailors slipped to fifth (out of six) that year with a record of 39–43. Pitcher Harvey Brooks (12–10) was named to the league All-Star team, as was shortstop W. Dubbs, who hit only .122.

It was 1928 before a minor league team again called Wilmington home. In that year the Eastern Carolina League was reorganized with the Wilmington Pirates as a charter member. The Pirates took the regular season title that first year with a 68–46 record. They lost in the playoffs, however, to Goldsboro, four games to three. Outfielder Frank Roscoe won the Triple Crown as he led the league in batting average (.387), RBIs (101) and home runs (36). Nineteen-year-old rookie pitcher Louis "Bobo" Newsom (15–6) would go on to pitch for nine different big league clubs in a 20-year career, winning 211 games.

The next season the Pirates again played well but finished 3½ games back, in third place, at 67–52. They lost in the playoffs to Rocky Mount, four games to two. Former major league pitcher Hank Thormahlen (14–2) led the league in strikeouts with 135 while catcher Rainey (.357) finished second in league batting with outfielder Roland Robins (.338, 88 RBIs) third. The Eastern Carolina League disbanded after the season.

Wilmington was without professional baseball until 1932, when the town took over the former Henderson franchise in the Class B Piedmont League. The new Pirates team, with a Boston Red Sox working agreement, fared poorly that season and finished 21 games out of first with a 62–78 record. All-Star outfielder Parker Perry batted .339 with 110 RBIs and led the league in home runs with only 19. The leading pitcher on the team was John Burns at 18–13.

The 1933 team had a mediocre season of 70–68 and finished fourth. The team's top pitcher was Junie Barnes (14–8), named to the league All-Star team. Outfielder Blackie Carter, who had played briefly for the New

York Giants, was the team's offensive leader and manager. Carter batted .303, driving in 76 runs and hitting 14 home runs. Catcher Gus Brittain, a native of Wilmington, had a good season and hit .308. Outfielder Johnny Peacock, on his way to a nine year major league career, hit .285 with seven home runs.

In 1934, the Pirates signed a working agreement with the Cincinnati Reds. The team posted a record of only 64–74 that season, but it was good enough for third place. Johnny Peacock (.297, 49 RBIs) and Gus Brittain (.301, 5 HRs) were returning players but the star of the team was outfielder Tommy Robello. Robello, who had played part of the 1933 season with Cincinnati, hit .344 with 84 RBIs and 17 home runs. Left-handed pitcher Junie Barnes (18–13), who led the league in strikeouts with 232, was called up to the Reds in September of that season and appeared in two games. Gus Brittain made it to the Reds in 1937, appearing in three games with one hit in six at-bats.

The Pirates of 1935 improved to a second place finish with a record of 69–65, 4½ games out of first. From that team, both All-Star first baseman Les Scarsella (.356, 103 RBIs, 120 runs) and outfielder Lee Gamble (.347, 191 hits) received September call-ups. Each played parts of four seasons with the Reds. Third baseman Arnie Moser, who would briefly make the Reds in 1937, batted .315 with 80 RBIs. Shortstop Eddie Miller (.283) made it to Cincinnati the next season. He spent 14 seasons as one of the National League's best shortstops and was named to the All-Star team four times. Wilmington's leading pitchers that season were Elton Hamilton (12–11) and Jake Mooty (12–10). Mooty would spend much of the next seven seasons in the major leagues. The Pirates franchise moved to Durham after the 1935 season and again Wilmington was left without professional baseball.

In 1946, with the boom of the minor leagues, the Class D Tobacco State League was formed with Wilmington as a member. The name "Pirates" was resurrected and play commenced at Legion Stadium. The 1946 team finished fifth in the six team league with a record of 52–66. Thirty-six-year-old Gus Brittain was hired as manager and again played for his hometown team. He led the team in batting with a .318 average in 61 games, playing almost every position on the team (including pitcher) before his late season suspension for fighting. All-Star shortstop Andrew Cullen (.283) scored 95 runs and led the league with 30 stolen bases. The Pirates' pitching staff was led by Nate Andrews (9–2) and George Brooks (14–12). Andrews, who had spent parts of eight seasons in the big leagues, began that season with the Cincinnati Reds, was released and then signed by the New York Giants. He won one game for the Giants (over the Reds) before deciding to retire to his native North Carolina. Andrews made a home for his family near Wilmington and agreed to help out the local Pirates. He lost his first two games but went on to win nine in a row. The 1946 season was also the first of four in Wilmington for one of the league's best hitters, outfielder Hargrove Davis (.326 in 66 games).

In 1947 the Pirates improved to 68–57, good enough for a third place finish. They qualified for the playoffs but lost to Sanford in seven games in the semifinals. Nate Andrews was named manager, and was 4–3 as a part-time pitcher. Outfielder Hargrove Davis hit .320 with 77 RBIs, while fellow outfielder William Benton hit .295 with 73 RBIs (along with 100 runs and 24 stolen bases). First baseman Harry Bridges also had a good season, hitting .312 with 94 RBIs. The pitching staff was led by All-Star Lewis Cheshire (19–8), John Edens (15–11) and Roy Lamb (14–8, 2.53 ERA).

The Pirates of 1948 posted a 76–62 record, finishing in second place to Sanford. Hargrove Davis won the league batting title with a .366 average while driving in 92 runs, and All-Star outfielder William Benton again had a great season, batting .351 with 123 RBIs and 120 runs. Pirate pitcher Lewis Cheshire (19–11) led the league in strikeouts (258) and ERA (2.35) and was again named to the league All-Star team. Once again the team lost in seven games in the first round of the playoffs, this time to Red Springs. The Pirates did lead the league in attendance, however, with 77,842, nearly twice the total of the second place team.

The next season the Pirates, now playing at Godwin Field on Shipyard Boulevard, dropped to last in the eight team league. Their record of 49–88 put them 33 games out of first. The Pirates, who had a working agreement with Baltimore of the International League, had good hitting but lacked in pitching. Hargrove Davis missed winning his second batting title by .0004 of a percentage point. He hit an impressive .4082 (with 106 RBIs) but Joe Roseberry of Fayetteville hit .4086. John Edens turned in an amazing performance, batting .362 with 70 RBIs while playing first, third and the outfield. He was also the team's best pitcher with an 11–10 record. First baseman Duncan Futrelle, playing half a season, hit .320 after coming over from the North Carolina State League. Attendance declined to 49,009, still good enough for third in the league.

Only 35,950 fans saw the Pirates of 1950 finish in sixth place, winning 56 games and losing 75. A farm team of the Cincinnati Reds, the Pirates had some decent talent but it was not enough. John Edens, named as the All-Star team's third baseman, returned and led the team with a .344 batting average. First baseman Dwight Teague (.327, 94 RBIs) also had a good season. That season proved to be the last for the Pirates, as the league disbanded after the season.

It was to be four-and-a-half decades before professional baseball returned to Wilmington. With the boom in the popularity of minor league baseball in the late 1980s it was only a matter of time before a growing city such as Wilmington got a team. It finally happened in 1995. The Port City Roosters of the Class AA Southern League, affiliates of the Seattle Mariners, came to town. Operated by Steve Bryant, owner of the Carolina Mudcats, the team was only in Wilmington on a temporary basis. A franchise without a city, the team had been in Nashville but had been displaced when a AAA team moved to town. It was decided that the team would play two seasons in Wilmington until a permanent home could be found. After the 1996 season, they moved to a new home in Mobile, Alabama. The goal of Bryant was to prove professional baseball can be successful in Wilmington and then have a permanent Class A team in the town. Roosters games took place on the campus of UNC–Wilmington at Brooks Field, a ballpark that was

The 1996 Port City Roosters included: *Back:* Trainer Paul Harker, Trey Moore, Ryan Smith, Ryan Franklin, Mac Suzuki, Derek Lowe, Johnny Cardenas, LaGrande Russell, Keifer Rackley, Jason Brosnan; *Middle:* Geronimo Newton, Jason Friedman, Rick Ladjevich, Giomar Guevara, Coach Henry Cotto, Manager Orlando Gomez, Pitching Coach Bryan Price, Jason Varitek, Matt Apana, Charles Gipson; *Front:* Craig Hanson, Mike Barger, Craig Griffey, Mike Hickey, Dean Crow, Manny Patel, Randy Jorgensen (from the collection of the author).

upgraded from 1,000 seats to 3,500 for the team. As a team the Roosters were not terribly successful in their first season; they finished eighth in the ten team league with a record of 62–80. First baseman James Bonnici (.283, 20 HR, 91 RBIs) and shortstop Desi Relaford (.287, 25 SB) played well and were both named to the league All-Star team.

The Roosters' second season was no better as the team dropped to last in their division and finished with the league's worst record (56–84). One of the Mariners' top prospects, Jose Cruz, Jr. (.282, 31 RBIs), whose father was a longtime big league standout, was promoted to Port City at midseason. Reliever Dean Crow saved 26 games and was named to the Double A All-Star team.

If a permanent team is to come to Wilmington, a new stadium will have to be built. Attendance figures for the Roosters were not encouraging: 110,173 in 1995 and only 68,463 in 1996, last in the league for both seasons (in 1995 the first place Mudcats drew 317,802). However, the low figures are probably due to several factors, including the league's smallest park, difficulty in parking on the university campus, and the fact that no beer can be sold at games due to the university location. With a better ballpark and location, Wilmington should be able to easily support a Class A team.

 ── *Wilson* ──

In 1908 the Wilson Tobacconists were charter members of the Class D Eastern Carolina League. The league folded prematurely on August 19 and the Tobs became league champions as they were in first place at that time with a record of 34–17. The team had several good players, including pitcher Hatton Ogle (11–2) and manager Earl Holt (.286), the league batting champion.

The league was reformed the next season and once again the Tobs finished on top. Their record of 49–41 was actually identical to that of Fayetteville, but the Tobs were awarded the championship based on their record versus that team. The Tobs slipped to second place for the 1910 season, posting a record of 40–38. Pitcher Bunn Hearn, who finished the season in the major leagues, led the league with a 16–10 record.

It was 1920 before Wilson fielded another professional team. That season the Wilson Bugs became members of the Class B Virginia League. The team played poorly, as most new teams do, and wound up in last place with a record of 44–71. Third baseman Wilson "Rasty" Walters' amazing .435 batting average led the league. Thirty-seven-year-old former major leaguer Al Schweitzer played left field and batted .263. Pitcher Bill Meehan, who had appeared in one game with the Philadelphia Athletics in 1915, was 14–12 for the Bugs.

The 1921 season marked the return of Wilson native Bunn Hearn. Hearn, having began his career in Wilson in 1910, spent several seasons in the major leagues. He turned in a 12–7 record for the Bugs in 1921. Outstanding pitchers Deacon Joliff (18–7), George Quinn (18–9) and Bill Meehan (17–8) teamed with Hearn and reliever Mark Webb (4–1) to lead the Bugs to a 72–51 record. Rasty Walters (.345) had another good year and future Wake Forest football coach Peahead Walker (.293) played well at shortstop. Catcher Lee Head, in the first season of a 20-year minor league career, hit .345. Many of the team's wins were not counted in the league standings because the team paid salaries greater than were allowed by league rules. The team from Rocky Mount suffered the same fate, and this decision, by baseball commissioner Landis, kept both teams out of the playoffs.

The Wilson team returned to the name

Tobacconists for the 1922 season. The Tobs played well and won the pennant with a record of 68–52. There has been some dispute over the official league statistics in 1922 but no one will disagree that Rasty Walters won the batting title. His average has been reported at both .374 and .422, but either way it was an outstanding season. Bunn Hearn, as player-manager, posted a 21–9 pitching record with an ERA of either 2.12 or 1.49. Peahead Walker again played well at shortstop and batted .330.

The Tobs continued to play well in 1923, again winning the league pennant with a record of 70–52. It was a close race, however, as they finished only two percentage points ahead of the Richmond Colts. Bunn Hearn, no longer managing, won 14 games and lost 10, while Rasty Walters hit .357 with 77 RBIs. New manager and longtime major leaguer Rube Oldring hit .342 playing left field. Catcher Lee Head, in his third season with Wilson, hit .310. Never making the big leagues, Head retired from baseball after the 1941 season with a lifetime batting average of .304.

The Wilson team, now known as the Bugs, dropped in the league standings of 1924 down to fifth place. Their record of 66–70 left them 10½ games out of first. Pitcher George Quinn, in his fifth season with Wilson, won 19 games and lost 15. Bunn Hearn broke even at 11–11. Rasty Walters batted .333 with 83 RBIs, an off year by his standards. The team improved only slightly in 1925, finishing in fourth at 68–64. Right fielder Floyd Trexler was the team's offensive leader with a .341 batting average and 27 home runs, and Rasty Walters hit .314 with 81 RBIs.

The Bugs just missed the league championship in 1926. Their record of 85–69 was second by only half a game to Richmond. In his seventh season with Wilson, third baseman Rasty Walters led the team in batting with a .332 average and 103 runs driven in. Bunn Hearn was back for his sixth consecutive season with the team, posting a 19–10 record and leading the league in ERA with 2.68. He again took over manager's duties

that season. Another former major league pitcher, Pol Perritt, was 5–7 for the Bugs. D.C. "Peahead" Walker hit .326 as a utility player.

Twenty-three games into the 1927 season, Rasty Walters left the team to sign with Rocky Mount of the Piedmont League. It marked the end of an era in Wilson. Walters hit .347 over his eight years in Wilson, totaling 1,155 hits and scoring 564 runs. Without a doubt he was one of the best hitters ever in the minor leagues. Unfortunately, he never made the majors. Walters' replacement with the Bugs, Joe Mellana, had a good season, hitting .329 and finishing the season with the Philadelphia Athletics. First baseman George Stanton, who would make it to the St. Louis Browns for 13 games in 1931, hit .347 for the Bugs, while Peahead Walker hit .283. The Bugs' Frank Riel was one of the league's best pitchers with his 20–11 record, while manager Bunn Hearn won 11 games and lost 8. Ray Moss, who was only 1–4 as a Bugs pitcher, went on to a decent big league career as a reliever with the Brooklyn Dodgers. The Bugs finished that final season in the Virginia League in fourth place with a record of 65–67. The team withdrew from the league after the season.

It was 1939 before another minor league team made Wilson its home. That season a group of Wilson businessmen bought the assets of the Coastal Plain League's struggling Ayden franchise. The team was moved to Wilson and renamed the Tobacconists (or Tobs). They had an average season, finishing at 64–61, sixth in the eight team league. Outfielder Luis Olmo was the team's leading hitter at .328 and was named to the All–Coastal Plain Team. Clanard "Firpo" Creason (11–8, 2.25 ERA) and John Threlfall (10–5, 3.51 ERA) were the team's two best pitchers. That year also marked the first for Municipal Stadium (later renamed Fleming Stadium). Originally a 3,500-seat park, it was built as a WPA project for a cost of $75,000. Home to all of the city's professional teams thereafter, the park is still used today for recreational baseball.

The Tobs of 1940, managed by Frank Rodgers, improved dramatically, finishing first in the league with a 77–49 record. Left fielder Earl Carnahan won the batting title with a .354 average and led the league in RBIs with 119. First baseman Phil Morris also hit .354 while outfielder Luis Olmo, who played only half of a season with the team, hit .348 with a league leading 18 home runs. The Tobs had an excellent pitching staff led by Firpo Creason (12–9), Monk Webb (11–7), Joe Talley (17–7) and Al Green (11–6). Despite all of their talent, they were upset in the first round of the playoffs by Kinston, the regular season fourth place team.

The Tobs were again on top in 1941. They turned in an impressive record of 87–30, finishing 23½ games ahead of second place Greenville. Earl Carnahan repeated as batting champion, this time hitting .370 and driving in 94 runs. Second baseman Irv Dickens (.289) led the league with 114 runs scored, while outfielder Fred Eason (.325, 89 RBIs) led with 18 home runs. Utility man Rich Hoyle hit .338 and scored 70 runs. As a team, the Tobs hit for an average of .298. Once again the Tob pitching staff was outstanding as John "Monk" Webb (23–4, 2.27 ERA) led the league in wins and Joe Talley (21–3) had a league best 1.93 ERA. Bill Herring, who had been hired to manage the team, turned in an impressive 16–3 record, followed by Fem Bissette at 12–6. This time the Tobs were not denied in the playoffs, beating Rocky Mount in the first round and Greenville, four games to two, in the finals to take the championship

The Coastal Plain League postponed operations after the 1941 season due to the outbreak of World War II, and Wilson and Rocky Mount from the CPL decided to join up with the Class D Bi-State League for the 1942 season. Wilson finished the season in first place with a record of 69–53 but lost to Rocky Mount in the first round of the playoffs. The Tobs third baseman Rich Hoyle won the batting title with a .338 average and scored a league leading 108 runs. His promising baseball career would end tragically when

he was killed in a plane crash during World War II. Star outfielder Earl Carnahan had yet another great season and was second in the batting race with a .337 average. Bill Herring continued his successes on the mound, going 16–4, while Red Benton (15–7) and Bill Koy (16–11) also pitched well. The Bi-State League suspended operations after that season. League play was never resumed, though several of the league's teams went on to form the Carolina League in 1945.

After being without professional baseball for three seasons, Wilson rejoined the Coastal Plain League when it resumed play in 1946. Led by third baseman Eddie Bauer (.319), second baseman Irv Dickens (.305), center fielder Johnny Wolfe (.314, 17 HR, 88 RBIs, 123 runs) and Earl Carnahan (.315), the Tobs finished the season in third place with a 67–57 record. In addition to their impressive offensive talent, the Tobs also had excellent pitching; Kelly Kee (16–5) and Red Benton (14–7) were the staff leaders. Unfortunately for the Tobs, they lost in the first round of the playoffs to Kinston, four games to three.

Manager Max Wilson, a left-handed pitcher, led the Tobs to a 79–61 first place finish in 1947. The talented club featured second baseman Irv Dickens (.323), outfielder Johnny Wolfe (.299) and shortstop Al Rehm (.284). Max Wilson, who had appeared briefly in the major leagues, was the ace of the pitching staff with a 15–4 record and 2.20 ERA. The Tobs defeated New Bern in the first round of the playoffs but lost to Kinston in the finals, four games to two. Wilson's attendance for the year was 138,548, establishing the all-time league record. In 1947 there were 148 Class D baseball teams in the nation. Of all of these the Wilson Tobs were second only to Alexandria (La.) of the Evangeline League in attendance.

The Tobs slipped to a disappointing sixth place finish in 1948 with a record of 61–79, 21 games out of first. Johnny Wolfe (.325), Irv Dickens (.302) and Al Rehm (.299) all returned and had good seasons, but they weren't enough to overcome the weakness of the pitching staff.

Dropping to the cellar of the Coastal Plain League in 1949, the Tobs turned in a record of 57–79. Once again, Irv Dickens (.315) and Al Rehm (.292) were the leaders of an otherwise weak team. Though he had an ERA of 2.98 and pitched 27 complete games, pitcher Fred Pittman received little support and finished with a record of only 15–16.

One of the league's legendary pitchers, Bill Herring, who had been with the Tobs before the war, returned to Wilson as manager in 1950. Second baseman Bobby Dingler (.299, 109 runs) led the team's offense with help from long-time veteran Irv Dickens (.287). Fred Pittman (16–6) was the star of the pitching staff while manager Herring posted an 8–2 record. The team managed to improve upon the previous season's last place finish, rising to fifth with a 68–70 record. Again the Tobs led the league in attendance (84,159), though the number of spectators at Municipal Stadium was decreasing every year.

The 1951 team, led by the versatile Jack McComas (.284, 20 HR, 95 RBIs) finished fourth at 69–57. McComas, the league RBI and home run leader, divided his time between second and third bases and the outfield. The pitching staff was led by Fred Pittman (15–7, 2.56 ERA), whose totals included a no-hitter against Rocky Mount. Reliever J.D. Thorne was the real star of the pitching staff, however, appearing in a league leading 46 games and compiling an 18–5 record. The Tobs upset Kinston in the first round of the playoffs but lost to New Bern in seven games in the finals. The team again led the league in attendance with 54,753; however, it was again a significant drop from the previous season.

The 1952 season, the last for the Coastal Plain League, saw Wilson finish in second with a 71–51 record. Jack McComas, who also happened to be the basketball coach at Atlantic Christian College, began the season as the Tobs' manager. He gave up his managerial duties when former Tob shortstop Al Rehm, who had been playing in Texas, returned to the team. Third baseman Gene Hassell was the Tobs' best all-around player that season, hitting .300, scoring 98 runs, stealing 40 bases and walking a league leading 142 times. He also led all third basemen with a .955 fielding percentage. The team's strong pitching staff featured Dick McCleney (18–10), who had an ERA of just 1.85. Another player of note on the team that season was black outfielder Ernest Canada (.269 in 17 games), one of just four veterans of the state's negro leagues to ever appear in the league. In their final season as a member of the Coastal Plain League, the Tobs were swept by eventual champion Edenton in the first round of the playoffs.

With the demise of the Coastal Plain League after the 1952 season, Wilson was without a team for three seasons. In 1956 the Reidsville franchise of the Class B Carolina League decided to move to Wilson in search of better attendance. The team, again using the name Tobs, played well until the last month of the season. They then proceeded to lose 24 of their last 34 games to finish in sixth with a 72–79 record. Pitcher Earl Hunsinger (14–9) led the league in strikeouts with 232, while Jimmie Coker — who led the team with a batting average of only .269 — would go on spend several seasons in the big leagues as a backup catcher. Even though attendance was second in the league — more than double what it had been in Reidsville — the team folded after the season.

Early in the 1957 season, the Kinston Eagles, a Washington Senators farm club, decided to move due to poor attendance. On May 10, the Kinston owner announced he was moving the team to Wilson. He failed, however, to refund the money of season ticket holders in Kinston. To remedy the situation, George Trautman, president of the National Association, ordered control of the team be turned over to someone else. There was talk of moving the franchise again but Wilson businessman Penn Watson saved it when he offered to take over operation of the team. On the playing field, the hapless team which had been renamed the Tobs finished last with a 51–89 record. The only player of note was outfielder and Mt. Holly, North Carolina, native Jimmie Hall (.233), who went on to have two All-Star seasons for Minnesota in the mid–1960s.

The Tobs, now a Baltimore farm club, improved slightly in 1958 to finish seventh with a record of 60–78. Outfielder Fred Valentine (.319), named the league's Player of the Year, won the batting title and would reach the Orioles at the end of the next season. Fellow outfielder Dave Nicholson, a highly regarded prospect, hit only .225 with 10 home runs. He made it to the big leagues but never met with much success due to his tendency to strike out (He struck out 175 times in 126 games with the White Sox in 1963.) A player on the team that season with a well-known name was Cal Ripken. Ripken, who hit only .216, made it to the big leagues as a coach, while his son, Cal, Jr., became one of the biggest star players of the 1980s and '90s. Another notable player on the team was pitcher Steve Dalkowski. Dalkowski was one of the fastest, if not *the* fastest, pitchers to ever throw a baseball. He was also one of the wildest. Dalkowski pitched in only eight games for Wilson after being demoted from Knoxville because of control problems. In those eight games he pitched only 14 innings, struck out an impressive 29 batters, walked an amazing 38 but gave up only seven hits. Dalkowski was then demoted to an even lower team. Though he never made the big leagues he did achieve an amount of fame for his pitching velocity. One year Dalkowski was invited to Orioles spring training. In one game there he faced the legendary Ted Williams. Supposedly after one pitch, a called strike, Williams dropped his bat and walked away. He admitted he never even saw the ball and said that Dalkowski was the fastest pitcher he had ever seen.

The Tobs made great improvements in 1959. Led by pitchers Bob Veale (12–5, 187 strikeouts), Don Dobrino (15–7) and Tom Butters, they finished in second place with a 71–58 record. The Tobs then advanced to the playoffs and did not lose a single game. They swept Durham 3–0 in the first round and Raleigh, four games to none, in the finals to take the pennant. Veale went on to win 120 big league games. Tom Butters made it to the majors for parts of four seasons and later became athletic director at Duke University. Another of the Tobs' pitchers, Al McBean (7–7, 4.28 ERA)—who didn't have a particularly good season—spent ten seasons in the major leagues as an above average reliever.

The Tobs (73–65) again finished second in 1960, but, in failing to win either half of the league's split season format, were excluded from the playoffs. Managed by future big league manager Jack McKeon, the Tobs once again had a working agreement with the Washington Senators. Pitcher Lee Stange (20–13) was the star of the team. McKeon returned in 1961 to lead the Tobs to the pennant. They dominated the league (83–56) and won both halves of the season, eliminating the need for a playoff. The Tobs had an excellent pitching staff, led by Bill Jones, Gary Dotter and Joel Kiger. The offense was powered by catcher-outfielder Chuck Weatherspoon (.271, 121 runs, 123 RBIs, 31 HR,) who hit an amazing seven grand-slam home runs.

The 1962 Tobs suffered from a weak offense and finished fifth in the league with a 65–75 record. Pitcher and North Carolina native Jim Roland (10–8, 1.98 ERA) went on to a ten year big league career. The 1963 season was a much more successful one for the Tobs. Led by third baseman Ron Clark (.301), they finished half a game behind Kinston in the league's East Division with a 77–67 record. They then faced Kinston in the playoffs and swept them in three games. In the finals the Tobs faced Greensboro. It was a hard fought series with the first two games going to extra innings. The Tobs then took the pennant by winning the third and deciding game, 7–6.

Nineteen sixty-four saw the team finish last in the East, winning 57 games while losing 82. The only player of note on the team was first baseman Rich Reese (.301), who went to spend several seasons with Minnesota. The next season was not much of an improvement as the Tobs turned in a 68–75 record, fourth in the East Division. Attendance really suffered and, at 26,850, was last in the league. The Tobs improved to third in their division in 1966 with a 72–65 mark, but attendance continued to drop, down to 23,500. Wilson fans did have a talented second base prospect named Rod Carew to cheer for. Carew hit .292 with the Tobs and stole 28 bases. The next season he debuted with Minnesota and won American League Rookie of the Year honors. He went on to become one of baseball's greatest hitters and was elected to the Hall of Fame in 1991.

Attendance dropped to a dismal 20,108 in 1967. The Tobs, who could manage no better than a fifth place, 61–72 finish, continued to lose and the fans stayed away. Attendance was down for every league team and Wilson was the worst. The 1968 team, led by manager Vern Morgan for the fourth consecutive season, showed slight improvement. The Tobs (71–68) finished in fourth place and actually qualified for the expanded playoff format the league used that season (eight of the league's twelve teams were included). They beat Portsmouth in the one game first round but then lost to Raleigh-Durham, two games to one, in the second round. Because of years of poor attendance (22,811 in 1968) the team was moved to Red Springs for the 1969 season.

Wilson returned to the Carolina League for a final season in 1973. For the first time since 1927 a Wilson team was called something other than the Tobs. The Wilson Pennants were unable to sign a player development contract with a major league team and had to operate as a co-op, but city officials did agree to spend $20,000 to renovate Fleming Stadium. The final full season of Wilson's long minor league history was not to be a successful one, however, as the Pennants finished last with a record of 52–88. Third baseman Richard Oliver (.269, 71 RBIs) played well and was the only player from Wilson named to the league All-Star team. The Pennants' attendance figures (45,132) were double that of the last Wilson team in 1968 and considerably more than any of the other North Carolina teams in the league, but the team nevertheless folded after the season.

Professional baseball did return temporarily to Wilson in 1991. The Carolina Mudcats of the Class AA Southern League played the first two months of the season at Fleming Stadium while their permanent home, Five County Stadium in Zebulon, was being completed.

Winston-Salem

Winston-Salem first fielded a professional baseball team in 1905. That season the Salisbury-Spencer franchise in the Class D Virginia–North Carolina League decided to relocate and moved to Winston-Salem on July 17. The league lasted only until August 18, when it disbanded due to financial difficulties. At that time the Winston-Salem team, managed by Earl Holt, was in third place (out of four) with a 34–42 record.

A new team, named the Twins, was organized in 1908 to become a charter member of the Class D Carolina Association, a league made up of teams from both Carolinas. Fourth place in the six team league was the best the team could manage that first season as they finished at 41–48. The next two seasons were no different, as the Twins again finished fourth, with records of 54–52 and 51–57. Ezra Midkiff (.277), the team's shortstop and leading hitter in 1910, would go on to spend two seasons as a utility infielder with the Yankees.

Finally in 1911 the Twins improved. Largely due to the performance of pitcher Josh Swindell (29–8), the team won the league pennant with a 72–37 record. Short-stop and manager Charles Clancy (.337) led the team in hitting, followed by first base-man Bill Schumaker (.330), who was playing in his first of several seasons with the Twins. Josh Swindell was sold to Cleveland at the end of the season and appeared in four games that September. Though he had an ERA of 2.08 in his 17 innings, he never returned to the big leagues.

In 1912, the Twins again played well but missed the league title, as their 63–47 record left them three games behind first place An-derson. First baseman Bill Schumaker (.283) led the league with 16 home runs and 73 runs scored. Pitcher Pete Boyle (27–10) was the league's winningest.

The Twins joined with the other North Carolina members of the Carolina Associa-tion to form a new league in 1913, the Class D North Carolina State League. It proved to be a successful season as the Twins captured the league title with a 66–49 record. Bill Schumaker (.298, 18 HR) was the team's best hitter and J.R. Lee (25–14), who led the league with 199 strikeouts, the best pitcher.

Led by outfielder Jim Hickman (.301, 20 HR) and left-hander Carl Ray (28–15, 317 SO), the Twins of 1914 again played well, sharing the league title with Charlotte. Though it was declared a tie, the Twins' record of 70–47 gave them a winning per-centage of .598, compared to Charlotte's 72–49 record and .595 percentage.

Despite having the league's leading hit-ter, outfielder Turner Barber (.324), the 1915 Twins dropped to fifth in the six team league. Their 53–69 record left them 22 games out of first. Barber was sold to Wash-ington in mid–August and hit .302 in 20 games. He would spend eight seasons in the majors, most of them with the Cubs, and re-tire with a career .289 batting average.

In 1916, the North Carolina State League used the split season format for the first time. Winston-Salem's Twins improved and fin-ished with the league's second best record overall (63–48), but were not involved in the playoffs since they won neither half of the season. Third baseman Harvey "Hob" Hiller hit .325 and stole 28 bases, while pitcher Whitey Glazner finished 21–7.

Like many other leagues across the country, the North Carolina State League suspended operations during the 1917 season due to the United States' entry into World War I. When the league halted play on May 30, the Twins had a record of 17–20. At that time the Twins' Harry Chancey was leading the league in hitting with a .366 average. Outfielder and pitcher Bud Davis, who had appeared in 21 games with the Philadelphia Athletics in 1915 at age 18, was hitting .323.

After being without baseball for the 1918 and 1919 seasons, Winston-Salem joined the new Class D Piedmont League in 1920. That team, like its predecessors, was called the Twins. Not very successful in its first season, the team finished fourth in the six team league with a 56–65 record, though 18-year-old outfielder Hobart Whitman did win the batting title with a .342 average.

In 1921, Winston-Salem remained fourth in the league standings with a 62–58 record. The Twins did, however, have some good hitting talent including Hobart Whit-man (.307) and shortstop Ernie Padgett (.294). Padgett would serve as the Boston Braves' starting shortstop in 1924 and 1925 and spend parts of five seasons in the big leagues.

The Twins of 1922 improved to third place, winning 66 games and losing 59. Sec-ond baseman Fred Heck hit .354, while outfielder Hobart "Rabbit" Whitman had another good season and hit .327. Rookie shortstop Fred "Dutch" Dorman, whose minor league playing career would last 26 seasons, hit .228. The pitching staff was led by Bill Harris (24–15, 2.69 ERA), who pitched a league leading 321 innings. Harris began the next season with the Cincinnati Reds.

The next two seasons were also mediocre ones. The Twins finished fourth in 1923 with a 59–64 record. Rookie outfielder Blackie Carter hit .251 that season. He would go on to spend 18 seasons, many of them in

North Carolina, as a minor league player and manager. Though he retired with a .313 lifetime minor league batting average he had only been called up to the majors for six games. Pitcher Alvin "General" Crowder, a Winston-Salem native, was 10–7 for the 1923 Twins. He would go on to spend 11 years in the major leagues, winning 167 games and twice leading the American League in wins. The 1924 season saw slight improvement for the Twins as they finished 61–58, good enough for third place. The stars of that team were catcher Jim Hamby (.339), third baseman Jerry Standaert (.332) and pitcher Bernie Thompson (18–13).

The Twins improved in 1925, winning the second half of the season and finishing with a league best overall record of 77–49. It was an all-around good team that season with both good hitting and pitching. Pitcher Charlie Sullivan (21–7, 127 SO) led the league in wins and strikeouts, while Bernie Thompson (13–6) led the league with a 2.39 ERA. The offense was powered by first baseman Walt Ammons (.334, 94 RBIs, 17 HR) and outfielder Carr Smith (.323, 74 RBIs).

Two players that had mediocre seasons with the Twins that year were brothers Rick (.241) and Wes Ferrell (9–7). The Greensboro natives would go on to be among the biggest stars of the major leagues in the 1930s. Rick spent 18 years as a catcher with the Browns, Red Sox and Senators. He retired in 1947 with a career .281 batting average and was elected to the Hall of Fame in 1984. Wes Ferrell pitched 15 seasons — mainly with the Red Sox and Indians — and retired with a 193–128 record. He was probably one of the best hitting pitchers ever, with a career average of .280 in 548 games. Ferrell hit 38 career home runs, including nine in the 1931 season, both major league records for pitchers. Chances are good that Wes Ferrell will one day join his brother in Cooperstown. As for the 1925 Winston-Salem Twins, they lost in the playoffs to Durham, four games to three, despite their talent.

The Twins slipped back to sixth place in 1926 with a 64–81 record. With the exception of the performances of first baseman–manager Art Bourg (.334, 97 runs) and center fielder Jete Long (.303, 15 HR, 107 RBIs), it was an unmemorable season. The 1927 season saw improvement as the Twins finished with the league's third best record: 79–64. Outfielder Richard "Rip" Wade (.329, 24 HR, 111 RBIs) had a great season, leading the league in home runs and RBIs. The Twins were a good hitting team as four other starters also topped .300. The pitching staff featured Charlie Sullivan (14–7, 2.04 ERA) and Harry Smythe (7–3, 2.02 ERA). Both made it to the majors for short stays.

Winston-Salem finally won the pennant in 1928. The Twins finished the season at 82–51, in first place but tied with High Point. In a seven game playoff series the Twins prevailed, four games to three. The team had been bought that year by legendary North Carolina baseball figure Bunn Hearn and his business partner, catcher Leo Murphy. Hearn served as manager while Murphy was his assistant. Both also played as Hearn posted a 13–9 record and Murphy hit .306. Overall, the Twins were a very deep and talented team that season. Third baseman Art Reinholz (.342, 80 RBIs) was the team's offensive star and finished the season with the Cleveland Indians. He played in the last two games of the season, going 1–3 at the plate, but never made it back to the majors again. Center fielder Gene Rye (.289, 12 HR, 68 RBIs) made it up to the Red Sox for 17 games in 1931. Al Smith was the league's leading pitcher with a 20–6 record. Despite winning the pennant, Hearn and Murphy sold the team after the season.

The Twins finished third in both 1929 and 1930. The 1929 team, led by pitcher Art Yeager (21–8) and right fielder Ralph Brown (.345, 94 RBIs), posted a 77–63 record, ten games out of first. Manager and outfielder George Whiteman (.267, 84 RBIs) finished out a baseball playing career that had begun in 1905. He played in 3,282 minor league games, still a record. The 1930 team, which won 70 games and lost 71, saw the debut of 19-year-old pitcher Van Lingle Mungo.

Mungo, who was 11–11 for the Twins, went on to a long career with the Dodgers and the Giants and was a three time All-Star. George Ferrell, the older brother of Rick and Wes, played for the Twins in 1930, hitting .330 with 105 RBIs. Though just as talented as his brothers, George never played a single game in the major leagues.

The Winston-Salem Twins dropped to sixth place in 1931. The team's 55–79 record left them 43 games behind first place Charlotte. Pitcher Bunn Hearn, who also served as the head baseball coach at the University of North Carolina, was back with the Twins as manager. He finished his long, distinguished playing career that season with a 1–5 record. A few players stood out on the overall average team, including left fielder Bill Diester (.292, 99 RBIs) and third baseman D.C. "Peahead" Walker (.296), later a sucessful football coach.

The Twins played decent baseball in 1932 and finished third at 69–62, but suffered from poor attendance. On August 20 the team moved to High Point in search of better attendance. Pitcher Al Smith (17–8) led the league with a 2.21 ERA. Outfielder Hank Lieber, on his way to a ten year big league career, led the team with a .362 batting average and 103 RBIs. A new Winston-Salem team, also called the Twins, was formed in 1933. It was not successful and finished in the league cellar with a 42–99 record. That team, managed by former major leaguer Jim Poole, suffered from average hitting and horrible pitching. The Twins' two best starters posted records of 15–24 and 5–19. Hobart "Rabbit" Whitman, who began his long minor league career with the Twins in 1920, returned to Winston-Salem to finish his playing days after spending the previous ten seasons in the International League. He hit an even .300 that season and retired with a lifetime .324 batting average. The team disbanded after the season due to the financial difficulties caused by the Depression.

Winston-Salem was without professional baseball from 1934 through 1936. In 1937, a new team was formed, again called

the Twins, and the city was readmitted into the Piedmont League. That team was the worst in the city's baseball history, finishing the season with a 35–105 record, 54 games out of first. In the first month of the season the Twins had a 28-game losing streak. The team was weak all-around with exceptionally poor pitching. Pitchers' records from that team include 7–16, 2–8, 1–6, 1–9 and 1–13. The 1938 season was only a slight improvement as the Twins finished at 46–92, again a very distant last place. Pitcher Ace Adams won 16 games and lost 10, a very good record considering how little offense the team had. He went on to spend a few seasons with the New York Giants. Pitcher Manuel Norris (14–18) led the league with 222 strikeouts.

The Winston-Salem Twins became the perennial cellar-dwellers of the Piedmont League. For six consecutive seasons the Twins finished last in the league — from 1937 through 1942, the team's final year in the Piedmont League. The records for the other last place seasons were: 1939, 54–84; 1940, 48–85; 1941, 54–82; 1942, 52–81. In 1941, legendary minor league manager Jake Atz was hired. Even he could not help the team win in what would prove to be the final season of his long career. There were very few "star" players on these teams. A couple that stood out were 1941 outfielder Dick Wakefield (.300) and 1942 pitcher Bobby Hogue (17–13). Both spent several years in the majors. Wakefield had an outstanding rookie season with the Tigers in 1943. Named to the All-Star team, he hit .316 and led the American League in hits (200) and doubles (38). This proved, however, to be the best season of his big league career. Pitcher Rufe Gentry, a native of Winston-Salem, turned in a 14–18 record for the 1941 Twins. He spent parts of five seasons with Detroit.

After the 1942 season, Winston-Salem dropped out of the Piedmont League. This was primarily due to the war, yet the team's poor quality of play was probably also a factor. In 1945, a new team was formed for membership in the new Class C Carolina

League. Winston-Salem's relationship with the Carolina League is one that has now lasted over 50 years. The city has fielded a team every season since 1945 — the only league member to do so.

It was not a memorable beginning in 1945 as the team, a St. Louis Cardinals farm club, finished sixth in the eight team league with a 61–76 record. George Ferrell returned to the team as player-manager in the second half of the season and hit .289. He retired from playing after the season at age 41. Since the war was still going on when the season began, many ballplayers were serving in the military. This left teams with a choice of players who were either too young or too old for military service. One such player for Winston-Salem was 17-year-old pitcher Johnny Klippstein (8–7). He would go on to spend 18 seasons in the big leagues.

Again managed by a legendary minor league player — this time Cecil "Zip" Payne — the Winston-Salem Cardinals improved a little in 1946, finishing in fifth place at 68–72 and missing the playoffs by one game. Playing in the outfield, Payne hit .344 with 53 RBIs. Another player of note on the team was outfielder Hal Rice (.335, 70 RBIs), who would spend seven seasons in the major leagues.

The Cards of 1947 were a talented team. Zip Payne returned as manager and had another great year at the plate, hitting .367 in 63 games. Led by All-Star pitcher Harvey Haddix (19–5, 1.90 ERA), first baseman Steve Bilko (.338, 29 HR, 120 RBIs) and outfielder Frank Gravino (.310, 16 HR, 78 RBIs), the team finished second in the league with an 85–57 record. They qualified for the playoffs but lost to Durham, four games to two. Winston-Salem fans gave the team great support as the Cards led the league in attendance with 223,507, over 70,000 more than the second place team. This is a figure no Winston-Salem team since has ever matched.

The 1948 season saw the Cardinals slip back to fifth place. They won 76 games and lost 65, missing the playoffs by one game. Zip Payne returned as manager, though he had

retired from playing at age 39. The Cardinals had no real standouts on the team, though shortstop Walter "Teapot" Frye was named to the league All-Star team. Outfielder Mel McGaha, who hit .390 in 17 games with the Cardinals, along with fellow outfielder Uell Clark, joined the team after recovering from injuries suffered in one of baseball's great tragedies. Five players were killed and thirteen injured in a head-on collision of a truck and a bus carrying the Duluth club of the Northern League. Duluth was also a St. Louis Cardinals farm club.

Led by outfielder Rip Repulski (.300, 20 HR, 88 RBIs) and pitcher Hisel Patrick (10–1), the Cards improved to second place in 1949. They finished three games behind Danville with a record of 84–61. In the playoffs, however, the Cards were swept by Raleigh, four games to none. First baseman Andy Phillip (.279, 8 HR) was also a professional basketball player. A former All-American at Illinois, he spent 11 seasons in the NBA and is now enshrined in the Naismith Basketball Hall of Fame.

The 1950 Winston-Salem Cardinals were one of the more talented teams to ever play in the state. They led the league all season long and finished 19 games ahead of second place Danville with an outstanding 106–47 record. The Cards were loaded with talented players, including third baseman–manager George Kissell (.312), outfielder J.C. Dunn (.307), shortstop John Huesman (116 runs, 43 stolen bases) and pitchers Wilmer "Vinegar Bend" Mizell (17–7, 227 SOs), Bobby Tiefenauer (16–8) and Lee Peterson (21–10). Tiefenauer and Mizell both made the big leagues with Mizell later becoming a U.S. congressman from North Carolina. In the playoffs, the Cards struggled against Reidsville in the first round but prevailed, three games to two. They had little trouble with Burlington in the final series, taking the championship in five games. The Cards' 16-game winning streak from that season still stands as the league record.

The Cards again took the Carolina League championship in 1951. They finished

Manager Zip Payne (left) and three unidentified members of the 1947 Winston-Salem Cardinals (courtesy Buddy Payne).

the regular season in second place at 81–58. Sweeping Raleigh in the first round of the playoffs, the Cards went on to defeat Reidsville, four games to one, in the finals. The star of the team was third baseman Ray Jablonski. Named as the league's Player of the Year, Jablonski hit .363 with 200 hits, 127 RBIs, 28 home runs and 45 doubles, leading the league in all of these categories. To this day he is still the only player ever to win the Carolina League Triple Crown (home runs, batting average and RBIs). Jablonski had a decent big league career, though he was never the star he had been with Winston-Salem. All-Star first baseman Joe Cunningham (.311) went on to a longer big league career, spending 12 seasons with three teams.

In 1952, for the first time in six years, the Cardinals did not lead the league in attendance as their paying fans dwindled to 60,118. They did have a decent season on the field, though, finishing in third place with a 74–63 record. In the playoffs, however, the Cards were easily swept by Durham. All-Star first baseman Paul Owens (.338, 105 RBIs, 98 runs) never made it to the big leagues as a player but did spend three seasons as manager of the Phillies.

The Cards dropped even lower in the league standings in 1953 with their 69–70 record, leaving them in sixth place. Pitcher Ted Wieand (12–5, 2.31 ERA) was the team's most notable player. After the season St. Louis dropped its working agreement with the team. Forced to operate as an independent in 1954 and with its name changed back to the Twins, the team finished last in the league. Their record of 44–94 left them 44 games out of first. The highlight of the season was pitcher Bill Washburn's no-hitter against the Hi-Toms on May 10.

The Twins were able to sign a working

agreement with the powerful New York Yankees in 1955. It was still a forgettable season, as the team finished seventh with a 65–73 record. The next season was even worse as the Twins returned to the league cellar with a 59–61 record. The team lacked both hitting and pitching, though outfielder Curt Hardaway (.306, 21 HR) did achieve league All-Star honors. Surprisingly, attendance was first in the league at over 81,000. This was due to renewed fan interest in the team as Ernie Shore Field — the home of baseball in Winston-Salem to this day — opened in April 1956.

The 1957 season saw some improvement as the team posted a 72–68 record, good enough for fourth place. Again a St. Louis farm club, the team name was changed to the Red Birds. Attendance was still first, and at 101,000 was 40,000 more than the next closest team. The star of the team, catcher Gene Oliver (.285, 30 HR, 94 RBIs), went on to spend ten seasons in the big leagues with St. Louis and several other teams. The results of the 1958 season were much the same as the Red Birds (69–68) finished fifth. Outfielder Jim Hickman (.245, 10 HR) spent the first half of the season with the team before being demoted. He would eventually play 13 seasons in the majors.

The next two seasons brought more disappointments for Winston-Salem baseball fans. The 1959 season saw the team finish in fourth place with a 67–62 record. The Red Birds actually qualified for the playoffs but were swept by Raleigh in the first round. First baseman and future big leaguer Fred Whitfield (.293, 25 HR, 103 RBIs) was named

The 1956 Winston-Salem Twins included: *Front:* Claset, MacKay, Zivkovich, Eisenhour (batboy), Ambrosino, H. Charnofsky, S. Charnofsky; *Middle:* Hinfey, Bronstad, Leja, Peterson (manager), Howerton, Dunn, Marshall (batboy); *Back:* Dietrich, Hardaway, Collis, Drummond, Thomas, Dick, Le Tarte (business manager). Pictured top left is Dr. Vernon Lassiter, president, and top right is Jimmy Wynne, sports director of WAIR (from the collection of the author).

to the league All-Star team. The following season the team slipped to fifth place (61–76). Third baseman Ed Olivares came close to winning the league's Triple Crown, leading the league with 35 home runs and 125 RBIs, but his .317 batting average was second to Greensboro's Phil Linz at .320. Olivares finished the season in St. Louis. He played in a total of 24 big league games over two seasons, hitting .143.

The 1961 season brought a new affiliation with the Boston Red Sox organization, a relationship that would last for 24 seasons. It did not help much in 1961 though, as the Winston-Salem Red Sox finished fourth. Their 68–72 record left them 15½ games out of first. Attendance, however, at 70,236, did lead the league. Pitcher Bill MacLeod (15–8) had a good season, leading the league in wins, strikeouts (208) and ERA (2.31). He appeared in two games for Boston in 1962 but never returned to the majors. Wilbur Wood, on the other hand, 8–5 for Winston-Salem, became one of baseball's best pitchers in the early 1970s with the White Sox. Four times he won 20 or more games.

The Red Sox improved to third in 1962 with 76 wins against 64 losses. They advanced to the playoffs to face Kinston but lost, two games to one. Outfielder Jim Gosger (.283, 19 HR, 83 HR) and pitcher Jerry Stephenson (11–5) led the team and both eventually reached Boston. The biggest future star on the team was Rico Petrocelli (.277, 17 HR, 80 RBIs). He went on spend more than a decade as Boston's starting shortstop and was twice named to the American League All-Star team.

The 1963 season saw the managerial debut of Bill Slack. He would manage the team, off and on, until 1984, putting in a total of 13 seasons with Winston-Salem. The Red Sox (67–76) posted another losing record and dropped to fourth in their division that season. The next year saw dramatic improvements as the team finished first in the West with an 82–57 record. They took the league pennant by first sweeping Greensboro and then Portsmouth in the finals. All-Star

outfielder Mike Page (.344) won the batting title. Before being promoted to AAA early in the season, pitcher Jim Lonborg turned in a 6–2 record. He went on to win 157 big league games. First baseman Tony Torchia, who hit .300, would later return to Winston-Salem to manage the team in 1976 and '77.

The Red Sox struggled in 1965, finishing third at 65–79. Returning first baseman Tony Torchia hit .324, but the only other notable player on the team was pitcher Sparky Lyle (5–5, 4.24 ERA), later a star reliever with the Yankees. Led in 1966 by first baseman and league batting champ Jose Calero (.330, 26 HR, 94 RBIs), and Player of the Year pitcher Robbie Snow (20–2, 1.75 ERA), the Red Sox returned to first place. They took their league best 82–58 record into the playoffs and defeated Burlington, two games to none. The finals were not so kind to the Red Sox as they were swept by Rocky Mount, 2–0.

Dropping one spot to second place in 1967, the Red Sox (69–68) advanced to the playoffs but lost a one game playoff to Lynchburg. The 1968 season was even less successful as the Red Sox finished fifth in the West with a 56–81 record. The highlight of the season was pitcher Ed Phillips' perfect game against Rocky Mount, in which he also hit a home run. A notable player on that team was pitcher Bill Lee (3–3, 1.72 ERA), who arrived midseason. The Red Sox of 1969 (77–67) missed first place in the West by one game, finishing second to Salem's Rebels. They advanced to the playoffs but were defeated by Burlington, two games to one. The star of the team, in his first of three seasons in Winston Salem, was pitcher Don Newhauser (11–3, 1.11 ERA).

The Red Sox finally took another league pennant in 1970. The team finished first in the no longer divided league with a 79–58 record. They had little trouble with Burlington's Senators in the playoffs, winning in straight games. Lynn McGlothen (15–7, 202 SO, 2.24 ERA) and Robert Snyder (13–5, 2.77 ERA) anchored the outstanding pitching staff, while the offense featured All-Star shortstop Juan Beniquez (.272, 30 SB).

Breaking even with a 67–67 record in 1971, the Red Sox dropped to fourth place. That team featured three future big league stars: first baseman Cecil Cooper (.379), shortstop Rick Burleson (.274) and outfielder Dwight Evans (.286). Cooper was the league's best player before being promoted to AA in June. He finished the season in Boston. A five time All-Star, Cooper spent most of his career in Milwaukee, never receiving the recognition he deserved for a potential Hall of Fame career. Evans may also be enshrined in Cooperstown one day. He and Burleson were both three time All-Stars.

Nineteen seventy-two saw the Winston-Salem Red Sox finish back in fifth place. It was an unmemorable season as the team posted a 65–74 record. The following season was an improvement as the Red Sox (77–62) won the second half of the season. Facing first half champion Lynchburg in the playoff, the Red Sox prevailed, three games to two, with the deciding game going to extra innings. Despite the team's good play, attendance was at its postwar low; only 30,235 fans came to see the Red Sox play.

Though the Red Sox (76–61) only won one game less in 1974, they finished in third, ten games behind the Salem Pirates. The team featured future big league pitcher Don Aase (17–8, 2.43 ERA). The Red Sox again played well in 1975, yet their good 81–62 record left them 10½ games behind Rocky Mount. Since Rocky Mount won both halves of the season, no playoff was held. Red Sox third baseman Ted Cox won the batting title with a .305 average.

The Red Sox had a great season in 1976, winning both halves and having a combined record of 80–57. Pitchers Rich Waller (13–0), Al Faust (11–5), and Breen Newcomer (14–6) led the outstanding pitching staff. Future big league pitcher John Tudor was 5–2 with a 2.74 ERA. Seven members of the team, including manager Tony Torchia, were named to the league All-Star team.

The 1977 season saw perhaps the greatest player to ever appear in a Winston-Salem uniform take to the field at Ernie Shore Stadium. Destined for Cooperstown, third baseman Wade Boggs, only 18 when the season began, hit .332 for the Red Sox. Unfortunately, the team was otherwise lacking in talent and finished with a league worst record of 61–77.

The Red Sox remained in the cellar in 1978, their record of 55–77 leaving them 31 games out of first. The following season saw a complete turnaround as the Red Sox finished with the pennant, winning both halves of the season. Their 85–55 record put them nine games ahead of the second place team. The Red Sox were a talented team with both good pitching and offense. All-Star outfielder Reid Nichols, who had a 30-game hitting streak during the season, hit .293 and led the league with 107 runs and 156 hits. The pitching staff was led by Mike Howard (12–3, 2.30 ERA).

For the 1980 season, the Carolina League split into Virginia and North Carolina halves. Winston–Salem (76–64) played decently but finished second to Durham in the North Carolina division. Home run leader Craig Brooks (.327, 24 HR, 83 RBIs), the league's All-Star designated hitter, provided much of the offense. In 1981 the Red Sox (72–67) finished with the second best record in their division, but failing to win either half of the season, they were not included in the playoffs. All-Star pitcher Mike Brown (14–4, 1.49 ERA), Boston's first round draft pick, had a great season. He made it to Boston in 1982 but never found much big league success.

The Red Sox had a horrible season in 1982. They finished the season with a record of 45–93, last in their division by 45½ games (surprisingly this was not the league's worst record, as Salem finished 39–101). Because of this, attendance dropped to 46,430, nearly half of what it had been two seasons earlier. The Red Sox did have a talented catcher in the part of David Malpeso (.317, 29 HR, 91 RBIs), the league leader in home runs.

Bill Slack returned for another stint as

manager with the team in 1983 and led the Red Sox (74–66) to a first place divisional finish. They won both halves of the season and advanced to the playoffs to face Lynchburg. Unfortunately they were little match for the extremely talented Lynchburg team and lost, three games to none. Future Boston star Mike Greenwell (.278) played outfield but missed much of the season with a knee injury. Greenwell returned to Winston-Salem in 1984 and had a much better season, hitting .306 with 16 home runs and 84 RBIs. He and first baseman Sam Horn (.313, 21 HR, 89 RBIs) were the standouts on a team that had returned to the league cellar. Now called the Spirits, with the first name change since 1961, the team finished the season with a 58–82 record.

The Boston Red Sox ended their long relationship with Winston-Salem after the 1984 season. The team, retaining the name Spirits, became a member of the Chicago Cubs farm system in 1985. The Spirits won the first half of the season then surprisingly finished last in the second half. Their combined record of 58–81 was the league's worst. The team did feature All-Star outfielder Dave Martinez (.342), the league batting champion and a future big leaguer. Amazingly, the Spirits went on to win the league championship. They swept Kinston in the divisional playoff thendefeated Lynchburg, three games to one, in the finals. This may be the only time in baseball history when a team with the worst record in its league has won its championship.

The Spirits repeated as league champions in 1986, winning both halves of the season in their division with a combined record of 82–56. Led by All-Star outfielder Doug Dascenzo (.327, 107 runs, 83 RBIs, 57 stolen bases), catcher Hector Villanueva (.318, 100 RBIs) and a good pitching staff, the Spirits defeated the favored Hagerstown Suns to take the pennant. Though the Spirits prevailed three games to one, it was a hard fought playoff with two games going to extra innings. Attendance (136,841) broke the 100,000 mark that season for the first time since 1957.

The 1987 Spirits (72–68) won the first half of the season in their division but dropped to last in the second half. They advanced to the playoffs, but lost in the first round to Kinston, two games to none. The next season was an average one as the Spirits finished third in both halves of the season with a combined record of 73–67. Outfielder Derrick May (.305, 148 hits), named to the league All-Star team, had a great season, as did pitcher Bill Kazmierczak (9–2, 1.34 ERA, two no-hitters) before being promoted. The results of the 1989 season were similar as the Spirits (64–71) again finished third in both halves of the season. All-Star pitcher Pat Gomez (11–6, 2.75 ERA) led that team.

The Spirits improved in 1990 and wound up with a combined record of 86–54. They were second, however, to Kinston in both halves of the season. Pitcher John Salles (14–5, 2.58 ERA) was one of the league's best. The 1991 season was almost identical as the Spirits again were second to Kinston, and the team turned in a combined record of 83–57. Two standouts on that team were pitcher Ryan Hawblitzel (15–2, 2.42 ERA) and third baseman Pete Castellano (.303, 88 RBIs), who was named the league's Most Valuable Player.

The 1992 season saw the Spirits finish last in the first half of the season with a 29–40 record. They improved in the second half to 37–33 and just missed the playoffs, finishing one game behind Peninsula. Designated hitter Corey Kapano won the batting title with a .318 average, while first baseman Andy Hartung (.278, 23 HR) led the league with 94 RBIs. After that season the Spirits switched their player development contract from the Cubs to the Cincinnati Reds.

The Spirits' 33–37 first half record in 1993 left them in third place. They improved in the second half, however, winning it with a 39–31 record. The Spirits took on Kinston in the first round of the playoffs and in the deciding game won on a ninth inning home run. In the finals they defeated league newcomer Wilmington (Del.) to take

The 1988 Winston-Salem Spirits included: *Front Row:* Ed Hrynkow (batboy), Steve Hill, Tim Wallace, Eric Woods, Juan Adames; *Second Row:* Tom Michno, Butch Garcia, Luis Cruz, John Lewis, Greg Smith, Jay Loviglio (manager), Geoff Burdick (batboy); *Third Row:* Mike Folga (trainer), Bill Kazmierczak, Jeff Schwarz, Brian Otten, Derrick May, Shawn Boskie, Heath Slocumb, Kelly Mann, Joe Housey (coach); *Fourth Row:* David Rosario, Jim Matas, Henry Gatewood, Phil Harrison, Francisco Tenacen, Glenn Sullivan, John Berringer (not pictured) (from the collection of the author).

the pennant, three games to one. The star of the team was league Player of the Year Bubba Smith (.301, 27 HR, 81 RBIs), the teams' designated hitter. All-Star outfielder Chad Mottola (.280, 21 HR) led the league with 91 RBIs.

Winning the first half of the season in 1994 and finishing with an overall record of 67–70, the Spirits advanced to the playoffs. They swept Durham in the first round but lost to Wilmington in the finals, three games to none. All-Star outfielder Pat Watkins (.290, 27 HR, 83 RBIs) led the team in hitting, while the pitching staff had two standouts: right-hander Chad Fox (12–5) and left-hander Will Brunson (12–7).

The team drew attention in 1995 not for its play on the field but rather for its name change to the Winston-Salem Warthogs. The Spirits had never been successful in marketing compared to many of the other teams in the league, and the team name was

changed to give a new, more marketable image. While most team names are traditionally based on local historical or geographical references, critics of the name Warthogs say there is no connection to the city.

On the playing field it was an average season. The Warthogs (69–58) finished second in the first half of the season and then third in the second half. The team had no real standouts, with catcher Paul Bako (.285) the leading hitter.

The Warthogs played well in 1996 and finished with a record of 74–65. They missed winning either half of the season, though, and were not involved in the playoffs. Outfielder Decomba Conner (20 HR, 33 SB) was named to the league All-Star team.

◆ ——— *Zebulon (Carolina)* ——— ◆

In 1991, professional baseball returned to Wake County for the first time in 20 years. Though Raleigh had always been the home to baseball in the county, the mandate that minor league teams could be located no closer than 30 miles from each other made it impossible for a team to move to that city due to its distance from Durham. Steve Bryant, owner of the AA Southern League's Columbus (Ga.) Mudcats and a native of Smithfield, North Carolina, wanted to relocate his team to Wake County. It was decided that the best location for the team would be the town of Zebulon. Located in the far eastern corner of the county, and the required distance from Durham, a site was chosen that would draw fans from Raleigh as well as from Wilson and Rocky Mount. Construction began on a new stadium and the team moved north.

When the 1991 season began, Five County Stadium, as the ballpark was named, was not complete. The Mudcats, a Pittsburgh farm club, were forced to play the first half of the season in Wilson's Fleming Stadium. The team finally moved into their new home in July. On the field it was not a good season as the Mudcats finished last in their division with a 66–76 record. Knuckleballer Tim Wakefield (15–8, 2.90 ERA) and reliever Victor Cole (1.91 ERA, 12 saves) were the stars of the team.

The 1992 season saw the Mudcats again finish last with a league worst record of 52–92. Outfielders William Pennyfeather (.337), who was promoted at midseason, and Scott Bullett (.270, 29 SB) were the team's standouts.

The Mudcats improved to 74–67 in 1993, the second best record in their division. At the ticket window the team had its most successful season yet, drawing 328,207 fans.

First baseman Rich Aude (.289, 18 HR, 73 RBIs) was the star of the team and finished the season in Pittsburgh. Blaine Beatty (7–3, 2.85 ERA) led the pitching staff.

In 1994 the Mudcats fielded their best team yet. With a record of 44–26, they easily won the first half of the season in their division. Unfortunately, they dropped to last in the second half with 30 wins and 40 losses. The Mudcats were led by All-Star outfielder and batting champ Trey Beamon (.323), along with league MVP Mark Johnson (.276, 23 HR, 85 RBIs), the team's designated hitter. Pitcher Gary Wilson (8–5, 2.56 ERA) was also named to the All-Star team. In the playoffs that season, the Mudcats defeated Greenville, three games to two. They faced Huntsville in the finals but lost, three games to one.

The Mudcats had a banner season in 1995. They won both halves of the season in their division and finished with a record of 89–55, best in the league. Attendance was also first as the team drew 317,802 to Five County Stadium. On the field the Mudcats were led by the league MVP, catcher Jason Kendall (.326, 71 RBIs, 87 runs), and All-Star pitchers Elmer Dessens (15–8, 2.49 ERA) and Matt Ruebel (13–5, 2.76 ERA). In the playoffs, the Mudcats beat Orlando and then took the league pennant by defeating Chattanooga, three games to two.

Though the 1996 season was not as successful as the previous, the Mudcats (70–69) still played well. With the second best record in their division, they advanced to the playoffs but lost to Jacksonville, three games to two. All-Star shortstop Lou Collier (.280, 29 SB), outfielder Charles Peterson (.275, 63 RBIs) and pitcher Jimmy Anderson (8–3) were among the team's best players.

Appendix 1:
The Negro Leagues

In North Carolina, as well as in the entire nation, baseball's greatest shame comes from its exclusion of black players for more than half a century. In the early days of professional baseball, a few black players appeared on teams in the North but this was soon ended by racial bigotry on the part of some players and managers, notably Hall of Famer Cap Anson.

It wasn't until 1946 that the first black player appeared on a minor league team that was a member of the National Association. That season Jackie Robinson was assigned to the Montreal Royals of the AAA International League by the Brooklyn Dodgers. Though this opened the door to the minor leagues for other black players, change came slowly, especially in the South. It was the end of the 1951 season before the color line was broken in North Carolina. The Danville Leafs of the Carolina League signed a local player named Percy Miller, Jr., who made his debut on August 10, 1951. He spent the final few weeks of the season with the team and played in North Carolina against other league teams. Two weeks after Miller's debut, the Granite Falls Rocks of the Class D Western Carolina League became the first team in the state to sign black players, as they signed five to help the team finish out the season (see **Granite Falls** entry). In 1952 a few more black play-

ers were given brief trials in the Coastal Plain League.

One of the first black players to spend an entire season with a team in the state was Cuban outfielder Daniel Morejon of the 1955 High Point–Thomasville Hi-Toms. "He didn't speak a word of English," said the team's former business manager. "If people would yell racial insults at him he would just smile and wave because he had no idea what they were saying." Morejon went on to be named the league's Player of the Year after hitting .324 with 86 RBIs.

Before minor league integration, however, the tradition of baseball was just as strong in the black community as it was in the white. No matter what color their skin might be, boys grew up playing baseball. Since black ballplayers were excluded from white teams they formed their own. This led to the formation of leagues and to professional teams that played each other for money. In the North the Negro leagues, as they were called, were much more organized. Concentrated black populations in urban areas such as New York and Pittsburgh made it possible for teams like the New York Cuban Giants and Pittsburgh Crawfords to prosper.

Just like in white baseball, the major league teams of the 1920s and '30s were located in the North and the Midwest, which

Dan Morejon (right) in 1955 with Hi-Tom teammates (courtesy High Point Museum Archives).

were more densely populated than the South. All of the cities of the South and their teams, both black and white, were relegated to minor league status. The larger the city, however, the higher the level of baseball they played. The larger cities had larger black populations which meant more fans at the ballpark, more money for the team and the ability to pay better ballplayers. Prominent Southern black teams of the era included the Atlanta Black Crackers, Birmingham Black Barons and the Memphis Red Sox. These teams eventually reached major status when they were incorporated into what was called the Negro American League in 1937. Still, they never achieved the fame that more established teams like the Homestead Grays or Kansas City Monarchs did.

"In the summer of 1947, a couple of black guys came to me wanting to rent the ball-park," recalls the former business manager of the Lumberton Cubs, Buddy Frasier. "I wasn't quite sure how to handle that so I told them I would get back to them. I went to the mayor of Lumberton and said to him, 'We got a couple of colored fellas wanting to rent the ballpark. What do you think I should do?' and he said, 'What do they want to do with it?' I told him they had said they were going to bring in teams from the Negro Southern League to play and he said, 'I don't see why not. Let 'em do it.' You could not imagine the quality of baseball those guys brought in. Teams from Memphis, Atlanta, New Orleans came through town and played each other — you know they lived out of their buses. Those were some talented ballplayers. They could have beaten any minor league team in the state."

North Carolina, too, had its black teams.

The 1948 Greensboro Goshen Red Wings included: *Back:* Charles Parks, Charlie Roach, Hubert Simmons, Benny Harrison, Herman Taylor, Johnson, Scooter Watkins, Brian Morris (business manager); *Front:* Clemente Verona, Joe Siddle, William Davis, Spud Chandler, Ed Ledwell, John Tonkins (courtesy William Davis).

Black youngsters banded together to form neighborhood teams and eventually town teams. In the 1930s and '40s it is probable that most towns in the state had both a black and a white team represent-ing them. The larger cities in the state had populations large enough to support professional black baseball. These teams had no governing body and the line between professional and semipro is difficult to distinguish, but some of the teams in North Carolina that played for money included the Asheville Blues, the Charlotte Black Hornets, the Durham Black Sox and the Winston-Salem Pond Giants. Still others were the Raleigh Tigers, the Kinston Grays, the Rocky Mount Crocodiles and the Greensboro Goshen Red Wings.

Most of these teams shared a ballpark with the white minor league team in their town, playing home games when that team was away. Much of their money also came from barnstorming, a practice that was also common in the Negro major leagues. Teams would meet to play a game anywhere a large enough crowd could be assembled. Fans would come out to see quality baseball even if neither team was the home team. According to one former player, proceeds from the gate would usually be split, with the winner taking 60 percent and the loser 40 percent. Some teams hired players on a game by game basis while others sometimes offered season long contracts.

In the late 1950s, black teams in North Carolina began to die out. Just like the Negro major leagues, integration brought about their demise. Many of the top black players were rapidly lost to organized baseball as new opportunities were opened to them. Black fans had always been allowed at white minor league games, though they had to sit in the "colored" bleachers. After integration, they could attend a minor league game and see talented black players, lessening the need for black teams.

Appendix 2:
The Textile Leagues

For many years, the textile mills of North Carolina provided some of the highest quality baseball in the state. Other industries sponsored baseball teams as well, but the textile mill teams were by far the most abundant. Though not truly professional, this type of baseball did play a large part in the development of the game within the state.

In many cases, minor league teams began as textile teams. This was particularly true in the towns of the North Carolina State League (the version which began in 1937). Landis, Cooleemee, Mooresville, Concord, and other towns, had all been home to teams sponsored by the mills. The popularity of the mill teams led many towns to take the next step, which was true professional baseball. In some cases, the mills remained involved and even owned and operated minor league teams.

Though mill teams were not members of professional leagues, they did often recruit professional players. Competition between mill teams was strong and just like in minor league baseball, it was sometimes necessary to look beyond local boys for talent. Good players were hired for a season or sometimes on a game by game basis. In some leagues, it was required that all players had to work for the mill. To get around this, players were hired and given token jobs with the understanding that the real reason they were there was to play baseball. "I remember there would be five or six of us ballplayers assigned to do a job that might only take two people. We mainly just stood around until it was time to play ball," recalls Ralph Hodgin, who played for Greensboro's Pomona Mills in 1934 and later went on to the major leagues.

Many towns had very successful textile teams. Cleveland Cloth of Shelby advanced to the final round at the 1935 semipro championships in Wichita, Kansas, before losing. The same was true for Elkin's Chatham Blanketeers in 1948. Perhaps the best textile team ever in the state was the McCrary Eagles of Asheboro. The mill spared no expense on its players and there were times when McCrary was quite possibly the best team in North Carolina, including the professional teams. Though Asheboro was larger than many towns that fielded professional teams, it never did. Minor league, Class D ball (which would have suited the size of the population) may have been a step down in the level of play that baseball fans there were used to.

Appendix 3:
Biographies

Following are short biographies of 20 people who have played an important part in the history of minor league baseball in North Carolina. Though there are probably many more who deserve mention here, these 20 were chosen because they give a good representation of the personalities that have been a part of the state's professional baseball history. Numbers in bold indicate that the player led the league in that category.

◆ —————— *Danny Boone* —————— ◆

James Albert "Danny" Boone was born in Samantha, Alabama, in 1895. The older brother of Ike Boone, who would also become a legendary hitter, Danny Boone began his baseball career as a pitcher, playing semipro ball after high school until being signed by the Atlanta Crackers of the Southern Association in 1919. He was sold to the Philadelphia Athletics at the end of that season and appeared in three games. Boone was back in Atlanta in 1920 and would spend the next several seasons being shuffled between the major leagues and various high minor league teams in the South. His longest stay in the big leagues came in 1923, when he spent the entire season as a reliever with the Cleveland Indians.

Boone first came to North Carolina in 1926 after signing on with High Point of the Piedmont League. After giving up pitching and switching to first base (and later to the outfield), Boone became the greatest hitter in the history of the Piedmont League. In five-and-a-half seasons in the league he won four batting titles. He also served as High Point's manager beginning in 1927.

Frustrated with the last place team, Boone left High Point in midseason 1931 for a higher paying managerial job in York, Pennsylvania. He spent the 1932 and '33 seasons, his final ones in baseball, as player-manager for Charleston (W.Va.) of the Class C Middle Atlantic League. Eventually returning to his native Alabama, Boone died in Tuscaloosa in 1968.

Boone's North Carolina record:

YEAR	CLUB	POS	G	AB	R	H	2B	3B	HR	RBI	SB	AVG
1926	High Point	1b	146	537	112	214	37	8	28	117	10	.399
1927	High Point	of-1b	108	392	71	134	27	3	12	57	17	.342
1928	High Point	of	128	468	123	196	40	11	38	131	11	.419
1929	High Point	of	140	513	116	191	30	6	46	125	17	.372
1930	High Point	of	128	488	124	188	46	4	25	113	15	.385
1931	High Point	of	73	268	61	104	14	2	20	76	5	.388

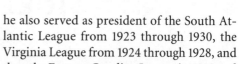

◆ —— Judge William Bramham —— ◆

Durham attorney William G. Bramham is one of the most important figures in minor league baseball history. Born in Kentucky in 1875, Bramham moved to Durham around 1900. He first became involved in professional baseball in 1902 when he helped organize the Durham team in the North Carolina League and served on the league's executive committee.

Bramham attended law school at the University of North Carolina, graduating in 1905. Though never actually a judge (he was given the nickname by his younger law school classmates), he did become a successful corporate attorney.

Next involved with baseball in 1912, Bramham helped establish the Carolina Association. In 1916, he was elected president of the North Carolina State League and remained at that position until the league disbanded due to World War I in 1917. In 1920, the Piedmont League was formed and Bramham was named as its first president. He helped guide that league from its Class D beginnings until it became a successful Class B circuit in 1932. The Piedmont League was not Bramham's only baseball job in the 1920s, however, as he also served as president of the South Atlantic League from 1923 through 1930, the Virginia League from 1924 through 1928, and then the Eastern Carolina League in 1928 and 1929.

In December of 1932, Bramham was elected to his most important baseball job when he became president of the National Association, the minor leagues' governing body. The minors had been struggling and they needed strong leadership. Bramham, who moved the National Association headquarters to Durham, dealt with many difficult issues in his tenure. He cracked down on gambling and enforced salary limits. A staunch defender of umpires, Bramham handed out stiff penalties for assaults on umpires by players and managers. He also had to deal with the development of major league farm systems and how much control the major leagues should have over the minors.

Though not always very popular for some of his decisions, the minor leagues grew and prospered because of Bramham's leadership. When he retired due to poor health after the 1946 season, the minors were on the verge of their greatest popularity.

 # —— Hargrove Davis ——

Wilmington native Hargrove "Hoggie" Davis was one of the best pure hitters in the state in the years following World War II. Probably the best hitter in the Tobacco State League, Davis played in the league all five seasons it existed. He won the batting title in 1948 and even though he hit .408 in 1949, Davis missed winning a second consecutive title by .0004 of a percentage point to Fayetteville's Joe Roseberry.

Davis attended Campbell College, then a two year school, from 1938 through 1940 and played both baseball and football. He then entered professional baseball, playing for teams in the Alabama State and SALLY leagues. From 1943 to 1945 Davis served in the U.S. Army Aviation Engineers.

Though he had potential major-league hitting ability, Davis lacked speed in the field; a motorcycle injury caused him to limp slightly. While continuing to play in the Tobacco State League, Davis began coaching at Campbell in 1947. During his tenure there he produced future major leaguers Cal Koonce and Jim Perry.

In the 1960s, Davis became Campbell's golf coach. He led his team to the NAIA national championship in 1968 and again in 1969.

Davis died in November of 1979.

Tobacco State League record:

YEAR	CLUB	POS	G	AB	R	H	2B	3B	HR	RBI	SB	AVG
1946	Wilmington	of	66	258	43	75	10	2	6	41	3	.326
1947	Wilmington	of	90	372	68	119	27	6	12	77	4	.320
1948	Wilmington	of	101	404	63	148	31	2	11	92	4	**.366**
1949	Wilmington	of	107	436	72	178	42	5	9	106	6	.408
1950	Red Springs	1b-of	38	141	24	51	13	2	1	30	1	.362

 ## *Willie Duke*

Willie Duke is one of the legendary figures in North Carolina's baseball history, not only for his playing career but for his involvement with the sport at all levels, particularly youth programs and American Legion ball. He also was one of the founders of Raleigh's Hot Stove League in 1950 and served as its president for many years.

Born at Franklinton in 1909, Duke played baseball at North Carolina State College. He graduated in 1933 and in 1934 signed his first pro contract with Nashville of the Southern Association. For the next several seasons he was a star in that league, eventually playing for six different teams. In 1938, Duke reached his highest level of professional baseball when he began the season with Minneapolis of the American Association. In 15 games with that team he hit .250 before being sent back to the Southern Association.

The 1943–45 seasons were spent as an officer in the U.S. Navy. In 1946, Duke finally returned to his home state to resume his baseball career, taking a job as the playing manager of the Clinton franchise in the Tobacco State League. He moved to the Carolina League and managed Durham in 1947 and '48 and Winston-Salem for part of the 1949 season. Duke finished his playing career in 1950 at age 41, playing the last half of the season with Rockingham in the Tobacco State League. His career batting average is .331.

Duke's playing record after returning to North Carolina:

YEAR	CLUB	LEAGUE	POS	G	AB	R	H	2B	3B	HR	RBI	SB	AVG
1946	Clinton	Tobacco State	of	96	238	106	129	29	6	27	109	15	**.393**
1947	Durham	Carolina	of	122	439	104	169	42	4	13	117	2	.385
1948	Durham	Carolina	of	110	346	104	123	36	7	12	89	3	.355
1949	Winston-Salem/ Danville	Carolina	of	119	413	80	144	37	1	22	106	3	.349

Willie Duke (standing, far left) was a member of this 1928 semipro Concord team (courtesy Hank Utley).

YEAR	CLUB	LEAGUE	POS	G	AB	R	H	2B	3B	HR	RBI	SB	AVG
1950	Greensboro/	Carolina											
	Raleigh		of	53	154	30	47	6	1	5	36	0	.305
	Rockingham	Tobacco State	of	38	138	37	48	11	3	4	35	2	.348

 ——————— *Rube Eldridge* ———————

Little is known about the life of pitcher Rube Eldridge outside of the baseball field. Born at Speiro, North Carolina, in 1888, Jesse Morgan "Rube" Eldridge first appeared in professional baseball in 1909. For nearly 20 seasons he was one of the best pitchers in the Southern minor leagues. Though Eldridge appears to have had the talent to achieve a higher level of baseball, only once did he leave the South, when in 1920 he pitched seven games for Columbus (Ohio) of the American Association. Possibly the opportunity never presented itself for him to advance to the major leagues, though more than likely he made good money in the minors and was able to stay closer to home.

Eldridge died at Glenola, North Carolina, in 1968.

Complete playing record:

YEAR	CLUB	LEAGUE	G	IP	W	L	H	R	BB	SO	ERA
1909	Greensboro	Carolina Assoc.	8	52	3	1	47	17	7	24	1.90
1910	Greensboro	Carolina Assoc.	27	234	11	16	210	69	39	115	2.08
1911	Greensboro	Carolina Assoc.	**38**	333	25	13	290	122	45	191	2.43
1912	Greensboro	Carolina Assoc.	33	288	13	**19**	280	91	44	153	2.22
1913	Col./Charleston	SALLY	34	265	10	16	264	111	43	121	2.58
1914	Charleston	SALLY	34	255	20	9	201	61	41	92	1.66
1915	Charleston	SALLY	25	206	14	8	167	61	28	79	2.14
	Frederick	Blue Ridge	7	61	2	3	62	28	7	22	2.80

YEAR	CLUB	LEAGUE	G	IP	W	L	H	R	BB	SO	ERA
	Portsmouth	Virginia	5	34	4	0	31	6	5	15	1.32
1916	Portsmouth	Virginia	24	161	6	10	158	78	15	53	3.41
	Raleigh	N.C. State	22	99	4	8	93	37	8	40	3.00
1917	Raleigh/Durham	N.C. State	15	105	6	5	104		10	37	3.17
	Mobile	Southern Assoc.	1	1	0	1	5	4	0	0	–
	Columbia	SALLY	7	61	5	2	63	17	6	19	2.07
	Hagerstown	Blue Ridge	7	43	4	1	27	7	6	15	1.26
1918						Did not play					
1919	Charlotte	SALLY	38	295	20	12	277	107	32	80	2.59
1920	Charlotte	SALLY	12	77	5	4	90	45	7	27	3.97
	High Point	Piedmont	22	159	13	6	122	33	11	41	1.36
	Columbus	American Assoc.	7	45	4	2	50	31	16	13	4.80
1921	High Point	Piedmont	43	286	15	19	284	112	22	89	2.96
1922	High Point	Piedmont	37	297	26	9	286	108	40	81	2.76
1923	High Point	Piedmont	35	254	20	10	281	127	38	59	3.79
1924	High Point	Piedmont	30	199	8	12	236	125	35	44	4.79
1925	Danville	Piedmont	27	215	14	9	234	108	40	67	3.77
1926	Greensboro	Piedmont	31	195	13	11	233	125	37	63	4.89
1927	High Point	Piedmont	37	226	15	12	266	124	38	54	4.06
1928–32						Did not play					
1933	Greensboro/ Wilmington	Piedmont	4	35	4	0	33	12	7	10	2.31
1934	Greensboro	Piedmont	1	9	1	0	9	3	1	5	3.00
		Totals:	611	4490	285	218	4403	1769	638	1646	2.83

 ## *Bunn Hearn*

Charles Bunn Hearn was born in Chapel Hill on May 21, 1891. He was a talented athlete as a boy and in 1910 enrolled at Elon College, where he pitched for the baseball team. That year was his only one as a college player as he signed on with Wilson in the Eastern Carolina League after the season. Toward the end of the season the Wilson club sold him to the St. Louis Cardinals. He pitched in five games with the Cardinals, finishing with a record of 1–3. For the next ten seasons Hearn was up and down between the major and minor leagues. He pitched for the Cardinals in 1911, Springfield in 1912 and Toronto in 1913. At the end of the 1913 season Hearn was called up to the New York Giants. In 1915 Hearn jumped to the Federal League and pitched in 29 games for Pittsburgh. He returned to the majors for 17 games in 1918 with the Boston Braves and another 11 games with the Braves in 1920.

During the 1917 offseason, Hearn began coaching college teams, first at the University of North Carolina. He returned to UNC the next year but was called up to the Braves. While with Boston he helped coach at Harvard. Later coaching stops included Elon College and Atlantic Christian (now Barton) College.

After the 1920 season, Hearn remained in North Carolina. In 1921 he joined the Wilson Bugs and helped lead them to the Virginia League pennant in 1922. Hearn remained with the Wilson team as a player through the 1927 season, serving as manager of the Bugs in 1926 and '27.

In 1928, Hearn and Leo Murphy, a catcher who had played briefly with the Pittsburgh Pirates, bought the Winston-Salem Twins of the Piedmont League. Hearn became the manager and president of the team. Even though the Twins won the pennant, Hearn and Murphy sold the team when the season ended.

In 1929 Hearn managed the Henderson Bunnies of the Piedmont League, a team that was named after him. The Bunnies did not have a good season as they finished 32½ games back with a record of 54–85. Hearn left the team at midseason.

After the 1931 season, Hearn left pro-fessional baseball and took a position as head coach at the University of North Carolina, a job he kept for many years. He died at Wilson in 1959.

Complete playing record:

YEAR	CLUB	LEAGUE	G	IP	W	L	H	R	BB	SO	ERA
1910	Wilson	Eastern Carolina	28	203	**16**	10	128	41	38	162	–
	St. Louis	National	5	39	1	3	49	22	16	14	5.08
1911	St. Louis	National	2	3	0	0	7	4	0	1	12.00
	Louisville	American Assoc.	22	124	2	11	146	82	38	52	–
1912	Omaha	Western	3	10	0	1	14	7	2	5	–
	Springfield	Three I	39	306	**27**	11	268	103	38	197	–
1913	New York	National	2	13	1	1	13	6	7	8	2.77
	Toronto	International	34	222	11	11	214	90	41	97	–
1914	Toronto	International	36	243	13	13	234	130	78	136	–
1915	Pittsburgh	Federal	29	176	6	11	187	73	37	49	3.27
1916	New London	Eastern	30	263	**22**	7	176	–	44	121	–
1917	Toronto	International	37	310	**23**	9	292	–	62	133	2.03
1918	Boston	National	17	126	5	6	119	43	29	30	2.50
1919						Did not play					
1920	Boston	National	11	43	0	3	54	34	11	9	5.65
	Toronto	International	14	99	8	4	112	47	14	45	3.45
1921	Wilson	Virginia	21	165	12	7	170	–	18	75	–
1922	Wilson	Virginia	28	203	17	8	197	–	20	107	**2.12**
1923	Wilson	Virginia	30	211	14	10	218	87	43	88	2.77
1924	Wilson	Virginia	24	183	11	11	188	76	34	54	3.15
1925	Wilson	Virginia	32	234	13	12	287	123	38	61	3.96
1926	Wilson	Virginia	32	218	19	10	218	79	25	74	**2.68**
1927	Wilson	Virginia	24	166	11	8	202	93	24	41	3.96
1928	Winston-Salem	Piedmont	24	167	13	9	170	73	26	64	3.29
1929	Henderson	Piedmont	7	37	1	5	55	26	5	11	–
	York	New York-Penn.	9	55	4	2	66	33	12	16	4.58
1930	York/Harrisburg	New York-Penn.	28	156	9	12	187	91	23	27	4.62
1931	Winston-Salem	Piedmont	8	56	1	5	84	53	9	18	–
	Minor League Totals:		510	3631	247	176	3626	1234	632	1584	–

 ───────── *Bill Herring* ─────────

Bill Herring is probably the greatest pitcher to have ever played baseball in east-ern North Carolina. While others may have had outstanding seasons, Herring excelled for seven, pitching for several teams.

A native of Wayne County, Herring attended Wake Forest University and earned a law degree while starring in baseball. He first entered professional baseball in 1935, when, near the end of a great semipro sea-son, his contract was sold to Portsmouth of the Piedmont League. Twice, in 1940 and

again in 1943, he got as high as the AA level but never got the call to go to the big leagues.

After the 1943 season, Herring entered the U.S. Navy as an officer, serving for two years and taking part in the Normandy In-vasion.

Returning to baseball in 1946, Herring took his first job as manager of his home-town Goldsboro Goldbugs. After managing that team for three seasons (as well as remaining one of the league's best pitchers), he moved up to the Class B Southeastern

League in 1949, taking over the reigns of the Pensacola club. It was back to North Carolina for a managerial position at Wilson in 1950.

Herring retired from playing in 1952

but continued to manage. His final managerial assignment came in 1964 with Burlington of the Carolina League.

Complete playing record:

YEAR	CLUB	LEAGUE	G	IP	W	L	H	R	BB	SO	ERA
1935	Goldsboro	Coast. Pl. (semipro)	–	–	–	–	–	–	–	–	–
	Portsmouth	Piedmont	–	<45	–	–	–	–	–	–	–
1936	Portsmouth	Piedmont	35	229	15	11	265	120	74	83	3.93
1937	Portsmouth	Piedmont	39	217	13	15	234	127	71	130	–
1938	Ayden	Coastal Plain	30	249	18	11	252	–	74	137	–
1939	Kinston	Coastal Plain	36	291	22	11	267	100	94	158	1.97
1940	Milwaukee	Amer. Assoc.	11	30	2	4	–	–	–	–	–
	Montreal	International	19	40	1	3	57	33	22	29	6.53
1941	Wilson	Coastal Plain	29	224	16	3	190	–	73	160	–
1942	Wilson	Bi-State	27	198	16	4	156	76	59	119	3.00
1943	Portland	Pacific Coast	24	121	8	5	128	50	41	44	2.90
1944–45		Military service									
1946	Goldsboro	Coastal Plain	33	225	21	6	188	–	34	187	–
1947	Goldsboro	Coastal Plain	41	211	14	11	–	–	51	150	1.79
1948	Goldsboro	Coastal Plain	38	204	19	7	186	72	50	149	2.60
1949	Pensacola	Southeastern	34	97	10	3	98	39	35	41	3.25
1950	Wilson	Coastal Plain	14	87	8	2	79	39	27	42	3.72
1951	Temple	Big State		Manager only							
	Panama City	Alabama-Florida									
1952	Panama City	Alabama-Florida	10	45	4	1	44	21	9	39	1.20

 ─────── *Minnie Mendoza* ───────

Christobal Rigoberto "Minnie" Mendoza was born in Cuba in 1933 and began playing professional baseball in 1954. Well-traveled in the first few seasons of his career, Mendoza would eventually play minor league baseball in several parts of the United States as well as in his native Cuba, Mexico and Canada.

In 1958, Mendoza was signed by the Washington Senators and sent to their Class C team in Missoula, Montana. Promoted to Charlotte in 1960, he began what would become a long relationship with baseball in that city.

Throughout most of the 1960s Mendoza was a mainstay of the Charlotte Hornets, earning league All-Star honors four times. In 1969 he was promoted to AAA Denver and, with one of the best seasons of his career,

earned a shot at the major leagues. Finally, in 1970 at age 36, Mendoza made the Twins out of spring training and appeared in 16 games as a utility infielder.

The 1971 season found Mendoza back in Charlotte, where he won his second Southern League batting title. After retirement in 1973, he began a minor league coaching career that has lasted in to the 1990s.

In 1992, Mendoza returned to his adopted home state of North Carolina in a baseball capacity, serving as manager of the Burlington Indians.

Complete professional record:

YEAR	CLUB	LEAGUE	POS	G	AB	R	H	2B	3B	HR	RBI	SB	AVG
1954	Greater Miami	Fla. Int.	ss	3	2	0	1	0	0	0	0	0	.500
	Nogales	Az.-Tex.	ss	101	436	89	141	35	2	16	79	6	.323
1955	Portsmouth	Piedmont	3b	129	467	65	124	18	4	3	52	4	.266
1956	Havana	Internat.	3b	4	12	0	1	0	1	0	0	0	.083
	Nuevo Laredo	Mexican	3b-ss	103	318	40	70	12	1	1	27	10	.220
1957	Albuquerque	Western	ss	21	77	10	14	3	1	1	8	0	.182
1958	Missoula	Pioneer	of-3b	23	85	10	23	3	1	0	11	0	.271
1959	Missoula	Pioneer	3b	126	487	105	174	32	9	12	94	8	.357
1960	Charlotte	SALLY	2b	138	516	71	152	21	8	2	43	0	.295
1961	Charlotte	SALLY	2b-3b-ss	139	536	62	151	16	5	1	41	7	.282
1962	Vancouver	Pac. Coast	3b	113	366	39	95	12	1	3	35	3	.260
1963	Charlotte	SALLY	3b	84	319	47	91	10	4	0	29	9	.285
1964	Charlotte	Southern	of-3b	125	473	67	143	19	2	8	47	7	.302
1965	Charlotte	Southern	ss-3b	141	549	64	151	20	4	5	42	12	.275
1966	Charlotte	Southern	3b	128	501	68	140	15	1	1	34	29	.279
1967	Charlotte	Southern	ss-2b	134	528	62	157	21	1	0	40	16	.297
1968	Charlotte	Southern	3b-ss	139	545	85	165	35	3	4	67	30	.303
1969	Denver	Am. Assoc.	ss-3b	139	582	97	194	23	2	0	48	4	.333
1970	Minnesota	American	3b-2b	16	16	2	3	0	0	0	2	0	.188
	Evansville	Am. Assoc.	3b-2b	84	314	37	87	14	0	2	16	8	.277
1971	Charlotte	Southern	3b-ss	131	516	80	163	18	3	1	55	9	.316
1972	Charlotte	Southern	3b-2b	135	516	51	128	18	2	2	41	5	.248
1973	Monterrey	Mexican	3b-2b	42	153	22	43	4	1	0	16	2	.281
	Minor League Totals:			2282	8707	1227	2502	366	62	67	868	176	.287

◆ ———————— *Jim Mills* ———————— ◆

The minor league baseball career of Jim Mills covered five-and-a-half decades. The career that began as a player in 1941 ended in 1996 when Mills retired from the front office of the Durham Bulls. During that time, Mills at one time or another held almost every job possible in minor league baseball. He has been a player, a manager, an umpire, a general manager, and a league president.

Mills, a native of Apex, attended N.C. State University on an athletic scholarship in 1940, as did his twin brother Joe. There they both played football, basketball and baseball. The brothers left school after one year and signed professional baseball contracts with the Boston Red Sox, who assigned them to the Class D team in Owensboro, Kentucky. Joe was released from the team but Jim played well, hitting .331 for the season.

Jim Mills was set to begin the next season with Class AAA Louisville but a draft notice changed those plans. He would go on to spend the next four years in the Army Air Corps, patrolling the Mississippi River and Central America. After the war, Mills was invited to spring training with the N.Y. Giants and offered a job playing for their minor league team in Knoxville, Tennessee. The owner of the Carolina League's Raleigh Capitals had also offered him a job and Mills decided to take it since it was closer to home.

Mills spent two seasons in Raleigh, helping lead the Capitals to league championships both years. He left in 1948 for a chance to be both a player and a manager with Concord of the North Carolina State League. The next season Mills moved over to the powerful Mooresville Moors to serve in the same capacity. In 1951 he left Mooresville for a managerial job with Rocky Mount of the Coastal Plain League. After only half a season, he resigned and shortly thereafter returned to his old job with Mooresville. There Mills remained through the 1953 season, when he retired as a player. After nine seasons as a minor league ball player, he finished with a career batting average of .310.

Mills returned to the Carolina League in 1954, this time as an umpire. The 1955 season was spent out of baseball as a sporting goods salesman, but in 1956 Mills took a job as the general manager of Fayetteville's Carolina League franchise. That club folded after the season and Mills returned to sporting goods.

The 1958 season began 14 consecutive years of Mills serving as a minor league general manager. The 1958 and '59 seasons were spent with the Wilson Tobs, 1960 with Savannah, and then 1961 through 1968 with the Asheville Tourists. Nineteen sixty-nine found Mills in Spartanburg, South Carolina, for one season and then it was back to Savannah in 1970. His final year as a general manager — 1971— was spent in Charleston, West Virginia.

In 1972, Mills took a job as a field representative for the National Association of Professional Baseball Leagues, the minor leagues' governing body. That job would last through 1981. In 1977, following the death of Wallace McKenna, Mills was elected to fill

the vacant presidency of the Carolina League. Perhaps his greatest successes in baseball came while guiding this league. When Mills assumed leadership, the once thriving league had fallen upon hard times and dropped to only four teams. By 1980, the league had grown to eight teams and attendance had risen from 167,000 to over 600,000. The expansion Durham Bulls — a league addition Mills worked hard for — drew over 175,000 in their first season back in the league. The Carolina League was prospering and attendance was continuing to grow when Mills left the presidency after the 1983 season.

Mills spent the 1984 season as a scout for the Pittsburgh Pirates. He then took a job with the Durham Bulls in 1985 and worked in their front office until retiring in 1996 at age 76.

Surprisingly, baseball was only Mills' summer job during much of his career. With his brother Joe, Mills spent 18 years as a college football and basketball referee, working games in the Atlantic Coast, Southeastern and other conferences. He had to give it up when he took the job with the National Association due to the amount of travel that job required.

Complete professional record as a player:

YEAR	CLUB	LEAGUE	POS	G	AB	R	H	2B	3B	HR	RBI	SB	AVG
1941	Owensboro	Kitty	of	109	411	70	136	24	3	3	46	16	.331
1942–45						Military service							
1946	Raleigh	Carolina	of	133	517	118	164	33	6	1	71	15	.317
1947	Raleigh	Carolina	of	118	467	77	130	36	3	4	67	15	.278
1948	Concord	N.C. State	of–3b	108	430	82	138	34	7	5	63	21	.321
1949	Mooresville	N.C. State	3b–of	112	430	108	166	26	8	6	79	13	.386
1950	Mooresville	N.C. State	3b–of	111	429	100	145	29	3	7	62	10	.338
1951	Rocky Mount	Coastal Plain	2b–of	54	211	39	60	10	1	6	40	5	284
	Mooresville	N.C. State	2b–of	62	220	37	64	13	1	3	36	2	.291
1952	Mooresville	N.C. State	of–1b	104	383	87	122	26	1	2	74	8	.347
1953	Mooresville	Tar Heel	of–3b	112	394	92	127	21	4	1	59	8	.323
		Totals:		1023	3892	810	1252	252	37	38	597	113	.322

Russell "Red" Mincy

Russell Mincy grew up in Lincolnton, North Carolina. After graduating from high school he played baseball for several textile mills around the area. In 1937, Mincy, then 20,

earned a tryout with the Valdese Textiles of the independent Carolina League. He didn't make the team but it led to another tryout with Gastonia in the same league. He did make that team, marking the beginning of a long, distinguished minor league career.

Mincy related this incident from 1940, when he was an outfielder for Tarboro:

> One night Waudell Mosser was pitchin' and he could throw hard. He was pitchin' to Phil Morris, Wilson's first baseman, who had a reputation for being pretty mean and apt to fight. Mosser threw close to him and knocked him down so Morris turned around to the catcher and said, "If you called for that pitch you're an s.o.b." Then he told Mosser, "If you threw it on your own you're an s.o.b." Dace Davis, who was the catcher, told Morris, "I didn't call for that one but I'm callin' for the next one" and down Morris went again. He and Davis then got into a scuffle and wrestled around a bit.

Mincy had some good seasons before the war but was frequently shuffled from team to team. After spending three years in the U.S. Navy during World War II, Mincy returned to professional baseball in 1946.

Like so many other talented minor leaguers robbed of their peak years by the war, Mincy was 29 and no longer a real major league prospect when he returned. A self-described "late bloomer," Mincy played his best baseball, however, after the war. For his last nine seasons, he batted .342.

Mincy first served in a managerial role in 1948 with Kingsport (Tennessee) before leaving at midseason for a job with his hometown Lincolnton Cardinals. He managed at Douglas, Georgia, in 1949 and then came back to North Carolina to take over the helm of the Marion Maruaders for the 1950 and '51 seasons.

After spending the 1954 season as player-manager with Fulton (Ken.) of the KITTY League, Red Mincy retired from professional baseball. He took a job with the North Carolina Department of Motor Vehicles as an officer in the Charlotte weight station and worked there until retirement in 1982.

Complete playing record:

YEAR	CLUB	LEAGUE	POS	G	AB	R	H	2B	3B	HR	RBI	SB	AVG
1937	Gastonia	Carolina (Ind.)	of	–	166	22	48	8	1	5	28	2	.289
1938	Salisbury	N.C. State	of	29	120	24	31	6	2	0	11	6	.258
	Huntington	Mountain State	of	79	306	66	97	21	7	8	56	17	.317
1939	Salem-Roanoke	Virginia	of	106	399	92	138	41	9	9	77	16	.346
	Kannapolis	N.C. State	of	<10	–	–	–	–	–	–	–	–	–
1940	Portsmouth	Piedmont	of	21	81	10	12	2	1	0	7	3	.148
	Tarboro	Coastal Plain	of	100	382	77	123	34	6	4	59	24	.322
1941	Harrisonburg	Virginia	of	17	62	16	17	4	2	1	15	2	.274
	Portsmouth	Piedmont	of	7	27	–	5	–	–	–	–	–	.185
	Rocky Mount	Coastal Plain	of	38	144	24	44	9	2	0	14	4	.306
	Jackson	Southeastern	of	34	125	18	32	8	0	1	15	1	.256
1942	Portsmouth	Piedmont	of	<10	–	–	–	–	–	–	–	–	–
	Lancaster	Interstate	of	29	106	13	22	2	1	0	9	1	.208
	Statesville	N.C. State	of	<10	–	–	–	–	–	–	–	–	–
	Salem-Roanoke/ Stanton	Virginia	of	29	111	21	34	7	1	0	16	2	.306
1943–45		Military service											
1946	Asheville	Tri-State	of	<10	–	–	–	–	–	–	–	–	–
	Pulaski/Kgsprt.	Appalachian	of	123	452	131	179	51	10	12	136	20	.396
	Chattanooga	Southern Assoc.	of	4	11	–	2	–	–	–	–	–	.182
1947	Charlotte/Knox.	Tri-State	of	138	522	85	164	35	11	2	90	3	.314
1948	Kingsport	Appalachian	of	41	132	23	44	9	1	1	33	3	.333
	Lincolnton	Western Carolina	of	57	189	46	61	10	3	2	44	3	.323
1949	Douglas	Georgia State	of	146	564	113	165	34	2	8	98	30	.293
1950	Marion	Western Carolina	of	110	382	98	161	32	8	4	104	14	.421
1951	Marion	Western Carolina	of	98	351	64	124	25	3	1	66	11	.353
1952	Shelby	Western Carolina	of	106	393	107	132	32	9	8	85	7	.336
1953	Shelby	Tarheel	of	110	395	87	138	32	11	9	101	6	.349
1954	Fulton	KITTY	of	61	181	41	50	9	1	4	52	4	.276

MARION MARAUDERS - 1950
RED MINCY MANAGER,
W-56   L-54

Russell "Red" Mincy (kneeling, third from right) managed the Marion Marauders in 1950 and 1951 (courtesy David Beal).

Eddie Neville

Born in Baltimore in 1922, Eddie Neville became probably the best left-handed pitcher in North Carolina in the late 1940s and early '50s. A star outfielder in high school, Neville first entered professional baseball in 1942 when he was invited to spring training by his hometown Baltimore Orioles. He failed to make the team, however, and was sent to Wilmington (Del.) of the Class B Interstate League. After only a few games, Neville was released and sent to Butler of the Class D Pennsylvania State Association. There he played well but an injury ended his season after only 22 games.

Neville joined the Army in January of 1943 and served until early 1946. He then returned home to Baltimore and played semipro baseball that summer. The following winter, Neville was offered a job playing baseball in the Canal Zone so he headed for Panama. He would eventually play seven seasons there and, after switching from outfielder to pitcher, compile a record of 50–17.

In the spring of 1947, Neville turned down offers to play in several major league farm systems for attractive pay offered by the independent Tarboro Tars of the Coastal Plain League. He dominated the league that first season in North Carolina, tying the league record with 28 wins, and followed it with another great performance in 1948. In 1949, Neville was promoted to

Durham of the Carolina League and continued to pitch outstanding baseball, winning 25 games.

The summer of 1950 found Neville in Toledo, Ohio, only one step from the major leagues. Like Durham, Toledo was a Detroit farm club and Neville seemed to be headed to the big leagues. It was not to be, however, as he failed to meet with much success at that level and finished the season at only 6–15 for the seventh place team.

After spending most of the 1951 season in Williamsport, Pennsylvania, Neville returned to Durham in 1952. He picked up right where he had left off in 1949 and again became one of the best pitchers in the Carolina League. When he retired in 1955, Eddie Neville had won 75 games for Durham, an all-time team record.

Neville went on to work for Duke University for many years. He died in 1989.

Complete pitching record:

Eddie Neville (courtesy Janet Neville).

YEAR	CLUB	LEAGUE	G	IP	W	L	H	R	BB	SO	ERA
1947	Tarboro	Coastal Plain	43	304	28	9	269	122	89	172	2.31
1948	Tarboro	Coastal Plain	25	176	15	4	204	82	53	59	3.22
1949	Durham	Carolina	40	274	25	10	252	12	69	154	2.59
1950	Toledo	Amer. Assoc.	35	174	6	15	181	98	94	72	4.14
1951	Toledo	Amer. Assoc.	6	16	2	0	19	8	7	5	2.81
	Williamsport	Eastern	32	162	7	11	176	77	73	95	3.39
1952	Durham	Carolina	30	215	17	9	186	53	61	95	**1.72**
1953	Durham	Carolina	41	**264**	21	8	243	99	74	138	2.28
1954	Durham	Carolina	43	216	12	11	267	128	52	119	3.83
1955	Albany	Eastern	6	35	1	3	49	24	14	24	4.63

◆ ───── *Cecil "Zip" Payne* ───── ◆

James Cecil "Zip" Payne was born in the Alamance County town of Swepsonville on April 9, 1909. Though he became one of the best hitters and outfielders in all of minor league baseball, he never advanced to the big leagues.

Reported to have rejected countless offers to play for high level major league farm clubs with a good shot at the big leagues, Payne accepted only one: He signed with the Pittsburgh Pirates in 1931 and was sent to Wichita, Kansas. Unhappy being so far from home, Payne secured his release and returned to North Carolina. He eventually settled in to playing for Class D teams near home where, for a player of his caliber, the money was good.

After spending the 1943 season out of baseball, Payne was convinced to return by George Ferrell, who was managing at Lynchburg. Stating that baseball had been good to him and he owed it to the game to help keep it going during the war, Payne signed on with Ferrell and his St. Louis Cardinals farm club. He played well and was sent to Rochester the next season, just one step from the big leagues. Past his prime, however, and no longer considered a big league prospect, Payne continued to play well but was returned to Lynchburg when that team needed a manager.

In 1946, Payne returned to baseball in North Carolina when the Cardinals offered him a job as playing manager with their Winston-Salem club.

Payne played his last games while serving as manager of the Fayetteville club in 1949. He left that team in midseason and took over as manager of the Reidsville Luckies in the Carolina League. The 1950 season — Payne's last in professional baseball — was spent as manager of the Mt. Airy Graniteers of the Blue Ridge League.

After retiring from baseball, Payne returned to his home in Mayodan and took a job working in security at the textile mill. He died in 1983.

Complete playing record:

YEAR	CLUB	LEAGUE	POS	G	AB	R	H	2B	3B	HR	RBI	SB	AVG
1929	Goldsboro	Eastern Car.	of	94	347	54	97	20	2	0	30	14	.280
1930	Columbia	SALLY	of	117	546	93	151	19	18	1	37	9	.277
1931	Wichita	Western	of	19	73	10	17	5	2	1	5	0	.233
	Henderson	Piedmont	of	41	150	19	36	8	2	0	9	0	.240
1932	unknown semipro			–	–	–	–	–	–	–	–	–	–
1933	Mayodan (semipro)	Bi-State	of	–	–	–	–	–	–	–	–	–	–
1934	Mayodan	Bi-State	of	79	333	64	125	32	6	14	50	2	.375
1935	Mayodan	Bi-State	of	110	458	95	177	30	9	14	60	0	.386
1936	Mayodan/Bassett	Bi-State	of-3b	102	432	86	153	29	12	12	75	1	.354
1937	Mayodan	Bi-State	of	115	476	102	167	44	9	18	85	2	.351
1938	Mayodan	Bi-State	of	108	439	80	155	46	12	4	97	4	.353
1939	Leaksville	Bi-State	of	114	455	110	177	38	12	12	126	8	.389
1940	Portsmouth	Piedmont	of	5	19	4	5	0	0	0	2	2	.263
	Leaksville	Bi-State	of	110	455	81	144	38	9	10	100	1	.316
1941	Leaksville	Bi-State	of	100	412	89	147	33	5	6	75	1	.357
1942	Leaksville	Bi-State	of	125	478	61	144	34	2	5	64	5	.301
1943							Did not play						
1944	Lynchburg	Piedmont	of	133	532	81	181	29	10	0	99	4	.340
1945	Rochester	International	of	51	182	26	55	5	3	1	34	3	.302
	Lynchburg	Piedmont	of	42	143	19	44	6	1	0	21	0	.308
1946	Winston-Salem	Carolina	of	93	334	52	115	23	4	4	53	1	.344
1947	Winston-Salem	Carolina	of	63	221	35	81	17	1	0	33	5	.367
1948	Winston-Salem	Carolina					Manager only						
1949	Fayetteville	Tobacco St.	of	14	37	3	8	1	1	0	9	0	.216
	Totals:			1635	6522	1164	2179	457	120	102	1066	60	.334

 ——————— *Jim Poole* ———————

Jim Poole's involvement with professional baseball in some capacity spanned nearly 50 years. He began his professional playing career in 1914 as a 19-year-old, playing a few games in the outfield with Newnan of the Georgia-Alabama League. From there Poole, who soon switched to first base, worked his way up through the minor leagues with stops in Charleston, South Carolina; Richmond; San Antonio; and Portland, Oregon. In 1925 he made the big leagues with the Philadelphia Athletics.

Poole was the Athletics' starting first baseman for two seasons, but after a slow start in 1927 he was sent to Minneapolis. The next several seasons would be spent playing with teams in the International League and the Southern Association, never again reaching the major leagues.

Poole's first managerial job came in 1933 when he was hired to take the helm of the Piedmont League's Winston-Salem Twins. It was his first return to his native state as a player since beginning his professional baseball career.

Poole's final games as a player came in 1946 when he spent 22 games with the Moultrie Packers of the Georgia-Florida League. The 1947 season was spent out of baseball, but for two years—1948 and '49—Poole

served as a scout for his old team, the Philadelphia Athletics. In 1950, he was hired in midseason to take over as manager of the Morganton Aggies in the Western Carolina League. Poole spent a few more seasons managing other teams in the South before returning to North Carolina in 1960, this time as both the owner and manager of the Rutherford County Owls of the Western Carolina League. After poor attendance, he moved the team to Belmont in 1961. Unfortunately, the team had little talent and disbanded after the season. Poole then retired from baseball. He died at Hickory in 1975.

Poole's playing record after returning to North Carolina:

YEAR	CLUB	LEAGUE	POS	G	AB	R	H	2B	3B	HR	RBI	SB	AVG
1933	Winston-Salem	Piedmont	1b	65	247	34	64	12	0	4	41	5	.259
1934	various semipro textile teams	–	–	–	–	–	–	–	–	–	–	–	–
1935	Mooresville (semipro)	Car. Textile	1b	–	259	51	88	19	1	13	–	–	.345
1936	Mooresville	Carolina (Ind.)	1b	–	158*	42*	63*	15*	1*	13*	54*	1*	.399*
1937	Mooresville	N.C.State	1b	93	378	68	130	36	0	14	83	13	.344
1938	Reidsville	Bi-State	1b	117	414	97	135	33	3	14	94	17	.326
1939	Martinsville	Bi-State	1b	22	81	11	26	9	0	1	22	1	.321
	Landis	N.C.State	1b	65	212	25	57	6	2	3	34	5	.269
1940	Thomasville	N.C. State	1b	14	48	5	12	2	0	1	8	0	.250
	Fulton	KITTY	1b	87	321	62	109	23	1	8	86	6	.340
1941	Ft.Pierce	Fla. E. Cst.	1b	114	387	63	119	17	2	6	67	10	.307
1942	Statesville	N.C. State	1b	82	314	54	101	20	2	7	60	3	.322
1943	Erwin	Appalach.	1b	82	274	55	87	24	2	2	49	5	.318
1944	Erwin	Appalach.	1b	17	9	2	1	0	0	0	2	1	.111
1945	Statesville	N.C. State	1b	3	6	0	0	0	0	0	2	0	.000
1946	Moultrie	Ga.–Fla.	1b	22	49	13	14	3	1	2	16	0	.286

* 1936 statistics are from midseason, the only ones available

Walter Rabb

Lenoir native Walter Rabb was a talented athlete as a boy. He attended Mars Hill Junior College and then went on to N.C. State, where he played both baseball and basketball. During the summers while in college he played semipro baseball and in the summer of 1936, Rabb was playing for Selma-Smithfield. "I was playing a fairly decent game of shortstop and Billy Hitchcock

was playing shortstop for Greenville. He was also the quarterback for Alabama and Bear Bryant said he had to come back and get ready for football about halfway through the season. So they came over and got me and I went and played for Greenville. It was a step upward in the semipro ranks; the Coastal Plain League was the prestige league in all of semipro baseball."

After getting a degree in physical education, Rabb took a job coaching football, boxing and baseball at Cary High School in 1937. After meeting Peahead Walker and Jim Tatum — two local football legends who also played baseball — Rabb decided to go back to the Coastal Plain League (which was now professional) and play with them at Snow Hill.

Walter Rabb was the best fielding shortstop in the Coastal Plain League during his seasons there and was named to the league All-Star team in 1940. His greatest achievements in baseball came after his short professional career ended. In 1947 he took the head baseball coach job at the University of North Carolina. Serving in that capacity for more than 25 years, he coached some great teams and produced dozens of minor league and several major league players.

Complete professional record:

YEAR	CLUB	LEAGUE	POS	G	AB	R	H	2B	3B	HR	RBI	SB	AVG
1937	Snow Hill	Coast. Plain	ss	70	252	41	61	7	1	0	26	5	.242
1938	Snow Hill	Coast. Plain	ss	104	391	52	121	9	4	6	59	9	.309
1939	Snow Hill	Coast. Plain	ss	14	59	7	19	2	0	1	7	1	.322
	Akron	Mid. Atlantic	ss	45	172	24	40	2	2	0	18	5	.233
	Augusta	South Atl.	ss	68	247	35	67	4	4	1	34	12	.271
1940	Snow Hill	Coast. Plain	ss	128	514	72	139	19	3	3	49	10	.270
		Totals:		429	1635	231	447	43	14	11	193	42	.273

 ## Charlie Roach

The name Charlie Roach in not as familiar to fans of minor league baseball as it should be. In the late 1940s and early '50s, Roach was one of the better third basemen in the state but was not allowed to join the ranks of minor league ball due to the color of his skin. Instead, he excelled with the teams in the state's Negro leagues.

Roach, a native of Reidsville, entered college at Winston-Salem State in 1942 and graduated in 1948 after taking two years off for service in the Army. While in college he played baseball with North Carolina A&T since Winston-Salem State did not have a team. Beginning with the summers while in college, Roach played with the black semipro teams of the state. At one time or another he played for the Asheville Blues, Greensboro's Redbirds and Goshen Redwings, and the Durham Eagles and Rams. In 1951, Roach was named by the National Baseball Congress as the best semipro third baseman in North Carolina.

Finally, in 1952, Roach was given the opportunity to join a white minor league team when the New Bern Bears of the Coastal Plain League hired him. The Bears' black trainer and bus driver, Phillip "Rabbit" Martin, knew Roach and recommended him to the team owners. Moved from third base to the outfield because of the team's fear that fans might throw things at him (they didn't, and according to Roach the fans treated him well), Roach played only a few games before a leg injury led to his release.

Since college graduation, Roach taught in the Durham public school system. This often made it difficult to play baseball since the season began before school got out. Roach attributes his leg injury at New Bern to a lack of conditioning since he was not able to attend spring training.

After New Bern, Roach worked out with Danville of the Carolina League later in that same season but did not sign with the team. He returned to semipro baseball and played for several more seasons while continuing his teaching career. Roach eventually became assistant principal of Durham High School in 1967 and served in that capacity until his retirement in 1985.

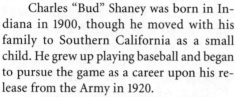

Bud Shaney

Charles "Bud" Shaney was born in Indiana in 1900, though he moved with his family to Southern California as a small child. He grew up playing baseball and began to pursue the game as a career upon his release from the Army in 1920.

Shaney worked his way up the minor league ladder and in 1923 was promoted to Milwaukee of the American Association. He spent part of 1924 with Milwaukee and at spring training in Florida in 1925 he thought he was ready for the major leagues.

Unfortunately, Shaney came down with malaria and was sent to Asheville in hopes that he would recover in the mountain climate. Shaney never again came as close to making the big leagues. Instead he became a star in places like Asheville and Charlotte.

After spending the 1942 season as the manager of the talentless Hickory Rebels, Shaney retired from baseball. He umpired for a few seasons and then took a job as the groundskeeper at Asheville's McCormick Field, a position he would hold for many years.

For three seasons, beginning in 1953, Shaney would take the mound again for the Asheville club for one game. His best outing of the three came in 1954, when at age 54, Shaney shut out his opponent for the five innings he pitched.

Complete professional record:

YEAR	CLUB	LEAGUE	G	IP	W	L	H	R	BB	SO	ERA
1922	Independence	Southwestern	32	233	19	8	195	90	61	152	2.59
1923	Independence	Southwestern	42	312	18	18	317	150	60	168	–
	Milwaukee	Amer. Assoc.	8	47	4	2	63	26	11	9	4.21
1924	Milwaukee	Amer. Assoc.	24	85	2	6	113	60	26	25	5.51
	Mobile	South. Assoc.	12	65	2	6	100	52	17	23	5.68
1925	Mobile	South. Assoc.	4	4	0	1	16	13	5	0	–
	Asheville	SALLY	38	233	13	10	271	126	54	86	3.86
1926	Asheville	SALLY	40	262	19	14	315	156	56	90	4.33
1927	Asheville	SALLY	41	273	15	14	271	110	46	95	2.74
1928	Asheville	SALLY	42	257	21	11	270	104	55	93	2.59
1929	Asheville	SALLY	37	255	17	12	295	128	62	92	3.67
1930	Williamsport	New York–Penn.	35	224	14	14	219	92	39	72	3.38
1931	Charlotte	Piedmont	39	280	24	10	258	126	67	161	–
1932	Charlotte	Piedmont	37	235	14	13	288	146	52	129	4.79
1933	Scranton/W-B	New York–Penn.	38	199	7	15	238	112	47	60	4.48
1934	Columbia	Piedmont	12	44	3	3	59	44	17	16	–
1935	Portsmouth	Piedmont	19	98	6	5	127	70	35	28	5.42
1936	Charlotte	Carolina (Ind.)	–	–	–	–	–	–	–	–	–
1937	Trenton	New York–Penn.	17	100	5	5	105	49	15	36	3.15
	Sydney	Cape Breton Coll.	5	31	3	1	19	4	5	23	0.29
1938	Spartanburg	SALLY	15	84	3	6	100	54	8	42	4.29
1939						Unknown semipro					
1940	Hickory	Tar Heel	33	194	12	10	202	98	25	111	3.71
1941	Asheville	Piedmont	1	8	0	1	9	4	0	0	4.50
1942	Hickory	N.C. State	30	179	8	9	199	94	16	88	2.92
1943–52						Did not play					
1953	Asheville	Tri-State	1	5	0	0	9	3	0	2	5.40
1954	Asheville	Tri-State	1	5	1	0	4	0	1	0	0.00
1955	Asheville	Tri-State	1	2	0	1	7	7	22	3	31.50

◆ ——————— *Emo Showfety* ——————— ◆

A native of Greensboro, Emil "Emo" Showfety played baseball at Elon College. After graduation in 1941, he signed on with Danville of the Bi-State League, where he had an excellent rookie season.

The 1942 season with Durham was another good one but like so many others, Showfety's baseball career was interrupted by World War II. After three years in the military, he was no longer considered a prospect. Instead, he returned to North Carolina and became a star in the Carolina League.

Showfety was one of the premier power hitters in the early years of the league, earning All-Star honors in 1947 and '48. He retired from baseball after the 1949 season and entered a long career in the men's clothing business.

Complete playing record:

Right: Emo Showfety and the 10 cases of Wheaties cereal he won in 1949 for hitting home runs in Greensboro's stadium that season (courtesy of Emo Showfety).

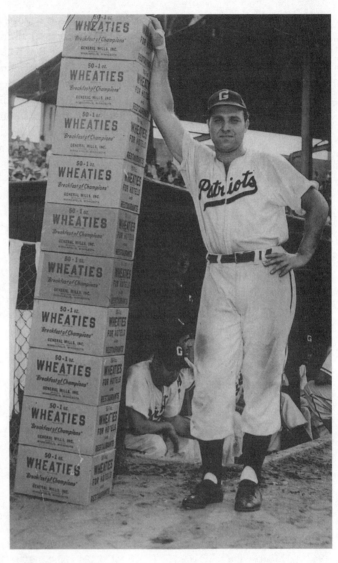

YEAR	CLUB	LEAGUE	POS	G	AB	R	H	2B	3B	HR	RBI	SB	AVG
1941	Danville	Bi-State	of	108	456	100	156	28	8	25	110	5	.342
1942	Durham	Piedmont	of	110	397	51	115	29	6	5	55	7	.290
1943–45					Military service								
1946	Raleigh	Carolina	of	82	312	59	107	24	6	13	69	5	.343
1947	Burlington	Carolina	of	95									
	Greensboro	Carolina	of	43									
	totals:			138	543	103	178	25	10	26	121	2	.328
1948	Greensboro	Carolina	of	142	567	95	**191**	38	8	19	105	1	.337
1949	Greensboro	Carolina	of	138	525	86	182	28	0	35	120	5	.347
	Totals:			718	2800	494	929	172	38	123	580	25	.332

◆ ——————— *Norman Small* ——————— ◆

Norman Small, a native of Long Island, New York, began his professional baseball career in 1934 with a Class D team in Martinsville, Virginia. He advanced through the minor leagues and in 1937 reached Durham of the Class B Piedmont League. There, reminiscent of the movie *Bull Durham*, Small was married at home plate between games of a doubleheader. The 1943 season found Small a member of the New York Giants organization playing for AAA Jersey City, one step from the big leagues. World War II interrupted that dream, however, as he was drafted into the army. After seeing action in both Europe and the Pacific, Small returned to baseball in 1946.

Baseball was flooded after the war with returning major leaguers. At age 32, Small was no longer considered a prospect and returned to Class D ball in Mooresville, North Carolina, his wife's home. He prospered there and became a legend. For five consecutive seasons he would lead the league in home runs. When Small retired from baseball after the 1953 season, he had played in 1,703 minor league games, hit 336 home runs, driven in over 1,400 runs and had a career batting average of .320.

Complete playing record:

YEAR	CLUB	LEAGUE	POS	G	AB	R	H	2B	3B	HR	RBI	SB	AVG
1934	Martinsville	Bi-State	of/p	40	123	24	37	12	3	2	–	–	.301
1935	Asheville	Piedmont	of	15	58	14	11	2	0	3	11	–	.190
	Greenwood	East Dixie	of	16	49	2	8	2	0	0	3	–	.163
	Martinsville	Bi-State	of/p	47	135	12	33	5	1	1	–	–	.244
1936	Landis	C. Car. Text.(semi)	of	14	47	–	23	–	–	–	–	–	.489
	York	New York–Penn.	of	2	7	1	1	0	0	0	0	–	.143
	Mooresville	Carolina (Ind.)	of	–	127*	27*	40*	8*	1*	10*	29*	0*	.315*
1937	Mooresville	N.C. State	of	35	148	44	58	12	2	12	51	5	.392
	Durham	Piedmont	of	88	318	49	87	18	7	2	42	8	.274
1938	Durham	Piedmont	of	69	276	40	76	9	9	5	43	6	.275
	Waterloo	Three I	of	9	29	3	2	0	0	0	2	0	.070
	Columbia	SALLY	of	21	78	10	32	6	1	2	16	1	.410
1939	Columbia	SALLY	of	111	455	60	123	24	10	6	54	5	.270
	Meridian	Southeastern	of	11	39	9	11	2	0	4	7	–	.282
1940	Mooresville	N.C. State	of	103	437	95	151	41	6	25	115	5	.346
1941	Mooresville	N.C. State	of	95	386	75	128	22	8	18	73	3	.332
1942	Mooresville	N.C. State	of	100	383	91	144	35	6	32	107	7	.376
1943	Jersey City	International	of	53	168	21	42	10	1	4	19	0	.250
1944–45							Military service						
1946	Mooresville	N.C. State	of	99	388	100	135	31	10	18	69	8	.348
1947	Mooresville	N.C. State	of	104	398	106	143	36	2	31	102	3	.359
1948	Mooresville	N.C. State	of	110	431	103	154	32	4	33	130	7	.357
1949	Mooresville	N.C. State	of	124	456	115	157	20	4	41	152	7	.344
1950	Mooresville	N.C. State	of	98	350	73	163	23	0	32	104	4	.294
1951	Hickory	N.C. State	of	126	485	106	165	35	6	37	127	4	.340
1952	Hickory	Western Carolina	of	20	82	15	28	10	2	2	13	0	.341
	Raleigh	Carolina	of	112	419	59	113	25	4	12	68	1	.270
1953	Mooresville	Tar Heel	of	95	385	75	131	31	1	14	87	6	.340
	Professional Totals:			1703	6483	1302	2073	443	87	336	1395	80	.320

* 1936 statistics are from midseason, the only ones available, and not included in totals

Harry Soufas

Harry Soufas was perhaps the greatest hitter in the history of the Coastal Plain League. He played eight seasons in the league for Snow Hill, Rocky Mount, Kinston and New Bern.

Born in Wilson in 1917, Harry Soufas was more of a football player while growing up. In 1936 he attended the University of North Carolina on a football scholarship, winning a spot on the freshman team. His football career soon ended after injuries and a promise to his parents to give it up. Soufas then transferred to Atlantic Christian College in his hometown of Wilson. That spring he met Peahead Walker, the Elon College football coach who was also the manager of Snow Hill's baseball team in the Coastal Plain League. Walker gave him a tryout and Soufas made the team as a first baseman.

Soufas had a good season that first year in professional baseball; he hit .307 and was named to the All–Coastal Plain team. The next season, still with Snow Hill, his batting average dropped due to injuries but he still hit a respectable .284 with 13 home runs. In 1939 Soufas had a great year. Batting .338 with 30 home runs, he was again the All–Coastal Plain League first baseman.

After the 1939 season Snow Hill sold his contract to the New York Yankees. The Yankees sent Soufas to Norfolk of the Piedmont League, a big step up in the minor leagues. He would spend two years in Norfolk before returning to North Carolina in 1942 as a member of the Rocky Mount Rocks of the Bi-State League. With the Rocks, Soufas would hit 29 home runs and be named league MVP.

The war interrupted Soufas's promising career. He would spend the next three years as a member of the military police in North Africa and Italy. After the war Soufas was offered a chance to play for Beaumont in the Texas League by the Detroit Tigers. He de-

Harry Soufas was player-manager of the 1946 Rocky Mount team (courtesy Harry Soufas).

cided against it and took a job in 1946 as player-manager of the Rocky Mount entry in the Coastal Plain League. The 1947 and '48 seasons — two of his best — were spent with New Bern.

After the 1948 season Soufas decided to retire and concentrate on a career in business after he had opened a sandwich shop and a pool room in New Bern. The Kinston Eagles talked him out of retirement and he played for them in 1949.

The 1950 season was the last for Harry Soufas. He returned to New Bern and played for the Bears for one final season. He then retired and went on to a career in insurance that lasted over 30 years.

Complete playing record:

YEAR	CLUB	LEAGUE	POS	G	AB	R	H	2B	BB	HR	RBI	SB	AVG
1937	Snow Hill	Coastal Plain	1b	79	290	46	89	14	–	7	47	4	.307
1938	Snow Hill	Coastal Plain	1b	111	408	69	116	19	–	13	57	7	.284
1939	Snow Hill	Coastal Plain	1b	121	447	92	151	25	–	30	104	3	.338
1940	Norfolk	Piedmont	1b	82	295	48	75	10	32	9	46	8	.254
1941	Norfolk	Piedmont	1b	37	114	12	27	3	11	0	16	2	.237
1942	Rocky Mt.	Bi-State	of	122	472	100	149	31	73	29	83	14	.316
1943–45								Military service					
1946	Rocky Mt.	Coastal Plain	1b	125	434	79	139	18	–	11	66	17	.320
1947	New Bern	Coastal Plain	1b	137	517	114	177	34	99	25	122	12	.342
1948	New Bern	Coastal Plain	1b	134	540	111	188	30	105	23	135	9	.348
1949	Kinston	Coastal Plain	1b	126	438	82	138	26	105	8	79	16	.315
1950	New Bern	Coastal Plain	1b	137	488	95	167	32	113	11	117	12	.342
		Totals:		1211	4443	848	1416	242	–	166	872	104	.319

◆ ─── *Matt Winters* ─── ◆

In an era when minor league players are lucky to spend an entire season with one team, Matt Winters is a rarity: He played three seasons with the Greensboro Hornets.

After spending a decade in the minors, Winters finally made the major leagues in 1989, when he appeared in 42 games with the Kansas City Royals. In 1990, he signed with the Nippon Ham Fighters of the Japanese Pacific League. In five seasons with that team, Winters was one of the top sluggers in Japan, hitting a total of 160 home runs.

As of this writing, Winters is a coach in the Florida Marlins minor league system.

Winters's Greensboro record:

YEAR	CLUB	POS	G	AB	R	H	2B	3B	HR	RBI	BB	AVG
1980	Greensboro	dh-of	112	363	72	116	15	2	20	92	58	.320
1981	Greensboro	of-dh	125	404	85	121	23	2	16	76	94	.300
1982	Greensboro	of	104	326	76	106	20	2	20	93	118	.325

Appendix 4:
About the Team Names

North Carolina towns and cities have been very creative when naming their local teams. There have been Moonshiners and Tourists, Bats and Owls, Jets and Rockets, Hornets and Bees, and Orphans, Twins and Triplets. There have also been Tars, Tarheels, and Tarbabies.

Many teams adopted the names of their major league affiliates. Most major league teams have been represented, some by more than one town. There have been the Cardinals, Twins, Pirates, Rangers, Senators, Indians, Orioles, Mets, Cubs, Reds, Yankees, Red Sox, Phillies, Browns, Giants, Blue Jays, Expos, Dodgers, Athletics, Braves, and Astros.

Some towns chose more traditional sports mascot names for their teams, such as Eagles, Colts, Knights and Chiefs. At least two towns named teams after the manager: Tarboro's Serpents (for Snake Henry) and Henderson's Bunnies (for Bunn Hearn). Some apparently chose a name because it had a catchy sound, such as the Ayden Aces or Burlington Bees. Others were plays on the town's name: High Point Pointers, Cooleemee Cools, Thomasville Tommies, Goldsboro Goldbugs and Snow Hill Billies, to name a few. Two others took names from their respective counties: the Williamston Martins (for Martin County) and the Tarboro Combs (for Edgecombe County).

While some team names were meant to be humorous, others reflected the natures of the towns. Teams in the tobacco producing areas of the state chose names such as Tobacconists, Leafs, Bulls (for Bull Durham tobacco), Luckies (for Lucky Strikes) and Auctioneers (for tobacco markets). Other prominent forms of industry in the state are also represented, such as textiles (Weavers, Spinners, Blanketeers, Towelers, and Millers) and furniture (Furniture-makers and Chairmakers). There have been the less specific Manufacturers and Farmers. Asheville's team was named the Tourists because of that city's tourist industry. Town histories can also be seen in team names. Greensboro's Patriots were named after the Revolutionary War battle fought near that city. Because of Edenton's colonial history, their team was called the Colonials. New Bern's Swiss heritage is reflected in the name Bears. A bear is the prominent feature of the town's crest.

Distinguishing geographical features have been used in names. The Elizabeth City Albemarles were named for that city's proximity to the Albemarle Sound. Teams in the mountains, due the altitude, have been the Skylanders and the Skylarks. Mt. Airy was the Graniteers because that town is home to the largest granite quarry in the world. Other teams have chosen more generic geographical names such as Rocks and Pines. Other distinguishing features such as military bases have led to names such as the Goldsboro Jets (for Seymour Johnson Air Force Base) and the Fayetteville Generals (for Ft. Bragg).

With the recent rise in the importance of merchandising, teams have picked names and logos that will sell well on shirts and hats. Catchy names such as Warthogs, Crawdads, Mudcats, and Bats have been on the rise in all of minor league baseball. Now even losing teams have the potential to make money if they have an attractive name and logo.

Appendix 5:
North Carolina
Major Leaguers

Hundreds of players have gone on to the major leagues from North Carolina teams. While most of the players listed here have played in the state on their way to the majors, many, especially in the period from the 1920s to the early '50s, came back to the minors after playing in the big leagues. This was common with managers, since a playing manager saved the team an extra salary.

The players in this list range from those who appeared in only one big league game to those who had as many as 20 or more seasons. It also includes players who may have appeared in just a few games with the respective minor league club. This is by no means a complete list. There are probably dozens of former players who have been inadvertently overlooked. Happily, the list grows every day as current minor league players are promoted.

An asterisk denotes election to the Hall of Fame.

Aase, Don (Winston-Salem) 1974
Abbott, Kurt (Charlotte) 1995
Abernathy, Tal (Leaksville) 1947; (Burlington) 1948
Abernathy, Ted (Roanoke Rapids) 1952; (Charlotte) 1959
Abreu, Bob (Asheville) 1992
Adams, Ace (Winston-Salem) 1938
Adams, Glenn (Greensboro) 1968
Aderholt, Morris (Charlotte) 1939, 1942; (Roanoke Rapids) 1951
Adlesh, Dave (Durham) 1963
Afenir, Troy (Asheville) 1984
Agee, Tommie (Burlington) 1962
Agosto, Juan (Winston-Salem) 1977–78
Akers, Bill (Durham) 1926–27
Alberro, Jose (Gastonia) 1992
Albosta, Ed (Durham) 1941
Aldred, Scott (Fayetteville) 1987
Alexander, Dale (Charlotte) 1925–26

Allard, Brian (Asheville) 1977
Allen, Bernie (Charlotte) 1961
Allen, Bob (Burlington) 1958
Allen, Johnny (Asheville) 1929
Alley, Gene (Asheville) 1961–62
Allison, Bob (Charlotte) 1956
Allred, Beau (Kinston) 1988
Alomar, Sandy, Jr. (Charlotte) 1993
Alusik, George (Durham) 1953
Alvarez, Wilson (Gastonia) 1987–88
Amaral, Rich (Winston-Salem) 1985
Ancker, Walter (Asheville) 1916
Anderson, Alf (New Bern) 1938–39
Anderson, Ferrell (Durham) 1942
Anderson, Hal (Asheville) 1925, 1937–39
Andrew, Kim (Asheville) 1974
Andrews, Mike (Winston-Salem) 1963
Andrews, Nate (Durham) 1932; (Greensboro) 1934; (Asheville) 1935; (Wilmington) 1946–47

Andrews, Rob (Asheville) 1973
Anthony, Eric (Asheville) 1988
Aponte, Luis (Winston-Salem) 1974–75
Aquino, Luis (Kinston) 1984
Aragon, Angel (Winston-Salem) 1926
Aragon, Jack (Asheville) 1950
Arias, Alex (Charlotte) 1990–91
Armas, Tony (Monroe) 1971
Arnold, Chris (Lexington) 1966
Arnsberg, Brad (Greensboro) 1984
Arntzen, Orie (Asheville) 1937–38
Arrigo, Gerry (Charlotte) 1961, 1963
Arroyo, Luis (Greenville) 1948; (Greensboro)
    1948–49
Ash, Ken (Rocky Mount) 1924
Aspromonte, Ken (Kinston) 1950
Assenmacher, Paul (Durham) 1984–85
Atz, Jake (Raleigh) 1901
Aude, Rich (Carolina) 1993
Ault, Doug (Gastonia) 1973
Avery, Steve (Durham) 1989
Ayala, Bobby (Greensboro) 1989
Babcock, Bob (Asheville) 1975
Bacsik, Mike (Gastonia) 1974
Bagby, Jim (Charlotte) 1935; (Rocky Mount)
    1936
Bagwell, Bill (Asheville) 1929
Bailey, Bob (Asheville) 1961
Bailey, Mark (Asheville) 1983
Bailor, Bob (Asheville) 1973
Baker, Frank (Kinston) 1968
Baney, Dick (Winston-Salem) 1967
Banks, George (Greensboro) 1959–60
Bankston, Bill (Charlotte) 1922–23; (Raleigh)
    1928
Barbare, Walter (Asheville) 1913
Barbee, Dave (Greensboro) 1925–26; (Bur-
    lington) 1942
Barber, Turner (Winston-Salem) 1915
Barfield, Jesse (Kinston) 1979
Barker, Len (Gastonia) 1974
Barmes, Bruce (Charlotte) 1951
Barnes, Junie (Wilmington) 1933–34
Barnes, Frank (Winston-Salem) 1927; (Greens-
    boro) 1928
Barnes, Red (Charlotte) 1933–35; (Rocky
    Mount) 1936
Barney, Rex (Durham) 1943
Barrett, Bob (Raleigh) 1923
Barrett, Tim (Gastonia) 1984
Barry, Rich (Greensboro) 1960, 1965
Barton, Vince (Kannapolis) 1937; (Hickory)
    1938
Bartosch, Dave (Asheville) 1938
Bass, Dick (Asheville) 1932
Bates, Buddy (Burlington) 1947–48
Bates, Frank (Asheville) 1897
Batista, Miguel (Charlotte) 1995

Batista, Rafael (Kinston) 1967
Bautista, Dan (Fayetteville) 1991–92
Bearse, Kevin (Kinston) 1988
Beers, Clarence (Asheville) 1940
Behney, Mel (Asheville) 1969
Belcher, Kevin (Gastonia) 1988–89
Belinsky, Bo (Asheville) 1970
Bell, Bill (Asheville) 1959
Bell, David (Burlington) 1990; (Kinston) 1992;
    (Charlotte) 1994
Bell, Jerry (Raleigh-Durham) 1971
Belle, Albert (Kinston) 1987–88
Belliard, Rafael (Shelby) 1980
Beniquez, Juan (Winston-Salem) 1969–70
Bennett, Dennis (Asheville) 1960
Bennett, Red (Kannapolis) 1939
Benzinger, Todd (Winston-Salem) 1984
Berenyi, Bruce (Shelby) 1977
Bernazard, Tony (Kinston) 1974
Berry, Neil (Winston-Salem) 1942
Berryhill, Damon (Winston-Salem) 1985
Bethea, Bill (Charlotte) 1964
Bevacqua, Kurt (Asheville) 1969
Bibby, Jim (Raleigh-Durham) 1968
Bielecki, Mike (Shelby) 1980
Biggio, Craig (Asheville) 1987
Bilko, Steve (Winston-Salem) 1947
Billingham, Jack (Salisbury) 1963
Billings, Dick (Burlington) 1966
Bischoff, John (Winston-Salem) 1920
Bishop, Charlie (Winston-Salem) 1946
Blackburn, Ron (Asheville) 1964
Blasingame, Don (Winston-Salem) 1953
Blass, Steve (Asheville) 1962; (Kinston) 1962
Blateric, Steve (Asheville) 1969
Blauser, Jeff (Durham) 1986
Blefary, Curt (Greensboro) 1962–63
Blethen, Clarence (Leaksville-Spray-Draper)
    1937
Blomberg, Ron (Kinston) 1968
Bloodworth, Jimmy (Charlotte) 1938
Bocek, Milt (Asheville) 1939–40; (Gastonia)
    1940
Boerner, Larry (Charlotte) 1929
Boggs, Wade (Winston-Salem) 1977
Bolton, Cliff (High Point) 1927–28; (Valdese)
    1938; (Charlotte) 1942; (Reidsville) 1947;
    (High Point–Thomasville) 1948–51; (Ruther-
    ford County) 1952; (Lexington) 1952
Bond, Walt (Burlington) 1958
Bonds, Bobby (Lexington) 1965
Booe, Everett (Greensboro) 1930
Boone, Bob (Raleigh-Durham) 1969
Boone, Danny (High Point) 1926–31
Borbon, Pedro, Jr. (Durham) 1990–91
Borders, Pat (Kinston) 1985–86
Borgman, Glenn (Charlotte) 1971
Bork, Frank (Kinston) 1962; (Asheville) 1962

Bosch, Don (Kinston) 1963; (Asheville) 1964–65

Boskie, Shawn (Winston-Salem) 1988; (Charlotte) 1989

Bosman, Dick (Lexington) 1964

Bostock, Lyman (Charlotte) 1972

Boswell, Dave (Charlotte) 1964

Bouton, Jim (Greensboro) 1960

Bowen, Ryan (Asheville) 1987; (Charlotte) 1995

Bowers, Stew (Rocky Mount) 1937

Bowles, Charlie (Durham) 1939; (Hickory) 1949; (Granite Falls) 1951

Bowman, Bob (Mt. Airy) 1947; (Morganton) 1948

Bradshaw, Dallas (Asheville) 1915

Bradshaw, George (Landis) 1946–47; (Statesville) 1949–50; (Morganton) 1951–52; (Charlotte) 1953

Brand, Ron (Kinston) 1962

Brandon, Darrell (Durham) 1963

Braxton, Garland (Greensboro) 1920; (Winston-Salem) 1939,40

Breeden, Hal (Kinston) 1967

Brett, Ken (Winston-Salem) 1967

Brewer, Tom (High Point–Thomasville) 1951

Brewster, Charlie (Durham) 1942

Bridwell, Al (Rocky Mount) 1920

Brillheart, Jim (Asheville) 1930–31

Brinkman, Ed (Raleigh) 1962

Brittain, Gus (Wilmington) 1933–34; (Rocky Mount) 1941

Brodie, Steve (Wilmington) 1909

Brondell, Ken (Salisbury) 1941

Bronstad, Jim (Winston-Salem) 1956

Brown, Alton (Roanoke Rapids) 1948–50

Brown, Bobby (Asheville) 1975

Brown, Earl (Asheville) 1932

Brown, Gates (Durham) 1961

Brown, Hal (Durham) 1946

Brown, Jimmy (Greensboro) 1933

Brown, Mace (Greensboro) 1930–31

Brown, Mike (Winston-Salem) 1981

Brown, Norm (Rocky Mount) 1939; (Greensboro) 1941

Brown, Oscar (Kinston) 1967

Brunet, George (Shelby) 1953

Brusstar, Warren (Rocky Mount) 1975

Bryant, Clay (Asheville) 1948

Brye, Steve (Charlotte) 1970

Bucher, Jim (Greensboro) 1933

Buddin, Don (Greensboro) 1953

Bumbry, Al (Asheville) 1972

Burbach, Bill (Greensboro) 1966

Burgess, Smoky (Fayetteville) 1947

Burgmeier, Tom (Durham) 1963

Burk, Mack (Asheville) 1959

Burke, John (Asheville) 1994

Burkhart, Ken (Asheville) 1940

Burleson, Rick (Winston-Salem) 1971

Burrows, Terry (Gastonia) 1991

Busby, Paul (Mayodan) 1939

Butcher, John (Asheville) 1977–78

Butcher, Max (Raleigh) 1946

Butler, Brett (Durham) 1980

Butters, Tom (Wilson) 1959; (Asheville) 1962

Buzhardt, John (Hickory) 1954

Caligiuri, Fred (Greenville) 1937–40

Camp, Howie (Charlotte) 1927

Campbell, Bill (Charlotte) (SL) 1972

Campbell, Paul (Rocky Mount) 1937

Campbell, Soup (Tarboro) 1937–38

Campos, Francisco (Charlotte) 1951

Canseco, Ozzie (Greensboro) 1983–84

Caraballo, Ramon (Durham) 1991

Carbo, Bernie (Asheville) 1968–69

Carew, Rod* (Wilson) 1966

Carlyle, Cleo (Charlotte) 1924

Carlyle, Roy (Charlotte) 1923, 1934

Carmona, Rafael (Wilmington) 1995

Carrasco, Hector (Asheville) 1992

Carreon, Mark (Shelby) 1982

Carter, Blackie (Winston-Salem) 1923; (Charlotte) 1932; (Wilmington) 1933–34; (Asheville) 1934; (Leaksville) 1934–35; (Salisbury) 1937–38; (Cooleemee) 1939; (Landis) 1940

Casanova, Paul (Burlington) 1963

Casey, Hugh (Charlotte) 1933

Cash, Dave (Gastonia) 1967

Cash, Ron (Rocky Mount) 1972

Cedeno, Andujar (Asheville) 1989

Cerutti, John (Kinston) 1982

Chambers, Johnnie (Greensboro) 1933–34

Chance, Bob (Burlington) 1962

Chaney, Darrel (Asheville) 1968

Chapman, Ben (Asheville) 1928

Chapman, Fred (Landis) 1949–50; (Elkin) 1951; (Mooresville) 1952; (Statesville) 1953

Chavez, Raul (Asheville) 1992

Chipple, Walt (Durham) 1943

Chism, Tom (Charlotte) 1977

Chrisley, Neil (Kinston) 1950

Christenson, John (Shelby) 1982

Christmas, Steve (Shelby) 1978

Churn, Chuck (Asheville) 1967

Cimino, Pete (Wilson) 1961–62; (Charlotte) 1963

Cisar, George (Leaksville-Spray-Draper) 1936

Citarella, Ralph (Gastonia) 1980

Clabaugh, Moose (High Point) 1927

Clark, Cap (Asheville) 1935

Clark, Phil (Fayetteville) 1987

Clark, Ron (Charlotte) 1963, 1964–65; (Wilson) 1963

Clark, Terry (Gastonia) 1980–81

Clendenon, Donn (Wilson) 1959

Clifton, Flea (Raleigh) 1930–31

Clines, Gene (Raleigh) 1966

Clinton, Lou (Greensboro) 1955–56

Clontz, Brad (Durham) 1993

Clough, Ed (Greensboro) 1930

Coble, Dave (Asheville) 1934; (Rocky Mount) 1940

Coffman, Kevin (Winston-Salem) 1989; (Charlotte) 1990

Coggins, Frank (Rocky Mount) 1964; (Burlington) 1965

Cohen, Alta (Rocky Mount) 1929; (Durham) 1929

Coker, Jimmie (Wilson) 1956

Cole, Victor (Carolina) 1991

Coleman, Joe (Burlington) 1965

Coletta, Chris (Winston-Salem) 1964

Collins, Rip (Durham) 1933

Colpaert, Dick (Asheville) 1963–66

Combs, Merrill (Greensboro) 1941

Comer, Wayne (Raleigh) 1962

Concepcion, Dave (Asheville) 1969

Conde, Ramon (Asheville) 1970

Conigliaro, Billy (Winston-Salem) 1966

Conley, Gene (Burlington) 1963–64

Cooke, Dusty (Asheville) 1928

Coombs, Danny (Asheville) 1967

Cooper, Cecil (Winston-Salem) 1971

Cooper, Gary (Gastonia) 1974

Cooper, Pat (Burlington) 1949–50

Cooper, Mort (Asheville) 1936

Cooper, Scott (Greensboro) 1987

Cooper, Walker (Asheville) 1939

Corey, Mark (Charlotte) 1977

Corkins, Mike (Lexington) 1965

Correll, Vic (Asheville) 1971

Corsi, Jim (Greensboro) 1983, 1985

Cosman, Jim (Raleigh) 1964

Covington, Chet (Goldsboro/Tarboro) 1939; (Greensboro) 1952

Cowley, Joe (Durham) 1980

Cox, Casey (Rocky Mount) 1962, 1964; (Burlington) 1963

Cox, Ted (Winston-Salem) 1975

Crawford, Pat (Charlotte) 1924

Crawford, Steve (Winston-Salem) 1978–79

Crespi, Frank (Shelby) 1937

Cress, Walker (Greensboro) 1941

Crocker, Claude (Asheville) 1946–48

Crockett, Davey (Wilmington) 1901

Cross, Lave (Charlotte) 1909–1911

Crouch, Bill (Winston-Salem) 1926

Crowder, General (Winston-Salem) 1923

Crowson, Woody (Thomasville) 1939–42; (Greensboro) 1947

Cruz, Jose, Jr (Port City) 1996

Cruz, Todd (Rocky Mount) 1974

Cubbage, Mike (Burlington) 1972

Cuellar, Charlie (Reidsville) 1939, 1940; (Leaksville-Spray-Draper) 1940–42

Cueto, Bert (Asheville) 1964

Cullen, Jack (Greensboro) 1960

Culler, Dick (Concord) 1936–37; (Reidsville) 1939

Cullop, Nick (Asheville) 1941

Culp, Ray (Asheville) 1960

Culver, George (Shelby) 1963; (Greensboro) 1963

Cunningham, Joe (Winston-Salem) 1951

Curry, Tony (High Point–Thomasville) 1958

Curtis, John (Winston-Salem) 1968

Cuyler, Milt (Fayetteville) 987

Dal Canton, Bruce (Asheville) 1966

Dalena, Pete (Greensboro) 1982

Daniel, Jake (Kannapolis) 1938; (Tarboro) 1948; (New Bern) 1949; (Burlington) 1949

Daniels, Fred (Mooresville) 1951, 1953

Darwin, Danny (Asheville) 1976

Dascenzo, Doug (Winston-Salem) 1986; Charlotte) 1995

Dasso, Frank (Rocky Mount) 1937

Dauer, Rich (Asheville) 1974–75

Daughters, Bob (Rocky Mount) 1937

Daviault, Ray (Asheville) 1956

Davis, Bud (Winston-Salem) 1917; (Raleigh) 1931; (Reidsville) 1937

Davis, Butch (Charlotte) 1988

Davis, Crash (Gastonia) 1937; (Durham) 1948; (Raleigh) 1949, 1951–52; (Reidsville) 1950

Davis, Jacke (High Point–Thomasville) 1958

Davis, Odie (Asheville) 1977

Davis, Ron (Durham) 1962

Davison, Scott (Wilmington) 1995

Dean, Chubby (Mt. Airy) 1946–47

DeCinces, Doug (Asheville) 1972

DeLeon, Jose (Shelby) 1980

Delker, Eddie (Asheville) 1937

DeMars, Billy (Asheville) 1947

Demeter, Steve (Durham) 1954

Dente, Sam (Greensboro) 1942

Derrick, Mike (Asheville) 1964; (Kinston) 1965

DeSilva, John (Fayetteville) 1989

Destrade, Orestes (Greensboro) 1982

Detweiler, Ducky (Red Springs) 1950; (Lexington) 1952

Deutsch, Mel (Greensboro) 1941

Diaz, Bo (Winston-Salem) 1975

Didier, Bob (Kinston) 1967

DiLauro, Jack (Rocky Mount) 1965

Dillman, Bill (Durham) 1966

DiPoto, Jerry (Kinston) 1990; (Charlotte) 1993–94

Dixon, Ken (Charlotte) 1984

Dixon, Sonny (Charlotte) 1941–42, 1946–47

Doak, Bill (Wilmington/Greensboro) 1910

Dobson, Pat (Durham) 1960, 1961

Dodd, Tom (Greensboro) 1981; (Charlotte) 1987

Doherty, John (Fayetteville) 1990

Doljack, Frank (Gastonia/High Point) 1938

Donaldson, John (Wilson) 1963

Doran, Bill (Salisbury-Spencer) 1927

Dotter, Gary (Wilson) 1961

Dougherty, Jim (Asheville) 1991
Doyle, Jeff (Gastonia) 1979
Drago, Dick (Rocky Mount) 1965–66
Dreisewerd, Clem (Asheville) 1938–39
Drew, Cameron (Asheville) 1986
Dubuc, Jean (Greensboro) 1928
Duff, Cecil (Rocky Mount) 1924
Duffalo, Jim (Kinston) 1956
Duffy, Frank (Asheville) 1968
Dunbar, Tom (Asheville) 1980–81
Duncan, Duke (Raleigh) 1916
Duncan, Taylor (Asheville) 1973–74
Dunn, Ron (Asheville) 1972
Duran, Dan (Gastonia) 1974
Durham, Leon (Gastonia) 1977
Dyer, Eddie (Salisbury-Spencer) 1928; (Greensboro) 1933
Dykstra, Lenny (Shelby) 1981–82
Early, Arnold (Greensboro) 1956
Early, Jake (Charlotte) 1937–38
Easley, Logan (Greensboro) 1983
Eaton, Zeb (Cooleemee) 1939; (Gastonia) 1952
Edwards, Bruce (Durham) 1942
Edwards, Doc (Burlington) 1960
Edwards, Jim (Salisbury-Spencer) 1929
Eichorn, Mark (Kinston) 1980
Eischen, Joey (Gastonia) 1990
Ellis, Dock (Kinston) 1965; (Asheville) 1966
Ellis, John (Kinston) 1969
Ellsworth, Steve (Winston-Salem) 1984
Embree, Alan (Burlington) 1990; (Kinston) 1992
Emery, Cal (Asheville) 1960
Ericks, John (Carolina) 1994
Etheridge, Bobby (Lexington) 1964
Ettles, Mark (Fayetteville) 1989
Estalella, Bobby (Charlotte) 1937–38, 1951
Evans, Al (New Bern) 1937
Evans, Dwight (Winston-Salem) 1971
Evans, Joe (Raleigh) 1926; (Winston-Salem) 1927
Evers, Hoot (Winston-Salem) 1941
Fahey, Bill (Burlington) 1970
Fanzone, Carmen (Winston-Salem) 1964–65
Farr, Jim (Asheville) 1979
Felderman, Marv (Lenoir) 1939
Fernandez, Frank (Greensboro) 1962, 1964
Fernandez, Tony (Kinston) 1980
Ferraro, Mike (Shelby) 1961
*Ferrell, Rick (Winston-Salem) 1925; (Kinston) 1926
Ferrell, Wes (Winston-Salem) 1925; (Leaksville-Spray-Draper) 1941; (Greensboro) 1946; (Marion) 1948
Ferriss, Dave (Greensboro) 1942
Fielder, Cecil (Kinston) 1984
Filson, Pete (Greensboro) 1980
Fine, Tommy (Rocky Mount) 1939
Finley, Bob (Rocky Mount) 1939
Firova, Dan (Winston-Salem) 1989

Fisher, Brian (Durham) 1982
Fisher, Harry (Asheville) 1952
Fisher, Jack (Wilson) 1958
Fittery, Paul (Asheville) 1925
Flair, Al (Rocky Mount) 1939
Flanagan, Mike (Asheville) 1975
Fletcher, Van (Elkin) 1949–50
Flinn, John (Asheville) 1974–75
Flood, Curt (High Point–Thomasville) 1956
Flowers, Bennett (Wilson) 1946
Flythe, Stuart (New Bern) 1937
Foley, Tom (Shelby) 1978
Folkers, Rich (Durham) 1967
Fontenot, Ray (Greensboro) 1980–81
Ford, Dave (Charlotte) 1976
Forsch, Ken (Greensboro) 1968
Fortune, Gary (Asheville) 1914–15, 1926
Foss, Larry (Asheville) 1961
Fossas, Tony (Asheville) 1980
Foster, Roy (Gastonia) 1964–65; (Raleigh) 1966
Foucalt, Steve (Burlington) 1971–72
Foy, Joe (Winston-Salem) 1963
Frazier, Joe (Leaksville-Spray-Draper) 1941
Frazier, Lou (Asheville) 1987
Freese, Gene (Burlington) 1953
French, Jim (Rocky Mount) 1964
Friday, Skipper (Raleigh) 1921–23
Friend, Owen (Raleigh) 1945
Frisella, Danny (Durham) 1967
Frye, Jeff (Gastonia) 1989
Fryman, Travis (Fayetteville) 1988
Fuller, Jim (Asheville) 1972
Fulton, Bill (Greensboro) 1984
Funk, Tom (Asheville) 1984–85
Gagne, Greg (Greensboro) 1980–81
Gakeler, Dan (Greensboro) 1985–86
Galasso, Bob (Asheville) 1973–74
Gamble, Lee (Wilmington) 1935
Gant, Ron (Durham) 1986
Garber, Gene (Raleigh) 1966–67
Garcia, Kiko (Asheville) 1974
Gardella, Danny (Shelby) 1940; (Williamston) 1940
Gardner, Chris (Asheville) 1989–90
Gardner, Glenn (Shelby) 1937; (Gastonia) 1938–39
Gardner, Larry (Asheville) 1925–27
Gardner, Rob (Wilson) 1963
Garman, Mike (Winston-Salem) 1967, 1969
Garrido, Gil (Burlington) 1962
Geary, Bob (Charlotte) 1915–16
Gebhard, Bob (Charlotte) 1969
Geddes, Jim (Asheville) 1971
Gehrman, Paul (Durham) 1937
Gelnar, John (Asheville) 1963–64
Genovese, George (Asheville) 1943
Gentile, Sam (Rocky Mount) 1940; (Greensboro) 1941
Gentry, Rufe (Landis) 1939; (Winston-Salem) 1941

Gettel, Allen (Snow Hill) 938; (Asheville) 1959

Gibbon, Joe (Kinston) 1962

Gibson, Paul (Shelby) 1978

Gibson, Russ (Raleigh) 1959–60; (Winston-Salem) 1961

Gibson, Sam (Asheville) 1924; (Reidsville) 1947; (Warsaw) 1948

Gil, Benji (Gastonia) 1992

Gilbert, Andy (Rocky Mount) 1940

Gill, Johnny (Salisbury) 1926

Gillenwater, Carden (Kinston) 1937

Girardi, Joe (Winston-Salem) 1987

Glazner, Whitey (Winston-Salem) 1915–16

Godby, Danny (Asheville) 1970

Goggin, Chuck (Salisbury) 1964

Gogolewski, Bill (Burlington) 1966

Gohr, Greg (Fayetteville) 1989

Golden, Jim (Kinston) 1971

Goldy, Purn (Durham) 1959

Goltz, Dave (Charlotte) 1970

Gomez, Leo (Charlotte) 1988

Gonzalez, Juan (Gastonia) 1987

Gonzalez, Luis (Asheville) 1988

Gooch, Lee (Durham) 1922; (Rocky Mount) 1927; (Fayetteville) 1928

Goodman, Billy (Durham) 1963

Gornicki, Hank (Asheville) 1937–39

Gosger, Jim (Winston-Salem) 1962

Gott, Jim (Gastonia) 1978–79

Graff, Milt (Asheville) 1963

Graham, Moonlight (Charlotte) 1902

Granger, Wayne (Raleigh) 1965

Gray, Ted (Winston-Salem) 1942

Grba, Eli (Salisbury) 1953

Green, Dallas (Reidsville) 1955; (High Point–Thomasville) 1957

*Greenberg, Hank (Raleigh) 1930

Greenwell, Mike (Winston-Salem) 1983–84

Greenwood, Bob (Asheville) 1959

Gregg, Tommy (Charlotte) 1995

Grieve, Tom (Salisbury)1966; (Burlington) 1967–68

Griffin, Ivy (Asheville) 1934

Griffin, Mike (Asheville) 1976–77

Griffin, Tom (Asheville) 1967

Grimes, Ray (Durham) 1917

Grimes, Roy (Durham) 1916–17

Grimm, Charlie (Durham) 1917

Groh, Heinie (Charlotte) 1928

Grossman, Harley (Charlotte) 1951

Guante, Cecilio (Shelby) 1980

Guerrero, Mario (Kinston) 1969

Guidry, Ron (Kinston) 1973

Guise, Lefty (Concord) 1938; (Lenoir) 1939

Guttierez, Cesar (Lexington) 1963

Haas, Bert (High Point–Thomasville) 1956

Haas, Dave (Fayetteville) 1988

Habyan, John (Charlotte) 1984–85

Haddix, Harvey (Winston-Salem) 1947

Hahn, Dick (Charlotte) 1940–41

Hajek, Dave (Asheville) 1990

Hall, Albert (Durham) 1980

Hall, Bob (Winston-Salem) 1942

Hall, Dick (Burlington) 1952–53

Hall, Drew (Winston-Salem) 1985

Hall, Jimmie (Kinston/Wilson) 1957; (Charlotte) 1958

Hall, Tom (Charlotte) 1968

Hamby, Jim (Rocky Mount) 1925

Hamilton, Jack (Winston-Salem) 1960

Hamilton, Steve (Burlington) 1958

Hammond, Chris (Charlotte) 1995

Handley, Gene (Mt. Airy) 1935–36; (Durham) 1936–37

Hargan, Steve (Burlington) 1962

Hargrove, Mike (Gastonia) 1973

Harkey, Mike (Charlotte) 1992

Harlow, Larry (Asheville) 1974

Harnisch, Pete (Charlotte) 1988

Harrah, Toby (Burlington) 1968–69

Harrington, Bill (Fayetteville) 1951

Harris, Bill (Charlotte) 1921; (Winston-Salem) 1922; (Asheville) 1926, 1927–28

Harris, David (Greensboro) 1923–24; (Wilson) 1926

Harris, Donald (Gastonia) 1990

Harris, Lum (Charlotte) 1937

Harrison, Roric (Salisbury) 1965; (Asheville) 1967

Hart, Bill (Asheville) 1939–40, 1952

Hartgraves, Dean (Asheville) 1988–89

Haselman, Bill (Gastonia) 1987

Hash, Herb (Rocky Mount) 1937–38

Hauger, Art (Winston-Salem) 1928; (Kinston) 1925–27

Haughey, Chris (Asheville) 1947

Hawkins, Wynn (Fayetteville) 1956

Hayes, Ben (Greensboro) 1979

Haynes, Joe (Charlotte) 1938

Hayward, Bill (Burlington) 1966

Hayworth, Red (Winston-Salem) 1940

Hazewood, Drungo (Charlotte) 1980

Hearn, Bunn (Wilson) 1910, 1921–27; (Winston-Salem) 1928, 1931; (Henderson) 1929

Hebner, Richie (Raleigh) 1967

Hedlund, Mike (Burlington) 1964

Heffner, Don (Salisbury-Spencer) 1929

Heflin, Randy (Rocky Mount) 1940; (Greenville) 1950

Hehl, Jake (Rocky Mount) 1923–25

Heine, Bud (Durham) 1923

Heise, Bob (Durham) 1967

Henke, Tom (Asheville) 1980–81

Henry, Bill (Asheville) 1968

Henry, Dwayne (Asheville) 1981

Henry, Ron (Charlotte) 1964

Henry, Snake (Greensboro) 1914; (Tarboro) 1937–38; (Kinston) 1939

Hermanski, Gene (Kinston) 1939–40; (Durham) 1943

Hernandez, Enzo (Greensboro) 1968

Hernandez, Jackie (Burlington) 1962

Hernandez, Jose (Gastonia) 1989

Herrera, Jose (Statesville) 1964

Hetzel, Eric (Greensboro) 1985

Heving, Joe (Asheville) 1927–28

Hiatt, Jack (Statesville) 1961

Hibbs, Jim (Asheville) 1969

Hickman, Jim (Winston-Salem) 1914; (Asheville) 1915–16

Hickman, Jim (Winston-Salem) 1958

Hidalgo, Richard (Asheville) 1993

Higbe, Kirby (Rutherford County) 1953

Hill, Glenallen (Kinston) 1985

Hill, Ken (Gastonia) 1985–86

Hiller, Hob (Winston-Salem) 1916

Hitchcock, Sterling (Greensboro) 1990

Hobson, Butch (Winston-Salem) 1973–74

Hodgin, Ralph (Reidsville) 1935, 1952–54; (Charlotte) 1937; (Winston-Salem) 1954; (High Point–Thomasville) 1955

Hodkey, Al (Greensboro) 1941

Hoerst, Frank (Mayodan) 1939

Hoffman, John (Durham) 1964

Hoffman, Ray (Charlotte) 1940–41

Hogue, Bobby (Winston-Salem) 1942

Holcombe, Ken (Asheville) 1940

Holland, Bill (Charlotte) 1939

Holman, Brian (Gastonia) 1984

Holman, Gary (Salisbury)1964

Holmes, Darren (Asheville) 1994

Holshauser, Herm (Salisbury-Spencer) 1926

Holt, Jim (High Point) 1921

Hood, Albie (Carlotte) 1929

Hooper, Bob (Tarboro) 1941; (Salisbury/Lexington) 1942

Hopper, Jim (Mooresville) 1948; (Landis) 1942, 1949

Horn, Sam (Winston-Salem) 1983–84; (Charlotte) 1993

Horton, Ricky (Gastonia) 1980

Hosley, Tim (Rocky Mount) 1969

Host, Gene (Kinston) 1952

Hottman, Ken (Asheville) 1971

House, Tom (Kinston) 1967

Howard, Larry (Statesville) 1964

Hubbard, Trenidad (Asheville) 1987

Hudgens, Jimmy (Charlotte) 1931

Hudler, Rex (Greensboro) 1980

Hudson, Charlie (Raleigh-Durham) 1968

Hughes, Bill (Raleigh) 1920–21; (Durham) 1936, 1938

Hughes, Dick (Winston-Salem) 1959

Humphreys, Bob (Durham) 1959

Hunter, Brian L. (Asheville) 1990

Hunter, Brian R. (Durham) 1988

Husta, Carl (Winston-Salem) 1930

Hutson, George (Asheville) 1972–73

Hyde, Dick (Charlotte) 1953

Illsley, Blaise (Asheville) 1986

Iorg, Dane (Burlington) 1972

Irvine, Daryl (Greensboro) 1985

Jablonski, Ray (Winston-Salem) 1951

Jackson, Chuck (Asheville) 1984

Jacobs, Jake (Charlotte) 1960

Jacobs, Spook (Thomasville) 1946; (Asheville) 1948

Javier, Stan (Greensboro) 1983

Jeffcoat, Hal (Shelby) 1946

Jefferson, Jesse (Asheville) 1972

Jeter, Derek (Greensboro) 1992–93

Jeter, John (Gastonia) 1966–67

Johnson, Bobby (Asheville) 1978

Johnson, Cliff (Raleigh-Durham) 1970

Johnson, Dave (Asheville) 1972

Johnson, Earl (Rocky Mount) 1940

Johnson, Ernie (Salisbury-Spencer) 1927–1928

Johnson, Ken (Asheville) 1941–42

Johnston, Rex (Asheville) 1961

Jolly, David (Mooresville) 1946–47

Jones, Andruw (Durham) 1996

Jones, Art (Salisbury-Spencer) 1929

Jones, Chipper (Durham) 1992

Jones, Cleon (Raleigh) 1963

Jones, Gary (Greensboro) 1967

Jones, John (Charlotte) 1927, 1928, 1929; (Asheville) 1927; (High Point) 1929, 1931; (Henderson) 1929, 1930; (Greensboro) 1931; (Durham) 1933

Jones, Sherman (Raleigh) 1963

Jones, Steve (Wilson) 1963

Jordan, Buck (Salisbury-Spencer) 1925–26; (Lexington) 1942

Jorgenson, Carl (Durham) 1938

Jorgenson, Mike (Raleigh-Durham) 1968

Jurak, Ed (Winston-Salem) 1976

Justice, Dave (Durham) 1986

Kahdot, Ike (Salisbury-Spencer) 1928–29

Karl, Andy (Rocky Mount) 1937

Kane, John (High Point)1923

Katz, Bob (Rocky Mount) 1938–39

Kearns, Ted (Charlotte) 1927

Kelly, Roberto (Greensboro) 1983–84

Kelly, Jim (Durham) 1913

Kelly, Pat (Wilson) 1964, 1965; (Charlotte) 1966

Kelly, Pat (Kinston) 1979

Kelly, Van (Kinston)1967

Kendall, Fred (Asheville) 1968

Kendall, Jason (Carolina) 1994–95

Kenders, Al (Asheville) 1960

Kennedy, Bill A. (Rocky Mount) 1941–42, 1946

Kennedy, Bill G. (Charlotte) 1941

Kennedy, John (Raleigh) 1962

Kennedy, Ray (Asheville) 1928, 1931

Kerfeld, Charlie (Asheville) 1983

Kerrigan, Joe (Kinston) 1974
Kiecker, Dana (Winston-Salem) 1984
Kiefer, Joe (Raleigh) 1923
*Killebrew, Harmon (Charlotte) 1956
King, Chick (Durham) 1952
King, Hal (Asheville) 1967
King, Jim (Winston-Salem) 1951
Kipp, Fred (Asheville) 1953
Kitsos, Chris (Asheville) 1951
Kleinhans, Ted (Greensboro) 1931–32
Klesko, Ryan (Durham) 1990
Klimkowski, Ron (Winston-Salem) 1965–66
Kline, Ron (Burlington) 1952
Kline, Steve (Greensboro) 1967
Kling, Rudy (Asheville) 1912
Klippstein, John (Winston-Salem) 1945
Kluttz, Clyde (Asheville) 1938
Knowles, Darold (Charlotte) 1962
Knudsen, Kurt (Fayetteville) 1988
Kolb, Gary (Winston-Salem) 1960
Komminsk, Brad (Durham) 1981
Kopshaw, George (Wilson) 1927
Kosco, Andy (Durham) 1960
Koshorek, Clem (Asheville) 1959
Kostro, Frank (Durham) 1957
Koy, Ernie (Durham) 1933
Kramer, Tom (Burlington) 1987; (Kinston) 1989–1990
Kraus, Jack (Durham) 1941
Kull, John (Fayetteville) 1909
Kvasnak, Al (Charlotte) 1942
Labine, Clem (Asheville) 1947
Laboy, Coco (Raleigh) 1964
Lacy, Guy (Charlotte) 1931–1933; (Mt. Airy) 1939
LaFrancois, Roger (Winston-Salem) 1978
Lahoud, Joe (Winston-Salem) 1966–1967
Lahti, Jeff (Greensboro) 1979
Lamabe, Jack (Wilson) 1956; (Gastonia) 1959
Lambert, Gene (Mayodan) 1939
Lamont, Gene (Statesville/Rocky Mount) 1966; (Rocky Mount) 1967–1968
Lancaster, Les (Winston-Salem) 1986
Landrum, Cedric (Winston-Salem) 1987
Landrum, Don (Reidsville) 1955
Landrum, Joe (Asheville) 1948
Lane, Jerry (Charlotte) 1951
Lane, Marvin (Rocky Mount) 1971
Lanier, Max (Asheville) 1935
Lanning, John (Asheville/Charlotte) 1934
Lanning, Tom (Asheville) 1934
Larker, Norm (Asheville) 1951
Lasher, Fred (Charlotte) 1963, 1964
Lasorda, Tommy (Concord) 1945
Lau, Charley (Durham) 1955
Law, Vern (Kinston) 1963
Lawing, Garland (Durham) 1940
Lazorko, Jack (Asheville) 1979
Ledbetter, Razor (Charlotte) 1914–15

Lee, Bill (Greensboro) 1930
Lee, Bill (Winston-Salem) 1968
Lee, Bob (Asheville) 1961, 1963
Lee, Terry (Greensboro) 1988
Leiber, Hank (Winston-Salem/High Point) 1932
LeJohn, Don (Asheville) 1959
Lemke, Mark (Durham) 1987
Lemon, Jim (Charlotte) 1954
Leskanic, Curtis (Kinston) 1990–91
Lesley, Brad (Greensboro) 1979
Levan, Jesse (Charlotte) 1954, 1955
Levis, Jesse (Burlington/Kinston)1989; (Kinston) 1990; (Charlotte) 1993
Lewis, Bill (Greensboro) 1931–1932
Lewis, Mark (Kinston) 1989; (Charlotte) 1993–94
Lima, Jose (Fayetteville) 1991
Limmer, Lou (Lexington) 1946–47
Lind, Jack (Asheville) 1967
Lindsey, Bill (Greensboro) 1982
Lines, Dick (Asheville) 1962
Linhart, Carl (Durham) 1948
Linz, Phil (Greensboro) 1960
LiPetri, Angelo (Asheville) 1959
Liriano, Nelson (Kinston) 1984–85
Lisi, Rick (Asheville) 1977
Livengood, Wes (Greensboro) 1932; (Lexington/Thomasville) 1937; (Durham) 1939–40; (Raleigh) 1949; (Kinston)1951
Livingston, Mickey (Charlotte) 1937
Loane, Bob (Durham) 1938
Lock, Don (Greensboro) 1959
Locklear, Gene (Asheville) 1970
Lofton, Kenny (Asheville) 1989
Lohr, Howard (Asheville) 1912
Lolich, Mickey (Durham) 1959–61
Lombardi, Phil (Greensboro) 1983
Lonborg, Jim (Winston-Salem) 1964
Long, Bob (Charlotte) 1987
Lopez, Al (Burlington) 1991; (Kinston) 1992; (Charlotte) 1993–94
Lopez, Arturo (Greensboro) 1963
Lopez, Javy (Durham) 1991
Lopez, Ramon (Burlington) 1960
Lovitto, Joe (Shelby) 1969; (Burlington) 1970
Lovullo, Torey (Fayetteville) 1987
Lowe, George (Asheville) 1915–16
Luebbe, Roy (Asheville) 1927–28
Luebber, Steve (Charlotte) 1971
Luskey, Charlie (Asheville) 1897
Luttrell, Lyle (Charlotte) 1954
Luzinski, Greg (Raleigh-Durham) 1969
Lyle, Jim (Charlotte) 1931–35; (Mooresville) 1938
Lyle, Sparky (Winston-Salem) 1965
Lynch, Ed (Asheville) 1978
Lynn, Red (Asheville) 1935
LLyons, Barry (Shelby) 1982
Lyons, Ed (Charlotte) 1942
Lyons, Hersch (Asheville) 1938–39

Lyons, Steve (Winston-Salem) 1981
Lyttle, Jim (Greensboro) 1967
Maas, Duke (Dunn-Erwin) 1949; (Roanoke Rapids) 1949; (Durham) 1953
Mack, Earle (Raleigh) 1914; (Asheville) 1916
Mackanin, Pete (Burlington) 1970
MacLeod, Bill (Winston-Salem) 1961
Maddox, Elliott (Rocky Mount) 1968–69
Magallanes, Ever (Kinston) 1988
Maggert, Harl (Rocky Mount) 1936; (Asheville) 1937
Mahaffey, Art (High Point–Thomasville) 1958
Mahlberg, Greg (Rocky Mount) 1974
Mallicoat, Rob (Asheville) 1984
Mallonee, Jule (Durham) 1925–26
Malone, Eddie (Asheville) 1940–41
Mangual, Angel (Raleigh) 1967
Mann, Johnny (Asheville) 1925
Mann, Kelly (Winston-Salem) 1988
Manrique, Fred (Kinston) 1980
Mantei, Matt (Charlotte) 1995
Manuel, Chuck (Wilson) 1965–66; (Charlotte) 1968
*Manush, Heinie (Rocky Mount) 1940; (Greensboro) 1941–42
Manzanillo, Josias (Greensboro) 1985
Marion, Red (Durham) 1937
Markell, Duke (Hickory) 1945
Marone, Lou (Asheville) 1966
Marshall, Ed (Salisbury-Spencer) 1926
Martin, Joe (Winston-Salem/High Point) 1932
Martin, John (Gastonia) 1980–81
Martin, Morrie (Asheville) 1946–47
Martin, Stu (Asheville) 1935
Martinez, Dave (Winston-Salem) 1985
Martinez, Dennis (Asheville) 1975
Martinez, Jose (Asheville) 1962–63
Martinez, Orlando (Wilson) 1961
Martinez, Ted (Raleigh-Durham) 1968
Martinez, Tippy (Kinston) 1973
Marty, Joe (Asheville) 1928
Mason, Mike (Asheville) 1981
Masters, Walt (Durham) 1924–25
Masterson, Walt (Charlotte) 1939
Mata, Vic (Greensboro) 1980–1982
Matarazzo, Len (Lexington) 1950; (Fayetteville) 1951–52
*Mathews, Eddie (High Point–Thomasville) 1949
Mathews, Terry (Gastonia) 1987; (Charlotte) 1995
Matlack, Jon (Raleigh-Durham) 1968
Mattingly, Don (Greensboro) 1980
Mattingly, Earl (Raleigh) 1928; (Asheville) 1929–30
Mauriello, Ralph (Asheville) 1954
Maxcy, Brian (Fayetteville) 1993
May, Darrell (Durham) 1993–94
May, Derrick (Winston-Salem) 1988
May, Jerry (Asheville) 1963–64

May, Lee (Rocky Mount) 1963
May, Milt (Gastonia) 1969
May, Pinky (Durham) 1933
Mayberry, John (Greensboro) 1968
Mayer, Ed (Greensboro) 1954
Mayer, Erskine (Fayetteville) 1910
Mauch, Gene (Durham) 1943
Maynard, Buster (Tarboro) 1938; (Burlington) 1950
McAuliffe, Dick (Durham) 1959
McBean, Al (Wilson) 1959
McBride, Ken (Greensboro) 1955–56
McCabe, Joe (Charlotte) 1964
McCall, Larry (Asheville) 1974–75
McCarty, Lew (Durham) 1926–27
McColl, Red (Charlotte) 1937
McCormick, Frank (Durham) 1936
McCrabb, Les (Lexington) 1937
McCurry, Jeff (Carolina) 1993–94
McDaniel, Von (Winston-Salem) 1958
McDowell, Roger (Shelby) 1982
McFarlane, Jesus (Asheville) 1961, 1965
McGhee, Bill (Winston-Salem) 1937–39
McGinn, Dan (Asheville) 1968
McGlothen, Lynn (Winston-Salem) 1970
McGriff, Fred (Kinston) 1983
McLean, Eldon (Asheville) 1932
McManus, Jim (Durham) 1955–56
McMichael, Greg (Burlington/Kinston) 1988; (Durham) 1991
McMillan, Norm (Winston-Salem) 1927
McRea, Frank (Asheville) 1930
Meacham, Rusty (Fayetteville) 1988–89
Meadows, Henry Lee (Durham) 1913–1914
Meadows, Louie (Asheville) 1982
Meads, Dave (Asheville) 1986
Meaney, Pat (Fayetteville) 1909
Medich, George (Kinston) 1971
*Medwick, Ducky (Raleigh) 1951
Meehan, Bill (Wilson) 1920–22
Meeks, Sam (Charlotte) 1947
Meers, Russ (Roanoke) Rapids1949
Mele, Dutch (Durham) 1938–1939
Mellana, Joe (Wilson) 1926–27
Melton, Lefty (Asheville) 1931
Mendoza, Minnie (Charlotte) 1960–61, 1963–68, 1971–72
Mercer, Bobby (Greensboro) 1965
Mercer, Mark (Asheville) 1978
Mercker, Kent (Durham) 1987–1988
Merritt, Jim (Charlotte) 1963
Mesa, Jose (Kinston) 1984–85
Michael, Gene (Kinston) 1962–63
Michaels, John (Rocky Mount) 1939
Midkiff, Ezra (Winston-Salem) 1910
Milacki, Bob (Charlotte) 1987
Miller, Bill (Lexington) 1945–47; (Statesville) 1948
Miller, Bruce (Asheville) 1971

Miller, Dyar (Asheville) 1972
Miller, Eddie (Wilmington) 1935
Miller, Eddie (Asheville) 1976
Miller, Orlando (Asheville) 1990
Miller, Stu (Winston-Salem) 1951
Milligan, Randy (Shelby) 1981
Milner, Brian (Kinston) 1980
Milosevich, Mike (Lumberton) 1950
Mirabella, Paul (Asheville) 1976
Mitchell, Keith (Durham) 1990
Mitchell, Monroe (Salisbury-Spencer) 1928; (Asheville) 1931
Mitterwald, George (Charlotte) 1967
*Mize, Johnny (Greensboro) 1930–31, 1933
Mizell, Wilmer (Winston-Salem) 1950
Mliicki, Dave (Charlotte) 1994
Moates, Dave (Burlington) 1970
Moloney, Rich (Asheville) 1971
Monbouquette, Bill (Greensboro) 1957
Money, Don (Raleigh) 1967
Monteagudo, Aurelio (Asheville) 1968
Montgomery, Bob (Winston-Salem) 1965
Montgomery, Monty (High Point–Thomasville) 1968–69
Monzon, Dan (Wilson) 1968; (Red Springs) 1969; (Charlotte) 1970
Moock, Joe (Raleigh-Durham) 1968
Mooney, Jim (Charlotte) 1930; (Asheville) 1933, 1937, 1939
Moore, Archie (Asheville) 1968
Moore, Bill (Asheville) 1932
Moore, Jackie (Durham) 1959
Moore, Jimmy (Winston-Salem) 1921
Moose, Bob (Gastonia/Raleigh) 1966
Mooty, Jake (Wilmington) 1935
Morales, Jerry (Raleigh-Durham) 1968
Mordecai, Mike (Durham) 1990–91
Morejon, Dan (High Point–Thomasville) 1955
Morel, Ramon (Carolina) 1995
Morgan, Eddie (Mt. Airy) 1946
*Morgan, Joe (Durham) 1963
Morgan, Vern (Asheville) 1960
Morlan, John (Monroe) 1971
Morman, Alvin (Asheville) 1992
Morris, Doyt (Kinston) 1939
Morrison, Jim (Rocky Mount) 1975
Morrison, Johnny (Asheville) 1926
Morton, Bubba (Durham) 1957
Morton, Carl (Kinston) 1966–67
Morton, Guy (Kinston) 1950; (Greensboro) 1954
Moser, Arnie (Wilmington) 1935
Moses, Gerry (Winston-Salem) 1965
Moss, Howie (Gastonia) 1937; (Salisbury)1941; (Gastonia) 1952
Moss, Ray (Wilson) 1927
Moulder, Glenn (Durham) 1941
Moyer, Jamie (Winston-Salem) 1985
Mueller, Heine (Asheville) 1934

Mulleavy, Greg (Raleigh) 1928
Munger, Red (Asheville) 1938–39
Mungo, Van Lingle (Fayetteville) 1929 (Winston-Salem) 1930; (Clinton) 1946–47
Munoz, Bobby (Greensboro) 1990
Munoz, Oscar (Kinston) 1990–91
Munson, Joe (Raleigh) 1920
Murcer, Bobby (Greensboro) 1965
Murphy, Herb (High Point) 1921
Murphy, Leo (Winston-Salem) 1928
Murray, Eddie (Asheville) 1974–75; (Charlotte) 1976
Murray, Matt (Durham) 1991, 1994
Murray, Ray (Tarboro) 1941
Murrell, Ivan (Durham) 1964, 1966
Muser, Tony (Winston-Salem) 1968
Mutis, Jeff (Kinston) 1989
Myers, Elmer (Raleigh) 1915
Myers, Lynn (Asheville) 1935–38
Myers, Mike (Charlotte) 1995
Nabholz, Chris (Charlotte) 1994
Nagel, Bill (Leaksville/Raleigh) 1947; (Raleigh/Reidsville) 1948; (Reidsville) 1949–50; (Burlington) 1951
Nagy, Charles (Kinston) 1989
Nagy, Mike (Winston-Salem) 1968
Nahorodny, Bill (Rocky Mount) 1973
Narleski, Bill (Rocky Mount) 1922; (Raleigh) 1925
Narron, Sam (Asheville) 1937; (Selma-Smithfield) 1947–48
Natal, Rob (Charlotte) 1995
Necciai, Ron (Salisbury) 1951; (Burlington-Graham) 1952–53
Neel, Troy (Burlington) 1987
Nelson, Gene (Asheville) 1979
Nen, Rob (Gastonia) 1988–89
Nettles, Graig (Charlotte) 1967
Neumeier, Dan (Asheville) 1971
Newhauser, Don (Winston-Salem) 1969–71
Newsom, Bobo (Raleigh/Wilmington/Greenville) 1929
Newsome, Dick (Greensboro) 1931, 1933–34
Nichols, Reid (Winston-Salem) 1979
Nichols, Rod (Kinston) 1987
Nichols, Roy (Salisbury) 1941
Nicholson, Dave (Wilson) 1958
Nied, David (Durham) 1989, 1990, 1991
Nieman, Butch (Greensboro) 1941
Nieves, Melvin (Durham) 1991–92
Nixon, Otis (Greensboro) 1980
Nordbrook, Tim (Asheville) 1972
Nordhagen, Wayne (Kinston) 1970–71
Noriega, John (Asheville) 1968
Nosek, Randy (Fayetteville) 1987
Nossek, Joe (Charlotte) 1961–62
Nunnally, Jon (Kinston) 1994
Oana, Prince (Hickory) 1937
O'Brien, Buck (Rocky Mount) 1915
O'Brien, Pete (Ashevillle) 1980

O'Brien, Syd (Winston-Salem) 1964
O'Dea, Ken (Greensboro) 1931
Odom, Dave (Sanford) 1941, 1946; (Wilmington/Angier) 1946
Ogea, Chad (Kinston) 1992; (Charlotte) 1993–94
Ogrodowski, Bruce (Greensboro) 1933
Oldis, Bob (Charlotte) 1951
Olin, Steve (Kinston) 1988
Oliva, Jose (Gastonia) 1990
Oliva, Tony (Charlotte) 1962
Olivares, Ed (Winston-Salem) 1960
Oliver, Al (Gastonia) 1965; (Raleigh) 1966
Oliver, Bob (Gastonia) 1963; (Kinston) 1964; (Asheville) 1965, 1966
Oliver, Gene (Winston-Salem) 1957
Oliver, Darren (Gastonia) 1989–90
Oliver, Tom (Durham) 1939
Olmo, Luis (Wilson) 1939–40
Olson, Gregg (Charlotte) 1988
Olwine, Ed (Greensboro) 1981
O'Neill, Emmett (Rocky Mount) 1940
Ordenana, Tony (Concord) 1949
Ortiz, Roberto (Charlotte) 1941
Osborn, Danny (Asheville) 1970
Osinski, Dan (Fayetteville) 1956
Osteen, Champ (Charlotte) 1912; (Asheville/Durham) 1913
Ostermueller, Fritz (Greensboro) 1931–32
Ostrowski, Joe (Greensboro) 1942
Osuna, Al (Asheville) 1987–88
Otis, Harry (Goldsboro) 1909
O'Toole, Denny (Asheville) 1971
Outen, Chick (Asheville) 1929
Paciorek, John (Statesvile)1964; (Asheville) 1967
Padgett, Ernie (Winston-Salem) 1921; (Charlotte) 1922
Pagan, Dave (Kinston) 1972
Page, Mike (Winston-Salem) 1964
Page, Vance (Durham) 1929
Pagliarulo, Mike (Greensboro) 1982
Palica, Erv (Asheville) 1946
Palmer, Dean (Gastonia) 1987
Papa, John (Asheville) 1965
Parilla, Sam (Burlington) 1964; (Raleigh-Durham) 1969Parker, Ace (Durham) 1949–52
Parker, Dave (Monroe) 1971
Parnham, Rube (Raleigh) 1915–16; (Durham) 1916
Parris, Steve (Carolina) 1995
Parrott, Mike (Asheville) 1975
Paschal, Ben (Charlotte) 1916, 1920–23
Pascual, Carlos (Charlotte) 1958
Patek, Fred (Gastonia) 1966; (Asheville) 1966
Pavlas, Dave (Winston-Salem) 1986
Pavlik, Roger (Gastonia) 1987–88
Peacock, Johnny (Wilmington) 1933–34
Peden, Les (Fayetteville) 1948
Peel, Homer (Winston-Salem) 1924
Pellagrini, Eddie (Rocky Mount) 1939

Pena, Alejandro (Charlotte) 1995
Pena, Orlando (High Point–Thomasville) 1956
Pena, Roberto (Asheville) 1962–64
Pennyfeather, William (Carolina) 1992
Perez, George (Asheville) 1961
Perez, Tony (Rocky Mount) 1962
Perritt, Pol (Wilson) 1926
Perry, Gerald (Durham) 1980
Perry, Herbert (Kinston) 1992; (Charlotte) 1994
Person, Robert (Burlington) 1989; (Kinston) 1990
Perzanowski, Stan (Asheville) 1971
Pesky, Johnny (Rocky Mount) 1940; (Durham) 1956
Peterson, Fritz (Shelby) 1964; (Greensboro) 1965
Petrocelli, Rico (Winston-Salem) 1962
Pettibone, Jay (Asheville) 1980
Pettit, Leon (Asheville) 1934
Pettitte, Andy (Greensboro) 1992
Petty, Jesse (Henderson) 1931
Phelps, Ray (High Point) 1926–27
Phillips, Buz (Valdese) 1936
Pico, Jeff (Winston-Salem) 1986
Pierce, Jack (Kinston) 1971
Pignatano, Joe (Asheville) 1953
Plaskett, Elmo (Asheville) 1962, 1964, 1966
Poff, John (Rocky Mount) 1975
Poholsky, Tom (Durham) 1945–46
Pointer, Aaron (Salisbury) 1961; (Durham) 1962
Poole, Jim (Winston-Salem) 1933; (Mooresville) 1936–37; (Reidsville) 1938; (Landis) 1939; (Thomasville) 1940; (Statesville) 1942, 1945
Portocarrero, Arnie (Fayetteville) 1950
Potter, Dykes (Greensboro) 1933; (Asheville) 1935–36; (Durham) 1941
Powell, Grover (Asheville) 1968
Pratt,Todd (Greensboro) 1986
Price, Jackie (Asheville) 1936
Price, Jim (Kinston) 1963
Prichard, Bob (Charlotte) 1939, 1941
Priddy, Bob (Asheville) 1961
Prim, Ray (Greensboro) 1930–31; (Durham) 1931
Pritchard, Harold (Asheville) 1964
Pryor, Greg (Rocky Mount) 1973
Purdin, John (Salisbury) 1964
Putnam, Pat (Asheville) 1976
Pyecha, John (Elkin) 1950; (Rutherford County) 1951; (Greensboro) 1952
Quilici, Frank (Charlotte) 1962, 1963, 1964; (Wilson) 1962, 1963
Quinones, Rey (Winston-Salem) 1984
Quintana, Carlos (Greensboro) 1986
Radatz, Dick (Raleigh) 1959, 1960
Rader, Doug (Durham) 1965
Ragland, Tom (Burlington) 1967; (High Point–Thomasville) 1968
Rainey, Chuck (Winston-Salem) 1975
Ramirez, Manny (Burlington) 1991 (Kinston) 1992; (Charlotte) 1993
Ramsey, William (Asheville) 1943

Rand, Dick (Winston-Salem) 1951
Randolph, Willie (Asheville) 1973
Rapp, Pat (Charlotte) 1995
Ratliff, Paul (Charlotte) 1963; (Wilson) 1963–64
Ray, Carl (Winston-Salem) 1914; (Greensboro) 1915, 1920
Ray, Jim (Durham) 1965
Raydon, Curt (Asheville) 1961
Redding, Phil (Charlotte) 1916
Redfern, Howard (Asheville) 1925
Redmon, Glenn (Asheville) 1971
Redus, Gary (Greensboro) 1979
Reed, Ron (Kinston) 1966
Reese, Rich (Wilson) 1964; (Charlotte) 1965
Regan, Phil (Durham) 1957
Reinbach, Mike (Asheville) 1972
Reinholz, Art (Raleigh) 1926; (Kinston) 1927; (Winston-Salem) 1928
Repulski, Rip (Winston-Salem) 1949
Regan, Phil (Durham) 1957
Renfroe, Laddie (Winston-Salem) 1986; (Charlotte) 1989
Reyes, Carlos (Durham) 1992
Reynolds, Craig (Gastonia) 1972
Reynolds, Shane (Asheville) 1989
Rhawn, Rocky (Asheville) 1940
Rhodes, Karl (Asheville) 1987
Rice, Bob (Greensboro) 1933–34
Rice, Hal (Asheville) 1942; (Winston-Salem) 1946
Rich, Woody (Valdese) 1936; (Greensboro) 1950; (Rutherford County) 1953–54; (High Point–Thomasville) 1954–56; (Charlotte) 1958
Richards, Paul (Asheville) 1929
Richardson, Gordy (Winston-Salem) 1959
Richardt, Mike (Asheville) 1979
Riddle, Elmer (Charlotte) 1937
Riddoch, Greg (Asheville) 1970
Ridzik, Steve (Greensboro) 1945
Righetti, Dave (Asheville) 1977
Rightnowar, Ron (Fayetteville) 1987
Ripkin, Billy (Charlotte) 1985–86
Ripkin, Cal, Jr. (Charlotte) 1979–80
Risley, Bill (Greensboro) 1988
Ritz, Kevin (Gastonia) 1986
Rivera, Dave (Asheville) 1977
Rivera, Mariano (Greensboro) 1991, 1993
Rivera, Roberto (Burlington) 1989; (Kinston) 1991–93
Rivera, Ruben (Greensboro) 1994
Robello, Tommy (Wilmington) 1934
Roberts, Dave (Asheville) 1964, 1965–66; (Kinston) 1964
Roberts, Ray (Wilson) 1927
Robertson, Bob (Gastonia) 1965; (Asheville) 1966
Robertson, Rich (Carolina) 1992
Robertson, Sherry (Charlotte) 1940
Robinson, Aaron (Snow Hill) 1937; (Fayetteville) 1954–55; (Winston-Salem) 1955

Rodriguez, Edwin (Greensboro) 1982
Rodriguez, Ellie (Greensboro) 1965
Rodriguez, Ivan (Gastonia) 1989
Rodriguez, Rosario (Greensboro) 1988
Rodriguez, Vic (Charlotte) 1983
Roettger, Oscar (Durham) 1939
Rohe, George (Asheville) 1912
Roland, Jim (Wilson) 1961, 1962; (Charlotte) 1962
Rollins, Rich (Wilson) 1960; (Charlotte) 1961
Roman, Bill (Durham) 1960
Rooker, Jim (Rocky Mount) 1965, 1966; (High Point–Thomasville) 1969
Roomes, Rolando (Winston-Salem) 1985–86
Rosario, Victor (Greensboro) 1986–1987
Rosen, Al (Thomasville) 1942
Rowland, Rich (Fayetteville) 1989
Ruberto, John (Asheville) 1970
Ruble, Art (Charlotte) 1925
Runge, Paul (Durham) 1980
Rusteck, Dick (Charlotte) 1971
Ryan, Ken (Greensboro) 1987
Rye, Gene (Winston-Salem) 1928
Sadek, Mike (Charlotte) 1969
Sadowski, Ed (Greensboro) 1953
Salas, Mark (Gastonia) 1980
Salmon, Chico (Durham) 1961
Salveson, Jack (Winston-Salem) 1932
Samuels, Roger (Asheville) 1983–84
Sanchez, Celerino (Asheville) 1967; (Greensboro) 1968
Sanchez, Rey (Gastonia) 1987
Sanders, Reggie (Greensboro) 1989
Sands, Charlie (Kinston) 1968
Sanford, Jack (Charlotte) 1940
Sanford, Mo (Greensboro) 1989
Sanguillen, Manny (Raleigh) 1966
Santana, Rafael (Kinston) 1979
Scarsella, Les (Wilmington) 1935
Schaffer, Jimmie (Winston-Salem) 1957
Scheid, Richard (Charlotte) 1989, 1995
Scheinblum, Richie (Burlington) 1964
Schemer, Mike (Salisbury) 1940
Schenz, Hank (Tarboro) 1940
Scherman, Fred (Rocky Mount) 1965, 1966
Schilling, Chuck (Raleigh) 1959
Schilling, Curt (Greensboro) 1987; (Charlotte) 1988
Schmidt, Dave (Asheville) 1980
Schmidt, Fred (Asheville) 1940
Schmidt, Jason (Durham) 1993
Schneck, Dave (Raleigh-Durham) 1968
Schroder, Bob (Lexington) 1964
Schueler, Ron (Kinston) 1967
Schultz, Joe (Kinston) 1937; (Asheville) 1937–38
Schwabe, Mike (Fayetteville) 1987
Schweitzer, Al (Wilson) 1920
Scott, Donnie (Asheville) 1980
Scott, George (Gastonia) 1964; (Winston-Salem) 1964

Seanez, Rudy (Burlington) 1986; (Kinston) 1989
Searage, Ray (Gastonia) 1978
Seats, Tom (Asheville) 1936
Sedgwick, Duke (Asheville) 1926
Sembera, Carroll (Durham) 1964
Semproch, Ray (Wilson) 1956
Sessi, Walter (Kinston) 1937; (Shelby/Thomas-
   ville) 1937
Settlemire, Merle (Charlotte) 1931–32
Sewell, Rip (Raleigh) 1931
Shannon, Mike (Winston-Salem) 1959
Sharon, Dick (Gastonia) 1969
Sharp, Bill (Asheville) 1971
Shave, Jon (Gastonia) 1991
Sheaffer, Danny (Winston-Salem) 1983
Shealy, Al (Kinston) 1926
Shearer, Ray (Asheville) 1951
Sheely, Bud (Greensboro) 1941–42
Sheets, Larry (Charlotte) 1983
Shellenback, Jim (Gastonia) 1963; (Asheville)
   1964–65
Shemo, Steve (Mayodan) 1939–40; (Winston-
   Salem) 1947
Shepherd, Keith (Kinston) 1989; (Charlotte) 1995
Shields, Steve (Winston-Salem) 1979
Shifflett, Garland (Charlotte) 1963–68
Shinault, Enoch (Asheville) 1917
Shirley, Mule (Lenoir) 1937; (Goldsboro) 1939
Shore, Ernie (Greensboro) 1913
Short, Chris (High Point–Thomasville) 1958
Shuey, Paul (Kinston) 1993–94; (Charlotte) 1994
Siebert, Sonny (Burlington) 1958, 1960
Sima, Al (Salisbury) 1942
Simms, Mike (Asheville) 1987
Simpson, Dick (Statesville) 1961
Simpson, Wayne (Asheville) 1968
Sims, Greg (Asheville) 1967
Sims, Duke (Burlington) 1961
Singleton, Ken (Raleigh-Durham) 1968
Sington, Fred (High Point) 1931
Sipek, Dick (Reidsville) 1948–51
Sisk, Tommie (Asheville) 1961
Sisler, Dick (Asheville) 1941–42
Skaggs, Dave (Asheville) 1974
Skinner, Joel (Shelby) 1980
*Slaughter, Enos (Raleigh) 1961
Slocumb, Heathcliff (Winston-Salem) 1987–1988;
   (Charlotte) 1990, 1993
Small, Aaron (Charlotte) 1995
Smalley, Roy (Shelby) 1946
Smith, Al (Winston-Salem/High Point) 1932
Smith, Bryn (Charlotte) 1977
Smith, Carr (Raleigh) 1923; (Winston-Salem)
   1920, 1925, 1926; (Wilson) 1926; (Greensboro)
   1928; (Leaksville-Spray-Draper) 1934
Smith, Daryl (Asheville) 1981
Smith, Dave (Durham) 1949
Smith, Elwood (Asheville) 1929

Smith, Frank (Raleigh) 1901
Smith, Frank (Statesville) 1946
Smith, George (Durham) 1958–59
Smith, George (Asheville) 1924
Smith, Greg (Winston-Salem) 1988
Smith, Keith (Greensboro) 1980–1981
Smith, Mayo (Wilmington) 1934–35
Smith, Mike (Durham) 1980
Smith, Pete (Charlotte) 1995
Smith, Vinnie (Greenville) 1938–39
Smith, Wib (Winston-Salem) 1927
Smith, Zane (Durham) 1983; (Carolina) 1993
Smythe, Harry (Asheville) 1926, 1927–29; (Win-
   ston-Salem) 1927; (Charlotte) 1942
Soderholm, Eric (Red Springs) 1969; (Charlotte)
   1969
Sodowsky, Clint (Fayetteville) 1993
Solaita, Tony (High Point–Thomasville) 1968
Solano, Julio (Asheville) 1982
Sosa, Sammy (Gastonia) 1987
Southworth, Billy (Asheville) 1935–36
Spanswick, Bill (Raleigh) 1969
Spence, Stan (Rocky Mount) 1936; (Kinston) 1949
Spencer, Ben (Rocky Mount) 1921, 1923–24; (Kin-
   ston) 1926
Spencer, Roy (Raleigh) 1921
Spicer, Bob (Lumberton) 1947; (Asheville) 1948
Spikes, Charlie (Kinston) 1971
Spinks, Scipio (Greensboro) 1968
Spriggs, George (Asheville) 1964
Springer, Russ (Greensboro) 1990
Staley, Gale (Salisbury-Spencer) 1925
Stallard, Tracy (Raleigh) 1958
Stange, Lee (Wilson) 1960
Stanley, Fred (Salisbury) 1966
Stanley, Joe (Raleigh) 1901
Stanton, Buck (Wilson) 1927
Stanton, Leroy (Raleigh-Durham) 1968
Stanton, Mike (Durham) 1988
*Stargell, Willie (Asheville) 1961
Starr, Dick (Asheville) 1948–49
Staton, Joe (Rocky Mount) 1971
Staub, Rusty (Durham) 1962
Stearns, John (Rocky Mount) 1972
Stein, Randy (Asheville) 1973
Steinecke, Bill (Concord) 1937–38; (Tarboro)
   1940
Steiner, Ben (Greensboro) 1942
Stennett, Rennie (Gastonia) 1969
Stephenson, Jerry (Winston-Salem) 1962
Stephenson, John (Raleigh) 1963
Stephenson, Walter (Mt. Airy) 1939
Stevens, Chuck (Williamston) 1937
Stevens, Dave (Charlotte) 1992
Stewart, Bill (Lexington) 1950
Stewart, Bunky (New Bern) 1951
Stewart, Neb (Sanford) 1941
Stewart, Sammy (Charlotte) 1977

Stillman, Royle (Asheville) 1972
Stocksdale, Otis (Raleigh) 1901; (Durham) 1902
Stone, Dean (Charlotte) 1952
Stone, George (Kinston) 1966
Stone, John (Asheville) 1939
Stottlemyre, Mel (Greensboro) 1962
Stottlemyre, Mel, Jr. (Asheville) 1985–86
Straker, Les (Greensboro) 1979
Strickland, Bill (Forest City/Lexington) 1936
Sukeforth, Clyde (Leaksville-Spray-Draper) 1936
Sullivan, Charlie (Winston-Salem) 1925, 1927–29
Sullivan, John (Durham) 1960
Sullivan, Marc (Winston-Salem) 1981
Sunkel, Tom (Asheville) 1932, 1935–36
Susko, Pete (Hickory) 1937–38
Sutko, Glenn (Greensboro) 1989
Swacina, Harry (Rocky Mount) 1922–23
Swanson, Art (Asheville) 1961
Swartzbaugh, Dave (Winston-Salem) 1991; (Charlotte) 1991–92
Swindell, Josh (Winston-Salem) 1911
Tabor, Greg (Asheville) 1981
Tackett, Jeff (Charlotte) 1987–88
Taitt, Doug (Raleigh) 1923
Tarasco, Tony (Durham) 1991
Tatlor, Arlas (Winston-Salem) 1926–28; (Raleigh) 1932Taubensee, Eddie (Greensboro) 1988
Tauby, Fred (Durham) 1927–30
Taveras, Frank (Gastonia) 1969–70
Tavarez, Jesus (Charlotte) 1995
Tavarez, Julian (Burlington) 1992; (Kinston) 1993; (Charlotte) 1994
Taylor, Bill (Asheville) 1980–81
Taylor, Bob (Lexington) 1963
Taylor, Ed (Winston-Salem) 1931
Taylor, Carl (Kinston) 1964; (Asheville) 1965–66
Temple, Johnny (Morganton) 1948
Tenace, Gene (Shelby) 1965
Tepedino, Frank (Greensboro) 1967
Terpko, Jeff (Burlington) 1971–72
Terrell, Jerry (Charlotte) 1971
Terrell, Walt (Asheville) 1980
Thomas, Andres (Durham) 1984
Thomas, Lee (Winston-Salem) 1956
Thomas, Red (Asheville) 1925
Thomas, Roy (Rocky Mount) 1973
Thomas, Stan (Burlington) 1972
Thomason, Erskine (Burlington) 1972
Thome, Jim (Burlington/Kinston) 1990; (Charlotte) 1993
Thompson, Danny (Charlotte) 1969
Thompson, Forrest (Newton-Conover) 1937; (Leaksville) 1938–39; (Thomasville) 1942; (Mooresville) 1945, 1951
Thompson, Jocko (Greensboro) 1941
Thompson, Mike (Salisbury) 1968; (Burlington) 1969
Thompson, Milt (Durham) 1980
Thomson, Bobby (Rocky Mount) 1942

Thorpe, Jim (Rocky Mount) 1909–10; (Fayetteville) 1910
Thrasher, Buck (Asheville) 1910
Tiant, Luis (Burlington) 1963
Tibbs, Jay (Shelby) 1981
Tifenauer, Bobby (Winston-Salem) 1950
Tillman, Bob (Raleigh) 1958
Timmerman, Tom (Durham) 1960
Timmons, Ozzie (Winston-Salem) 1992
Tipton, Eric (Kannapolis) 1938
Tischinski, Tom (Rocky Mount) 1963
Toliver, Freddie (Greensboro) 1980–81; (Carolina) 1993
Tolleson, Wayne (Asheville) 1978
Tolson, Chick (Charlotte) 1924
Tomberlin, Andy (Durham) 1988–89
Tomlin, Dave (Asheville) 1970
Toporcer, Specs (Rocky Mount) 1936
Toppin, Rupe (Burlington) 1966
Torres, Gil (Charlotte) 1937–39, 1940, 1942
Torres, Rusty (Greensboro) 1967; (Kinston) 1969
Torrez, Mike (Raleigh) 1965
Tovar, Cesar (Rocky Mount) 1962
Townsend, Leo (Raleigh) 1928; (Henderson) 1929–31
Tracewski, Dick (Asheville) 1955
Trachsel, Steve (Winston-Salem) 1991; (Charlotte) 1992
Treadway, Red (Wilson) 1941
Tremie, Chris (Hickory) 1993
Tresh, Tom (Greensboro) 1959
Tudor, John (Winston-Salem) 1976
Tuero, Oscar (Newton-Conover) 1937
Turbeville, George (Asheville) 1938–39
Turner, Jim (Winston-Salem) 1925; (Greensboro) 1926, 1928–29; (Salisbury-Spencer) 1927
Twitchell, Wayne (Asheville) 1967; (Greensboro) 1968
Tyack, Jim (Asheville) 1936–37
Tyson, Turkey (Durham) 1947; (Lumberton) 1949; (Rockingham) 1950; (Rocky Mount) 1948, 1952
Uhlaender, Ted (Wilson) 1962, 1963; (Charlotte) 1963, 1964
Umphlett, Tom (High Point — Thomasville) 1951
Unser, Al (Gastonia) 1939; (Winston-Salem) 1940, 1942
Valdes, Marc (Charlotte) 1995
Valdespino, Sandy (Charlotte) 1959
Valdez, Julio (Winston-Salem) 1976
Valentine, Fred (Wilson) 1958
Vander Meer, Johnny (Durham) 1936
Van Dusen, Fred (High Point–Thomasville) 1957; (Asheville) 1960
Van Slyke, Andy (Gastonia) 1980; (Carolina) 1993
Vargas, Eddie (Shelby) 1979
Varney, Pete (Asheville) 1971
Veach, Al (Wilmington) 1929; (Winston-Salem) 1930; (Charlotte) 1933

Veal, Coot (Durham) 1952
Veale, Bob (Wilson) 1959
Velez, Otto (Kinston) 1971
Verban, Emil (Asheville) 1940–41
Veres, Randy (Charlotte) 1995
Villanueva, Hector (Winston-Salem) 1986
Viox, Jim (Rocky Mount) 1925; (Raleigh) 1928
Voiselle, Bill (Rocky Mount) 1940; (Greensboro) 1941
Von Hoff, Bruce (Asheville) 1969
Wade, Ben (New Bern/Durham) 1940
Wade, Gale (Asheville) 1949
Wade, Jake (New Bern/Goldsboro) 1941
Wade, Rip (Winston-Salem) 1927
Wade, Terrell (Durham) 1993
Wagner, Charlie (Charlotte) 1935; (Rocky Mount) 1936
Wagner, Paul (Carolina) 1992
Wakefield, Dick (Winston-Salem) 1941
Wakefield, Tim (Carolina) 1991, 1993
Walbeck, Matt (Winston-Salem) 1991; (Charlotte) 1992
Walker, Dixie (Greensboro) 1928
Walker, Frank (Rocky Mount) 1920–24
Walker, Luke (Asheville) 1964–65
Walker, Mike (Burlington) 1986; (Kinston) 1987
Walker, Tony (Greensboro) 1979
Wall, Donne (Asheville) 1990
Waller, Ty (Shelby) 1978
Walsh, Joe (Rocky Mount) 1937
Walters, Bucky (High Point) 1929
Walters, Dan (Asheville) 1985–85
Walton, Danny (Salisbury) 1966; (Asheville) 1967
Ward, Duane (Durham) 1983
Wares, Buzzy (Asheville) 1914
Washington, LaRue (Asheville) 1976
Waslewski, Gary (Kinston) 1962–63, 1964; (Asheville) 1964
Watkins, Bob (Asheville) 1967
Watson, Art (Asheville) 1914
Watson, Bob (Salisbury) 1965
Watson, Mule (Asheville) 1912
Waugh, Jim (Burlington-Graham) 1953
Weathers, Dave (Charlotte) 1995
Weaver, Jim (Burlington) 1959
Weiser, Harry (Charlotte) 1912, 1914
Webster, Mitch (Kinston) 1980
Wehner, John (Carolina) 1991
Weiand, Ted (Winston-Salem) 1953
Wells, David (Kinston) 1983–84
Wells, Terry (Asheville) 1986
Wendell, Turk (Durham) 1989–90
Wentzel, Stan (Burlington) 1953–54
Wert, Don (Durham) 1959–60
Wertz, Vic (Winston-Salem) 1942
Wetherby, Jeff (Durham) 1986
Whitaker, Steve (Shelby) 1962–63; (Greensboro) 1964

White, Abe (New Bern) 1946
White, Elder (Edenton) 1952; (Wilson) 1959
White, Ernie (Asheville) 1937
White, Mike (Burlington) 1959
White, Richard (Carolina) 1992–93
White, Roy (Greensboro) 1962, 1963
Whited, Ed (Asheville) 1987
Whitehouse, Len (Asheville) 1977
Whiteside, Matt (Gastonia) 1991
Whitfield, Fred (Winston-Salem) 1959
Whitfield, Terry (Kinston) 1973
Whitmore, Darrell (Burlington) 1990; (Kinston) 1992
Whitt, Ernie (Winston-Salem) 1973
Wicker, Kemp (Goldsboro) 1929
Wickersham, Dave (Burlington) 1955; (Gastonia) 1959
Wilborn, Claude (Salisbury) 1938; (Cooleemee) 1939
*Wilhelm, Hoyt (Mooresville) 1942, 1946–47
Wilke, Harry (Asheville) 1926
Wilkerson, Curtis (Asheville) 1981
Wilkins, Rick (Winston-Salem) 1989; (Charlotte) 1990
Williams, Pappy (Kinston/Rocky Mount) 1948; (Greenville) 1949
Williams, Walt (Durham) 1963
Williams, Woody (Leaksville) 1934–35
Willingham, Hugh (Durham) 1932
Willis, Mike (Asheville) 1973–74
Wilson, Duane (Greensboro) 1953
Wilson, Max (Wilson) 1947–48
Wilson, Mutt (Greensboro) 1928
Wilson, Teddy (Statesville) 1942, 1961; (Durham) 1946; (Shelby) 1960
Windle, Willis (Salisbury-Spencer) 1927
Winters, Matt (Greensboro) 1980–1982
Wise, Hugh (Asheville) 1934–35
Wissman, Davis (Asheville) 1963
Witt, George (Asheville) 1961
Wockenfuss, John (Shelby) 1969
Wolcott, Bob (Wilmington) 1995
Wolf, Wally (Durham) 1962
Womack, Dooley (Greensboro) 1960, 1961
Womack, Sid (Rocky Mount) 1925
Wood, Jake (Durham) 1958
Wood, Ken (Charlotte) 1956
Wood, Spades (Salisbury-Spencer) 1929
Wood, Wilbur (Raleigh) 1960; (Winston-Salem) 1961
Woodal, Larry (Asheville) 1915
Woods, Ron (Kinston) 1962, 1964–65; (Asheville) 1963–64; (Rocky Mount) 1966
Woodson, Dick (Thomasville) 1966; (Charlotte) 1968
Woodward, Rob (Winston-Salem) 1983
Wright, Ab (Greensboro) 1932
Wright, George (Asheville) 1978–79
Wright, Jamey (Asheville) 1994

Wright, Ken (Winston-Salem) 1965
Wright, Taffy (Charlotte) 1933
Wright, Tom (Durham) 1946
*Wynn, Early (Charlotte) 1938–1940
Wyrostek, John (Kinston) 1937–1938
*Yastrzemski, Carl (Raleigh) 1959
Yancy, Hugh (Asheville) 1971
York, Jim (High Point–Thomasville) 1969
Young, Cliff (Gastonia) 1984
Young, Kevin (Carolina) 1991
Yount, Eddie (Newton-Conover) 1948–51

Yuhas, Eddie (Winston-Salem) 1947
Zepp, Bill (Charlotte) 1969
Zernial, Gus (Burlington) 1946
Ziem, Steve (Durham) 1984, 1988–89
Zimmerman, Jerry (Greensboro) 1955
Zinser, Bill (Kinston) 1940
Zisk, Richie (Gastonia) 1968
Zosky, Eddie (Charlotte) 1995
Zupcic, Bob (Charlotte) 1995
Zuvella, Paul (Durham) 1980

Bibliography

Beam, John Mark III. *They Played Here: Sports History in the High Point Area*. High Point, NC: High Point Historical Society, 1990.

Blake, Mike. *The Minor Leagues: A Celebration of the Little Show*. New York: Wynwood Press, 1991.

Browning, Wilt. *The Rocks: The True Story of the Worst Team in Baseball History*. Asheboro, NC: Down Home, 1992.

Chadwick, Bruce. *Baseball's Hometown Teams: The Story of the Minor Leagues*. New York: Abbeville, 1994.

Filichia, Peter. *Professional Baseball Franchises: From the Abbeville Athletics to the Zanesville Indians*. New York: Facts on File, 1993.

Fite, Howard "Doc." *Four Indian Summers*. Charlotte, NC: Delmar, 1984.

Gaunt, Robert. *We Would Have Played Forever: A History of the Coastal Plain League*. Robert Gaunt, 1996.

Green, Ernest J. *The Diamonds of Dixie: Travels Through the Southern Minor Leagues*. Lanham, MD: Madison, 1995.

Hoie, Bob. "The Minor Leagues." In *Total Baseball*, edited by John Thorn and Pete Palmer. New York: HarperCollins, 1993.

Johnson, Lloyd. *The Minor League Register*. Durham, NC: Baseball America, 1994.

Johnson, Lloyd, and Miles Wolff, eds. *The Encyclopedia of Minor League Baseball*. 2d ed. Durham, NC: Baseball America, 1997.

Kirkland, Bill. *Eddie Neville of the Durham Bulls*. Jefferson, NC: McFarland, 1993.

Lamb, David. *Stolen Season: A Journey Through America and Baseball's Minor Leagues*. New York: Random House, 1991.

O'Neill, Bill. *The Southern League: Baseball in Dixie, 1885–1994*. Austin, TX: Eakin, 1994.

Pietrusza, David. *Minor Miracles: The Legend and Lure of Minor League Baseball*. South Bend, IN: Diamond Communications, 1995.

Smith, Leverett T. "1946: Bill Kennedy's Fabulous Year." Society for American Baseball Research, *Minor League History Journal*, vol. 2. no. 1 (1993): 38–40.

Sullivan, Neil J. *The Minors: The Struggles and the Triumph of Baseball's Poor Relation from 1876 to the Present*. New York: St. Martin's Press, 1990.

Sumner, Jim L. *Separating the Men from the Boys: The First Half-Century of the Carolina League*. Winston-Salem, NC: John F. Blair: 1994.

Sumner, Jim L. "The North Carolina State Professional Baseball League of 1902." *North Carolina Historical Review* 64 (July 1987): 247–73.

Sumner, Jim L. "William G. Bramham: The Czar of Minor League Baseball." *Carolina Comments* 37 (July 1989): 116–122.

Terrell, Bob. *McCormick Field: Home of Reality*. Asheville, NC: Bob Terrell, 1991.

Tygiel, Jules. "Black Ball." In *Total Baseball*, edited by John Thorn and Pete Palmer. New York: HarperCollins, 1993.

Utley, R.G., and Scott Verner. *The Independent Carolina Baseball League, 1936–1938: Baseball Outlaws*. Jefferson, NC: McFarland, 1998.

◆ ———— *Other Sources* ————

Various guidebooks published by Spalding, Reach and *The Sporting News*, 1905–1985.

Baseball America Alamanac, 1986–1997. Durham, NC: Baseball America.

South Atlantic League Record Book, 1990 ed.

Carolina League Record Book, 1986 ed.

Various programs and media guides from current minor league teams.

Index

242

Index